RELIGIOUS PLURALISM
AND INTERRELIGIOUS THEOLOGY

RELIGIOUS PLURALISM AND INTERRELIGIOUS THEOLOGY

The Gifford Lectures—An Extended Edition

Perry Schmidt-Leukel

ORBIS BOOKS

Maryknoll, New York 10545

ORBIS BOOKS
Maryknoll, New York 10545

Fathers and Brothers
MARYKNOLL™

Founded in 1970, Orbis Books endeavors to publish works that enlighten the mind, nourish the spirit, and challenge the conscience. The publishing arm of the Maryknoll Fathers and Brothers, Orbis seeks to explore the global dimensions of the Christian faith and mission, to invite dialogue with diverse cultures and religious traditions, and to serve the cause of reconciliation and peace. The books published reflect the views of their authors and do not represent the official position of the Maryknoll Society. To learn more about Maryknoll and Orbis Books, please visit our website at www.maryknollsociety.org.

Library of Congress Cataloging-in-Publication Data

Names: Schmidt-Leukel, Perry, author.
Title: Religious pluralism and interreligious theology : the Gifford lectures—an extended edition / Perry Schmidt-Leukel.
Description: Maryknoll : Orbis Books, 2017. | Includes bibliographical references and index.
Identifiers: LCCN 2016031476 (print) | LCCN 2016045240 (ebook) | ISBN 9781626982307 (pbk.) | ISBN 9781608336951 (ebook)
Subjects: LCSH: Religious pluralism. | Religions—Relations. Dialogue—Religious aspects.
Classification: LCC BL85 .S359 2017 (print) | LCC BL85 (ebook) | DDC 201/.5—dc23
LC record available at https://lccn.loc.gov/2016031476

To my former students and colleagues at Glasgow University and all friends in this warm-hearted city.

*There are as many paths toward God as there are breaths
of the human beings.*
—Traditional Hadith

"How many ways are there to God?"—"As many as there are people."
—Joseph Ratzinger
Salt of the Earth

Contents

Acknowledgments   *xi*

1. **A Preliminary Orientation**   **1**
   Religious Pluralism   1
   Interreligious Theology   8

PART ONE: RELIGIOUS PLURALISM

2. **Pluralist Awakenings in Christianity**   **17**
   The Emergence of the Pluralist Option   17
   Doctrinal Presuppositions   21
      Saving Faith   22
      The Concept of God and Divine Revelation   24
      Jesus Christ   26
   Prospects and Developments   28

3. **Judaism and the Many Covenants**   **32**
   A Prelude to Jewish Pluralism   32
   The Traditional Background   34
   Toward a Theology of Multiple Covenants   36
   "No Religion Is an Island"   39

4. **Submission to a Divinely Willed Diversity: Islamic Pluralism**   **42**
   The Meaning of *islām*   43
   Diversity and Universality   45
   The Impact of Islamic Mysticism   48

5. **Is Hinduism a Pluralist Religion?**   **54**
   Vivekananda's Presentation of Hinduism   54
   Some Retrospective Observations   58
      Pro-Pluralist Tendencies in Hindu History   58

Anti-Pluralist Tendencies in Hindu History   61
Hindu Approaches to Islam and Christianity   63
Hinduisms and Pluralism Today   65
    The Legal Battle between the Ramakrishna Mission   65
    and the State of West Bengal
    On the Position of the Hindutva Movement   66
    Toward an Alternative Pluralism   68

6. **The Difficult Road to Pluralism in Buddhism**   **71**
    Of Blind Men, Elephants, and Rafts   71
    Theravāda Buddhism and Religious Pluralism   74
        Doctrinal Obstacles   74
        Two Possible Starting Points   77
    Pluralist Approaches in Mahāyāna Buddhism   82
        Traditional Mahāyāna Approaches to Religious Diversity   82
        Pluralist Moves   85

7. **Pluralist Inclinations in Chinese Religions**   **90**
    Unity and Diversity of Religions in China   90
    Daoist and Confucian Attitudes toward Religious Diversity   94
    Regulated Pluralism and Multiple Participation   97
    Contemporary Discourses   100

PART TWO: INTERRELIGIOUS THEOLOGY

8. **From Religious Pluralism to Interreligious Theology**   **109**
    Pluralisms across Religious Traditions   109
    Religious Pluralism and the Vision of a Global Theology   114
    Religious Pluralism versus Religious Diversity?   119
    Religious Pluralism and the Need for an Ongoing Dialogue   124
    An Interim Conclusion   128

9. **Interreligious Theology: Principles and Methodology**   **130**
    Four Key Principles of Interreligious Theology   130
        A Theological Credit of Trust   130
        The Unity of Reality   133
        Tied to Interreligious Discourse   136
        An Open Process   138
    Methodological Issues   139
        Perspectival: Facing the Confessional Dimension   140
        Imaginative: Seeing through the Eyes of the Other   141

Comparative: Seeking Reciprocal Illumination   143
Constructive: Mutual Transformation   144

10. The Prophet and the Son   **147**
The Son   148
  The Critique of "the Son"   148
  Understanding "the Son"   151
  Toward a Synthesis   154
The Prophet   158
  Understanding "the Prophet"   158
  The Critique of "the Prophet"   159
  Toward a Synthesis   160

11. The Son and the Buddha   **164**
Between Demonization and Sanctification   164
  Christian Perspectives   164
  Buddhist Perspectives   167
Acknowledging the Buddha   171
  An Atheist Philosopher?   171
  A Mind from Beyond   173
Acknowledging the Son   178
Conclusion   182

12. The Buddha and the Prophet   **185**
Historical Perspectives   185
  Early Muslim Views   185
  Early Buddhist Views   190
Dialogical Perspectives   193
  Tracking Down the Problem   193
  Acknowledging the Buddha   196
  Acknowledging the Prophet   199

13. Toward an Interreligious Theology of Creation   **204**
The Buddhist Critique of a Divine Creator   207
Some Important Modifications   211
A Synthesizing View   217

14. A Fractal Interpretation of Religious Diversity   **222**
The Theory of Fractals   223
Observations from Intercultural Philosophy   225
Observations from Comparative Religion   227

Interreligious Theology and the Fractal Interpretation   232
     of Religious Diversity
     The Basic Idea   233
     Hints at a Fractal Approach in Current Interreligious   237
          Theology
The Fruitfulness of the Theory   243

References   *247*

Index   *279*

Acknowledgments

This book is based on two series of lectures: Part 2 contains a revised version of the Gifford Lectures, which I was honored to deliver in October 2015 at the University of Glasgow. It was a marvelous experience to be back to Glasgow Uni with its more than five hundred years of impressive intellectual history. I am extremely grateful to the distinguished members of the Gifford Committee for granting me this excellent opportunity of presenting and discussing my thoughts on interreligious theology in such a prestigious lecture series.

Most of the material in Part 1 was presented during a series of lectures in October 2014 at the Zheijiang University of Hangzhou on the invitation of Professor Zhicheng Wang. As in the past, Hangzhou is still an exciting place of intense multireligious encounter, but nowadays it is also an internationally renowned center of academic study of this encounter. Some of the findings presented in Part 1 are also published in condensed form in my contribution to *Twenty-First Century Theologies of Religions: Retrospection and New Frontiers* (Leiden: E. J. Brill, 2016), a volume edited by E. Harris, P. Hedges, and S. Hettiarachchi in honor of Alan Race. A German variant of chapter 5 has been published in *Ordnungen religiöser Pluralität: Wirklichkeit—Wahrnehmung—Gestaltung*, edited by U. Willems, A. Reuter, and D. Gerster (Frankfurt a.M.: Campus-Verlag, 2016). Chapter 13 is in part a revised version of an earlier essay published in *Ching Feng: A Journal on Christianity and Chinese Religion and Culture* 10, no. 1–2 (2010–11). I thank the publishers for the permission to reuse parts of these publications in the present book.

The research behind this book was mostly enabled by the support of the Cluster of Excellence "Religion and Politics" of the University of Muenster, which provided me with three terms of research leave. In these days, when the modern concept of many universities is to view their professors more as research managers than as researchers, such "leaves" have become invaluable for those among us who still cling to a more old-fashioned profile of the professorial vocation.

My gratitude also goes to my wife, Doris, who dedicated much of her time to the proofreading of the manuscript, and to Teresa Jesionowski, who as a professional copy editor also helped in amending my Teutonic English. I am grateful to Maria Angelini for skillfully steering the production process.

I thank Robert Ellsberg of Orbis Books for his keen interest in the publication of these lectures. Orbis is one of the international publishing houses that has been firmly committed to the fostering of interreligious exchange and reflection for many decades. In 1987, Orbis published the papers of the so-called Rubicon-Conference in *The Myth of Christian Uniqueness: Toward a Pluralistic Theology of Religions*, edited by John Hick and Paul F. Knitter, which marked a decisive stage in the development of religious pluralism. Finally my gratitude goes to Paul Knitter who, by then, together with John Hick edited the Rubicon papers and now, thirty years later, has provided a helping hand in arranging the publication of this book with Orbis. It is an immense joy to see my new book appearing with the same publisher who produced so many of the books that are treated in this one—a fact that is almost reminiscent of the fractal structures which, as I will suggest in the subsequent pages, can be discerned in religious diversity and which require wise and constructive attitudes in our dealings with them.

1

A Preliminary Orientation

RELIGIOUS PLURALISM

It is uncontroversial that our planet hosts a wide range of religious traditions, and people have never ever been more aware of the actual extent of this diversity than today. What is controversial is how one should interpret religious diversity and deal with it. This has become a challenge to the religions themselves. Within each of the major religions we find a range of different approaches to religious diversity, both in terms of how to understand it doctrinally and how to relate to it practically. The first half of this book deals with one set or type of approaches, the one that I call "pluralist." When I use the terms "pluralist" or "religious pluralism," I am not referring to the fact of religious plurality or religious diversity but rather to a particular *interpretation of religious diversity*. "Religious pluralism" designates a specific theory and evaluation of religious diversity. This theory first assumes that religious truth exists—and in a sense must exist—in a diversity of forms, which are then assessed as equally valid despite their being different. "Religious pluralism," as used in this book, is not simply an interpretation of religious diversity, but it is itself a *religious* interpretation. This interpretation, as I argue, can be developed only from within the different religious traditions. In the first part of this book, I focus on the developments of pluralist approaches in Christianity, Judaism, Islam, Hinduism, Buddhism, and the Chinese religions. But before I go into the particularities of pluralist approaches within these religious traditions, I would like to begin by making some remarks about the rationale and general features of religious pluralism.

Humans have apparently been religious right from their early evolutionary beginnings and there is obviously more than just one religion in the world. Both of these facts call for some explanation. To the atheist or naturalist the phenomenon of religion is largely a product of delusion and deceit. It is, for example, interpreted as a relic from the early childhood of humanity, when humanity had not yet risen to a rational understanding and exploration of reality (Auguste Comte). Or it is seen as a phenomenon of human self-estrangement, as a projection of human ideals and fears on some imagined supernatural being (Ludwig Feuerbach); or as a projection of psychological (Sigmund Freud), social (Émile Durkheim), and economical (Karl Marx) structures reflecting human ideals and values, or feelings of lostness and guilt, or various power mechanisms in society and human reactions to them. In more recent days, religion has also been explained as the result of an in-built neurological structure supposed to serve some evolutionary purpose (Dean Hamer, Lionel Tiger, Michael McGuire, et al.). What all these different theories have in common is that they provide non-religious interpretations and explanations of religion. That is, they assume that religious understandings of reality are basically wrong. On this premise they try to explain why religion, although being wrong, is nevertheless such a widespread phenomenon. They tend to see the diversity of religions as a further confirmation of their atheistic or naturalistic premise. On the assumption that religion, if it were true, should be far more homogeneous than it actually is, the fact of religious diversity seems to support their view that religion is basically false.

However, it is not only from a nonreligious perspective that religious diversity requires some explanation and interpretation. Religions too have to confront questions such as why their own religion is not the only one in the world, why there are any other religions at all, and why other people follow other religious ideas and practices. An astonishing fact, often overlooked, is that the traditional religious interpretations of religious diversity have not been that much different from the nonreligious ones. One could even argue that some religious interpretations have been, in a sense, forerunners of the nonreligious ones. Like naturalists, many traditional religious thinkers also assumed that all religions are wrong—with just one single exception, which is their own religion. In a sense, nonreligious interpretations have just adopted this religious view on religious others, without making that particular exception. Penn Jillette, an American illusionist and committed atheist, made that point jokingly clear:

> The Jews say: "Christians and Muslims are wrong." The Christians say: "Jews and Muslims are wrong." The Muslims say: "Jews and Christians are wrong." The Atheist says: "You are all right."[1]

The negative interpretation of religious diversity, so widespread among traditional religious views, clearly undermines the credibility of each reli-

---

[1] http://www.atheismus-info.de/warum.html (my re-translation).

gious perspective. This was already emphasized in the eighteenth century by David Hume when he compared the rival religious views to a case in court. If there are a number of witnesses all refuting each other, whom should the judge believe? Presumably none of them.[2]

Is it inevitable for religions to take such a negative stance on religious diversity as they have often done in the past? Or are there any other options that they might choose? Since Alan Race published *Christians and Religious Pluralism: Patterns in the Christian Theology of Religions* in 1983,[3] a typology has spread around the globe that lists three different options for a religious interpretation of religious diversity: exclusivism, inclusivism, and pluralism. However, looking more carefully at the various debates since the 1980s, one will note that these three terms are not always used strictly in the same sense. Despite the pervasiveness of Race's classification, its different handling by different authors has created a significant amount of confusion.[4] As a result, some scholars have rejected the tripolar classification as altogether useless and misleading. It is, however, possible to refine this typology in such a way that it becomes logically comprehensive, coercive, and universally, that is, interreligiously applicable.[5]

Each of the major religious traditions, in its own way, proclaims a path leading to an ultimate well-being, salvation, or liberation, which is connected to some kind of transcendent or ultimate reality. If one takes these claims seriously—as at least the followers of these religions tend to do—the principal question raised by the fact of religious diversity is to what extent the different religious messages of salvation might be true. The first possible answer is that none of them is true, which would be the atheist or *naturalist*[6] position. As Bertrand Russell once stated: "I think all the great religions of the world . . . both untrue and harmful."[7] A second answer is that none of the central religious messages is true except that of one's own religion. This is the *exclusivist* position. A third possible answer is that more than one is true, but only one is so in a uniquely superior sense. This is what I call the *inclusivist* position. A fourth answer is that more than one of these religious messages is true, although none is superior to all the rest, so that at least some are equally valid. This would be the *pluralist* position.

Thus, if we extend the tripolar classification to four options and interpret them in the way I just suggested, one can easily recognize the *logically*

---

[2] Hume 2000, 121–22.
[3] Race 1983.
[4] For past and present debates about the typology see Harris, Hedges, and Hettiarachchi 2016.
[5] See Schmidt-Leukel 2005b.
[6] I prefer the designation "naturalist" because atheism is sometimes confused with nontheism, while the position of naturalism denies all forms of transcendent reality whether theistic or nontheistic.
[7] Russell 1992, 9.

comprehensive character of the scheme resulting from its strictly disjunctive nature. That is:

- The religious claims of teaching a path of salvation are either all false (*naturalism*) or they are not all false.
- If they are not all false, then either only one of them is true (*exclusivism*) or more than one is true.
- If more than one is true, then there is either one singular maximum of that truth (*inclusivism*) or there is no singular maximum, so that at least some are equally true (*pluralism*).

If we understand the classification in this way it is logically comprehensive, that is, there is no position left, which would not be covered by one of these four options.

But can there be degrees of truth? I think one may reasonably argue that among the various proclaimed paths of salvation, one particular path might be superior to others in that it is entirely or nearly free from any errors, or that it is most efficient, most direct, most clear, and so on, whereas other paths might have too many errors, or they might be potentially misleading, less clear, or leading to lesser though still to some extent desirable goals, and so on. Thus there can be degrees of truth, if "truth" is related to the path. This alerts us to an important point: "Religious pluralism"—as defined here—is not identical with the assumption that there are no valid criteria by which one could assess or grade different religious proclamations or paths. To deny the possibility of this kind of critical assessment would amount to *relativism* but would not be religious pluralism, although religious pluralism is often confused with relativism. Relativism holds that no religion can justifiably claim superiority for its own message because there are no criteria to support such a claim. In contrast, pluralism holds that there are indeed valid criteria that allow for a reasoned assessment of religions, but that on the normative basis of these criteria several religions are doing equally well so that none of them is evidently superior to all the others. Pluralism is essentially different from relativism.[8]

Pluralism is also different from religious *tolerance*. The ideal of religious tolerance consists in enduring or "tolerating" ideas and practices that one believes to be wrong. Tolerance is the toleration of what we do not like. This is the crucial and precious point of tolerance. Tolerance thus presupposes a negative assessment of what one tolerates. This implies that one can never tolerate everything. Some ideas and practices may be so harm-

---

[8]Like agnosticism, relativism would not constitute a further position but a second- or even third-order claim articulating serious doubts over the availability of any norms of judgment.

ful that their toleration would cause greater evil than their non-toleration. Therefore, the negotiation of the limits of tolerance needs to be subject to a permanent social discourse, while the spirit of tolerance is to set these limits as wide as possible and to be as flexible as possible. But all of this means that religious pluralism must not be confused with tolerance: Although tolerance presupposes a negative assessment of what one should tolerate, religious pluralism is the expression of a positive assessment. It is not about the toleration of other religions but about their genuine appreciation. The ideal of tolerance is indispensable on the social and political level, where the society as a whole will always be asked to tolerate views and practices that diverge from the views and practices of the majority. And tolerance is similarly indispensable in the religious sphere. For no religious pluralist will ever regard everything in the world of religious diversity as equally valid. Pluralists will not endorse exclusivist and inclusivist positions. And presumably there will always be people rejecting religious pluralism. Hence, tolerance remains important. Religious pluralism cannot replace religious tolerance, nor is religious pluralism a requirement of tolerance. Religious pluralism is just something different. It holds that religions are not only capable of tolerating each other but that they can also develop genuine forms of reciprocal appreciation.

So the tripolar classification of options, defined, interpreted, and expanded in the way I just suggested, covers all logical possibilities. If at least one of the key questions in any theology of religions is how to understand and assess the messages of salvation proclaimed by other faiths, there is no position left, which is not covered by the scheme. *Agnosticism* does not constitute an additional position but, as a kind of second-order claim, articulates one's felt inability to assume any one of the four positions. Moreover, it is a stance that is not taken by the religions, because they affirm (though not necessarily as infallible knowledge) at least the truth of their own message of salvation.

If the classification covers all possible options, it is useless to look for any further alternatives. Because of logical reasons such alternatives do not exist. Any feasible position in relation to the initial question is just either one of the four principal options or a version of it as it may emerge from further possible subdivisions. Hence we may focus our intellectual efforts on considering which of the four options appears to provide the most reasonable or most probable answer to the question raised by the diversity of religious claims to salvation. Rejecting all four possible positions would amount to a refusal to answer—or even to seriously deal with—the question that religious diversity inevitably poses.

The discussion about the interpretation of religious diversity has indeed been extensive and fervent over the last five decades, and I will not try to summarize it here. I want to point out only that one of the most significant features of the pluralist position, which distinguishes it from naturalism, exclusivism, and inclusivism, is its *positive assessment* of religious diversity. From a naturalist perspective religion is, after all, an evil, the evil of delusion and deceit. Religious diversity is therefore ultimately a diversity of evils, which makes things not really better but worse. The world would be a better place without religion, and many atheists dream with John Lennon of a future when there is "nothing to kill or die for, and no religion too." The religious positions of exclusivism and inclusivism are also unable to arrive at an ultimately positive evaluation of religious diversity. According to religious exclusivism other religions are false *because* they differ from one's own religion, or from a specific subform of that religion, which is regarded as being uniquely true. According to religious inclusivism other religions are not entirely false, but they are inferior or insufficient *to the extent* that they differ from one's own religion. If one's own religion or denomination is seen as the highest expression of religious truth, others can be true only inasmuch as they resemble one's own faith, and they are false to the extent that they differ. So according to both, exclusivism and inclusivism, religious difference or diversity is perceived as ultimately negative. It indicates either falsity or at least inferiority.

Only religious pluralism seeks to combine religious difference with equal validity. It is therefore the only option that allows for a positive assessment of religious diversity. In this sense John Hick, one of the major representatives of religious pluralism, once argued that "we need a pluralistic theory which enables us to recognise and be fascinated by the manifold differences between the religious traditions, with their different conceptualisations, their different modes of religious experience, and their different forms of individual and social response to the divine."[9]

In the past, each of the major religions has been aware of the existence of at least some other religions, while none of them has had the kind of comprehensive awareness of religious diversity that we have today. More important, in the past we find only relatively few attempts of achieving a good and deep understanding of other religions, that is, an understanding that tries to understand the religious other as he or she understands himself or herself. The history of interreligious encounter comprises plenty of religious controversy but hardly any examples of interreligious dialogue. The difference between the two is that in religious controversy one seeks to identify the weaknesses and shortcomings of the other in order to demonstrate the superiority of one's own faith, whereas in genuine dialogue one looks for the strengths of the religious other, for the insights contained

---

[9]Hick 1985a, 39.

in the other's tradition in order to learn from them. The widespread lack of sound knowledge, understanding, and dialogical spirit in the past may, at least in part, explain why traditionally all of the major religions have favored exclusivist or inclusivist interpretations of religious diversity, so that one hardly finds any truly pluralist and only few examples of proto-pluralist positions.

Exclusivist or inclusivist superiority claims have been expressed by the religions in their own characteristic ways. Christian, Jewish, Muslim, Hindu, Buddhist, Daoist, or Confucian forms of exclusivism and inclusivism differ from each other in that they reflect the specific features of their own tradition. This observation has an important implication, namely that any pluralist approaches will also need to be developed in ways *specific to the respective religious traditions.*[10] Pluralist approaches, as found within the different religions, are not only characterized by their joint vision of a legitimate diversity of equally valid paths of salvation/liberation/right-living. They need to give this vision plausibility against the particular background of their respective religious heritages. To every religious pluralist it is therefore, on the one hand, essential to demonstrate some continuity between the pluralist approach and his or her own religious tradition. But, on the other hand, every pluralist will also have to be critical of those elements within one's own respective tradition that support its claims of an either exclusivist or inclusivist superiority. In this twofold sense of being faithful to and being critical of one's own tradition, pluralist approaches have to be tradition-specific through and through.

In this respect, John Hick's view, expressed in *An Interpretation of Religion*, that pluralism offers a "religious but not confessional interpretation of religion"[11] has often been misunderstood as if Hick were aiming at a position above all the existing religions. Yet he makes it very clear, in the same work, that a "genuinely pluralistic hypothesis will thus inevitably call, at least by implication, for further development within each of the traditions."[12] He further suggests that each of the major religions "has within it . . . the resources for a pluralist understanding of the religious situation" and that supporters of a pluralist view can only work toward it from within their own tradition.[13] Pluralism is not, as so many of its critics hold, a metatheory beyond or even independent of the real religious traditions. It is not something like a new religion claiming its own superiority above all others. On the contrary, pluralism can exist only as Christian pluralism,

---

[10]As has also been implicitly affirmed by David Griffin (2005b, 4).
[11]Hick 1989, 1.
[12]Ibid., 2.
[13]Ibid., 377–78.

Jewish pluralism, Muslim pluralism, and so on. It is these tradition-specific features on which I focus in the subsequent chapters.[14]

INTERRELIGIOUS THEOLOGY

How will the development of pluralist positions affect the ways in which religions do their "theology"? I take "theology" in a broad sense, which also includes the intellectual reflection within predominantly nontheistic religions.[15] The theological reflection of major religious traditions has been based, so far, predominantly on their own scriptures and scriptural traditions. The religious other was taken into account, if at all, only to mark it off as the other. The otherness of other religions was used as an instrument of defining and distinguishing the identity and truth of one's own faith over against that of the religious other. This will change significantly if religions adopt a pluralistic understanding of religious diversity. If religiously relevant truth is understood as being no longer confined to one's own religion, any theological reflection that looks for truth can no longer be satisfied with drawing only on the sources of one's own religious tradition.

I dare to prognosticate that theology, instead of being an essentially denominational enterprise, will become increasingly interreligious. In the future it will also draw on other religions when reflecting on major questions of human life and will reconsider, and further develop, the answers that have been given in one's own tradition in a fresh comparative light. It will also reflect on one's own tradition in order to see what possible contribution might be made to the issues on the agenda of a global interreligious theological inquiry. Thus after discussing in more detail in chapter 8 why and how interreligious theology is the next step following that of taking a religiously pluralist position, chapter 9 expounds the key principles and methodological features of interreligious theology. Chapter 13 gives an example of the creative speculative potential in interreligious theology, whereas chapters 10–12 address the difficult question of how interreligious theology might deal with the confessional nature of religious beliefs as it is expressed, for example, in confessing Muḥammad as the final *Prophet*, Jesus as the *Son* of God, and Gautama as the *Buddha* in whom one takes one's refuge.

The concluding fourteenth chapter presents a new interpretation of reli-

---

[14]General overviews are offered by four handbooks, which provide excellent information on the religions' specific understandings of religious diversity (Meister 2011; Schilbrack 2017), their mutual relations (Cheetham, Pratt, and Thomas 2013), and their approaches to dialogue (Cornille 2013).

[15]As those Buddhist scholars did when they published their reflections under the title *Buddhist Theology* (Jackson and Makransky 2003).

gious diversity, suggesting that this diversity is marked by fractal patterns. That is, the diversity as it is found on the global level replicates, to some extent, in the diversity found within the major religious traditions and is finally rooted in the diversity of religious possibilities of the human psyche and the human mind. This view is different from both the theories that assume an essential identity and those that postulate a radical incommensurability between the religions: On a fractal interpretation, religions resemble each other precisely *in* their diversity. As I will show, one important implication of this view is that interreligious theology is far more continuous with tradition-specific theology than one might initially expect.

Although interreligious theology and religious pluralism are closely interconnected, the need for theology to become interreligious is not felt only among religious pluralists. Interreligious theology responds to the fact that every society in the world is undergoing an unstoppable religious pluralization. As already mentioned, in the past the fact that our world hosts an immense diversity of religions has either been completely or largely hidden to the vast majority of people, including the most learned ones. Today, however, it has become almost common knowledge. Of course, there have always been encounters with religious diversity in former societies, but nothing that would equal in scope and intensity the current situation. In many contemporary metropolitan cities, religious diversity happens on site. And there is nothing to indicate that this development will stop. In contrast, it is very likely that in numerous countries the process of religious pluralization will further increase. Even if this development does not proceed at the same pace in all parts of the world, and even if there are some singular attempts of reestablishing religiously homogeneous zones, it is hardly feasible that in the long run we would ever return to largely mono-religious cultural realms. This implies that the awareness of living in a world of tremendous religious diversity will continue to intensify. This has repercussions on the self-understanding of each single religion. The theological reflection as it takes place within all other religions is going to accompany and influence the development of self-reflection and auto-interpretation of each religion permanently. It is for this reason that in every religion "theology" is likely to become in various degrees, but altogether increasingly so, "interreligious theology."

Interreligious theology, especially in conjunction with religious pluralism, presents a serious alternative to three other reactions triggered by the ongoing process of religious pluralization. The sociologist Peter Berger describes these as secularization, fundamentalism, and relativism. Although Berger has turned away from the secularization theory in the form that modernity will necessarily lead to a decline of religion, he nevertheless still maintains that religious pluralization fosters secularism inasmuch as it deprives "religion of its taken-for-granted quality." "Pluralism," says Berger, "undermines religious certainty."[16] That is, religious diversity triggers secularism in the sense of skepticism. This is somewhat reminiscent of David Hume, whose comparison of religious diversity with a case in court where all witnesses mutually refute their testimonies I mentioned earlier. Hume's argument is based on the premise—as Hume explicitly states—that "in matters of religion, whatever is different is contrary." Therefore, "there is no testimony . . . that is not opposed by an infinite number of witnesses."[17] This, however, is far from self-evident. Interreligious theology, in conjunction with religious pluralism, questions this premise and tries to show, as will be pointed out in the course of this book, that by no means all religious difference and diversity must be taken as incompatible.

The loss of certainty that comes along with pluralization causes many people to experience existential anxiety, to which, according to Berger, fundamentalism and relativism are different but similarly flawed and dangerous reactions. Fundamentalism fights this anxiety by its attempt to restore the certainty of premodern, in the sense of prepluralist, societies. This attempt is destined to fail because in contrast to the premodern situation, the fundamentalist's worldview is not based on givenness, but on choice. Yet choices are unstable, and hence an element of insecurity is lurking in the back of the fundamentalist's position. Psychologically this is combated by fanaticism, which makes fundamentalism dangerous. Relativism deals with the uncomfortableness of uncertainty in a different way: by a kind of self-deceit. The relativist is allowed to feel certain about at least one thing, which is the uncertainty of everything. Relativism thus suffers from the well-known aporia that it declares as absolute truth that there is no absolute truth. Apart from this epistemic flaw, the social dangers of relativism lie, according to Berger, in that it cultivates the "art of mistrust," which "translate(s) affirmations of truth or virtue into expressions of allegedly underlying interests that have nothing to do with truth or virtue—interests of power, or greed, or lust."[18] Whereas fundamentalism tends toward fanaticism, relativism, Berger writes, "moves individuals toward moral nihilism."[19] Interreligious theology may function as an antidote against all three of these side effects of religious pluralization: the tendency to undermine the credibility of all religions, as well as the potential to bring about fundamentalism and relativism.

That interreligious theology is a valid alternative over against skepticism, fundamentalism, and relativism is reflected in a further phenomenon that

---

[16]Berger 2014, 20.
[17]Hume 2000, 21.
[18]Berger 2014, 11.
[19]Ibid., 66.

accompanies religious pluralization. The intensified awareness of different religions does not only lead to a rejection of all of them in favor of atheism or naturalism or to a fundamentalist rejection of all apart from one's own or to nihilistic relativism. There are not a few people who welcome religious diversity as a natural, or should we say "supernatural," resource from which they can gain helpful impulses and orientations in relation to their personal spiritual life. Several sociological studies have confirmed that the number of people with multireligious identities is clearly on the rise in the West. In Asia and East Asia, that is, in cultural realms with a long and comparatively intensive experience of religious diversity, the phenomenon is widespread and in some regions regarded as more or less normal.[20] The religious practice of people who draw for their own spirituality on sources from various religious traditions is usually highly eclectic and subjective and does not display, in most cases, the standards of academic reflection. Nevertheless, it may express the attempt to develop one's own private version of an "interreligious theology." However, there are those who practice their multireligious belonging with an extremely high level of intellectual sophistication.[21] People with different degrees of multireligious identities seem to represent on a micro level a development which on the macro level of our global society indicates the overall future of theology.

As an additional reason underlining the need for an interreligious theology, I would like to adduce the conflict potential inherent in religious diversity. The last two decades have more than enough reminded us of this fact. I am not suggesting that interreligious theology will be the universal remedy. Unfortunately, but definitely, it is not as simple as that. The roots, causes, and reasons of interreligious conflicts are far too complex to allow for just one cure. Various factors of a political, economic, ethnic, legal, and historical nature, and so on, often play a crucial role when religious diversity turns into interreligious conflict. But the religious factor is undeniably part of the complex situation. It is not the case that in religious or interreligious conflicts, religion is entirely innocent and simply the victim of abuse. It may be correct that religions are frequently used to increase conflicts that are basically rooted in nonreligious causes and motives. Yet this is possible only because one can be sure that religions are suitable instruments for this kind of use or misuse. If you wish to burn down a house, you will use petrol, not water. If there were nothing within the religions themselves that contains seeds of conflict, that is, if religions were peaceful through and through, it would be impossible to misuse religion for instigating or fueling religious conflicts. This insight may further underline the need for

---

[20]For a recent treatment of religious hybrid identities in India and the United States see Rajkumar 2015.
[21]See, for example, Knitter 2009 and the examples studied in Drew 2011.

an interreligious theology. In this way religions can jointly address, self-critically examine, and, if possible, solve, or at least control, the religious roots of interreligious conflicts.[22]

In this respect, the adoption of a pluralist position by various theologians and scholars and an uncounted number of ordinary people within the various religions is already significant progress. For, as I argued above, in contrast to exclusivism and inclusivism, religious pluralism does not regard religious diversity as an evil. If the exclusivist is convinced that one's own religion is the only true religion in the world, or if the inclusivist believes that one's own faith is uniquely superior to all others, both the exclusivist and the inclusivist will quite naturally harbor the wish that ideally everybody should become a member of one's own religion. In itself, that is, on its own premises, this is a morally good wish, because it expresses the intention that everybody should ideally be able to enjoy the benefit of belonging to the exclusively true or uniquely superior religion. It would be immoral to hold that other people should remain in error about the true goals and purpose of life or should remain satisfied with inferior forms of revelation while the fullness of truth is to be enjoyed by only a chosen few. However, the honest and subjectively innocent wish that ideally everybody should become a member of one's own religion implies that ideally all other religions should be replaced by one's own faith. If different religions harbor and cultivate such intentions this creates much of the conflict potential that comes along with religious diversity.

The question of one's overall attitude to religious diversity translates into numerous far more specific and detailed issues regarding the relation between particular beliefs and the corresponding practices of different religions. Tackling these issues will be one of the major tasks of interreligious theology. Hans Küng was, and still is, right when he declared that "there can be no peace among the nations without peace among the religions" and that "there can be no peace among the religions without dialogue between the religions."[23] But in order to fulfill the hope implied by this dictum, dialogue needs to become permanent. It needs to become a habitual feature of the theological reflection in every religion; that is, it needs to take the form of interreligious theology. Although the practical necessity of interreligious dialogue is thus evident, dialogue cannot and must not be reduced to interreligious diplomacy or interreligious crisis management. For, on the one hand, some of the conflict potential between the religions is rooted in their beliefs. A purely pragmatic approach to dialogue would therefore be unable to deal satisfactorily with this aspect. On the other hand, theological dia-

---

[22]See Schmidt-Leukel 2009, 13–29.
[23]Küng 1991, 105.

logue cannot dispense with the question of truth. On the contrary, dialogue within the realm of religion needs to be dialogue seeking truth—similar to dialogue or discourse in philosophy, the natural sciences, and the social sciences. Perhaps we may never achieve in this life an irrefutable and infallible guarantee of having found the truth. But this must not mean that we give up the serious search for truth. For this resignation would make us even more liable to errors and mistakes. Interreligious theology is therefore the form that theology assumes when it takes religious truth claims seriously, those of one's own religious tradition and those of all others. Taking them seriously means to search for possible truth in all of the religious testimonies.

PART ONE

RELIGIOUS PLURALISM

2

Pluralist Awakenings in Christianity

THE EMERGENCE OF THE PLURALIST OPTION

The biblical scriptures do not contain an elaborate theology of religions but a number of different verses that can and are in fact quoted in support of each of the three possible options: exclusivism, inclusivism, and pluralism.[1] Christian exclusivists often draw on verses such as "I am the way, and the truth, and the life. No one comes to the father except through me" (Jn 14:6), and "There is no other name under heaven given among mortals by which we must be saved" (Acts 4:12). But there are also verses that seem to support an inclusivist option, for example, that God "has not left himself without a witness" among the nations (Acts 14:17) and that "in every nation anyone who fears him and does what is right is acceptable to him" (Acts 10:35). A Christian pluralist could refer to passages such as Amos 9:7, which states that God has not only liberated Israel from Egypt but also "the Philistines from Caphtor and the Arameans from Kir." Or one could draw on 1 John 4:7, which says indiscriminately that "everyone who loves is born of God and knows God." Neither explicitly nor implicitly does the Bible endorse just one particular option in the theology of religions. It is rather open to different interpretations. Even more important, it does not deal with other major religious traditions, neither with Hinduism or Buddhism, nor with Confucianism or Daoism, which were all unknown to the biblical authors. Nor, of course, does the Bible say anything about Islam, which came into existence much later. However, an adequate theology of religions can only be developed by taking into account a profound knowledge and understanding of the other religions themselves. The only religion that still exists and figures prominently in the Bible is Judaism. But this was not "another religion." The biblical discourse, including the New Testament, is itself an inner-Jewish discourse.

---

[1]For overviews on Christian attitudes toward religious diversity see the anthology Plantinga 1999, the summary in Schmidt-Leukel 2013b, and the contributions to Race and Hedges 2008.

This changed to some extent during the patristic period. By then various church fathers leaned toward an inclusivist view, seeing "seeds of the *logos*," that is, divine revelation in rudimentary form, in other religions while Jesus Christ was understood as the unique and full embodiment of the *logos*. Others tended toward exclusivist positions, which became increasingly harsher and, from the fourth century onward, developed into the dominant strand of Christian theology. The concept of "a religion" in the modern sense did not yet exist. What we would now call the classical Greek and Roman religions were perceived by Christian theologians as "pagans," and under massive Christian pressure they disappeared from the Roman Empire. Jews were also not seen as a different religion but as the people of the old covenant who had deliberately rejected the new one and hence attracted divine wrath and punishment. Islam, once it had come into existence, was not understood as another religion either, but as a Christian heresy that had been brought by a false prophet. The exclusivist dictum of "no salvation outside the Church" was thus directed not at "other religions" but, as the standard formula has it, at the three groups of Pagans, Jews, and "false Christians."[2] The latter group was by no means small: "More Christians were persecuted by the Roman Empire *after* the conversion of Constantine than before."[3]

If one were to look for early signs of theological moves toward a pluralist understanding, one would have to turn to those small Christian minorities who lived among the major non-Christian religions and had a better knowledge of them—for example, the Nestorians in India and China. There are indeed indications that at least something like protopluralist leanings existed among them. The famous Nestorian stele of Xi'an in China (erected in 781) quotes with approval an imperial proclamation that displays pluralist tendencies: "Right principles have no invariable name, holy men have no invariable station; instruction is established in accordance with the locality, with the object of benefiting the people at large."[4] In India the Portuguese synod of Diamper (1599) condemned the view, which it ascribed to the Nestorian Indian Thomas Christians, that "everyone may be saved in his own law; all which are good and lead men to heaven."[5] As we will see below, it was also a Nestorian bishop who first acknowledged a true prophetic mission of Muḥammad.[6]

In the Western churches, theology of religions gained new attention during the later Middle Ages, when Judaism and Islam began to be seen

---

[2]For a brief overview see Dupuis 1997, 84–109.
[3]Fredriksen 2014, 108.
[4]Horne 1917, 385.
[5]Aleaz 2005, 163.
[6]See chapter 10.

as religions in their own right, and in particular after the "discovery" of the Eastern religions in early modernity. In the works of Nicolas Cusanus (1401–64), Herbert of Cherbury (1583–1648), Matthew Tindal (1657–1733), and Enlightenment philosophers and theologians such as Gotthold Ephraim Lessing (1729–81), Immanuel Kant (1724–1804), and the early Friedrich Schleiermacher (1768–1834), we find new attempts of interpreting religious diversity, which point in a pluralist direction. Toward the end of his influential speeches *On Religion*, published in 1799, Schleiermacher, for example, held: "As nothing is more irreligious than to demand general uniformity in mankind, so nothing is more unchristian than to seek uniformity in religion."[7] By and large, however, religious pluralism became an elaborate option of Christian theology only during the second half of the twentieth century, after the knowledge about other religions rapidly improved from the late nineteenth century onward.[8] Several lines can be discerned along which religious pluralism emerged.

First of all, and most important, pluralism developed as a result of serious *interreligious dialogue*. A number of pioneers of religious pluralism had entered dialogue as exclusivists or inclusivists. But as understanding improved through their dialogue with people of other faiths, they became convinced that claims to Christian superiority could no longer be justified. Prominent examples of Christian theologians who became religious pluralists because of their dialogical experiences are Raimon Panikkar (1918–2010), Stanley Samartha (1920–2001), Henri Le Saux / Swami Abhishiktananda (1910–73), Lynn de Silva (1919–82), Aloysius Pieris, Seiichi Yagi, Paul Ingram, Wilfred Cantwell Smith (1916–2000), John Hick (1922–2012), Rosemary Radford Ruether, and Leonard Swidler.

Second, pluralism emerged from various attempts at understanding religious diversity from a *historical* and *philosophical* perspective. Early moves toward a pluralist approach are already found in the very last writings of Ernst Troeltsch (1865–1923) and Paul Tillich (1886–1965).[9] But the main features of a consistent pluralistic hypothesis were, from the 1960s and '70s onward, developed by Raimon Panikkar,[10] Wilfred Cantwell Smith,[11] and in particular the philosopher and theologian John Hick.[12] Until today, Hick's work exerts a major influence on discussions about pluralism and

---

[7] Schleiermacher 1958, 252.

[8] As a rather early example one might quote the Theosophists, some of whom, like Annie Besant (1847–1933), on the basis of their experiments in multireligious experiences, started displaying features of a pluralist interpretation of religious diversity.

[9] See Troeltsch 1980; Tillich 1966. On Tillich see also chapter 8.

[10] See, for example, Panikkar 1978; 1981; 1987; 1993; 1995; 2010.

[11] See, for example, Smith 1963; 1967; 1977; [1963] 1978; 1979; 1989.

[12] See, for example, Hick 1973; 1982; 1985a; 1989; 1993a; 1995; 2001.

its further development. An impressive list of other systematic theologians and philosophers of religions made significant contributions which partly build on Hick's ideas, complement them, or present alternative versions of pluralism—for example, Alan Race, Gordon Kaufman, Langdon Gilkey, Wesley Ariarajah, Glyn Richards, Peter Byrne, Maurice Wiles, Keith Ward, Leonard Swidler, Chester Gillis, and Roger Haight.

One theologian, whom I have not mentioned so far, but whose work is highly influential within and beyond Christian religious pluralism is the Roman Catholic theologian Paul Knitter. He represents a third important strand in the development of pluralism, which combines the theology of religions with impulses from *liberation theology*. At a crucial stage in the development of liberation theology the question arose of how its concern for the poor can be realized in those parts of the so-called Third World where the majority of the poor belong to non-Christian religions. This question triggered intensive controversy and debate within the Ecumenical Association of Third World Theologians (EATWOT). Some liberation theologians argued in favor of an exclusivist approach, criticizing non-Christian religions as oppressive, along the lines of Karl Marx, and idolatrous, along the lines of Karl Barth, in contrast to the supposedly uniquely liberating gospel. Others, however, opted for a pluralist approach, suggesting that the poor are God's people regardless of their religious affiliation, so that interreligious alliances can be formed in which the liberating elements from all religious traditions should be employed in service of a joint commitment to the common good. Some prominent representatives of this view are the Sri Lankan theologians Aloysius Pieris and Tissa Balasuriya (1924–2013), the Indian Felix Wilfred, and today José Maria Vigil.[13] Paul Knitter was also strongly influenced by Aloysius Pieris and integrated central features of liberation theology with his own version of pluralism, giving it thereby a decisively practical-political orientation.[14]

Finally, a fourth line that contributed to the development of religious pluralism is *feminist theology*. The principal concern of feminism to unmask and overcome any sociocultural structures confining women to an inferior role has quite naturally an intercultural and interreligious dimension. Feminist theologians who do not reduce religion to a mere sociocultural phenomenon are therefore interested in combining their feminist concern with a theological understanding of the relation between Christianity and non-Christian religions. Their sharpened sensitivity for the ambivalences of Christianity regarding the gender issue has prepared a number of them to approach non-Christian religions with a similar attitude: a readiness

---

[13]Vigil 2008.
[14]See, e.g., Knitter 1987; 1995; 1996; 1997.

to discover similar ambivalences in all the religious traditions, that is, to identify both oppressive as well as liberating features. Various feminist Christian theologians thereby have arrived at a pluralist understanding—for example, Chung Hyun Kyung, Ursula King, Marjorie Hewitt Suchocki, Manuela Kalsky, Rosemary Radford Reuther, and Jeannine Hill Fletcher.

DOCTRINAL PRESUPPOSITIONS

After this rough overview,[15] let me now turn briefly to some of the central doctrinal questions that are to be addressed by a Christian and pluralistic theology of religions.[16] A general starting point for, I suppose, all Christian pluralists is the tension between the Christian belief in God as universal love and the exclusivist assumption that more or less all non-Christians are destined for eternal damnation. In a lecture from 1972 John Hick called this "a paradox of gigantic proportions."[17] Already in 1961 Wilfred Cantwell Smith had given this problem a positive twist: If God is as has been revealed in and through Christ, we need to assume that God also responds to the faith of non-Christians:

> If the Christian revelation were *not* true, then it might be possible to imagine that God would allow Hindus to worship Him or Muslims to obey Him or Buddhists to feel compassionate towards their fellows, without His responding, without His reaching out to hold them in His arms. But because God is what He is, because He is what Christ has shown Him to be, *therefore* other men *do* live in His presence.[18]

There is no doubt that this is a position that can also be endorsed by Christian inclusivists. Yet as has been shown in chapter 1, inclusivist positions maintain a claim to Christian superiority and hence cannot advance to a genuine theological appreciation of religious diversity. Pluralists therefore grapple with those features of their respective religious tradition that support superiority claims in both exclusivist and inclusivist forms. Within Christianity the theological debate is focused on the understanding of saving faith, the nature of God and divine revelation, and the status and redemptive role of Christ.

---

[15]For more details see Schmidt-Leukel 2008b; 2010b.

[16]An extensive treatment of these issues is found in Schmidt-Leukel 2005a (an English translation is forthcoming as Schmidt-Leukel 2017b).

[17]Hick 1973, 122.

[18]Smith 1963, 139. The text is, as Smith (1963, 4) tells, from a lecture of 1961.

Saving Faith

The question of how to understand the *saving nature of faith* features prominently in the work of Wilfred Cantwell Smith. Throughout his academic work
Smith has emphasized the personal nature of religion and religious studies.
To Smith, "Religious Studies" is not a neutral enterprise but is carried out by
individual persons with their specific views reflecting in many respects their
own time and context.[19] The concept of "religions" is, according to Smith,
highly misleading if it creates the impression of stable, fixed realities. In
this sense, the idea of "a religion" is a reified abstraction. What we find in
reality are not things called "religions" but diverse and constantly changing
religious traditions plus the individual faith of religious people who keep the
traditions alive and are, in turn, themselves influenced by these traditions.[20]

In relation to the understanding of religious faith, Smith insists on
distinguishing sharply between "faith" as a personal attitude and "belief"
or "beliefs" as part of the religious traditions. According to Smith, *faith*
"stands for an inner experience or involvement of a particular person";[21] it
signifies "what his tradition means to him," or "what the universe means
to him, in the light of that tradition,"[22] and especially "the impingement
on him of the transcendent, putative or real."[23] In contrast, *beliefs* take the
shape of doctrinal propositions. They express what people in a particular
religious tradition at a specific time and place hold to be true. "Believing"
is thus "the holding of certain ideas,"[24] whereas "faith" is "an orientation of
the personality, to oneself, to one's neighbor, to the universe; . . . a capacity to live at a more than mundane level; to see, to feel, to act in terms of,
a transcendent reality."[25] Regarding the theological question of salvation,
Smith holds that "faith" is decisive, not "belief." It is "faith" that saves,
or better: "God through faith."[26] "One's faith," so Smith writes, "is given
by God; one's beliefs by one's century."[27] Personal faith is nourished by
and articulates itself in the respective religious traditions. From this Smith
draws two important conclusions: First, if faith finds expression in different religious traditions, then "faith differs in form, but not in kind."[28] And
second, if the different traditions nourish the faith of the people living in

---

[19]See Smith 1959.
[20]See Smith [1963] 1978.
[21]Ibid., 156.
[22]Ibid., 159.
[23]Ibid., 156.
[24]Smith 1979, 12.
[25]Ibid.
[26]Smith 1989, 169.
[27]Smith 1977, 96.
[28]Smith 1989, 168.

and by them, the religions can be understood theologically as channels of divine revelation. That is, divine reality becomes manifest in the lives of individual persons through their religious traditions.[29] A Muslim is thus saved by faith of an Islamic form, a Buddhist by faith of a Buddhist form, a Jew by faith of a Jewish form, and so on.[30]

John Hick adopted this idea from Smith, but held that the word "faith" is linguistically too much linked to the theistic religions and is still too close to the intellectual act of believing, instead of expressing the kind of holistic existential attitude that Smith had in mind. Hick therefore suggested to replace the term "faith"—in the sense used by Smith—with the formula: "transformation from self-centeredness to Reality-centeredness,"[31] whereby "Reality" or just "the Real" signifies transcendent or ultimate reality, independently of whether this is conceived of in personal or impersonal terms.[32] On the one hand, Hick generates this formula from an analysis of the concepts of salvation and liberation as found in the various religious traditions.[33] On the other hand, the formula represents a further development of his earlier concept of human life as a "soul-making" or "person-making process" which he had coined in the context of his discussion of theodicy, that is, the problem of evil.[34] In fact, there is a substantial connection between the problem of evil and a valid theology of religions: If a credible answer to the problem of evil is based on the idea of life's meaning as a soul-making process, then this must be valid for all human beings. And this leads to the question of how this process is reflected and possibly supported by other religions.

One advantage of Hick's formula is that it allows for—and in fact requires—the establishment of criteria that determine whether that salvific transformation is truly happening. According to Hick these are the kind of spiritual and moral qualities that the New Testament calls "the fruit of the spirit" (Gal 5:22–23). The central criterion among them is, according to Hick, "love" (*agape*) or "compassion" (*karuṇā*).[35] On this normative basis he can argue that "religious traditions and their various components . . . have greater or less value according as they promote or hinder the salvific transformation."[36] As far as human observation can tell, says Hick, none of the major religious traditions appears to be evidently superior to all the others[37]—and I think that in this he is clearly right. Paul Knitter's approach

---

[29]Ibid., 172ff.
[30]Ibid., 168.
[31]Hick 1985a, 28–30.
[32]Hick 1989, 10–11.
[33]Ibid., 36–55.
[34]Hick [1966] 1990, esp. 252–61.
[35]Hick 1989, 164.
[36]Ibid., 300.
[37]E.g., Hick 1985a, 36.

is—in a sense—a further elaboration of this aspect inasmuch as Knitter emphasizes the social and political dimension of the salvific transformation. When he characterizes his own model as "soteriocentric," he takes, like John Hick, the soteriological potential of the religions as the crucial criterion for their theological assessment. Knitter has also referred to his approach—in more Christian terms—as "Kingdom centered."[38] Turning one's life toward God and toward one's neighbor corresponds the twofold commandment, which Jesus declared to be the highest rule of God's kingdom, that is, of the reign of God: to love God with all one's heart and one's neighbor as oneself. This translates easily into Hick's formula of a transformation from self-centeredness to Reality- or God-centeredness, which proves to be genuine if it results in a loving and compassionate attitude toward one's neighbor. But is this translation of "Reality-centeredness" into "God-centeredness" correct? How do Christian pluralists understand God?

The Concept of God and Divine Revelation

I do not suggest that all Christian pluralists share the same understanding of God. But most of them tend to de-emphasize the idea that humans could have an adequate conceptual grasp of God. If God—as some Christian theologians certainly hold—can best and most adequately be described as the Trinity of Father, Son, and Holy Spirit, the concepts of God or transcendent reality that we find in all other religions must be judged either as simply wrong or at best as insufficient inasmuch as they approximate, or diverge from, this one and only true understanding of God as the Christian Trinity—an understanding that the Christian tradition supposes to have been revealed in fact by God. This way of establishing Christian superiority is criticized by Christian pluralists with two major objections: First, revelation should not be misunderstood as the revelation of any doctrinal propositions or texts but as the self-communication or manifestation of the Divine in human experience within specific historical contexts. Doctrinal expressions are not themselves revealed but emerge from the specific circumstances under which humans experience the presence of the Divine. In short, they do not describe the Divine reality itself but signify specific human experiences of the Divine. For example, to John Hick different religions are not different expressions of the same experience, but expressions of different experiences with the same divine reality.[39] This argument is supported by

---

[38]Knitter 1996, 118–21.

[39]See Hick 1989, 295, 350–51. Regarding the question of whether conceptual interpretation is secondary to the experience or whether experience is shaped and structured by conceptual interpretation, Hick holds the latter view and, therefore, in this respect, agrees with Stephen Katz and George

a second one, according to which God's transcendence implies that God's reality is necessarily greater than anything that human words or concepts can express. Christian pluralists claim—and again I think rightly so—that this has been affirmed by the vast majority of the Christian church fathers, that is, by the widely influential theologians of the Christian tradition.

Much of John Hick's work is marked by the attempt to cast these two arguments in a consistent epistemological form. Employing Kantian terminology, he distinguished between "the Real *an sich*," that is, the divine reality in itself, beyond human experience, and "the Real" as it is reflected in human thought and experience. The latter appears in the history of religions in the form of the different personal representations and impersonal concepts or images of the Ultimate, which Hick calls the *personae* and *impersonae* of the Real. Hick's use of the Kantian model and Kantian terminology has led to various misunderstandings and misrepresentations of his position. Several critics assumed that Hick would say—with Kant—that God cannot be experienced and known at all because of our epistemological limitations, although Hick explicitly stated that he holds—against Kant—that humans are able to genuinely experience God.[40] However, God, the Transcendent or "the Real," can only be experienced in those ways that our specifically human capacities permit. Our epistemic apparatus is bound by the confinements of our nature and by concepts that are inevitably part of a conceptual scheme and as such are also of a limited, de-*fining* character, whereas the transcendent reality in itself is supposed to be an *in*-finite reality. We can therefore never experience the Real as it is *in itself*, that is, *in its infinity*, but only in the finite ways predetermined by our limited cognitive capacities, that is, as the particular *personae* and *impersonae* of the religions. This conclusion is not the outcome of a Kantian epistemology but is primarily derived from the metaphysical affirmation of the *transcendence* of God or Ultimate reality, an affirmation that is found in all the major religious traditions.[41] So if it needs to be affirmed that God is ultimately an ineffable or—as Hick says—transcategorial reality,[42] one cannot claim that the Christian Trinity is the most adequate description of this reality.

Will the pluralists' emphasis on the limits of the human capacity to understand God conceptually, that is, their subscription to the Christian apophatic tradition, undermine the very starting point of their rejection of exclusivism? Can one still hold that there is a conflict between the faith in God's universal love and the belief in the eternal damnation of all non-

---

Lindbeck (cf. Hick 1989, 170–71, 296, 360–61). This is often neglected by those among Hick's critics who accuse him of ignoring religious differences.

[40]Hick 1989, 243.

[41]Hick 1985a, 39–40.

[42]Hick 2001, 76–89.

Christians, if such faith in God's love is quenched or even destroyed by the affirmation of God's "transcategoriality"? Can pluralists still trust that non-Christians too live in the saving presence of God, because God, as Smith had phrased it, "is what Christ has shown Him to be"?[43] Hick has replied to this objection by pointing out that one can affirm divine ineffability and nevertheless still call the Real "benign" or "good" if this is not understood as an intrinsic attribute but as relating to valid experience of the Real in its relation to us: "Our human nature, with its range of concepts and languages, is such that from our point of view the Real, experienced in a variety of divine phenomena, is benign, good."[44]

Jesus Christ

Another major pillar of traditional Christian superiority claims is the belief that Jesus Christ is the unique incarnation of God, or more precisely of the "Word of God," the divine *logos*, in human form and thus the climax of Divine revelation, which inevitably makes Christianity superior to all the other faiths. Christian pluralists respond to this in two different ways: First, by questioning the concept of "incarnation" and, second, by questioning the assumption of a unique incarnation. But these two ways are in the end convergent, because pluralists suggest an understanding of incarnation that renders the assumption of a unique incarnation implausible.

In 1977 John Hick edited the book *The Myth of God Incarnate*, in which he criticized a literal understanding of the classical Chalcedonian Christology as meaningless. To say that Christ had both a true human nature (with all the human attributes) and a true divine nature (with all divine attributes) would make as little sense as saying that a certain geometrical figure has at the same time both the nature of a circle and that of a square. He thus suggested that the doctrine of incarnation should be taken as a mythological statement that expressed, with the help of classical Greek mythology, the authentic and valid experience of Jesus as a human mediator of the Divine presence.[45] Later on Hick replaced the term "mythological" with "metaphorical"[46] and held that the metaphor of incarnation signifies "an intersection of the divine and the human . . . that occurs in different ways and degrees in all human openness and response to the divine initiative."[47]

In his major monograph *Jesus Symbol of God*[48] the Roman Catholic

---

[43]See above at n. 16.
[44]Hick 2001, 86.
[45]Hick 1977.
[46]Hick 1993a.
[47]Hick 1993b.
[48]Haight 1999.

theologian Roger Haight argued that an understanding of incarnation along the lines that John Hick suggested would not require a complete rejection of the traditional two-natures Christology but rather call and allow for its reinterpretation in terms of symbolic mediation. Each symbol, Haight writes, has two natures: the nature of the symbol itself and the nature of the reality that is symbolized. On the one hand, the symbol points beyond itself to the symbolized reality; on the other hand, the symbolized becomes present in and through the symbol. In that sense Jesus can be understood as a symbol of God: being fully human, Jesus points beyond himself to the reality of God while God becomes present in and through the life of Jesus to other human beings. Haight agreed with Hick that, depending on its interpretation, incarnation does not necessarily require the idea of uniqueness or onliness. If incarnation is understood in the sense of symbolic mediation, it is compatible with the assumptions of several symbolic mediations of God, each taking a different and specific form.[49] Similarly Raimon Panikkar had argued since the 1980s that Jesus is just one manifestation of the inner unity of God and human (later he spoke of the "cosmotheandric" unity of God, human, and cosmos), revealing that unity in a particular and unique way, while other manifestations in different religious contexts may reveal this unity in their own ways.[50] Paul Knitter coined the formula that the "uniqueness of Jesus' salvific role can be reinterpreted in terms of *truly* but not *only*."[51] Hick called this "an excellent formulation."[52]

For Christian pluralists the status of Jesus as "savior" depends on his role as revealer. Jesus is savior inasmuch as he embodies God's saving word. Christian pluralists usually reject the idea that Jesus Christ constituted salvation by an act of atoning self-sacrifice. Salvation is rooted in the love and mercy of God, and the life of Jesus, including his crucifixion, does not constitute but represents God's love in such a way that it transforms human lives.[53] As Roger Haight has it: "The term *salvation* can be understood generically as indicating that Jesus communicates God in a way that makes people whole (or healed, or healthy) or eternally fulfilled in their being."[54] This view, as Knitter replies, allows us to "affirm both Jesus and Buddha as saviors; in the recognition that both of them 'saved,' mainly by revealing and teaching."[55]

---

[49]Haight 2005, 164.
[50]See Panikkar 1981, 14–15, 27, 52–53, 164; 1987, 112.
[51]Knitter 1997, 7.
[52]Hick 1997, 81.
[53]On the helpful distinction between a constitutive and representative understanding of Jesus' salvific role see Ogden 1992, 92–98.
[54]Haight in Knitter and Haight 2015, 59.
[55]Knitter in ibid., 63.

PROSPECTS AND DEVELOPMENTS

Pluralist theologies have been met with a wave of criticism blaming them as "non-Christian," "a form of paganism," "unbelief," "polytheistic," "colonialist," "crypto-imperialist," "relativistic," "agnostic," and so on. In 2000 the Roman Catholic Church issued *Dominus Iesus*, a document specifically written to condemn religious pluralism, including some forms of a too open-minded inclusivism such as that of Jacques Dupuis (1923–2004).[56] After *Dominus Iesus* the Roman Catholic Church proceeded with sanctions and investigations against various Catholic pluralists. Astonishingly little has been done in terms of seriously engaging with the pluralist arguments, or in terms of developing a more persuasive alternative.[57] There are, however, two more recent lines of theological thought that are often taken as alternatives to a pluralist position. Let us see to which extent this might be a fair perception.

Some critics have accused pluralist approaches as *not being truly "pluralistic"* because of the pluralists' assumption that the major religions are all related—though in different ways—to one and the same ultimate reality.[58] This kind of criticism may have two different implications. In one variant, it presupposes that a truly pluralistic approach would have to assume that only one religion is related to ultimate reality, while the others are not: "Their Gods are different from our God."—"So are there several Gods?"— "No, just one."—"Which one?"—"Ours."—"Then none of 'their Gods' is the true God."[59] So this way of emphasizing difference and diversity is actually identical with exclusivism. To be sure, exclusivism is a possible interpretation of religious diversity. Yet in what sense would it be "pluralistic"? It divides the world of religions in two groups: the one religion that is truly related to ultimate reality and all the others that are on a par in that they erroneously think to be related to the ultimate. I find it difficult to see why this should be more pluralistic than the pluralist theology of religions. And it would certainly not do any better justice to the self-understanding of other religions.

In a different variant, the criticism of being not truly pluralistic can be based on the presupposition that genuine pluralism would have to assume the existence of more than one ultimate reality and that different religions

---

[56]See Dupuis 1997.

[57]Becker and Morali (2010) offer for the most part of the volume just a restatement of what they consider to be the orthodox Roman Catholic position. The critical engagement with the challenge of pluralist positions remains peripheral (see the contributions of D'Costa and Rebernik, ibid., 329–56).

[58]This question will be pursued further in chapter 8.

[59]A somewhat similar conversation is related in Ariarajah 1985, 1.

are different because they relate to different ultimates. This idea is sometimes referred to as *polycentric pluralism* in contrast to a *monocentric pluralism* which presupposes one ultimate reality as the central focus of different religions. The idea of a plurality of ultimate realities, however, seems to be self-refuting. If there are several different ultimates, none of these would be "ultimate" in an ultimate sense. It would be a diversity of somehow limited, that is, finite realities, but not of truly ultimate realities. Some proponents of polycentric or "deep pluralism" have therefore suggested that what appears as different ultimates are in fact different aspects of one complex ultimate reality. This assumption underlies the concept of religious pluralism as it is found in *process theology*,[60] especially in the work of John Cobb,[61] and in the somewhat similar ideas of Steven Kaplan.[62] However, if the different religions are focused on different aspects of one complex ultimate reality, one religion might still be superior to all the others inasmuch as it has the most adequate understanding of this complex ultimate reality—an understanding that covers all of its aspects in the most appropriate form. The latter is the view of Mark Heim, who holds that the Christian Trinity is the most comprehensive concept of ultimate reality and that other religions are related—unknowingly—to different aspects of the Trinity.[63] This is no longer a pluralist, but clearly an inclusivist approach. Hence the demand for a more pluralistic pluralism is at times a concealed rejection of religious pluralism in favor of either exclusivist or inclusivist positions. Nevertheless, the positions of John Cobb and Mark Heim, and similarly that of Raimon Panikkar, encourage more reflection about the mutual relations between the different concepts of the ultimate, that is, in Hick's terminology, between the different *personae* and *impersonae* of the Real. This is indeed stimulating for the further development of religious pluralism and interreligious theology, as will be explained in more detail in chapters 8 and 14.

Given the explicit and sharp rejection of religious pluralism by the Roman Catholic Church, some (primarily Roman Catholic) theologians have suggested a moratorium for the theology of religions. Theology should focus on comparative studies before it would be fit to freshly address the issues of a theology of religions.[64] This understanding represents one, but by no means the only, type of *comparative theology*.[65] Perhaps it would be

---

[60]The label "process theology" indicates its dependence on the so-called process philosophy of Alfred North Whitehead (1861–1947).

[61]Griffin 2005a; Cobb 1999.

[62]Kaplan 2002.

[63]Heim 1995; 2001. See also chapter 14 below.

[64]Fredericks 1995; 1999; Clooney 1993; 2010.

[65]Keith Ward and Robert Neville are distinct exponents of a different approach in comparative theology. See, for example, Neville 1991, 155–69; Ward 1994, 3–49.

even more true to say that it does not represent one of its types but one of its rather short-lived phases. For as is becoming increasingly evident, the consistent exclusion of the theology of religions discourse from comparative studies would deprive such studies of their theological nature. That is, they would just be doing the job of "comparative religion." If, however, comparative theologians want to live up to the theological element of their work, they cannot exclude the issue of truth and of different religious truth claims from their comparisons and will thereby inevitably enter the field of theology of religions.[66] It is therefore no surprise to notice that James Fredericks and Francis Clooney, who most explicitly asked for a moratorium and for eschewing theology of religions, have in fact disclosed their personal preference for Christian inclusivism.[67] Comparative theologians of the "next generation"—for example, Kristin Kiblinger—have convincingly argued that some proponents of comparative theology "gave up on theology of religions prematurely."[68]

Yet if comparative theology is not understood as an alternative to the theology of religions but rather as a complementary strand of research, it can make important contributions to the kind of "global" or "universal theology" that pioneers of religious pluralism such as Wilfred Cantwell Smith and John Hick were aiming at. According to Smith, we need a "theology that will interpret the history of our race in a way that will give intellectual expression to our faith, the faith of all of us."[69] This kind of "world theology" can be realized only by means of a global multireligious colloquium that looks at the whole religious history of humankind as its source of reflecting on humanity's perennial questions.[70] In this sense, comparative theology can be seen as a formidable instrument for doing interreligious theology. Why and how a pluralist theology of religions requires interreligious theology will be further discussed in chapter 8. But before doing so, let us take a longer look at the development of pluralist approaches in other major religious traditions.

A decisive moment in the development of Christian pluralism was the publication of *The Myth of Christian Uniqueness: Toward a Pluralistic Theology of Religions.*[71] This book emerged from a conference that had taken place in 1986 in Claremont, California, and entered the history of contemporary theology under the name of the "Rubicon Conference." The image is taken from an event in the history of the Roman Empire, when Julius

---

[66]Schmidt-Leukel 2009, 90–104; Hedges 2010, 52–55; Hedges 2014a.
[67]See Clooney 1993, 194–95; Fredericks 2010, xv.
[68]Kiblinger 2010, 42.
[69]Smith [1981] 1989, 125.
[70]Schmidt-Leukel 2012; 2014; Vigil 2010.
[71]Hick and Knitter 1987.

Caesar in the middle of the first century BCE had crossed the river Rubicon in order to march with his troops toward Rome. Since then "crossing the Rubicon" became a common dictum indicating that one has reached a crucial decision, a point of no return. The explicit aim of the Rubicon Conference was to cross the Rubicon of Christian claims to superiority, regardless of whether these take the form of exclusivism or inclusivism, because neither of these two versions permits a positive assessment of religious diversity. It was therefore the aim of the Rubicon Conference, as Langdon Gilkey expressed it, to combine the perception of religious diversity with the notion of theological parity.[72]

How to understand religious diversity has become a matter of serious concern in each of the major religious traditions.[73] If, as I argued in chapter 1, exclusive or inclusive claims to superiority prevent by their internal logic a positive evaluation of religious diversity, then this is not just a Christian problem, but one that each religion has to confront. For, traditionally, each of the major religions understands itself as either uniquely true or uniquely superior in relation to all the other faiths. This raises the question of whether there are any efforts in the other major religious traditions to arrive at a position that combines the awareness of religious diversity with the notion of religious parity. Do these traditions also harbor a theological potential that allows them to cross their own Rubicon of absoluteness? What forms do exclusivist and inclusivist superiority claims take within the doctrinal framework of Judaism, Islam, Hinduism, Buddhism or Chinese religions? And what form, therefore, does religious pluralism take if developed from within those religions? Eighteen years after the Rubicon Conference, such questions were at the center of a follow-up conference held in Birmingham in 2004. Some of its papers were published under the title *The Myth of Religious Superiority: Multifaith Explorations of Religious Pluralism.*[74] It showed that the discussion about a religious understanding of religious diversity is indeed a vital issue in all the major faiths. Twenty years before, in 1984, John Hick had stated that "it is for the adherents of each of the great traditions to look critically at their own dogmas in the light of their new experience within a religiously plural world." As we will see, to some extent such critical revision with the prospect of arriving at a pluralist position has indeed been started and will now be considered in more detail.

---

[72] Gilkey 1987, 37.
[73] A useful overview is presented by Hedges 2014b.
[74] Knitter 2005.

3

Judaism and the Many Covenants

A PRELUDE TO JEWISH PLURALISM

On November 10, 1965, the Jewish theologian Abraham Joshua Heschel (1907–72) presented his official inaugural lecture at the Union Theological Seminary in New York, where he had been appointed as visiting professor. It was the night after the great blackout due to power failure in New York,[1] which Heschel briefly mentions in his lecture as an event when people felt a very strong fellowship and an "awareness of being one."[2] Heschel gave his lecture the illuminating title "No Religion Is an Island," signaling his view that in the contemporary world all religions have become interdependent and "involved with one another." "Today religious isolationism is a myth."[3] Heschel's words indeed apply to all religions, but they are of specific relevance to Judaism. As an ethnic religion bound to a particular people with its long and bitter experience of living in exile as a persecuted minority, Judaism could survive and maintain its identity only because—to some extent—it isolated itself from other religions and other people. According to Heschel, the time has come to enter into a new period of history, and so he ended his lecture with a call for interreligious cooperation, including the sharing of "insight and learning."[4]

Heschel's lecture became a highly influential text within contemporary Jewish reflection about the relationship between Judaism and other faiths.[5] Although he arguably did not arrive at a fully pluralist position, he certainly came fairly close to it.[6] Heschel questioned traditional Jewish thinking about

---

[1]Unfortunately the editors of the reprint of Heschel's lecture mistakenly gave the date of the power failure as "April 1966"; see Heschel 1991, 4.

[2]The widespread story that nine months later this experience "of being one" led to an increase of New York's birth rate by 35 percent is apparently just a nice tale.

[3]Heschel 1991, 6.

[4]Ibid., 22.

[5]Goshen-Gottstein 2007.

[6]For Jewish voices discussing Heschel's pluralism see Kasimow 1991; Hartman 2002, 169–92; Goschen-Gottstein 2009.

other faiths and affirmed crucial foundations on which religious pluralism rests: God transcends every religion and cannot be equated with any one among them. Ultimate truth transcends all concepts and words. "Revelation" is therefore "always an accommodation to the capacity of man," so that "one truth comes to expression in many ways of understanding." As a consequence, says Heschel, one needs to assume that the existence of religious diversity is the will of God for this present aeon.[7] "The Jews do not maintain that the way of the Torah is the only way of serving God."[8] It is worth mentioning that all of this was said in 1965—that is, well before the time when John Hick began to develop his pluralist theology, which was during his years as H. G. Wood Professor in Birmingham from 1967 onward.[9]

Subsequent to World War II, Jewish theology has initially been preoccupied with two topics: Reflection on the Holocaust and its theological implications, on the one hand, and the establishment of the modern state of Israel, on the other hand.[10] After Heschel's powerful impetus, there has been a gradual increase in voices addressing the question of how Judaism should see other religions and understand itself in relation to them. A crucial role was naturally played by Jewish interest and participation in the Christian theological attempts to overcome Christian anti-Judaism. Many Christians were keen on developing a theology that affirmed Judaism's ongoing value as a non-Christian religion and abandoned any idea of converting Jews to Christianity. Such efforts have been met with much approval on the Jewish side. They also triggered the reverse question of how Judaism sees Christianity. A remarkable answer to this was given by the Jewish declaration *Dabru Emet*, published in 2000 and initially signed by more than 220 rabbis and scholars from many different branches of Judaism. In *Dabru Emet* the outlines of a pluralist, or perhaps protopluralist, position can be discerned. For the declaration does not only say that "Jews and Christians worship the same God"; it also states: "Christians know and serve God through Jesus Christ and the Christian tradition. Jews know and serve God through the Torah and the Jewish tradition."[11] Both Jesus Christ and the Torah, as two different media of revelation, and the two traditions based on them are presented in strict parallelism without ranking one above the other.

Today more and more Jewish theologians feel the necessity of commenting

---

[7] Heschel 1991, 13–15.

[8] Ibid., 19.

[9] See Hick's autobiography—Hick 2002, 159–237. A first and brief proto-pluralist passage appears in Hick 1968, 80f. Yet there is no evidence that Hick had been aware of Heschel's lecture (as has also been confirmed by Thomas Ruston, who kindly checked the John Hick archive at Birmingham University).

[10] Lubarsky 2005. See also Lubarsky 1990, which deals primarily with modern predecessors of a Jewish pluralism.

[11] The text of the document is found at http://www.jcrelations.net/Dabru+Emet+-+A+Jewish+State ment+on+Christians+and+Christianity.2395.0.html?L=3.

about their faith's relation to other religions, for example, Islam, Hinduism, and Buddhism.[12] In the past, Jewish relations with Islam had their bad and their good times. For most of the time, Judaism could exist and sometimes even flourish under Muslim rule. Though much of anti-Muslim polemics is found in the Jewish tradition, there are also Jewish voices that have spoken of Islam with high regard.[13] The Yemenite Jewish philosopher Nethanael ibn al-Fayyumi (d. c. 1164), for example, accepted Muḥammad as a prophet to the Muslims but not to the communities that preceded them.[14] As is well known, medieval Jewish spirituality consciously borrowed from Sufism. Abraham Maimonides (1186–1237), the son of Moses Maimonides (d. 1204), could even declare that the ways of the biblical prophets have in his days become the ways of the Muslim Sufis from whom Jews should now relearn them.[15] Today Jewish-Muslim relations suffer heavily under the political struggle over Israel/Palestine. Nevertheless, there are Jewish voices who do remind fellow Jews and Muslims of how much both traditions have in common theologically.[16] As Jewish interest in Islam was once animated by the wish to learn from Sufi spirituality, Jewish relations to Hinduism[17] and even more so to Buddhism are currently determined by a strong interest of Jews in the various forms of Eastern meditation. This is most apparent in the fairly large number of so-called JuBus (or Bujus), that is, Jews who either converted to Buddhism or see themselves as both Jews and Buddhists.[18] Such developments have clearly contributed to the efforts among contemporary Jewish theologians of rethinking and revising traditional Jewish understandings of religious diversity.

THE TRADITIONAL BACKGROUND

Jewish pluralists often emphasize that Judaism is, in principle, in a better position to arrive at a positive assessment of other religions than Christianity or Islam, because, in contrast to their Abrahamic sister faiths, Judaism never saw itself as a religion destined for all humanity. In addition, many Jews will presumably agree with Michael Kogan that it would be "theologi-

---

[12]For brief overviews see Langer 2003; Ravitzky 2006. A detailed survey of traditional and contemporary elements and models of Jewish theologies of religions is offered by Brill 2010, and of Jewish relations to Christianity, Islam, Hinduism, and Buddhism by Brill 2012. See also the contributions to Goshen-Gottstein and Korn 2012.

[13]See overviews in Fenton 2012 and Brill 2012, 145–201.

[14]Solomon 1996, 94. See also Jospe 2012, 107–9.

[15]See Fenton 1981, 7–8.

[16]See, for example, Fenton 2012; Firestone 2013.

[17]See Goshen-Gottstein 2012a; Holdrege 2013.

[18]Gez 2011; Katz 2013.

cal madness" if Jews, being altogether not more than 15 million people, would hold that they are "the only bearers of truth" and that God would be concerned exclusively with the "religious welfare" of such a small group.[19] Like their Christian counterparts, Jewish theologians also employ the argument of God's universal care: "If God is truly concerned with the fate of all humanity, God would not have disclosed Godself fully and finally to a particular people, allowing the rest of humanity to wallow in darkness and ignorance."[20] Nevertheless, traditionally the Jewish position too has been either exclusivist or inclusivist. The Jewish theologian Ruth Langer summarizes succinctly that from the perspective of biblical Judaism all other peoples were seen as "uniformly idolatrous," and hence as "theologically . . . all total outsiders, uniform in their failure to recognize Israel's God."[21] A more positive perspective was offered by the rabbinic teaching of the Noahide Laws, first testified to in the third century CE.[22] According to this doctrine God's covenant with Noah comprises all peoples in the world and is based on seven laws. That is, people should abstain from (1) idolatry, (2) murder, (3) robbery, (4) sexual immorality (including incest and adultery), (5) blasphemy, and (6) eating from a living animal. (7) They should have just laws and "an effective judiciary to enforce the preceding laws."[23] Those among the non-Jews who live up to these commandments were supposed to have their "share in the world to come," that is, to partake in ultimate well-being.[24]

The crucial question, however, was and still is whether non-Jews actually comply with these laws. As far as the moral rules are concerned, that is, abstention from sexual immorality, from murder, theft and vivisection,[25] the rabbis recognized that non-Jewish nations usually do have respective legal regulations and that non-Jewish individuals often keep these commandments. Far more difficult was their assessment in relation to the prohibition of idolatry and blasphemy. Are not all non-Jewish religions clearly idolatrous? But as long as non-Jews are uniformly perceived as idolaters, the rabbinic teaching of the Noahide Laws does not overcome Jewish exclusivism. The salvation of non-Jews would be only a theoretical

---

[19]Kogan 2005, 113.

[20]Cohn-Sherbok 2005, 124.

[21]Langer 2003, 264.

[22]*Sanhedrin* 56a; *Tosefta Avodah Zarah* 8:4; later understood in relation to Gn 2:16 and 9:4. For summaries see Novak 1989, 26–41; Langer 2003, 266ff.; and Brill 2010, 51ff. For a comprehensive study see Novak 1983.

[23]Brill 2010, 51.

[24]Langer 2003, 271; Brill 2010, 41.

[25]The interpretation, however, is tricky. On the basis of Genesis 9:4, the sixth of the Noahide Laws could also be understood as the prohibition of blood, i.e., of any meat that had not been prepared by kosher slaughtering. In that case it would be a far more restrictive condition. For a contemporary discussion see Clorfene and Rogalsky 1987, 96–100.

but not a practical possibility. And non-Jewish religions would rather be obstructive than instrumental in terms of salvation. At a relatively early stage, some rabbis introduced the argument that what constitutes idolatry and blasphemy in an objective sense, as, for example, the classical Roman cult, would not necessarily count as idolatry subjectively. Thus, a religious practice or doctrine that would clearly be idolatrous and blasphemous if observed or held by a Jew could nevertheless be innocent for a non-Jew if he or she subjectively intends to worship the true God. Some even argued that non-Jews are permitted to relate to God indirectly through their pagan idols because a direct and unmediated relation to God is only open to Jews. Later on some rabbis were inclined to extend such considerations to Christians and Muslims.[26]

In this version, the concept of the Noahide Laws clearly reflects an inclusivist form of the superiority claim. The superior nature of the Jewish religion is not questioned and has its foundation in the belief in the particular election of the Jewish people. At the same time it is affirmed that some salvific elements are found in other religions as well and can contribute to the eschatological well-being of their members. Particularly in modern times, but with roots already in the work of Maimonides (1138–1204), the concept was even expanded to the idea that Christianity and Islam are divinely ordained ways of preparing the gentiles for the final messianic revelation of Israel's God as the only true God and allowing the righteous non-Jews to participate in the messianic world.[27]

TOWARD A THEOLOGY OF MULTIPLE COVENANTS

Jewish pluralists of today relate to these traditional ideas in continuity and critique. The teaching of the Noahide Laws is often regarded as a step in the right direction, but as insufficient in not doing justice to the specific form or character of the other religions. It is therefore seen as in need of a contemporary reinterpretation.[28] In this sense Michael Kogan holds: "We must now apply it in ways we never have before, dealing for the first time with the specific claims of other faiths and their followers rather than simply lumping them all together as 'Gentiles.'"[29]

The pluralists tend to interpret the Noahide Laws as a theological expression of a divine covenant that comprises all humankind, Jews and non-Jews alike, and involves essential spiritual and moral values binding for all human

---

[26]Novak 1983, 124–29; Langer 2003, 268ff.
[27]Langer 2003, 270; Brill 2010, 67ff.
[28]Langer 2003, 267.
[29]Kogan 2005, 112.

beings. Yet on the basis of this general covenant between God and humanity, and in addition to it, there exists a range of special covenants between God and specific peoples. These special covenants find their expression in the different religions, including Judaism. That is, Judaism does indeed have a special election, but having a special election is nothing unique. Other peoples too have their own special election, and therefore no Jewish superiority claim can be based on it.[30] To quote Michael Kogan once more: "Instead of being *the* chosen people, my people begin to see themselves as *a* chosen people."[31]

This idea is found in Jewish dialogues not only with Christianity and Islam but also with Eastern religions. When in 1990, during the official Jewish-Buddhist dialogue in Dharamsala, the Dalai Lama questioned the Jewish participants about their concept of the Jews as "the chosen people," Irving Greenberg replied: "Chosenness means a unique relationship of love. But God can choose others as well and give a unique calling to each group. Each has to understand its own destiny and can see its own tragedy not simply as a setback but as an opportunity."[32] Quite evidently Greenberg here applied the idea of multiple elections to the Tibetan people and to their religion. Another example can be given from Jewish-Hindu dialogue. The "First Jewish-Hindu Leadership Summit," which was held in Delhi, February 5–6, 2007, was jointly convened by a delegation of the Chief Rabbinate of Israel and a group of leaders of various Hindu branches. In point 1 of the final declaration it is stated that both Hinduism and Judaism "teach faith in one supreme being who is the ultimate reality, who has created the world and its blessed diversity and who has communicated divine ways of action for humanity for different peoples in different times and places."[33]

Within the theological framework of multiple covenants and elections, Jewish pluralists assume a legitimate diversity of ways in which human beings know God or Transcendence. They differ, however, on how the legitimacy of this diversity is to be understood. Some Jewish pluralists follow the line of John Hick and focus primarily on the human factor. As Raphael Jospe puts it, the limitations that account for the religious differences do not result from what is spoken, that is, from revelation, but rather from what is heard.[34] Pluralism, therefore, "does not imply a strong relativistic conception of multiple truths, but of multiple perspectives on the truth."[35]

---

[30]Langer 2003, 269–70.

[31]Kogan 2005, 114.

[32]Kamenetz 1995, 95.

[33]The text of the declaration and various other documents are found at http://www.millenniumpeace summit.org/Hindu-Jewish_Summit_Information.pdf.

[34]See Jospe 2007 and 2012.

[35]Jospe 2012, 121.

Dan Cohn-Sherbok[36] sees the teachings of the various religions as rooted in different, but equally legitimate and authentic human experiences of a Divine mystery that exceeds all human forms of expression.[37] The differences between the religions are not the result of different divine revelations, but "reflect differences in the historical, social, and cultural factors."[38] A number of Jewish pluralists,[39] however, for example, David Hartman (1931–2013),[40] Norman Solomon,[41] Elliott Dorff,[42] Irving Greenberg,[43] Michael Kogan,[44] and Jonathan Sacks,[45] take a more conservative position. They tend to emphasize that the different human experiences of transcendence are the result of different divine activities. God addresses different peoples in different revelations and thus, as one might say, "speaks" different languages. In that sense Michael Kogan asks: If the apostle Paul says in the First Letter to the Corinthians (9:22) that he became "all things to all people so that by all means some might be saved," then "why cannot God do the same thing?"[46] Yet also according to these theologians none of the revelations substantiates religious superiority claims. This is for two reasons: First, no revelation, even if it derives directly from God, is capable of expressing in human terms the complete truth about the infinite nature of God. And second, none of these revelations is meant by God to be universal but has its validity and meaning within God's particular dealings with a specific people.

Especially the latter point has been strongly affirmed by David Hartman. According to Hartman, the root of religious superiority claims lies in a confusion of the language of creation with the language of revelation. Through creation God relates to every human being qua human being. Creation has therefore a truly universal dimension. Revelation, however, is not universal, but particular and specific. Revelation always occurs within history and in relation to a specific people as part of a concrete relation between God and this people. In revelation God speaks the language of a particular people and speaks to this particular people in a specific situation. Revelation can

---

[36]See Cohn-Sherbok 1994.

[37]See Cohn-Sherbok 2005, 125–28.

[38]Ibid., 125.

[39]On contemporary Jewish pluralists see their brief portraits in Brill 2010, 129–49. It is puzzling that Dan Cohn-Sherbok, although being an important voice of liberal Jewish pluralism, is not even mentioned in any of Alan Brill's overviews (see Brill 2010; 2012).

[40]See Hartman 1990.

[41]See Solomon 1991; 1996; 2005.

[42]See Dorff 1982; 1996.

[43]See Greenberg 2000; 2004; 2006.

[44]See Kogan 2008.

[45]See in particular Sacks 2002. It is on the basis of this edition that A. Brill—I think rightly—puts Sacks in the pluralist camp (see Brill 2010, 144ff.). In the revised edition (Sacks 2003), due to the pressure from Sacks's opponents, many of the more pluralist statements were either watered down or deleted.

[46]Kogan 2005, 118.

therefore not be universalized.[47] "Revelation, as I understand it, was not meant to be a source of absolute, eternal, and transcendent truth. Rather, it is God's speaking to human beings within the limited framework of human language and history."[48] According to Hartman, the diversity of religions reminds us of "the limitations of human finitude" and shows us "that one's own faith commitment does not exhaust the full range of spiritual options."[49]

"NO RELIGION IS AN ISLAND"

In whatever way it may be construed, the idea of multiple covenants and multiple revelations is no doubt a truly pluralist approach. But does it overcome the isolationism against which Abraham Heschel warned when he claimed in his prophetic lecture that "no religion is an island"? If each people has its own covenant with God and its own specific revelation, destined by God for this particular people, why should such revelations be of any interest or use to other people? Does this concept leave any significant room or any serious need for interreligious exchange and interreligious learning? David Hartman affirms that "the experience of diversity . . . brings home to Jewish spiritual consciousness the important empirical fact that no one person or community exhausts all spiritual possibilities."[50] But this in itself does not yet entail whether, and if so how, this consciousness could or should lead to anything more than the sheer acknowledgment of such limitations.

Alon Goshen-Gottstein has linked such questions to Heschel's legacy in suggesting that the awareness of human and spiritual limitation can function as an incentive to help each other: "To follow Heschel is to be able to cultivate the space of heart and mind and those particular relationships by means of which we can really help each other address and fulfill our deepest spiritual yearnings."[51] As an example, Goshen-Gottstein refers to the persistent attraction that Indian religions have for many Jews, which he interprets as a longing for the rich and still vivid tradition of how to cultivate an awareness of God's presence. Even more important, he is convinced that Hindu spirituality can indeed fulfill this lack and thus be an example of interreligious spiritual aid.[52] A similar view has been defended by the Jewish pluralist and spiritual authority Zalman Schachter-Shalomi

---

[47]Hartman 1990, 246–47.
[48]Ibid., 248.
[49]Ibid.
[50]Hartman 1990, 265.
[51]Goshen-Gottstein 2007, 111.
[52]See Goshen-Gottstein 2012a, 269–72.

(1924–2014).[53] On his understanding interreligious learning could provide the kind of reciprocal inspiration that "helps the worshiper to worship, the meditator to meditate, the adorer to adore."[54] And so he confessed of himself that Buddhism had helped him deepen his Jewish practice and his understanding of Jewish texts.[55]

When Christian theologians produced the pluralist manifesto *The Myth of Christian Uniqueness*,[56] they suggested that one way to cross the Rubicon of Christian claims to absoluteness was the bridge of mysticism.[57] Schachter-Shalomi stands for those among the Jewish pluralists who similarly believe that the mystical tradition of Judaism provides the foundation for a new Jewish self-understanding that also embraces other faiths.[58] Goshen-Gottstein shares the view that mysticism facilitates the accommodation of the religious other. "Perhaps with mysticism comes a healthy kind of relativizing of one's own tradition that opens the gates to greater acceptance of all traditions, because they come to be seen as relative expressions of a greater view of reality."[59]

A different but complementary response to the danger of isolationism is presented by Ephraim Meir. He does not draw on Jewish mysticism but on the strong philosophical tradition of Jewish dialogical thinking, which he combines with a pluralist approach in the theology of religions. His starting point is the view "that one's own religious identity is intimately linked to the religious identity of other persons: one knows oneself only through the other."[60] This, according to Meir, is also true for religious identity. But he does not stop at affirming religious difference in order to reassure oneself of one's own religious identity. According to Meir, genuine dialogue means both affirming difference and transcending it. Otherwise no understanding between different people would be possible. In understanding the other, it may well occur that one learns from him or her some aspects of religious life that are also important to oneself. This "trans-difference," as Meir calls it, avoids both religious uniformity and "a narrow confessionalism that does not contribute to an intercultural and interreligious dialogue concerning what touches the depth of our human existence."[61] Trans-difference "creates an 'open' identity that has otherness in itself."[62] This is a thrilling insight. Far from denying the crucial awareness of our limitation, the otherness that is

---

[53]On Schachter-Shalomi see Linzer 1999 and Brill 2010, 134–37.
[54]Schachter-Shalomi 1977, 412.
[55]Schachter-Shalomi 2003.
[56]See chapter 2.
[57]See Hick and Knitter 1987, x–xi.
[58]See Brill 2010, 134–37.
[59]Goshen-Gottstein, 2012b, 324.
[60]Meir 2014, 126. See also Meir 2013; 2015.
[61]Meir 2014, 135.
[62]Meir 2015, 160.

part of an open identity is understood as relatedness. The religious other is not made redundant by claiming the other's presence in us. The presence of otherness rather means that there is a potential, an inclination, a longing in us that finds fulfillment through encounter with the real other—reciprocally—and thus leads to a new "we."[63]

Jewish pluralists are surely right when they claim that for Judaism the step toward a pluralist theology of religions is not too big. But the step from feeling and actually being isolated in an exclusivist understanding of election to a new identity as a living part of a larger "we" is a really big one. This may also explain why such moves are partly met by harsh opposition. In 2002 Jonathan Sacks published his book *The Dignity of Difference*,[64] in which he took a moderately pluralist approach. It raised fierce protest on the side of some orthodox Jewish theologians. Although Jonathan Sacks was, at that time, the chief rabbi of the United Hebrew Congregations of the Commonwealth, his critics declared his views to be heretical. Two influential rabbis among his critics demanded in a public statement that Sacks should recall the book because its views about other religions were "irreconcilable with traditional Jewish teachings."[65] When their view was supported by Rabbi Yosef Shalom Elyashiv, a chief authority among orthodox Jews, Rabbi Sacks stopped the further distribution of the first edition of his book and replaced it with a revised second edition, in which several of the more pluralistic statements were watered down or deleted.[66] The unambiguous statement—"Judaism, Christianity and Islam are religions of revelation—faiths in which God speaks and we attempt to listen"[67]—disappeared completely from the revised edition. Sacks had given what I think to be the right reply to such reactions even before they occurred. At the end of his book he stated that recognizing and appreciating the spiritual value of other religions does not mean to diminish one's own faith. It is just the other way round:

If we cherish our own, then we will understand the value of others. We may regard ours as a diamond and another faith as a ruby, but we know that both are precious stones. But if faith is a mere burden, not only will we not value ours. Neither will we value the faith of someone else.[68]

In the revised edition these sentences remained unaltered.

---

[63]Ibid., 204.
[64]Sacks 2002.
[65]Rocker 2003.
[66]Sacks 2003.
[67]Sacks 2002, 19.
[68]Ibid., 209.

4

Submission to a Divinely Willed Diversity: Islamic Pluralism

To Muslim pluralists the point of departure is significantly different from that of their Jewish counterparts.[1] For, similar to Christianity but unlike Judaism, Islam, in its vast majority, traditionally asserted a claim to universality, seeing itself as the one religion destined by God for everyone. To be sure, the Qur'ān repeatedly emphasizes that God has sent his messengers to every people so that there exists a plurality of authentic revelations (5:19; 5:48; 10:47; 14:4; 35:24). Yet at the same time Muḥammad is proclaimed as the "seal" of the prophets (33:40). According to traditional interpretation this does not just mean that the revelation brought by Muḥammad serves as the decisive criterion in assessing and confirming all other valid revelations. Being the seal is further understood as implying that with Muḥammad God's sending of prophets has come to an end.[2] Even more important, the majority of the Islamic tradition interpreted the sending of Muḥammad, his transmission of the Qur'ān, and the resulting foundation of Islam in such a way that all other religions, based on earlier revelations, are thereby surpassed and superseded or, to use Muslim terminology, they are "abrogated." In other words, after Muḥammad Islam is the one and only religion destined for all people, while the validity and legitimacy of other religions has expired.[3]

---

[1]For a detailed survey of Islam's relation to other faiths in past and present see Waardenburg 2003; an extensive collection of essays is offered in Ridgeon 2012; a number of divergent contemporary views is found in Khalil 2013. Muslim self-understanding in the context of interfaith dialogue is the topic of Boase 2005 and of Ridgeon and Schmidt-Leukel 2007. For a brief overview of Muslim pluralist ideas see Amirpur 2014 and Michel 2014.

[2]See also chapter 10.

[3]This is the main argument in Legenhausen's "non-reductive pluralism." Non-Islamic religions do contain divinely revealed truth but with the advent of Muḥammad their time has expired. Since then the only legitimate religion destined for all is Islam. One may nevertheless hope that those who mistakenly follow another religion might still be saved by the grace of God (see Legenhausen 2005, 64–72). On the basis of the definitions that I suggested (exclusivist, inclusivist, pluralist—see chapter 1 above) this would not count as a pluralist but—at best—as an inclusivist position. "Pluralism," as defined here, is for Legenhausen a form of unbelief (*kufr*), because it is incompatible with submission to God's final

"So the understanding for centuries within the mainstream Islamic tradition was that, in order to be saved and to experience salvation with God, one must be Muslim."[4] Muslim pluralists begin their criticism here.

THE MEANING OF *ISLĀM*

A first important point in the arguments of Muslim pluralists is the distinction between *islām* with a small "i," and Islam with a capital "I." With a small "i," *islām* signifies an existential attitude, that is, submission to the will of God, which is the literal meaning of the Arabic word. With a capital "I," *Islam* denotes a sociocultural phenomenon, that is, the religion of Islam. According to the pluralists, Qur'ānic verses that seem to affirm the universal and exclusive validity of Islam as a religion speak in fact of *islām* with a small "i." Muslim exclusivists frequently refer to verses such as "The Religion [*dīn*] before Allah is Islam"[5] (3:19) and "If anyone desires a religion other than Islam, never will it be accepted of him; and in the Hereafter he will be in the ranks of those who have lost" (3:85). According to the pluralists, such verses do not speak of the institutionalized religion called "Islam" but of the religious attitude of submission to God. This makes a crucial difference, because the realization of *islām* as a spiritual attitude is not confined to Islam as a religion. Therefore, the many and manifold religions "can be appreciated as being, at their origins, so many modes of 'submission' to God."[6] As a confirmation of this view, pluralists often cite Sūrah 42:13:

> The same religion has He established for you as that which He enjoined on Noah—That which We have sent by inspiration to thee—and that which We enjoined on Abraham, Moses, and Jesus.

The understanding of *islām* as an existential attitude that is not confined to the religion of Islam is reminiscent of Wilfred Cantwell Smith's distinction between *faith* and *belief* or *tradition*. Whereas "belief" refers to a doctrinal conviction and "tradition" to the sociohistoric dimension of religion, "faith" signifies the kind of personal attitude and orientation that is seen as decisive in one's relation to God.[7] Indeed it was Smith himself who suggested an understanding of *islām* along the lines of his own understanding of faith

---

revelation, the exclusive acceptance of Islam as an institutionalized religion (see ibid., 66).
[4]Ramadan 2013, x.
[5]All quotations from the Qur'ān are taken from the translation by 'Abdullah Yūsuf 'Alī ('Alī 1999).
[6]Shah-Kazemi 2012, 98.
[7]See chapter 2 above.

already in 1967,[8] and some of the Muslim pluralists, in particular Mahmoud Ayoub and Hasan Askari (1932–2008), were strongly influenced by Smith. While Ayoub had been born into a Muslim family and converted to Christianity as a teenager, it was under the influence of Wilfred Cantwell Smith with whom he studied at Harvard that Ayoub rediscovered and finally returned to his Muslim roots.[9] Askari had met Smith in India. Ataullah Siddiqui reports Askari's statement that he is following Smith "through and through,"[10] and Askari himself explicitly mentions his indebtedness to Smith's distinction between faith and belief/tradition.[11]

Muslim pluralists such as Mahmut Aydin,[12] Mahmoud Ayoub,[13] Asghar Ali Engineer (1939–2013),[14] Farid Esack,[15] and Abdulaziz Sachedina[16] base their interpretation on a number of detailed exegetical elaborations. Frequently their discussions center on Sūrah 2:62, which reads:

> Those who believe and those who follow the Jews and the Christians and the Sabeans—any who believe in Allah and the Last Day, and work righteousness, shall have their reward with the Lord: on them shall be no fear, nor shall they grieve.

This verse is taken as key evidence that even after the appearance of Muḥammad other faiths can still be valid paths of salvation. Against the traditional view that this verse is abrogated by verses such as those cited above (3:19 and 3:85), that is, by verses supposed to state that the only religion acceptable to God is Islam, the pluralists produce two weighty counterarguments: First, Sūrah 2:62 expresses a divine promise and not a legal directive. Whereas legal directives can be abrogated, divine promises cannot. Second, verse 2:62 is repeated in almost identical words in Sūrah 5:69, that is, in one of the last Sūrahs of the Medinan period, dating back to the end of Muḥammad's prophetic ministry, which clearly speaks against its supposed abrogation.[17] So why should a verse be reaffirmed if it had been allegedly abrogated before?

---

[8]Smith 1967, 104ff.
[9]See A. Siddiqui 1997, 97–98.
[10]Ibid., 110.
[11]Askari 1991, 124.
[12]See, e.g., Aydin 2000; 2001; 2005; 2007; 2014.
[13]See, e.g., Ayoub 1997; 2007.
[14]See Engineer 2005; 2007.
[15]See Esack 1997.
[16]See Sachedina 2001.
[17]See Aydin 2007, 48–49; Esack 1997, 162ff.; Sachedina 2001, 32ff.

DIVERSITY AND UNIVERSALITY

In addition to their view that a salvific attitude is not confined to Islam as a religion, Muslim pluralists point out that the Qur'ān itself affirms diversity, including religious diversity, as something positively willed by God, as—in the words of Mahmut Aydin—"a divinely ordained system of human co-existence."[18] This is supported by a number of different arguments. A key role is played by the concept of multiple divine revelations. If it is possible to refute the view that with the sending of Muḥammad all religions based on previous revelations are abrogated, the numerous Qur'ānic statements that God has sent messengers to every people in the world become a cornerstone of Muslim pluralism. In Sūrah 14:4 the Qur'ān states that all prophets were sent to teach in the language of their people. Pluralists take this as not only referring to different languages as such, but as to include the different sociocultural and historical contexts, which are inevitably reflected in every language. That is, even if the messengers who were sent to every people all brought a message that is in essence the same, it was nevertheless transmitted in a variety of forms reflecting cultural diversity and results in a diversity of religions.[19]

If religious diversity is, at least to a significant extent, due to the diversity of the human recipients of revelation, it still remains an open question of how this diversity relates to the supposed unity of the divine message. Can this unity be spelled out in terms of the common features shared by a variety of different revelations? Or is the unity of revelation to be seen only at the level of its divine subject whose transcendent nature goes beyond every human conceptualization? In a detailed study of John Hick, Rifat Atay has opted for what he calls "moderate pluralism." He suggests that—in Hick's terminology—"the Real" has a constitutive role and "positive contribution" within the different revelations "even though all are expressed in imperfect human languages."[20] The "moderation" that Atay has in mind is thus a moderation of divine ineffability: "Nobody has the full, absolute truth . . . but revelations containing portions of the Truth."[21] Nevertheless, "moderate pluralism" is still pluralism. Atay concurs with Hick that no religion can be established as uniquely superior to all the others.[22]

If religious diversity is divinely ordained, it has a specific purpose that

---

[18] Aydin 2014, 229.

[19] E.g., Esack 1997, 166; Aydin 2007, 37; Engineer 2005, 212–13.

[20] Atay 2014, 281.

[21] Ibid., 366.

[22] See ibid., 277. I therefore disagree with Michel's (2014, 175–76) characterization of Atay as an inclusivist.

Muslim pluralists see also revealed in the Qur'ān. On the one hand, religious diversity should work as a positive incentive to religious communities to encourage one another and compete with each other in good works as is expressed in Sūrah 5:48 (similarly in 2:148):

> To each among you have We prescribed a Law and an Open Way. If Allah had so willed, He would have made you a single People, but [His Plan is] to test you in what He hath given you; so strive as in a race in all virtues. The goal of you all is to Allah.

On the other hand, the purpose of religious diversity is seen in the value of mutual relatedness and dependence.[23] According to Sūrah 49:13, God created humankind "of a male and a female" and as "nations and tribes, that ye may know each other." To "know each other" is understood as an exhortation to perceive each other as mutually enriching and enter into deep and fruitful relations. Ashgar Ali Engineer puts it like this: "In knowing one another's national or tribal or religious differences we are able not only to understand but also to learn from one another, and so to fashion a richer unity."[24] Muslim pluralists therefore emphasize the need to overcome traditional prejudices about other religions and the need to take the other seriously in his or her self-understanding, that is, to "know" the other from his or her own religious sources.[25]

The Muslim feminist theologian Jerusha Tanner Lamptey has recently presented a theology of religions that focuses on the question of religious identity and difference.[26] According to Lamptey religious differences cannot be solely explained in terms of the different messengers and the different cultural contexts of their prophetic message. At least today, the members of all the major religions are living not only within the particular cultural contexts to which their original revelations were supposedly adapted. And there is not only difference, but, as taught by the Qur'ān, an essential identity in the prophetic message. According to Lamptey, the Qur'ān does not teach any clear-cut religious boundaries: "The religious 'other' of the Qur'ān is unique and perplexing in that it is an 'other' that is simultaneously the same as and different from the 'self.'"[27] Lamptey therefore suggests a more radical interpretation of the two Qur'ānic motifs of knowing one another and of competing in good works. The divinely willed purpose of religious difference is "to perpetually challenge individuals" and "to con-

---

[23]See, e.g., Aydin 2007, 53; Sachedina 2001, 27.
[24]Engineer 2005, 216.
[25]E.g., Esack 1997, 152; Sachedina 2001, 35; Ayoub 2004, 318.
[26]Lamptey 2014a.
[27]Lamptey 2014b, 213.

tinually raise questions about boundaries," including religious ones.[28] The religious other must be seen as a "proximate other" who is never wholly other nor ever completely the same. This requires more sophistication in the theological assessment and evaluation of religious difference. If religious diversity is part of the divinely intended diversity in all creation, it cannot be the object of any negative assessment. Divine judgment is confined to differences in terms of the individual's "submission" (*islām*) to God, that is, as an evaluation of how serious this submission is lived out. But this "hierarchical difference" in individual faith or submission does not coincide with the "lateral difference" as it exists between religious communities. "Hierarchical evaluation is never fixed or holistically applied to an entire lateral religious group because it is not ascribed on the basis of communal affiliation; hierarchical religious evaluation is individually assessed."[29] In other words, various degrees of seriousness in individual submission to God can be found across the different religions but do not result in any ranking of the religions themselves.

The efforts of Muslim pluralists in developing a genuine appreciation of religious diversity do not lead them to an abandonment of all universal claims. Instead, they tend to reinterpret Islam's universality as a confirmation of religious pluralism. In this sense, it is often confirmed that Muḥammad had indeed a mission and a message for all human beings, but with the qualification that his mission must not be misunderstood along the lines of exclusivism. On the contrary, part of Muḥammad's prophetic mission was precisely to warn people against exclusivist attitudes. For example, Sūrahs 2:111ff. and 5:18 reprimand Jews and Christians because of their exclusivist self-understandings, rejecting their views of possessing the sole path of salvation and being God's only elected people. According to Muslim pluralists, Muslims have to take care to not make the same kind of mistake.[30]

Farid Esack conceives Muḥammad's prophetic mission in terms of two primary functions: On the one hand, it entails a critical challenge for people of other religions to remain faithful to the revealed essence of their own faith and not to distort it. On the other hand, it entails the call to *islām* in the sense of submission to God's will, which can either be lived out within the context of one of the existing revelations or on the basis of the Qur'ānic revelation, that is, within the context of Islam as an institutionalized religion.[31]

Mahmut Aydin describes the universal dimension of the Qur'ānic message in deliberate analogy to Paul Knitter's understanding of Christ's uni-

---

[28]Lamptey 2014a, 252–53.
[29]Lamptey 2014b, 220.
[30]See Aydin 2007, 37, 41; Esack 1997, 18ff.; Ayoub 1997, 112.
[31]See Esack 1997, 172ff.

versal role.[32] According to Knitter, God's revelation in Christ should be seen as "universal, decisive and indispensable" but not as "full, definitive and unsurpassable."[33] Aydin holds that exactly the same can be said about God's revelation through the Qur'ān. The essential statements of the Qur'ān on the relationship between humans and God are universally valid and relevant; they are normative; and they are "indispensable" in the sense that they can enrich and transform the life of everyone. But they cannot exhaust the fullness of God's truth; they do not exclude the existence of "other norms for the divine truth outside" the Qur'ān; and they do not entail "that God could not reveal Himself in other ways apart from the Qur'ān at other times."[34] This is in line with the approach of Mohammed Arkoun (1928–2010),[35] who bases his own version of pluralism on a hermeneutical theory of revelation emphasizing that the infinite Word of God becomes inevitably contextual, fragmented, and finite as soon as it is "sent down to the earth."[36] Muslim pluralists recall that the limitation of the Qur'ānic revelation is taught by the Qur'ān itself when it says, as in Sūrah 31:27 (and similarly in 18:109): "And if all the trees on the earth were pens and the ocean (were ink), with seven oceans behind it to add to its (supply), yet would not the Words of Allah be exhausted."

THE IMPACT OF ISLAMIC MYSTICISM

The Sūrah just quoted touches on a third central motif of Muslim pluralists, as it is emphasized in Islamic mysticism (Sufism): Divine infinity is always channeled through finite media, like the sea poured in a jar or the ocean inhaled by the fish, to paraphrase Rūmī.[37] Yet no finite medium can ever encompass divine infinity. In the end, only God is absolute, but never anything that is finite, limited, or created—including religions. Divine revelation therefore takes its measure at the human recipient: "The Real becomes manifest to His servants in the measure of their knowledge of Him," as Ibn 'Arabī (1165–1240) has put it.[38] This view makes room for the pluralist idea that different revelations, different finite media, are compatible with one infinite reality mediated by them. Within the rich tradition of Islamic mysticism one therefore finds a number of statements pointing in a

---

[32]See chapter 2.
[33]See Knitter 1997, 8ff.
[34]Aydin 2007, 49–50.
[35]See Arkoun 2002, esp. 66–125. See also Arkoun 1989; 1998.
[36]Arkoun 2002, 74.
[37]*Maṭnawīye Ma'nawī* 6:812–17.
[38]*Al-Futūḥāt al-makkiya* III 215, 32. Quoted in Chittick 1994, 163.

pluralist direction.[39] Al-Junayd (9th and 10th c.), for example, is quoted as saying: "The water takes its colour from the vessel containing it," that is, although water looks different in a red, green, or blue glass, it is always the same water. Ibn 'Arabī commented that whoever understands these words "would not interfere with the beliefs of others, but would perceive God in every form and in every belief."[40] Dschalāl ad-Dīn Rūmī (1207–73) used a different image to make a similar point:

> The light's not different, though the lamps may differ. . . .
> It's due to viewpoint, kernel of existence,
> That Muslim, Jew, and Magian show a difference.[41]

The relativity of all religious differences in view of God's inconceivable absoluteness is the major theme of those Muslim pluralists who are influenced by Sufism.

Abdolkarim Soroush, who draws strongly on Rūmī and Hafez, understands religious diversity primarily in terms of hermeneutics: it reflects the inevitable diversity of meaning and interpretation inherent in and generated by religious experience:[42] "God has appeared to each person in a particular light and each person has interpreted this appearance in a different way."[43] In this respect Soroush finds himself in basic agreement with John Hick's distinction between the Real as it is in itself and as it is experienced and thought of by human beings.[44] But Soroush also emphasizes the "immersion" of divine truth in its diverse human vessels. At the human level truth inevitably turns into a variety of truths: "It is imperative . . . , instead of seeing the world as consisting of one straight line plus hundreds of crooked and broken lines, to see it as consisting of an aggregate of straight lines which meet, run parallel and overlap: truths immersed within truths."[45] Understanding the religions as reservoirs of valid but nevertheless diverse and multifaceted meaning is also the key idea in Tariq Ramadan's 2010 book, which is subtitled *Developing a Philosophy of Pluralism*.[46]

Another major representative of an Islamic pluralism informed by Islamic

---

[39]This does not imply that they actually were pluralist. It rather appears that they were usually inclusivists with pluralist inclinations. See also Kalisch 2007, 73–75; Legenhausen 2005, 67–69; Carney 2008.

[40]*Fuṣūṣ al-ḥikam* 27; R. A. Nicholson 1911, vi.

[41]*Maṯnawīye Ma'nawī* 3:1255, 1259; Rūmī 2013, 77–78.

[42]See Soroush 2000; 2009.

[43]Soroush 2009, 130.

[44]Ibid., 131–34. Conversely, Hick has commended Soroush as one of the most advanced thinkers in contemporary Islam (see Hick 2010, 108–20). On Hick and Soroush see also Amirpur 2014, 197–98.

[45]Soroush 2009, 136.

[46]See Ramadan 2010.

mysticism is Hasan Askari (1932–2008). According to Askari, "all religions . . . are relative to the Absolute Truth,"[47] and each religion is in danger of "equat[ing] one's own religious doctrine with the Transcendent."[48] As mentioned before, Sūrah 3:67 is generally understood by Muslim pluralists as confirming that true *islām* in the sense of submission to God can be practiced in different religions. Askari agrees with this interpretation but gives it a much more radical twist. To Askari this verse implies that one must never absolutize one's own faith: "By 'islam' (primordial and universal) the particular and the historical Islam is abolished. But what is *in principle* abolished is not in historical fact annulled: the abolition of the particular by the universal has to be enacted within the practice of the particular."[49] That is, the awareness of the relativity and limitation of one's own religious tradition has to become an essential element of how one practices one's own religion. Religious diversity is therefore seen as a spiritually important fact: By making religions aware of their finitude, it can work as an antidote against their self-absolutizing inclinations, while it encourages all religions to enrich and fertilize each other through their encounter and exchange.[50]

In his contributions to the theology of religions, Askari too has paid particular attention to the question of religious identity.[51] In this respect his approach displays the influence of mysticism as well as that of Wilfred Cantwell Smith. Askari was one of the pioneers of Muslim-Christian dialogue and was closely involved with the dialogue activities of the World Council of Churches. Through this commitment he became increasingly convinced that dialogue, in order to be genuine, should be conceived less as a dialogue between religious communities or institutions but between individual unique persons. That is, in interfaith dialogue one should guard oneself against the danger of encountering each other as representatives of collective religious identities. For this would automatically turn unique persons into religious stereotypes, both in their self- and in their partner-perception.[52] "There is a world of difference in looking at the other as a representation of his religion or ideology and the experience of that very other as a presence, as a person."[53] Stripping off our preconceived prejudices and projections so that we can meet as persons has wide-ranging

---

[47]Askari 1985, 191. See also Askari 1977; 1991.

[48]Askari 1985, 196.

[49]Ibid., 199. Shah-Kazemi repeatedly quotes the first part of this statement in order to criticize Askari (e.g., Shah-Kazemi 2006a, 252). But if one looks at the whole quotation one wonders whether it is really that different from what Shah-Kazemi proposes as his alternative: "universal Islam transcends particular Islam whilst simultaneously affirming it" (Shah-Kazemi 2006a, 259).

[50]Askari 1985, 204–5.

[51]Unfortunately Lamptey (2014a) has not taken any note of Hasan Askari.

[52]Askari 1991, 124.

[53]Ibid.

consequences. According to Askari, the human person is, at the bottom of his or her heart, just as little objectifiable as the Divine reality. If we empty ourselves of all traces of our collective identities, whether religious, racial, national, cultural, or whatever, we arrive at a kind of emptiness that reflects the emptiness or imagelessness of Ultimate Reality itself. After experiencing that at the deepest level our nature is not defined by any kind of collective identity, religious or otherwise, one will acquire a new understanding of religious differences: "Then one may return as a visitor to all the contents and constructs of one's religious consciousness, now both empty and full. One can then sit before the other from another culture or tradition, both as a portrait of one's own religion and culture and also as an empty mirror into which one can see both oneself and the other."[54]

A special strand among the Muslim pluralists is constituted by the so-called *perennialist* or *traditional school*, with Frithjof Schuon (1907–98)[55] and Seyyed Hossein Nasr[56] as probably their best-known representatives.[57] This school also has deep roots in Islamic mysticism and Neoplatonism. It therefore shares the conviction of the relativity of every religion in relation to the absoluteness of God. But the traditional school is particularly keen on emphasizing that this conviction does not amount to religious relativism. Taken on its own, says Nasr following Schuon, each religion which is based on genuine revelation has absolute validity because it owes its existence to the absolute reality of God and because it is able to relate humans to the Divine. For the same reasons, however, religions are also only "relatively absolute." That is, they are "not the Absolute as such" but are "relatively absolute within a particular religious universe."[58] Religions can be equated to different solar systems for which each sun is—and has to be—the one and only sun, although in fact there is more than just one sun. Today the basic tenets of the traditional school are creatively developed by Reza Shah-Kazemi.[59] Shah-Kazemi himself hovers between an inclusivist and a pluralist attitude.[60] On the one hand, he claims "Islam as the best religion,

---

[54]Ibid., 138.

[55]See Schuon 1953; 1963; Nasr 1991.

[56]See Nasr 1989. For a comparison of Nasr's pluralism with that of John Hick see Aslan 1998.

[57]For an overview see Oldmeadow 2010, 3–47.

[58]Nasr 1999, 171.

[59]See Shah-Kazemi 2006a.

[60]Shah-Kazemi is critical of John Hick and Muslim pluralists like Arkoun, Esack, Sachedina, and Askari, because he accuses them of sacrificing the particular of religions to the universal. In distancing Nasr's pluralism from Hick's, Shah-Kazemi follows closely Nasr's critique of Hick as found in Nasr's *Knowledge and the Sacred* (cf. Nasr 1989, 287–97, with Shah-Kazemi 2006a, 166–67, 249ff.). While in *The Other in the Light of the One* and elsewhere in his writings Shah-Kazemi shows some sympathy for the "attitude of superiority" (Shah-Kazemi 2006a, 244), he is far more critical of superiority claims in his later work *The Spirit of Tolerance in Islam* (Shah-Kazemi 2012, 102–7).

because it recognizes and respects all religions."[61] On the other hand, he understands the difference between revealed religions as "the results of different combinations of the specific divine qualities which lie at the roots of each of the religions"[62]—a position that will hardly allow for the idea that one such combination is better than the others.

Some of the Muslim pluralists tend to confine their discussion of religious diversity to the three Abrahamic religions. This is noticeably different among those pluralists who are influenced by Islamic mysticism. Imtiyaz Yusuf, a Muslim pluralist of Indian background who teaches at a Buddhist university in Thailand, speaks of "the Buddha and Muḥammad . . . as enlightened prophets who overcame the impediments of religious ignorance."[63] Schuon has also written extensively and appreciatively on Buddhism,[64] Askari,[65] and Shah-Kazemi on Hinduism.[66] In addition, Shah-Kazemi drafted the document *Common Ground Between Islam and Buddhism*, which presents "Buddhism as a true religion or *dīn*" to Muslims, and "Islam as an authentic *Dharma*" to Buddhists.[67] I will come back to the issue of Muslim-Buddhist relations in far more detail in chapter 12.

The effort of distinguishing pluralism from relativism is not only found in the traditional school. Muslim pluralists are generally keen on distancing themselves from relativism. They draw on the Qur'ān in order to formulate criteria by which valid religions can be discerned. In order to be universalizable, such criteria may be Islamic but without being exclusively so. Usually these involve the following two criteria: the clear relation of a religion to transcendence (that is, "monotheism" in an expanded sense that would also include nontheistic concepts) and its teaching of just ethical norms.[68] Particularly Farid Esack understands the latter in a way that is in basic agreement with Paul Knitter's liberation theology.[69] Despite such attempts, Muslim pluralists have been as much accused of relativism as their Christian counterparts. Over the past years various fatwas were issued condemning religious pluralism as a dangerous heresy unacceptable to Islam.[70] But as in Christianity or in Judaism strong opposition against pluralism has not been able to terminate the debate.

---

[61]Shah-Kazemi 2013, 98.

[62]Shah-Kazemi 2012, 110.

[63]I. Yusuf 2010a, 181. See also I. Yusuf 2005 and 2010b.

[64]Schuon 1993.

[65]Askari 1991, 71–79.

[66]Shah-Kazemi 2006b.

[67]Shah-Kazemi 2010a, 7.

[68]See, e.g., Ayoub 1997, 110; Esack 1997, 174–75.

[69]See Esack 1997, 14, 258.

[70]E.g., "Ruling on the call to unite all religions" (April 27, 2000). http://islamqa.info/en/10213. On the antipluralist fatwa in Indonesia (2005) see Gillespie 2007 and Basya 2011. On Budhy Munawar-Rachman, one of the leading Muslim pluralists in Indonesia, see Sinn 2014, 421–41.

In the ninth section of his *The Natural History of Religion* (1757) David Hume blames Judaism, Christianity, and Islam as being naturally intolerant, narrow-minded, and ready to condemn the religious other. The reason for this commonality is, according to Hume, their joint monotheism. The belief in only one true God, Hume states, is inseparably linked with the belief in only one true religion, and thus there is interreligious strife and hatred. Therefore, Hume presents polytheism as the praiseworthy opposite allegedly marked by a spirit of tolerance and agreeableness. Since then, the contrast between the supposedly absolutist, aggressive, and exclusivist nature of the Abrahamic religions, on the one hand, and the peaceful, tolerant, and pluralist mood of Eastern religions, on the other, has developed into a widespread cliché.[71] When in 1996 Josef Ratzinger, by then still head of the Vatican's Congregation for the Doctrine of the Faith, condemned the Christian pluralistic theology of religions as a relativist heresy, he pointed to "the philosophical and theological vision of India" as one source of religious pluralism.[72] There is no doubt that exclusivist tendencies are strong in all three of the Abrahamic religions. But as this brief survey of pluralist approaches has demonstrated, they also harbor the potential for developing a genuine appreciation of religious diversity. With the next three chapters I turn to the religions of the East and look into their potential for religious pluralism. As will become clear, the widespread cliché is less true than it appears. Eastern religions have their own forms of superiority claims and thus raise their own specific challenges for those who wish to move toward a truly pluralistic approach.

---

[71]See, e.g., Assmann 1997, 1–8.
[72]Ratzinger 1996. For John Hick's reply see Hick 2001, 157–60.

5

Is Hinduism a Pluralist Religion?

VIVEKANANDA'S PRESENTATION OF HINDUISM

Perceptions of Hinduism as the pluralistic religion per se are found not only among Westerners. It is also in line with the self-representation of various modern Hindus. According to Arvind Sharma, for example, the difference between the pluralism of John Hick and the characteristic Hindu attitude to religious diversity is only in particulars but not in essence.[1] Like no one else, it was Swami Vivekananda (1863–1902) who introduced to the West the image of Hinduism as *the* pluralist religion per se. During the World's Fair in Chicago in 1893, an interreligious assembly was convoked, the first so-called World Parliament of Religions.[2] Hinduism was represented by the then fairly unknown Vivekananda, who was only thirty years old. No one could guess that he should emerge as the uncontested star of the Parliament. Already in his brief address at the Parliament's opening session Vivekananda presented his pluralistic image of Hinduism. Rhetorically gifted, he earned enthusiastic applause when he—as a Hindu—addressed his predominantly Christian audience as "Sisters and Brothers of America," thereby expressing his idea of an inner kinship of the religions.[3]

In this short opening address Vivekananda stated: "I am proud to belong to a religion which has taught the world both tolerance and universal acceptance. We believe not only in universal toleration, but we accept all religions as true."[4] Yet Vivekananda also called Hinduism the "mother of religions,"[5] which indicates that he gave this religion a special status. In his main address, delivered eight days later, Vivekananda further elaborated

---

[1] See A. Sharma 1990, 163.
[2] On this event see Seager 1993; Lüddeckens 2001.
[3] A podcast of this speech is found on YouTube. Its text, together with all Vivekananda's other addresses during the Parliament are found in Vivekananda 1989, 1:3–24.
[4] Vivekananda 1989, 1:3.
[5] Ibid.

on his views. Here it became clear that he called Hinduism the "mother of religions" because Hinduism—and Hinduism alone—gives room to each form of religion, as he phrased it: from the "highest" philosophy of Vedānta to the "low ideas" of idolatry and mythology, from "the agnosticism of the Buddhists" to the "atheism of the Jains."[6] Hinduism, according to Vivekananda, is "the common religion of all sects of India."[7] And this diversity of Indian religions, all encompassed by Hinduism, reflects the diversity of all religions, because for Vivekananda it is true of "each and all" forms of religion that they have a place in Hinduism.[8] To Vivekananda this was not just a descriptive statement but indicative of his normative definition of Hinduism as the mother religion, which accepts all other religions as her children, that is, "as true."

Vivekananda gave two explanations of his claim that "we" as Hindus "accept all religions as true." First, the difference between the absolute nature of the Divine and the relative nature of the religions. This difference can never be removed, but the absolute can be experienced and thought by means of the relative, that is, through the finite representations of the absolute in form of its different religious images and symbols. Moreover, the different religions are like different coats. Not every coat will fit everybody; therefore, there has to be a diversity of coats, that is, of religions.[9] This is a truly pluralist scenario in that it combines diversity with equality.

But Vivekananda also gave a second explanation, which is considerably less egalitarian. The second explanation is based on the idea of progressive stages of spiritual growth and development. Similar to a child whose needs differ from those of an adult, those who are on a lower stage of spiritual development need different forms of religious practices and ideas than those on a more advanced stage. Different religions therefore also reflect different levels of spiritual maturity. But all religions are necessary, including the lower ones, for, as Vivekananda expressed it, the "child is the father of the man."[10] That is, the lower religions are inevitable as preliminary stages in spiritual maturation. The difference between religions is thus not one between error and truth but between lower and higher truth.[11] This second line of interpreting religious diversity is clearly not pluralistic but represents a form of inclusivism. Indeed, Vivekananda does not conceal that he regards his own religious tradition, Advaita Vedānta, as the highest form of religion, superior to all others:

---

[6]Ibid., 6.
[7]Ibid., 13.
[8]Ibid., 6.
[9]Ibid., 16–17.
[10]Ibid., 17.
[11]Ibid. See also Vivekananda 1989, 2:500.

Would to God that the whole world were Advaitins tomorrow, not only in theory, but in realization. But if that cannot be, let us do the next best thing; let us take the ignorant by the hand, lead them always step by step just as they can go, and know that every step in all religious growth in India has been progressive. It is not from bad to good, but from good to better.[12]

The main parameter indicating the different religious levels or stages is, according to Vivekananda, the concept of God. At the lowest level, God is imagined as a nonworldly personal power. On a more advanced level, God is recognized as not only transcendent but also immanent. On the third and highest level the full nondual unity between God and Soul is realized.[13] It is not difficult to recognize in these three stages the three major branches of Vedānta, the dualist Dvaita Vedānta, located by Vivekananda at the lowest level, the semidualist Viśiṣṭādvaita Vedānta at the medium level, and finally, as an expression of the supposedly highest level, the nondualist school of Advaita Vedānta. Yet Vivekananda falters when he applies this scheme to the non-Hindu religions because apparently he holds that not all religions contain all three levels, at least not in the same elaborate way. In relation to the supposedly highest stage he claims that its "ideas are expressed in some religions, and in others only hinted. In some they were expatriated."[14] The clearest expression of the highest stage is found in the Hindu school of Advaita Vedānta, which lifts this—and together with it Hinduism in general—above all other religions. In particular, Hinduism stands out by being fully aware of these three levels and by understanding their necessity in terms of stages within a progressive development. This is the reason why Hinduism has space for all the different forms of religion and different stages of truth. In this, according to Vivekananda, Hinduism has discerned "unity in variety" as "the plan of nature."[15] This is what distinguishes Hinduism from other religions, which falsely absolutize their own particular form of religion as the one and only religion, destined for all humanity. The acceptance of its own internal diversity enables Hinduism to accept religious diversity in general, and it is this capacity that makes it, according to Vivekananda, superior to all the other religions.

The background of Vivekananda's position becomes clearer if we look at

---

[12]Vivekananda 1989, 3:424. This stands in startling tension to Vivekananda's critique of a "patronizing way" in one's attitude to other religions. See Vivekananda 1989, 4:182. While Rambachan 1989 puts more emphasis on Vivekananda's pluralist tendencies, he characterizes him in Rambachan 2009, 155–56, as an inclusivist.

[13]See, for example, Vivekananda 1989, 1:322–27.

[14]Ibid., 323.

[15]Ibid., 17.

a speech that he delivered in 1897 in Lahore in today's Pakistan. His topic was "The Common Bases of Hinduism."[16] As the name of a specific religion, the word "Hinduism" had come into use only during the eighteenth and nineteenth centuries, when the British employed it as an umbrella term for the large number of religious traditions and local cultic practices of India which could not be allocated to one of the more clearly defined religious communities such as Islam, Christianity, Zoroastrianism, Sikhism, Buddhism, or Jainism.[17] The term "Hinduism" was applied to a large group of religions that did not exhibit a uniform profile, but was highly diverse or even heterogeneous. In this situation, the influential Neo-Hindu reformers of the nineteenth century tried to establish their own specific understanding of Hinduism as the normative one. Vivekananda responded to this situation by simply declaring that the essential and distinctive feature of Hinduism is its lack of uniformity. What makes Hinduism special is precisely its nature as a unity of highly diverse traditions. Hinduism does have, as Vivekananda underlines, some common principles. But these are as "broad as the skies above our heads" so that they give sufficient space for all of Hinduism's actual diversity.[18] Now, that is at the end of the nineteenth century, it is, says Vivekenanda, crucial for the various Indian religions such as Vaishnavites, Shaivites, the worshippers of Shakti, Ganesha, and Surya, and so on, the adherents of different philosophical schools, and even the Jains and the Buddhists to understand themselves in a new way, namely as different branches and sects of one common religion called "Hinduism" and to put an end to all of their sectarian hostilities. According to Vivekananda, this is mandatory because it lays the religious foundation of India's national unity and identity and indeed of its worldwide mission. For Vivekananda's understanding of India's destiny among the nations is that India should proclaim to all the world its insight into the inner unity of the many faiths. This view, as Wilhelm Halbfass has shown, is characteristic of many Neo-Hindu thinkers:

> Hinduism alone was supposed to provide the framework for the fulfillment of the universal potential inherent in the various religions. Accordingly, it was not considered merely as one religion among

---

[16]Vivekananda 1989, 3:366–84.

[17]Initially, the meaning of the term "Hindu" was geographical. It first referred to the inhabitants of the Indus valley and later on to those of the whole subcontinent (see Michaels 1998, 27–47; Lipner 1998, 1–21; Malinar 2009, 15–25; Llewellyn 2005). It first assumed religious connotations when, in the context of the North-Indian Sant and Bhakti movements, the term began to be used as referring to the non-Muslims in India. But it is controversial whether this already implied the idea of "Hinduism" as a distinct religion (see Lorenzen 1999). The latter use became widespread only during the British colonial period.

[18]Vivekananda 1989, 3:371.

many, but rather as a comprehensive and transcending context for these other religions. The traditional relationship of the "totality" of Hinduism to the Hindu sects became the model for the relationship between Hinduism and the world's religions.[19]

The problems of this position are evident: The first problem is in the claim that Hinduism is superior to all other religions in that it alone is supposedly able to understand and affirm the unity in religious diversity. Although the claim is presumptuous, it may have had some credibility in the nineteenth century. Today, however, with the development of pluralist approaches in a number of religions, it is no longer persuasive. The second problem is that this kind of superiority claim depends on the concept of Hinduism as *a* religion. The concept was retrospectively, and at a fairly late stage, applied to a number of different religious traditions, which up to that time had not understood themselves as belonging to one religion. It is this conceptual application which turned "Hinduism" into a more or less pluralistic religion by definition. But with these two observations alone the question of the pluralist nature of Hinduism is not yet sufficiently answered. Vivekananda was fully aware that the construction of "Hinduism" as the comprehensive religion of India is the work of his own time.[20] Yet he argues that the underlying insight into the legitimate diversity and inner unity of religions has a long and well-established history in Indian thought and can therefore legitimately be regarded as the principal feature of the newly conceived religion of "Hinduism." So his argument rests on a historical claim. It is therefore helpful and necessary to look briefly into India's religious history in order to see to what extent this claim might be justified.[21]

SOME RETROSPECTIVE OBSERVATIONS

Pro-Pluralist Tendencies in Hindu History

The history of Indian religions provides indeed numerous examples of the combining and linking of different deities, beliefs, and practices. Vivekananda frequently quotes the well-known verse from an early part of the Vedas (*Ṛg Veda* 1:164, 46):

---

[19]Halbfass 1988, 346. See also Richards 1985; Coward 1987; and Schmidt-Leukel 2013c.

[20]Vivekananda 1989, 3:368.

[21]For overviews on traditional and contemporary Hindu attitudes to religious diversity see Balasubramanian [1992] 2004; Clooney 2003; Coward 1987a; Halbfass 1991, 51–85; Long 2013.

They call it Indra, Mitra, Varuṇa, Agni, and it is the heavenly bird that
flies. The wise speak of what is One in many ways; they call it Agni,
Yama, Mātariśvan.[22]

Highly influential has also been an idea, found in the ancient Puruṣa myth
(*Ṛg Veda* 10:90), according to which the different gods are interlinked because they all emerged from the sacrifice and dissection of one single divine
organism, the Puruṣa. Another frequent motif is the construction of families
of deities with many different branches. The various gods allocated to the
same family are often interpreted as representing different aspects of what
is ultimately understood as being one and the same god. This is also true
of the fact that the male Hindu gods are usually presented in conjunction
with a female consort, who does not simply represent a second deity but the
female or energetic aspect of that god. Another pattern of linking different
deities, which is particularly common in Vaishnavism, is the belief that one
god can be the incarnation of a different one.[23] Popular deities like Krishna
or Rāma, who were originally independent gods, became thus venerated
as incarnations (*avatāras*) of Vishnu. In the Bhagavadgītā (4:6–8) Vishnu
reveals through Krishna that by means of his magical power (*māyā*) he,
the unborn and immutable God, assumes from time to time human form in
order to reestablish the Dharma—a term which here implies truth, order,
and religion—whenever the Dharma is threatened by decay, rewarding the
good and destroying the evildoers.

The various patterns of linking and combining different deities are often
connected to some sort of hierarchization as, for example, when the different
gods are seen as manifesting different aspects or vigors of the one supreme
God. When the deities are related to one large family, there is always one
god seen as the center or head of that family. Such hierarchical patterns usually imply a grading in terms of value. A good example is Krishna's famous
statement in the Bhagavadgītā that those who sacrifice to other gods will
receive their reward in fact from him, or more precisely, from Vishnu who
is incarnate in Krishna. Yet the reward received through other gods is only
of a subordinate and preliminary nature, whereas those who turn directly
to Krishna or Vishnu are promised the highest reward of ultimate salvation
(Bhagavadgītā 7:20–23; 9:23–25). Also in the Bhagavadgītā, we find the
beginnings of the later widespread idea that there are three valid paths to
salvation: First, the "path of works" (*karmamārga*), that is, the comple-
tion of the traditional caste duties as prescribed in the Vedas and Shastras.
Second, the "path of knowledge/insight" (*jñānamārga*), that is, the path of

---

[22]Doniger 1981, 80.
[23]See Parrinder 1997.

renunciation and ascetic strife for liberating insight. And third, the "path of the love of God" (*bhaktimārga*), that is, the path of dedicating oneself wholeheartedly to the veneration of god and relying completely on god's redeeming grace. According to the Bhagavadgītā, these three ways are not equally suitable to all individuals. In particular the "path of knowledge" is for most people far too harsh and demanding (12:1–8). And whereas the "path of works" underlies certain restrictions in caste and gender, the "path of the love of God" has the advantage that it is open to people from all castes and sexes and even to those who have gravely violated their obligations (see 9:29–34; 18:65–66). Thus in the Bhagavadgītā we find elements of a hierarchization of religious paths: The "path of knowledge" is praised as particularly ambitious, but this is also its major deficit. Similarly, the "path of works" is not available to people from the lowest or no caste and is of limited value to women. The easiest, unrestricted, and hence preferred way is the "path of *bhakti*, the love of God."[24] In such grading of the different paths according to different needs, we encounter an idea that we have already met in the thoughts of Vivekananda: that not all forms of religions are equally suitable to all people and that therefore the differences between individuals require a diversity of religions or religious paths.

In the course of the further religious development in India, the idea that different ritual practices, different spiritual paths, different gods, and different images of God correspond to differences in the spiritual capacities of individual human beings became more and more prominent. It is known under the term *adhikāra-bheda*, meaning "difference in the capacities."[25] Regarding the interpretation of religious diversity, this involves two important aspects: On the one hand, religious diversity is seen as something positive inasmuch as it serves different spiritual needs. On the other hand, this positive assessment of religious diversity does not entail the equal value of religions. For according to the concept of *adhikāra-bheda*, the differences in the individuals' spiritual capacities are usually understood in terms of different stages within a progressive line of spiritual development, as we have also seen in the thought of Vivekananda. So if the different religions correspond to lower or higher stages of spiritual insight and maturation, we arrive at a hierarchical interpretation of religious diversity: Thus one's own religion is understood as being the most mature and hence as that which is, in a typically inclusivist manner, superior to all the others. The idea of different spiritual stages with different religious needs and capacities is deeply rooted in Indian thinking. It goes back to the hierarchical caste system and the belief in karma and reincarnation. Once belief in caste, karma, and re-

---

[24]See also Malinar 2007, 188–91, 200–202.
[25]See Raghavan 1966, 76; A. Sharma 2005, 13–15; Halbfass 1991, 72–73.

incarnation have been combined, which happened through the Upanishads, the belief was born that one could ascend over a series of different lives from a lower caste or form of rebirth to a higher one, according to one's karmic or spiritual development. The concept of *adhikāra-bheda* transfers this widespread pattern to the realm of different religions or different religious practices. In this guise it became prominent in Neo-Hinduism.[26]

Apart from tendencies, which are pluralism friendly—although in a limited way and with strong inclusivist overtones—the Indian history of religions also knows of several examples of harsh interreligious polemics and even violent conflicts between different religious groups, which clearly display exclusivist attitudes.

Anti-Pluralist Tendencies in Hindu History

According to the classical Vedic view the revelation of the *dharma*, that is, the cosmic order and truth, is bound to a particular collection of texts, the Vedas, to the language of these texts, Sanskrit, and to a particular people, the Āryas. What makes the Āryas special is their role as custodians of the truth, while religious traditions of the other peoples, the "Barbarians" (*mleccha*), "are disregarded or, less frequently, explicitly dismissed."[27] In relation to the religious traditions of India a crucial line of demarcation was drawn between two groups, those who formally accepted the Vedas as revelation (*śruti*), the *āstikas* ("affirmers"), and those who rejected the Vedas, the *nāstikas* ("deniers"), such as the materialists (*cārvakās*), the Buddhists and the Jains. Mutual polemic was particularly strong between these two groups. For example, according to Śaṅkara (7th or 8th c.), the major representative of Advaita Vedānta, the Buddha had taught nothing but confused doctrines. Therefore "the Buddhist view should be abjured in every way by all who desire the highest good,"[28] that is, salvation. Kumārila (7th c.), the chief representative of the orthodox Hindu Mīmāṃsā school, not only extensively criticized the Buddha in his writings[29] but it is also reported that he advised King Sudhanvan to solve the problem of the Buddhists by simply killing all of them, including their old and young ones.[30] The *Viṣṇupurāṇa*, an influential Vaishnava scripture from the fourth or fifth century, "suggests," as Klaus Klostermaier summarizes, "complete excommunication of the Buddhists: all social contact must be broken, even looking at a heretic necessitates lengthy expiations. The Hindu who dines with a

---

[26]See Neufeldt 1987 on the strong presence of this idea in the Ramakrishna Mission.
[27]Halbfass 1991, 53. See also Halbfass 1988, 320.
[28]Brahma-Sūtra-Bhāsya II, 2, 32. Gambhirananda 2004, 426.
[29]See Clooney 2001, 143–47; Halbfass 1991, 59–62, 95–97.
[30]See Halbfass 1998, 176–77; Hazra 1995, 387.

Buddhist goes to hell. Buddhists are considered as unclean, whatever their caste-affiliation may have been."[31] Another Vaishnava text, the *Kalkipurāṇa*, which is influenced by the *Viṣṇupurāṇa* and was presumably composed around the beginning of the second millennium, prophesies about Kalkin, the future incarnation of Vishnu, that he will bring the Golden Age of Truth (*satyayuga*) by exterminating in a final apocalyptic battle all followers of Jainism and Buddhism.[32]

Buddhist polemic against Hinduism was similarly harsh. In the *Mahāvaṃsa*, the most important among the Buddhist chronicles of Sri Lanka, perhaps dating from the sixth century, a war between the Singhalese ruler Duṭṭagāmaṇī and the Tamil ruler Eḷāra, which took place in the second century, is retrospectively made up and celebrated as a war to the glory of the Buddha. After he had won the war, Duṭṭagāmaṇī felt remorse because he caused the death of several thousand Tamils. But a group of eight enlightened Buddhist saints (Pāli: *arahats*) consoled the king with the words that in fact he had caused the death of only one and a half human beings, a Buddhist monk and a Buddhist layperson. "The heretical and evil others who died were like animals." The Arahats further assured the king that he would not have to fear any negative karmic consequences of his deeds but "will make the Buddha's Faith shine in many ways."[33] In a later Buddhist text from the thirteenth century the anti-Tamil and anti-Hindu polemic is further increased. Tamils are here addressed as "Tamil dirt" and as "enemies of the Buddha's teaching."[34] High tribute is paid to a sort of Buddhist Hercules who protects Buddhism by regularly killing Tamils by catching them by their legs and literally ripping them apart and removing their corpses at night with the help of the deities.[35]

Hindu-Buddhist hostilities were not merely rhetorical. Buddhist texts report repeated persecutions of Buddhists by Hindu rulers.[36] Until today Hindu Tamils are victims of Buddhist hegemony in Sri Lanka. One will have to agree with the judgment of Indian historians such as Lal Mani Joshi, Kanai Lal Hazra, and R. C. Hiremath that the continuous rivalry and hostility between Hindus and Buddhists was one of the major reasons for the final

---

[31]Klostermaier 1979, 66.

[32]Cf. Bhatt 1982; Schmidt-Leukel 2013b. See also chapter 12.

[33]After the new English translation Guruge 2005, 573–74. As Sven Bretfeld has shown, the text is most likely the revision of an earlier version according to which the king could not fall asleep because of his enthusiasm about his victory. The Buddhist Arahats then appeared in order to calm him through the recitation of Buddhist texts (see Bretfeld 2001, xxxv–xxxvi). According to Wilke 2006, 203n95, the derogative designation of the Shaivite Tamils as "animals" might be a polemic allusion to Shaiva-Siddhanta terminology, which calls the human souls "cattle" whose fetters are cut asunder by Shiva.

[34]Bretfeld 2001, xxxix–xl.

[35]*Rasavāhinī* (B) 31. Cf. Bretfeld 2001, 135ff.

[36]Through Puṣyamitra (187–151 BCE) who terminated the rule of the pro-Buddhist Mauriya dynasty, and through Mihirakula in Kashmir (6th c.) and Śaśaṅka in Gauḍa (7th c.), both being Shaivites.

demise of Buddhism in India.[37] Thus, contrary to Vivekananda, one has to state that in the case of Hinduism and Buddhism, religious diversity was not preserved in traditional India.

Hostilities and polemics are found not only between the *āstikas* ("affirmers") and *nāstikas* ("deniers") but also among the *āstikas* themselves, that is, among those religious traditions that affirmed the Vedas. Well known are the various tensions between the representatives of traditional Brahmanism on the one hand and the devotees of Vishnu or Shiva on the other hand.[38] There were also conflicts between Vaishnavites and Shaivites or between the followers of different religious philosophies who—to paraphrase Karl Marx—did not only take their recourse to the weapon of arguments but also to the argument of the weapons.[39] Thus Vivekananda's appeal to a supposedly always tolerant and even pluralist Indian tradition is, at best, only partly correct. And that part of the tradition on which he could draw with some justification did not hold an egalitarian understanding of religious diversity but a hierarchical, inclusivist one.

Before I proceed to the contemporary situation, a few brief remarks shall be added about Hinduism's relation to Islam and Christianity in modern times. For these relationships are as important to the more recent debates as is the earlier traditional background which I just sketched.

Hindu Approaches to Islam and Christianity

Islam became increasingly present in India since the end of the first millennium and Christianity mainly since the arrival of the Portuguese in the sixteenth century.[40] Both appeared in India as religions of conquerors, a fact that has put a tremendous burden on the encounter between them and Hinduism.[41] Therefore, much polemic, tension, and conflict is found in the relationship between Hinduism and Islam and between Hinduism and Christianity. But there were also some attempts of understanding and integration, which, unfortunately, were not too successful.[42]

A particularly interesting case is the tendency within the so-called *nirguṇa-bhakti* movements to combine elements from Muslim and "Hindu"

---

[37]See Joshi 1983, xvi; Hazra 1995, 385–88; Hiremath 1994, 97.

[38]See Klostermaier 1989, 53–60.

[39]Ibid., 333–35.

[40]Some smaller Christian groups existed in India at least since the sixth century and perhaps still earlier. But before modernity, Christianity remained a small and locally confined phenomenon that had not been given much attention.

[41]For an analogous historical plight in Buddhist-Christian and Buddhist-Muslim relations see below, chapters 11 and 12.

[42]See the overview in Ram-Prasad 2005; 2006; 2007.

(i.e., non-Muslim)[43] spirituality and relativize the boundaries between the two religious traditions. Guru Nānak (1469–1539), for example, proclaimed the message: "There is neither Hindu nor Muslim,"[44] which meant for him that in the eyes of God it does not matter whether one is Hindu or Muslim. After his death, his following, coming from both religious traditions, developed into an independent religious movement. At least since the fifth guru, Guru Arjan (1563–1606), the followers of the new movement interpreted Nānak's message in the sense of "There are those who are neither Hindu nor Muslim," or—as we read in their canonical writings—"We are neither Hindus nor Muslims,"[45] meaning: We are a separate religious community, the community of the Sikhs, which is different from Hinduism and Islam. Thus a movement that began as an attempt at weakening religious boundaries led to the formation of a new religion with new demarcations. On the side of Islam one could point to the interreligious inclinations of Akbar the Great (1542–1605) who was probably influenced by Guru Nānak and the like-minded Muslim poet Kabīr (d. 1518). Akbar's great-grandson Dara Shikoh (1615–59) became famous for getting the Upanishads translated into Persian. He entertained close relations with the Sikhs and believed in the inner unity of Muslim and Hindu traditions. Such ideas did not remain without effect in India,[46] but they did not become Islamic mainstream either.

Testimonies of a more intensive engagement of Hindus with Christianity are not found before the period of the Neo-Hindu reformers. An early major figure in this respect was Rām Mohan Roy (1772–1833), who saw in Jesus an inspiring like-minded guru. Roy established the influential association Brahmo Samāj, which since then represented the interreligious open-minded branch of Neo-Hinduism. Vivekananda too had initially been a member of the Brahmo Samāj until he became a disciple of the mystic Ramakrishna (1836–86). Ramakrishna clearly believed in the traditional idea of *adhikāra-bheda* (difference in spiritual capacities): "God Himself has provided different forms of worship. He who is the Lord of the Universe has arranged all these forms to suit different men in different stages of knowledge."[47] Ramakrishna explicitly included Buddhism, Islam, and Christianity in what he considered the divinely prescribed forms of religion. After Ramakrishna's death, Vivekananda established the Ramakrishna Mission in order to spread Ramakrishna's ideas in his own, that is, Vivekananda's, interpretation.

---

[43]See the remarks in footnote 17 above.
[44]Cf. McLeod 1984, 21–22.
[45]*Adi Granth* 1136.
[46]See Ali 2004; Ramey 2008.
[47]Nikhilananda 2005, 126.

It is this line of Neo-Hinduism that has become responsible for the image of Hinduism as a pluralist religion. However, Neo-Hinduism had also a quite different face, and this reflects the polemical exclusivist strand as it is also found in India's religious history. A distinctive example is Dayananda Saraswati (1824–83). In 1875, Saraswati established the Arya Samāj, which after the Brahmo Samāj became the second major and highly influential association of Neo-Hinduism. In his main work "The Light of Truth" (*Satyārtha Prakāśa*), Dayananda presented a modernist and rationalist interpretation of the Vedas and ruthlessly criticized all religious ideas and practices diverging from his own views: not only those of some major Hindu traditions, but also those of Jainism, Buddhism, Islam, and Christianity. According to Dayananda, all these religions contradict human reason. On the Bible he wrote that it "contains hundreds of thousands of things that are condemnable."[48] And Christians who put their faith in Jesus "have deluded themselves, and who knows how long they will continue to do so."[49] On the Qur'ān Dayananda passes the judgment "that this book can neither be the work of God nor that of an enlightened person, nor does it contain knowledge."[50] It rather "increases the sufferings of the human race by making man a beast, and disturbs the peace of the world by promoting war and by sowing the seeds of discord."[51] Both the inclusivist and semipluralist tendencies that can be discerned in Ramakrishna and Vivekananda and the exclusivist tendencies as represented by Dayananda still exert their influence on the interpretation of religious diversity in contemporary India. In the case of the Hindutva movement they have formed a kind of amalgam. But before I turn to this, I would like to address an interesting legal development.

HINDUISM AND PLURALISM TODAY

The Legal Battle between the Ramakrishna Mission and the State of West Bengal

The legacy of Vivekananda led to one of the most paradoxical cases of recent Indian legal history. One of the activities of the Ramakrishna Mission, which Vivekananda founded in 1897, consists of running schools. In order to become exempt from the public control of their schools, the Ramakrishna Mission tried to achieve the legal status of a minority religion, called "Ra-

---

[48]Saraswati 1984, 648.
[49]Ibid., 645.
[50]Ibid., 719–20.
[51]Ibid., 720.

makrishnaism." This status would have granted the mission the right to run their schools according to its own rules. In order to achieve its recognition as a minority religion, the Ramakrishna Mission argued that Ramakrishna-ism is clearly different from Hinduism. As one reason they produced the argument that "other religions (including Hinduism) do not believe that all religions are different paths leading to the same goal, but claim absolute authority in all matters to the exclusion of all others."[52] Thus, in contrast to its founder, Vivekananda, the Ramakrishna Mission now declared that Hinduism is not a pluralist religion and that only Ramakrishnaism teaches the equal validity of different religions. The legal case between the Rama-krishna Mission and the State of West Bengal took more than fifteen years and was only settled in 1995 after a decision of the Indian Supreme Court which rejected the claim of the Mission to be a religion on its own. In its reasoning the Supreme Court defined the nature of Hinduism by present-ing a list of seven characteristic features. Among these seven points we find the "Spirit of tolerance and willingness to understand and appreciate the opponent's point of view based on the realisation that truth was many-sided" (no. 2), and the "Recognition of the fact that the means or ways to salvation are many" (no. 5).[53] Thus, by the way of this highly paradoxical circuit, Vivekananda's understanding of Hinduism as a pluralistic religion has finally entered a supreme legal decision—against the intentions of the Ramakrishna Mission, whose views can be regarded as historically more justified. The ambiguities of Hinduism regarding its understanding of re-ligious diversity become fully visible when we turn to the position of the nationalist Hindutva ("Hindu-ness") movement.

On the Position of the Hindutva Movement

One of the leading Hindutva ideologists was Madhav Sadashiv Golwalkar (1906–73). Golwalkar had been a member of the monastic Ramakrishna order for several years and was influenced by the ideas of Ramakrishna and Vivekananda.[54] He was also influenced by Keshav Baliram Hedgewar (1889–1940), another major figure in the Hindutva movement. After Hedge-war's death in 1940, Golwalkar became his successor as the leader of the paramilitary Rashtriya Swayamsevak Sangh (RSS) (= National Volunteers

---

[52]"Supreme Court to RK Mission: 'You're Hindus,'" *Hinduism Today*, September 1995. http://www.hinduismtoday.com/modules/smartsection/item.php?itemid=3536.

[53]*Bramchari Sidheswar Bhai & Ors. etc. v. State of West Bengal etc.* (Supreme Court 1995 AIR 2089). See http://www.indiacourts.in/bramchari-sidheswar-bhai—ors.etc.-vs.-state-of-west-bengal-etc._79c61d83-230d-4337-a335-97a14f32c86b.

[54]On the religious background of Golwalkar, see Gantke 1998.

Organization), one of the three institutional pillars of Hindutva.[55] The other two are the Vishva Hindu Parishad (VHP) (= World Hindu Council) and Bharatiya Janata Party (BJP) (= Indian People's Party).

It is not difficult to rediscover Vivekananda's central ideas in Golwalkar's writings, such as the affirmation of one single divine reality, the inadequacy of human concepts to fully grasp ultimate reality, and the view of religions, including Christianity, Islam, and Hinduism, as different but valid approaches to the divine.[56]

> According to our ways of religious belief and philosophy, a Muslim is as good as a Hindu. It is not the Hindu alone who will reach the ultimate Godhead. Everyone has the right to follow his path according to his own persuasion. . . . The God of Islam, Christianity and Hinduism is thus the same and we are all His devotees.[57]

But according to Golwalkar, only Hinduism is able to affirm this insight:[58] Buddhism has betrayed its mother religion of Hinduism,[59] and the Abrahamic religions, Judaism, Christianity, and Islam, are by their inner nature absolutist and intolerant.[60] Hinduism has therefore a special role to fulfill, a worldwide mission: Because only Hinduism can discern the inner divine unity in the diversity of religions and cultures, it is Hinduism's role to provide the ideas on which a true solidarity of all humans may be established: "It is the grand world-unifying thought of Hindus alone that can supply the abiding basis for human brotherhood."[61] It is therefore "the sacred duty" of India, for the benefit of all humanity, to care for Hinduism and keep it in sound condition. This implies the protection of Hinduism against the pernicious impact of the absolutist religions, that is, in particular against Christianity and Islam.[62] From this Golwalkar concludes a politics of harsh religious inequality so that in India Christianity and Islam must never have the same legal position as Hinduism.[63]

What emerged from Vivekananda's heritage is at best a kind of primus-inter-pares pluralism, holding that religions are in principle equally valid but that Hinduism is superior inasmuch as it is the only religion capable of

---

[55]For a brief overview on Hindutva see Randeria 1996.
[56]See Golwalkar 1996, 490–92.
[57]Ibid., 490, 492.
[58]Ibid., 6, 161, 337.
[59]Ibid., 70–71.
[60]Ibid., 103, 159–60.
[61]Ibid., 6.
[62]Ibid., 6, 348.
[63]See Frei 1996; Klostermaier 2000, 145; J. Sharma 2007, 83–87.

affirming this view without self-contradiction, whereas all other religions are suffering from various absolutisms. In the case of the Hindutva movement this version of pluralism serves to justify religious inequality and a politics of religious intolerance. Will Hinduism be able to overcome such tendencies?

Toward an Alternative Pluralism

In this respect the inner development of Mahatma Gandhi (1869–1948) is highly instructive. Gandhi initially shared the view that Hinduism is superior in that it alone is capable of appreciating the spiritual value of all religions.[64] Yet Gandhi realized the paradoxical nature of this view. From 1930 onward, he tried to develop an understanding of religious equality that would include Hinduism and not result in a new form of Hindu superiority. To this end he drew on two interconnected elements: On the one hand, he maintained the conviction that truth ultimately transcends all words. All doctrines and doctrinal systems are thus inevitably imperfect, including religions. Truth in its ultimate sense cannot be identified with any one among them, and Hinduism is no exception. On the other hand, he combined this view with his understanding that the true essence of religion can be realized only through a *practice* that is equally available to all religions. While Gandhi initially taught that "God is truth," he now reversed the sentence and held that "truth is God," thereby referring to a truth that can never become one's doctrinal possession and can only be authentically pursued in religious, particularly nonviolent, practice.[65] This shift to practice seems to have the potential of undermining any claims to Hindu superiority that are based on Hinduism's supposedly unique doctrinal ability of correctly interpreting religious diversity.

Gandhi's rather fragmentary considerations are taken up by the contemporary American Hindu Jeffery Long, who explicitly relates his own approach to Gandhi.[66] The Hindu claim to superiority, says Long, can be overcome only if Hindus affirm unambiguously that "eternal truth" (*sanatana dharma*) is not equivalent to any specific historical or linguistic articulation of truth, not even to that of Hinduism. Long directs this position explicitly against the Hindutva ideology and intends it as a basis for a genuinely pluralist approach. According to Long, genuine Hindu pluralism needs to dismiss the idea that Hinduism is all-encompassing and has nothing to learn from

---

[64]See Jordans 1987, 10.

[65]See Rao 2005, 51ff. For a comparison of Gandhi and John Hick see Sugirtharajah 2012. For John Hick's own views on Gandhi see Hick and Hempel 1989, 21–23, 85–89; Hick 2008, 161–78.

[66]See Long 2007, especially 101–70. For his reference to Gandhi see ibid., 135–36. See also Long 2005.

others.[67] The "eternal truth" is what underlies all religions in their totality. It is not identical with one particular religious tradition but is approximated by the religions' mutual openness in their search for a deeper understanding of truth.[68] In that sense, he sees polycentric forms of religious pluralism, as based on process philosophy or the ancient Jain philosophy of *anekāntavāda* ("not-one-sidedness"), as more congenial to genuine pluralism than the monocentric variants.[69]

Another contemporary Hindu pluralist is Anantanand Rambachan, a native of Trinidad and Tobago. Rambachan is self-critically aware that

> [m]ost of the Hindu models for interpreting religious pluralism are inclusive. Other traditions and viewpoints are accepted but only within the general framework that they are growing towards and will arrive at one's own position. There are higher and lower truths along a single continuum.[70]

Being firmly rooted in the Advaita Vedānta school of Hindu philosophy, he knows that this also applies to inner Hindu diversity and questions this kind of traditional ranking.[71] To him, however, this is an open question. He subscribes to the fundamental insight that all human expressions are inadequate to express ultimate reality. But it would be naïve, superficial, and in the end dangerous to conclude from this that *all* religious beliefs are equally true.[72] Different images of the divine are interlinked with different values and norms. The image of a vengeful God is likely to foster a different way of living than the image of a loving God.[73] To Rambachan the decisive criterion for distinguishing higher from lower truths is their potential "to sustain dignity and justice for all human beings."[74] Yet this criterion will not lead to a clear ranking of large religious traditions, because each one among them has its own specific deficits. As a consequence, they need a theology of religions that encourages them to be self-critical and "to question and challenge each other."[75] This is the function of dialogue. Rambachan lays open how much Christianity, but also Buddhism, have challenged his Hindu beliefs, thereby leading him to a creative reformulation of Advaita

---

[67]Long 2005, 134–35.

[68]Ibid., 155.

[69]See Long 2005 and Long 2009, 170–71. For the distinction between monocentric and polycentric see chapter 2.

[70]Rambachan 2000a, 1.

[71]See ibid., 2.

[72]See Rambachan 1999.

[73]Rambachan 2000b, 6.

[74]Rambachen 2001, 2.

[75]Ibid.

Vedānta.[76] A significant outcome of this process is his book *A Hindu Theology of Liberation.*[77]

In emphasizing the need and possibility of interreligious learning as a means of spiritual maturation, Long and even more so Rambachan give the traditional idea of *adhikāra-bheda* ("difference in the capacities") a new and constructive twist. There is indeed something like spiritual maturation marked by different stages of insight and accompanied by different levels of truths. But these are found *within* the various religions, and the kind of maturation may take some hitherto unexpected forms. This understanding has also the potential to overcome the *primus-inter-pares* variant of Hindu superiority claims. It can acknowledge that the capacity of relativizing one's own religion in light of the transcendent nature of ultimate truth is not the exclusive property of Hinduism but something that is also possible in other religions on the basis and within the framework of their own religious dynamics. The great Hindu scholar Radhakrishnan (1888–1975) at times expressed the opinion "that every religion has possibilities of such a transformation."[78] Comparing religions to different colleges, he speculated that instead of changing one's college it would be more important to improve the standard of all colleges "with the result that each college enables us to attain the same goal."[79] This statement may be ambiguous. It can be read in the sense of the Neo-Hindu's patronizing mentality that it is their mission to raise all other religions to the same high level that is exclusively found in Hinduism. But it can also be read in the optimistic sense that all of the major religions are indeed able to rise above their exclusivist or inclusivist superiority claims by means of their own religious potential. Ending with this ambiguous perspective may be somewhat frustrating, but I think it realistically mirrors where Hinduism stands in relation to the question of religious pluralism.

---

[76]E.g., Rambachan 1992, 43; 2006, 5; 2009, 179–80; 2011; 2012.
[77]Rambachan 2015.
[78]Radhakrishnan 1956, 204.
[79]Radhakrishnan [1927] 1974, 35.

6

The Difficult Road to Pluralism in Buddhism

OF BLIND MEN, ELEPHANTS, AND RAFTS

Vivekananda's master, Ramakrishna, illustrated his understanding of religious diversity by using the famous parable of the blind men and the elephant:

> Once some blind men chanced to come near an animal that someone told them was an elephant. They were asked what the elephant was like. The blind men began to feel its body. One of them said the elephant was like a pillar; he had touched only its leg. Another said it was like a winnowing-fan; he had touched only its ear. In this way the others, having touched its tail or belly, gave their different versions of the elephant. Just so, a man who has seen only one aspect of God limits God to that alone. It is his conviction that God cannot be anything else.[1]

This parable is often used to illustrate a pluralist interpretation of religious diversity: The religions are marked by different understandings of ultimate reality because they are constituted by different limited impressions of it. However, using this parable for pluralism should be done with caution. The crucial question is whether we are all in the situation of the blind men or whether there are some who can rightly claim that they are in an advanced position, seeing the elephant in its true shape. John Hick commented on the parable: "The advocate of the pluralist understanding cannot pretend to any such cosmic vision."[2] In this respect, Ramakrishna's version of the parable is ambiguous. It could imply that he understands himself as someone who knows more of the elephant than the blind ones know and that he takes the

---

[1] Nikhilananda 2005, 240–41.
[2] Hick 1985a, 37.

Advaita Vedānta view of the formless nature of the ultimate as the most advanced position. However, Ramakrishna continues to explain that "God has form and He is formless too. Further, He is beyond form and formlessness. No one can limit Him."[3] This statement seems to express his view that God transcends any human concept, even those concepts that try to grasp God as "formless," as ungraspable. In that sense, no one could legitimately claim to have a full or perfect grasp of God, which would indeed constitute a pluralist premise. And the premise would not be stated on the basis of a "cosmic vision" that claims to surmount or even supersede all religions, but as an expression of confidence from within one such limited religious perspective.

The story of the blind men and the elephant exists in many different versions. It is still widespread in India today. It also made its way to the world of Islam and is found among a number of medieval Muslim writers. Rūmī, for example, used it in the third book of his *Masnavi* in order to illustrate the limitation of ordinary knowledge as contrasted with mystical insight.[4] The earliest versions of the parable are found in the scriptures of the Jains and the Buddhists. In the Udāna of the Buddhist Pāli canon (*tipiṭaka*), the blind men are summoned and brought to the elephant on the order of a king with healthy eyes who arranges the spectacle for his private entertainment. When toward the end of the story the blind men come into heavy conflict about their contradictory descriptions of the elephant and finally start fighting each other with their fists, "the king was delighted."[5]

In its Buddhist version the parable has no pluralist implication. The blind men are compared to the rival teachers at the time of the Buddha and the elephant to the true Dharma. The blind men's understanding of the Dharma, as the text explicitly says, is too limited for pointing out the way to ultimate salvation. Their attachment to their own views keeps the Buddha's rivals within the bondage of *saṃsāra*, the cycle of rebirth: "They sink in the middle of the stream. . . . They do not go beyond *saṃsāra*"[6]—an image which is related to the metaphor of *nirvāṇa* as the "further shore." Only Buddhas show the path to liberation, the means to cross over the stream of *saṃsāra*. A Buddha, therefore, is not one of the blind ones; he knows ultimate reality as it truly is.[7] The whole section in the Udāna ends with a further, rather unambiguous simile: The light of the other teachers resembles the light of a glowworm, whereas the light of the Buddha shines like the sun: "When that illuminant arises, the glowworm's light is quenched and shines no more."[8]

---

[3]Nikhilananda 2005, 241.
[4]*Maṭnawīye Ma'nawī* 3:1260–92. Rumi 2013, 78–80.
[5]Udāna 6:4; Ireland 1997, 88.
[6]Udāna 6:6–7; Ireland 1997, 90–91.
[7]See Udāna 6:5–10. See also the fine analysis in Grünschloß 1999, 202–5.
[8]Udāna 6:10; Ireland 1997, 93.

There is a motif in the Pāli canon, which recommends to the Buddhist ascetic an abstention from all views. Part of this recurrent motif is the criticism of those religious teachers who cling to their personal view by considering it as "the highest in the world," while disputing and disparaging all other views. This motif coincides with the Pāli canonical version of the elephant and the blind narrative in that the latter likewise entails a critique of those who are "deeply attached to their own views," "see only one side of things," and "engage in quarrels and disputes."[9] A particularly pertinent example of the exhortation to abstain from such one-sidedness and dispute is found in Sutta-Nipāta (verses 796–803). This text says that by not clinging to any viewpoint, a wise ascetic "does not consider himself 'superior,' 'inferior' or 'equal.'" Such a one "has gone to the further shore, never more to return."[10] Given that the "further shore" refers to the Buddhist soteriological goal of *nirvāṇa*, the question arises of whether the abstention from all views would also include the Buddhist teaching. Verse 803 speaks without any qualification of "not adhering to such doctrines of truth"[11] and uses the word *dhamma* (= *dharma*) which is also used to signify the Buddhist teaching. Is this then an early anticipation of the Mahāyāna teaching according to which the ultimate truth is beyond all verbal explication?[12] The commentarial tradition of Theravāda Buddhism decided otherwise and interpreted verse 803 as referring only to the sixty-two "wrong doctrines."[13] In an early and influential Mahāyāna scripture the parable of the elephant and—in this case—just one blind man touching only the elephant's leg and thus wrongly inferring from this the shape and color of the whole elephant, is applied to those Buddhists who wish to follow the superior Mahāyāna path but rely only on the non-Mahāyāna teachings instead of the higher Mahāyāna wisdom.[14] But then this higher wisdom consists in ultimately transcending all conceptual teachings.

It is certainly a strong and influential strand in both Theravāda and Mahāyāna Buddhism that one should see the Buddhist doctrines only as a raft that is needed for crossing over the stream of *saṃsāra* and reaching the further shore of *nirvāṇa*.[15] That is, the Buddhist teaching should be taken only as a means and one should not be attached to it: Once the other shore

---

[9]Udāna 6:4; Ireland 1997, 89.

[10]Sutta-Nipāta 799, 803; Saddhatissa 1985, 34–35.

[11]*dhammāpi tesaṃ na paticchitāse.*

[12]For such tendencies in other texts of the Sutta-Nipāta, see also Gómez 1976.

[13]See Nyanaponika 1977, 322.

[14]*Aṣṭasāhasrikā-Prajñāpāramitā-Sūtra* III, 235. See Conze 1995, 163–64.

[15]The parable of the raft is found in *Majjhimanikāya* 22 and 38. It is explicitly referred to and quoted in the "Diamond Sūtra" (*Vajracchedikā Prajñāpāramitā-Sūtra* 6), an influential Mahāyāna scripture. There is also an indirect reference to *Majjhimanikāya* 22 in Nāgārjuna's *Mūlamadhyamakakārikā* 24:11, where Nāgārjuna refers to the simile of the snake which provides the title for this *Majjhimanikāya* 22.

is reached, the raft is no longer needed. Can other teachings likewise function as a raft? Or is it only the Buddhist teaching that enables one to reach the "further shore"? In the Pāli canon, as often also in the Mahāyāna world, there is a clear distinction between the wrong or deficient teachings of the Buddha's rivals and the right teaching of the Buddha as the only suitable vehicle of salvation.

> So I have shown you how the Dhamma is similar to a raft, being for the purpose of crossing over, not for the purpose of grasping.... When you know the Dhamma to be similar to a raft, you should abandon even the teachings, how much more so things contrary to the teachings.[16]

Thus while the Buddhist teaching is not to be confused with the wrong teachings of others, one should nevertheless not be attached to it. Is it possible to develop a Buddhist pluralism against this background?[17] Can the Buddha, the enlightened one, be declared as one of the "blind men"? Or can the supposedly blind ones be declared, against the teaching of the Buddha, as in fact other enlightened teachers being on a par with the Buddha? Can there be several rafts that take one to the other shore? Or are all other rafts destined to "sink in the middle of the stream"?

THERAVĀDA BUDDHISM AND RELIGIOUS PLURALISM

Doctrinal Obstacles

Within Theravāda Buddhism, Buddhist superiority claims are based on two crucial tenets: First, the belief that only the Four Noble Truths and the Noble Eightfold Path as taught by the Buddha will lead to liberating insight. This is clearly stated in the *Dhammapada* (273–74), a highly influential collection of sayings:

> Of paths, the eightfold is the best.
> Of truths, the four statements....
> Just this path, there is no other
> For purity of vision.[18]

---

[16]*Majjhimanikāya* 22:13–14 (PTS MN I, 135). See Ñāṇamoli and Bodhi 2001, 229.

[17]For overviews on Buddhist attitudes to other religions see Burton 2011; Harris 2013; Kiblinger 2005; Schmidt-Leukel 2008a; Schmidt-Leukel 2017a. A collection of essays on Buddhist attitudes to specific other faiths and to religious diversity as such is offered in Schmidt-Leukel 2013a.

[18]Carter and Palihawadana 2000, 49.

The second pillar of Buddhist superiority claims is the belief that in each world system there cannot be more than one full Buddha at the same time, that is, there can be only one who teaches the Four Noble Truths, shows the path to liberation, and establishes the salvific community, the Saṅgha, which preserves the Dharma and continues to teach it for the sake of gods and men.[19] Buddhism does affirm that there are many Buddhas, but they either exist in different worlds or at different times—hence the qualification that they cannot exist in one world simultaneously. Yet how should this "simultaneously" be understood? Does it refer to one generation or to some longer period or even to the whole duration of one particular world? In the semicanonical scripture "The Questions of King Milinda" (*Milindapañha*) this doctrine is the subject of a longer discussion that provides some important clues.

The respective section begins with King Milinda questioning the Buddhist monk Nāgasena about the Buddha's uniqueness with the following argument:

> Already by the appearance of one Buddha has this world become flooded with light. If there should be a second Buddha the world would still be more illuminated by the glory of them both.

Nāgasena rejects King Milinda's argument with the words:

> This world system, o king, is a one-Buddha-supporting world; that is, it can bear the virtue of only a single Tathāgata. If a second Tathāgata were to arise the world could not bear him, it would shake and tremble, it would bend, this way and that, it would disperse, scatter into pieces, dissolve, be utterly destroyed.

Apparently the author or redactors of the *Milindapañha* were themselves not fully satisfied by this initial reply and felt the need to add some further reasons, among which we find the following:

> If . . . two Buddhas were to arise together, then would disputes arise between their followers, and at the words: "Your Buddha, our Buddha," they would divide off into two parties.

And Nāgasena continues that if there were two Buddhas in the world,

---

[19] E.g., *Majjhimanikāya* 115:12–19; *Aṅguttaranikāya* 1:15:10; *Dīghanikāya* 19:1–14.

then the passage (of Scripture) that the Buddha is the chief would become false, and the passage that the Buddha takes precedence of all would become false, and the passage that the Buddha is the best of all would become false.

Finally, to Nāgasena, it is natural that everything supreme in the world is unique. There is also only one supremely evil being, Māra, and thus similarly there can also be only one supremely virtuous being, the Buddha.[20]

So what we find in the *Milindapañha* is first the interpretation that in one world there can be only one Buddha at a time because the Buddha is a uniquely supreme being; second, the insistence on the authority of the scripture which claims the uniqueness of the Buddha; and third, the fear that a plurality of enlightened Buddhas might easily lead to religious strife and rivalry. For our inquiry into the Buddhist attitudes to religious diversity, the third argument is of particular interest because it addresses the issue of interreligious strife and competition. But why should only the simultaneous existence of two or more Buddhas create interreligious quarrels? The usual Buddhist claim that all the other teachers are simply unenlightened, are just "blind men," is by no means less likely to produce religious conflict. Nevertheless, the third argument gives us an important hint of how to interpret the otherwise unexplained meaning of "simultaneously." This clause seems to be determined by the existence of the Buddhist Saṅgha. A "Buddha" is defined as someone who rediscovers, by means of his enlightenment, the Dharma in a world in which the Dharma has been forgotten and disappeared. And through the re-gained knowledge of the Dharma, a Buddha newly establishes a Saṅgha, which lives by the Dharma and transmits it until it finally will fall again into oblivion. Thus, if there should be several Buddhas in one world, they can exist only successively and can succeed each other only after the Saṅgha of the previous Buddha and the knowledge of the Dharma have fully disappeared. This, however, implies that other religious communities, which exist simultaneously with the Buddhist community, cannot be established by a fully enlightened being, a Buddha, and hence are not to be regarded as salvific communities, as Saṅghas.

The combination of the doctrines that only the Buddhist path leads to salvation and that in any possible world there cannot be simultaneously more than one Buddha or Saṅgha substantiates an exclusivist position and hence makes it very difficult for Theravādins to develop a pluralist interpretation of religions.

---

[20]See *Milindapañha* 4:6:4–10. All translations from Rhys Davids 1894, 47–51.

Two Possible Starting Points

There are two teachings in early Buddhism that are sometimes regarded as providing possible starting points for breaking up Theravāda exclusivism and thus eventually paving the way for pluralism. The first one is the doctrine of the *paccekabuddha* (Sanskrit: *pratyekabuddha*). According to early Buddhism there are three types of enlightened beings: A *Buddha* in the full sense of the word (*samyaksambuddha*), that is, as has been said above, someone who discovers the Dharma in a world in which it is unknown or forgotten, who therefore attains enlightenment without the help of a Buddha (that is, not in his current life although in past lives he was indeed inspired by previous Buddhas), and preaches the Dharma in such a way that he leads others to enlightenment and thereby establishes a Saṅgha. The second type of an enlightened being is an *arhat* (Pāli: *arahat*). He has attained enlightenment through the teaching of a Buddha and is also able to lead others toward enlightenment, but does not establish any new Saṅgha. The third type of enlightened being is the *pratyekabuddha*. He is someone who, like a full Buddha but different from the *arhat*, attains enlightenment without the help of a Buddha. He also teaches at least some aspects of the Dharma (usually morality), but does not establish a Saṅgha and does not lead others to salvation. The doctrine of the *pratyekabuddha* thus clearly implies that early Buddhism accepted the possibility of someone achieving liberating insight without having heard the doctrine of the present Buddha. There is a chance of salvation/liberation for those who did not hear the teachings of the Buddha (in their present lives) and are not "Buddhists" in any formal or institutional sense. This view, however, has been severely restricted by a doctrinal development within Theravāda Buddhism according to which *pratyekabuddhas* can only exist at a time when neither a full Buddha nor a Saṅgha exist.[21]

The second starting point for developing a pluralist position within the Theravāda Buddhist tradition is found in the influential *Mahāparinibbāna Sutta* (= *Dīghanikāya* 16).[22] When asked by the ascetic Subhada whether there is truth in the teachings of the Buddha's rival teachers, the Buddha explained that saints of all four grades, that is, including enlightened *arhats* (*arahats*), could indeed be found in the communities of other teachers *if* their teachings contained the Noble Eightfold Path. But he continues that the rival communities actually do not include saints of any degree, which—by implication—means that their teachings do not entail the Noble Eightfold Path.

---

[21]See Vélez de Cea 2013, 99–104.
[22]This must not be confused with the Mahāyāna Buddhist *Mahāparinirvāt Sūtra.*

On the basis of these two points, that is, the affirmation (in conjunction with the *pratyekabuddha* doctrine) that one can find liberating insight independently of knowing the Buddha's teaching and the affirmation that other religions could, at least in theory, lead people to salvation if their teachings contained the Noble Eightfold Path, the famous Sri Lankan Theravāda Buddhist scholar Kulatissa Nanda Jayatilleke (1920–70) developed an inclusivist position. Some religions, he argues, may be entirely false and unwholesome, but others, he mentions the "higher religions," may contain certain true elements, that is, elements of the Noble Eightfold Path, and may thus be able to make a positive contribution to the spiritual development of their followers, perhaps even to their liberation/salvation. But because of their being different from Buddhism, other religions are not on a par with it.[23] In a critical reply to Jayatilleke, the monk-scholar, Ven. Dhammavisuddhi, refuted Jayatilleke's interpretation of the *pratyekabuddhas*.[24] According to Dhammavisuddhi, the traditional Buddhist teaching merely entails the possibility of attaining *nirvāṇa* (Pāli: *nibbāna*) outside the Buddhist community, but not "within other religious frameworks," that is, not by following other religious teachings and practices. According to Dhammavisuddhi, the path taught by the Buddha is the only path leading to salvation. It can be discovered independently of Buddhism, but it is and remains unique, distinct from all other teachings. Even if there are some commonalities between the Buddhist and other religious paths, these are not sufficient to qualify those other paths as salvific. Moreover, other religions contain actual impediments on the path to liberation. Therefore, "any other religious man seeking liberation has to cut off his affiliation to the disciplinary system to which he belonged. This admits the fact that while remaining an adherent of any other religious system no person could find liberation."[25]

Dhammavisuddhi does not completely deny the possibility that other religions, depending on the extent to which they contain elements of truth, might positively contribute to the spiritual development of their members. But contrary to Jayatilleke, he denies that other religions may guide their adherents all the way to the ultimate goal of liberation. This reflects the probably most widespread Theravāda position: a limited form of inclusivism which grants some other religions that they might help their members to achieve a better rebirth and possibly a more favorable disposition for the attainment of *nirvāṇa*. But it is also a type of exclusivism in that it denies to other religions the potential of showing their members the way to final

---

[23]See Jayatilleke's frequently mentioned essay "The Buddhist Attitude to Other Religions," reprinted in Schmidt-Leukel 2013a, 4:88–108, esp. 99ff.

[24]See Dhammavisuddhi's paper in Schmidt-Leukel 2013a, 4:109–16.

[25]Ibid., 114.

liberation. In terms of doctrinal content, the major reason why other faiths are regarded as deficient is usually identified as their belief in a theistic God. This has also been the position of the highly reputed Theravāda monk-scholar Nyanaponika (1901–1994):

> Theism is regarded as a kind of karma-teaching (*kammavāda*), in so far as it upholds the moral efficacy of actions. Hence, a theist, if he leads a moral life, may (like anyone else doing so) expect a favourable rebirth and possibly one in a heavenly world that resembles his own conceptions of it, though it will not be of eternal duration as he may have expected. If, however, fanaticism induces him to persecute those who do not share his beliefs, this will of course have grave consequences for his future destiny. God belief, though not excluding favourable rebirth, is as a variety of eternalism (*sassata-diṭṭhi*) an obstacle to final deliverance. It is an expression of the craving for continued existence (*bhava-taṇha*).[26]

Theravāda pluralists are therefore faced with a double task: They have to engage with the twofold claim to uniqueness (of the path and the Buddha) and to address the crucial question of whether the theistic religions are irreconcilable with the nontheistic nature of Buddhism.

J. Abraham Vélez de Cea, a scholar of Buddhism, and a practitioner of Theravāda Buddhism and Christianity, has recently suggested a move toward pluralism based on parts of the Pāli canonical tradition.[27] He cites the doctrine of the *pratyekabuddhas* as strong evidence against Buddhist exclusivism and criticizes the widespread Theravāda teaching that restricts the existence of *pratyekabuddhas* to those times when there is neither a full Buddha nor a Saṅgha as unfounded by the canonical scriptures.[28] Unfortunately, however, Vélez de Cea takes no notice of the contemporary inner-Theravāda debate of whether or not non-Buddhist religious teachings may have any positive role in a *pratyekabuddha*'s achievement. Moreover, if non-Buddhist religious teachings were able to lead their members to salvation, these people would be, technically speaking, not *pratyekabuddhas* but *arhats*, because in that case they did not achieve liberating insight on their own (like a *pratyekabuddha*), but with the help of a specific religious tradition. This would presuppose that the founders of these non-Buddhist traditions are Buddhas in the full sense. Yet this is clearly in conflict with the Theravāda doctrine that there cannot exist two full Buddhas and Saṅghas

---

[26]Nyanaponika 1981, 2.
[27]Vélez de Cea 2013.
[28]Ibid., 99–105.

simultaneously. Vélez de Cea does not pay sufficient attention to the impact of this doctrine on the question of the status of other religions and their founding figures.[29]

As mentioned above, the first difficulty for a pluralist position within Theravāda Buddhism is the belief that only the Four Noble Truths and the Noble Eightfold Path will lead to liberating insight. In accordance with this belief, Theravāda Buddhism holds that all Buddhas, in all worlds and at all times, always teach the Four Noble Truths and the Noble Eightfold Path. Thus, even if one would admit that there could be more than one Buddha in the same world and at the same time, their teachings would have to be more or less identical. This hardly leaves any space for the appreciation of religious diversity. Again, Vélez de Cea has tried to figure out a way of how Theravāda Buddhism might overcome this obstacle. He draws on the simile of the *siṃsapā* leaves, found in the Pāli canon.[30] Just as a handful of *siṃsapā* leaves is much less than all the *siṃsapā* leaves in a little wood, the Buddha has taught his disciples only very few things and not everything he knows. He only taught them what is necessary for liberation. The obvious point of the simile is to underline that the Four Noble Truths and the Noble Eightfold Path are necessary and sufficient knowledge, while all the other things that one could know are either "unbeneficial" or "irrelevant to the fundamentals of the holy life," as is explicitly stated in the text.[31] Vélez de Cea, however, argues that this interpretation follows a dogmatist attitude which is in tension with the non-dogmatist approach displayed at other parts of the Theravāda Buddhist canon. He thus suggests reading the simile of the *siṃsapā* leaves as an affirmation that the Dharma is much more than what the Buddha taught, so that other aspects of the Dharma are possibly found in other religious traditions. Without any careful examination of these religions, Theravādins should not dogmatically exclude that such other aspects of the Dharma might also be relevant to the holy life, that is, that they might be conducive to liberation.[32] This appears to be a very significant and challenging suggestion. But it needs to be seen to what extent Vélez de Cea's view will find approval among Theravādins.[33]

As far as I am aware, there is only one Theravāda Buddhist thinker who developed a pluralist position. This was the Thai reformer Bhikkhu Buddhadāsa (1906–1993). He argued that the fundamental means of achiev-

---

[29]Ibid., 100ff.

[30]*Saṃyuttanikāya* 5:437–38.

[31]Bodhi 2000, 1858.

[32]Vélez de Cea 2013, 145–56.

[33]One example is perhaps Pinit Ratanakul of the Mahidol University in Thailand. He holds, under some influence by Buddhadāsa, that the experiential attitude of Buddhism "leaves it open for others to discover other aspects of truth for themselves" (Ratanakul 2014, 8).

ing salvation are not only found in Buddhism but also in Christianity, Islam, and Hinduism, though with different emphases and in different forms.[34] Buddhism puts its emphasis on "wisdom," Christianity on "faith" (which he interprets as confidence and trust), and Islam on "will-power." The ways centering on the development of these three different spiritual qualities form an inner unity, so that despite the differences in emphasis, all three are present in each of the three religions. Doctrinal differences between the religions are explained by Buddhadāsa as a result of their exposure to different cultural influences.[35] In order to support this view, Buddhadāsa draws not on a Buddhist authority but, interestingly, on the statement in the Qur'ān that there is a messenger for each nation (10:47).[36]

In order to reconcile doctrinal contradictions, Buddhadāsa employs a hermeneutics that is based on a Buddhist understanding of teachings as means to produce spiritually wholesome attitudes. The term "God," if properly interpreted, can thus be seen as referring to the same absolute reality as the Buddhist term Dharma, or *dhamma* (Pāli).[37] The reason that permits this identification is that both terms foster the realization of selflessness: "The mind which is free from the feeling of self or ego is the mind which has reached God or Dhamma in the highest sense."[38] Buddhadāsa thus clearly rejects the widespread Buddhist view that belief in a theistic God is always an expression of attachment. In relation to Christianity, Buddhadāsa held that even "the few pages of the Sermon on the Mount" are "far more than enough and complete for practice to attain emancipation."[39] Accordingly, Buddhadāsa referred to Jesus as a Buddha.[40]

So Buddhadāsa dealt with the two major obstacles for a pluralist position within Theravāda Buddhism in two different ways. In one sense, he retained the idea that there is only one path leading to salvation, but assumed that this path is in fact taught by several religions although in different forms. Among these different forms, the realization of selflessness can be discerned as the central aspect. And so he concludes: "The goal of all religions is salvation, and throughout history all religions have shown the way to salvation."[41] As a consequence of his position Buddhadāsa negated the teaching of only one Buddha per world system. He could do so only because of his specific religious hermeneutics. According to Buddhadāsa, all religious terms, including the Buddhist ones, have a standard meaning

---

[34]Buddhadāsa 1967, 12ff., 24–25, 38–39.
[35]Ibid., 24–25.
[36]Ibid., 8.
[37]Ibid., 69ff.
[38]Ibid., 43.
[39]Ibid., 29.
[40]Ibid., 105ff.
[41]Swearer 1989, 169.

and an ultimate meaning. In the ultimate sense, the word "Buddha" refers not to a particular human being but to the highest truth of the *dhamma*. Only through the realization of this truth does someone become a Buddha. Hence, by implication, everybody who realizes the highest truth and teaches it is a Buddha in the ultimate sense.[42] Similarly, Buddhadāsa held that the term "Son of God" can be applied "to those who can lead the world to perfect understanding of the dhamma."[43] Thus Jesus is a Buddha and Gautama a "son of God."[44]

As we have seen above, the interpretation of the religious teachings as practical means for salvation has its legitimate roots in early Buddhism. But it became particularly strong in Mahāyāna Buddhism, and the Mahāyāna influence on Buddhadāsa is obvious.[45] This certainly helped him move beyond the narrow limits of Theravāda orthodoxy and its heavy exclusivist leanings.

PLURALIST APPROACHES IN MAHĀYĀNA BUDDHISM

Traditional Mahāyāna Approaches to Religious Diversity

Mahāyāna Buddhism offers somewhat better conditions for the development of a pluralist position because it takes a more flexible approach on the two major doctrinal obstacles. First, in at least some of its forms, Mahāyāna Buddhism has weakened the belief that there can be only one Buddha at a time, and in its later forms, it generally assumes that all sentient beings participate in the common Buddha-Nature, which is in some cases not only identified as their true self but also as the ultimate reality in and of everything. Although the Mahāyāna conviction that all beings participate in the Buddha-Nature does not necessarily imply that the Buddha-Nature is fully manifest in more than one being in the same world and at the same time, there is an inclination in some branches of Mahāyāna to treat eminent figures or patriarchs of their schools as more or less equal to Buddhas and sometimes to speak of their teachings as "Sūtras."[46] Moreover, Mahāyāna Buddhism developed[47] the widespread view that there is not just one form of the Dharma but 84,000 different Dharma gates, which correspond to the

---

[42]Ibid., 129–30. See also Buddhadāsa 1967, 105–6.

[43]Buddhadāsa 1967, 106.

[44]This will be further discussed in chapter 11.

[45]For the Mahāyāna influence on Buddhadāsa see Jackson 2003, 69–99, 129–200.

[46]As, for example, in the famous case of the so-called Ch'an Buddhist "Platform-Sūtra." See Yampolsky 1967, 125n1.

[47]The beginnings of this teaching are already found in the Pāli canon (*Theragāthā* 1024), but it became far more prominent in Mahāyāna Buddhism.

84,000 types of human defilements and ignorance, that is, the diversity of forms that the Dharma assumes reflects the vast variety of different individual dispositions.

This comparatively greater openness to diversity is intrinsically linked to two central Mahāyāna notions, first, the notion of the "two truths," that is, the distinction between "conventional" or "relative truth" (*saṃvṛti satya*) and "ultimate" or "absolute truth" (*paramārtha satya*), and, second, the notion of "skillful means" (*upāyakauśalya*). Whereas "absolute truth" is beyond thought and expression, "relative truth" employs ordinary conceptual schemes and is seen as instrumental in finally achieving the metaconceptual understanding of "absolute truth." For this reason "relative truth" is often identified with the various "skillful means" adapted to the different spiritual needs of the people and used by a Buddha or Bodhisattva in guiding them on their way to enlightenment.

There is another typically Mahāyāna doctrine that one might regard as conducive to a more positive interpretation of religious diversity, the doctrine of different religious ends. But this notion clearly leads to an inclusivist rather than pluralist conception.[48] According to Mahāyāna Buddhism, one can deliberately aim at becoming one of the three types of enlightened beings. That is, one can try to become an *arhat* or a *pratyekabuddha* or a Buddha in the full sense. If one wants to become a Buddha, one has to follow the Bodhisattva path. "Bodhisattva" is the technical term for a being who is on its way to become a Buddha. The two most important virtues that a Bodhisattva needs to cultivate in order to achieve the goal of buddhahood are compassion and wisdom. The wish to become a Buddha is understood as an expression of compassion, because it means to seek enlightenment not primarily for one's own sake but for the sake of all others. Only as a Buddha, not as an *arhat* or *pratyekabuddha*, one can be of optimal assistance to all others. The doctrine of three different religious ends, and correspondingly three different paths leading to these ends, does therefore not involve the idea that these paths are of equal value. Mahāyāna Buddhism is entirely built on the conviction that the Bodhisattva path is the superior one, from which it concludes that Mahāyāna Buddhism is also superior to the non-Mahāyāna schools that are supposed to lead their followers only to the inferior or preliminary ends, but not to the highest goal of buddhahood. Thus traditionally the various Mahāyāna schools displayed an inclusivist understanding of other forms of Buddhism. The teachings of one's own school were regarded as comprising the best understanding of the two truths and as providing the most suitable means for achieving the highest form of enlightenment. Other Buddhist schools, including other

---

[48]See also Kiblinger 2005, 78–89.

Mahāyāna schools, were seen as less advanced. Particularly in the Chinese cultural sphere this approach was often developed into elaborate forms of hierarchical ranking of different teachings (*panjiao*) with the teachings of one's own school always on top.

But what was the relation of Mahāyāna Buddhism to non-Buddhist teachings and religious traditions? As far as other Indian religions are concerned, there is frequently not much difference between Theravāda and Mahāyāna Buddhism. Both often displayed primarily an exclusivist attitude, that is, the conviction that none of the non-Buddhist religions would lead to ultimate liberation. But the Bodhisattva ideal in conjunction with the doctrine of "skillful means" led some Mahāyānists to the belief that highly developed supernatural Bodhisattvas might also manifest themselves as Hindu deities in order to lead the Hindus at least some preliminary steps into the right, that is, the Buddhist, direction.[49] The same pattern was found in China. Initially the non-Buddhist teachings of Daoism and Confucianism were rejected by most of the Chinese Buddhists as useless, that is, as not making any positive contribution to the people's spiritual development. For example, the fourth Chinese Huayan (Hua-yen) patriarch, Chengguan (Ch'eng-kuan, 738–839), held that Daoism is only able to lead its followers to hell (a Buddhist hell, of course). As many others of the earlier Chinese Buddhists, he classified Daoism and Confucianism as "outer teachings" (*waijiao*) which are of a purely mundane or worldly nature and of no avail when it comes to the issues of liberation or salvation.[50] However, Chengguan's disciple and successor, Zongmi (Tsung-mi, 780–841), the fifth patriarch of Huayan, included Daoism and Confucianism into his ranking of teachings, although at the very bottom level. According to Zongmi, Daoism and Confucianism can be regarded as having some provisional and preparatory value.[51] As we will see in the next chapter, in the course of time scholars from Daoism, Confucianism, and Buddhism developed the idea of the "harmony of the three teachings" (*sanjiao heyi*). Although this idea entails some significant protopluralist aspects, in particular the view that all three religions need and complement each other, it was usually still employed in an inclusivist, hierarchical fashion. That is, although all three traditions affirmed the necessity of the other two, one's own tradition was seen as most important and as superior. Hanshan Deqing (1546–1623), for example, a leading Buddhist monk of the Ming Dynasty, assessed Confucianism, Daoism, and Buddhism in terms of three hierarchical stages "from dealing with the

---

[49]See Schmidt-Leukel 2008a, 143–71, especially 154ff.
[50]See the contribution of Imre Hamar in Schmidt-Leukel 2013a, 1:252–62.
[51]See Schmidt-Leukel 2013a, 1:263–89; Zhiru 2013.

world" (Confucianism), "to forgetting the world" (Daoism), and finally "to transcending the world" (Buddhism).[52]

In order to arrive at a Mahāyāna pluralist understanding of religious diversity it is therefore not enough to simply expand the conceptual tools of "two truths" and "skillful means" so that they include non-Buddhist faiths. The point is to overcome the deep-seated inclination of inclusivist hierarchical ranking. So far, however, this has been done only rarely and merely in initial or rudimentary ways.

Pluralist Moves

Frequently the fourteenth Dalai Lama is understood as a good example of a Buddhist pluralist. In his writings one finds statements that, at first sight, sound rather pluralistic, as, for example: "We cannot say that there is only one religion and that one religion is the best, or that a particular religion is the best."[53] In his 2010 book *Toward a True Kinship of Faiths*[54] he rightly states: "The challenge before religious believers is to genuinely accept the full worth of faith traditions other than their own. This is to embrace the spirit of religious pluralism."[55] But will the Dalai Lama's own ideas meet this standard? This remains more than dubious. He defines "pluralism" as according "validity" to other faiths, but not as according *equal* validity.[56] Being a religious pluralist, according to the Dalai Lama, would not exclude maintaining the doctrines of one's own faith "as representing the definitive truth."[57] In the end, his version of pluralism amounts to the identification of a basic equality and "full worth" of the major religions only in terms of their positive moral potential. Apart from that, the Dalai Lama holds the traditional view that a diversity of religions is necessary as the different mental dispositions of people require different spiritual means.[58] Yet these different dispositions and the respective means are apparently still inter-preted hierarchically, as at the time when he wrote about forty years ago: "Therefore, other teachers, their doctrines, and practitioners can be refuges, but not final refuges."[59] Apparently, he has not changed his mind. He still seems to assume that the religion that is in an objective sense closest to the truth and hence most adequate to the highest levels of spiritual progress is

---

[52]Brook 2013, 298–99. See also Chu 2006; Gentz 2008; 2013b.
[53]Dalai Lama 1995, 26.
[54]Dalai Lama 2010.
[55]Ibid., xi.
[56]Ibid., 147.
[57]Ibid., 157.
[58]Ibid., 154–61.
[59]Dalai Lama 1977, 35. See also Dalai Lama 1988, 12–13, 22–23.

his own version of tantric Buddhism.[60] Like the Theravādin Nyanaponika, the Dalai Lama too suggests that the beliefs and practices of theistic religions may lead their adherents to rebirth in a heavenly world. For this kind of goal "does not require the practice of emptiness, the understanding of reality."[61] The key to this way of understanding religious diversity is the belief that via reincarnation people can gradually advance through different forms of religions until they finally become fit for the ultimate truth, which is supposedly found exclusively in one's own religion or school.[62] This is very much the same pattern that is found in the Neo-Hindu adoption of the traditional Hindu idea of *adhikāra-bheda*, that is, of the individual differences in spiritual maturation, which require a diversity of hierarchically ranked religious teachings.[63]

According to the Buddhist Lama and Professor of Indo-Tibetan Buddhism, John Makransky, the similarities in ethical and spiritual qualities that the major religions are able to cultivate constitute sufficient evidence to suppose that they are all rooted in the same ultimate reality.[64] Moreover, according to Makransky, one should not assume that a particular type or school of Mahāyāna Buddhism possesses the most adequate concept of ultimate reality. The crucial insight of Mahāyāna philosophy is that the highest insight is beyond all human words and concepts so that no religious doctrine, not even Buddhist ones, should be taken as absolute truth or as truth in the highest sense (*paramārtha satya*). This too may sound like pluralism, but Makransky remains inclusivist. He argues that Buddhist philosophy is superior because it offers the best foundation for the insight into the transconceptual nature of highest insight and provides the best technical means for achieving it, whereas other religions tend to absolutize their notions of the ultimate and cling to them.[65] Thus again one finds a striking similarity with Neo-Hinduism. For Makransky's suggestion that the ultimate transcends all religious concepts but that this has been most clearly understood and realized by Mahāyāna Buddhism is structurally very similar to the primus-inter-pares pluralism of some Neo-Hindus.[66]

Nevertheless, Makransky widens his inclusivist approach to a startling extent, allowing even for the possibility that non-Buddhists may have realized some aspects of ultimate reality "more deeply through their modes

---

[60]See Dalai Lama 1988, 20–21; 2010, 159–60.

[61]Dalai Lama 1988, 23.

[62]See on this Williams 1991, 519–20; Compson 1996; and the analysis of the Dalai Lama's position in D'Costa 2000, 72–92.

[63]See chapter 5. See also Neufeldt 1987, 79, for the similarity between Hinduism and Buddhism in this respect.

[64]See Makransky 2008, 60–61.

[65]Ibid., 61–62; Makransky 2003a, 358ff.

[66]See chapter 5.

of understanding and practice than I have yet as a Buddhist because they are not Buddhists."[67] He reinterprets the notion of "skillful means" in terms of the sociohistorical conditionality of all religious teachings and communities,[68] and admits that his own Buddhist position, including its specific understanding of what counts as the "fullest spiritual fulfilment," is also part of a "historically conditioned tradition." From this he concludes that, in the end, he cannot step out of his "own conditioned perspective to fully understand and *rank* the possible fulfilments of other world religions (or even other Buddhist traditions)."[69] This admission, I suggest, brings him fairly close to pluralism, at least to some form of potential pluralism, that is, to a pluralism that does at least not exclude the possibility of other religions' equal validity.[70]

Something similar may be said about the position of Rita Gross (1943–2015), another scholar and practitioner of Tibetan Buddhism. Gross strongly emphasizes the Buddhist view to assess religious teachings on the grounds of their pragmatic value and spiritual efficacy. According to Gross, there is no good reason to assume that enlightenment is restricted to Buddhists. But its attainment may become easier through "Buddhist teachings and practices."[71] She admits that this is an inclusivist position, but she does not want to exclude the possibility and even the need of mutual interreligious learning. This, however, implies "that no religion has all the answers,"[72] which tends to go beyond inclusivism. Gross pleads for a position that is critical of exclusivism and inclusivism without taking the next step of affirming pluralism: "Simply put, I find it much more cogent to declare that Christianity, or any other religion, is *not* the only true religion than to claim that many or all religions are at least partially true. Faithful to my Buddhist sensibilities, I always prefer negative to positive language."[73] The way forward is, per Gross, the direct encounter with members of other religions thereby seeking a deeper understanding of their beliefs and practices.[74]

Another move toward pluralism was made by Masao Abe (1915–2006) during the later years of his life. Abe was a well-known representative of Japanese Zen Buddhism. He reinterpreted the *dharmakāya* in a characteristically Zen Buddhist manner as "boundless openness" and "formless emptiness," claiming that each religion, whether based on a personal God

---

[67]Makransky 2011, 131.

[68]Makransky 2003b.

[69]Makransky 2011, 130. My emphasis.

[70]Within Christianity, the idea of possible or potential pluralism has been suggested by Ogden 1992, 83–84, 103.

[71]Gross 2005, 86.

[72]Ibid.

[73]Gross 2014, 79.

[74]See ibid., 330–37.

or on an impersonal absolute, "must go beyond its substantial, self-identical principle and awaken to the dynamic, self-negating 'Boundless Openness' as the ultimate Ground."[75] Abe insisted that this suggestion should not be misunderstood as a new form of "Buddhist imperialism," but that it points to the necessity and, by implication, capacity of all the major faiths to transcend their own doctrinal fixations.[76] Abe, whose views had been informed by many years of intensive dialogue with Christianity, regarded such openness as a sound basis for mutual understanding and transformation:[77] Buddhism could help Christianity in liquefying its hard dogmatic ideas while Christianity could help Buddhism in gaining a better perception of the reality of history and its ethical challenges.[78]

Some innovative moves toward a Buddhist pluralist interpretation of religious diversity have also been suggested by Pure-Land Buddhists. Alfred Bloom, an American Pure-Land Buddhist, holds that through their different personal or impersonal concepts all major religions point to a reality beyond words and concepts, but legitimately and inevitably refer to this reality with their tradition-specific images and ideas. From the perspective of Pure-Land Buddhism these variegated representations of the ultimate can be interpreted as compassionate means by which the ultimate itself, seen in his tradition as Amida Buddha, enables different people in different contexts to achieve final liberation.[79] An analogous structure underlies the pluralist approach of the Japanese Pure-Land Buddhist John Shunji Yokota. He too identifies the "religious ultimate" as a reality not remaining in itself but "going forth and actualizing itself in our concrete, everyday lives."[80] This encourages him to identify Amida Buddha with the "Christ" who was incarnate in Jesus.[81] Moreover, he calls for a multireligious process of mutual transformation in order to arrive at "a fuller and truer vision of reality" through which each tradition achieves a more adequate understanding of itself.[82]

Slightly more cautious and tentative are the approaches of Kenneth Tanaka and Ryūsei Takeda. Tanaka is unambiguous in rejecting the traditional Buddhist approach of hierarchizing the various religious teachings. He affirms the *possibility* of different religions being equally valid paths of salvation but according to the ultimate goals of their respective traditions. Unfortunately, he refrains from specifying how these different goals relate

---

[75]See Abe 1985, 187.
[76]Ibid., 187–88.
[77]Ibid.
[78]See Abe 1995, 3–16.
[79]See Bloom 2013, 303–4.
[80]Yokota 2005, 92.
[81]See chapter 11.
[82]Yokota 2005, 91. See also Yokota 2000.

to each other.[83] For Ryūsei Takeda's sort of open or potential pluralism this inquiry into specific forms of interfaith relations is precisely the kind of question to which an answer must not be preconceived but should be expected as emerging from interfaith dialogue.[84]

Thus there are contemporary Buddhist scholars expressing their uncomfortableness with Buddhism's exclusivist or inclusivist superiority claims. But there is also considerable hesitation in adopting a fully pluralist position. Part of that hesitation is the sense that doctrinal differences between Buddhism and other religions are too severe to reconcile such differences with a pluralist interpretation. They don't want to exclude a pluralist position but feel that more dialogue is needed before a more confident affirmation of pluralism becomes feasible. Buddhadāsa, for example, held that "Buddhists . . . can accept all the passages of Christianity as in agreement with the Buddha's teaching, *if they are allowed to interpret the language of Dhamma in the Bible in their own terms.*"[85] The problem, however, is whether such reading would also find the assent of Christians or if they would simply feel misunderstood or misrepresented. This shows how much the development of religious pluralism, if it is seen as a movement from within the different religious traditions, is interlinked with the need for an interreligious theology. But before I pursue this point in more detail, a final look shall be taken at the development of pluralist approaches within the realm of Chinese religions.

---

[83]See Tanaka 2008, 69–84.
[84]See Takeda 2013, 261–62.
[85]Buddhadāsa 1967, 7.

7

Pluralist Inclinations in Chinese Religions

UNITY AND DIVERSITY OF RELIGIONS IN CHINA

China looks back on a long and rich experience of religious diversity. The roots of Confucianism and Daoism stretch back to the sixth century BCE. Buddhism infiltrated into China from the first century CE onward. In the sixth and seventh centuries, Manichaeism, Zoroastrianism, and Christianity came from Iran to China via Central Asia. Islam settled into the northwestern parts of China during the seventh and eighth century. There is also some evidence that small Jewish communities were present from the eighth and ninth centuries onward.[1] In addition to and across these well-known religious traditions there is the large phenomenon of Chinese popular or folk religion with animistic and shamanistic elements, ancestor worship, divination practices, geomancy, observation of specific rituals, festivals, and so on. Although folk religion has not developed its own institutional form, it often shapes the lives of ordinary Chinese people, while also both influencing and drawing on the institutionalized traditions.

In the course of time, some of the components making up religious diversity in China became so much interlinked that some scholars tend to speak of "Chinese religion" in the singular.[2] There are, however, several other suggestions of how to classify and structure religious life in China. One way is to distinguish between indigenous and foreign religions. Only Confucianism, Daoism, and the ancient, pre-Confucian forms of primal religion could count as indigenous religions in a strong sense.[3] Yet this prompts the question of where to place Buddhism and folk religion that has, along with its ancient Chinese elements, plenty of Buddhist ingredients. Strictly speaking, Buddhism would have to count as an imported, foreign religion and was indeed often classified as such in the past, as, for example,

---

[1] For an overview on the advent of "foreign religions" in China see Ching 2002, 170–201.
[2] See Gentz 2013a, 1. See also below at note 11.
[3] Ching 2002, 222.

when Buddhism, alongside Christianity, Manichaeism, and Zoroastrianism, became subject to the great persecution of foreign religions in the middle of the ninth century. However, Buddhism became so strongly interwoven with Daoism, Confucianism, and folk religion that it is usually treated as "indigenous." In fact, the reciprocal influence between all these religious traditions was massive. Chinese Buddhism absorbed much of Daoist spirituality and Confucian ethos. Daoist principles such as naturalness and spontaneity became fundamental in many forms of Chinese Buddhism plus their Korean, Vietnamese, and Japanese offshoots. Buddhist monks of the Tang dynasty (618–907) could even celebrate a Confucian virtue such as filial piety as equivalent to the learning of Buddhist Sūtras and as an unsurpassable practice in the imitation of the Buddha.[4] Conversely, it was the interaction with Buddhism that contributed significantly to the development of Daoism's institutional forms such as temples, monasteries, orders, rituals, and so on, and Neo-Confucianism reinvented itself by absorbing to a startling extent Buddhist and Daoist influence.[5] Because of the reciprocal interpenetrations some scholars regard Chinese Buddhism as "totally sinologized" and, thus, count it among the indigenous religions.[6]

This raises questions about foreign or "imported" religions such as Islam and Christianity. They too underwent—and still undergo—their own processes of sinification. Xinzhong Yao and Yanxia Zhao have argued that despite the fact that "Islam and Christianity have gone far beyond their traditional boundaries to penetrate the heart and mind of mainstream Chinese people," they nevertheless remain alien insofar as they "continue to retain their original characteristics."[7] This assessment would tacitly imply that Chinese Buddhism, in contrast to Islam and Christianity, is indigenous because it lost its original characteristics, a view that seems hard to substantiate. In fact, since 1912, Islam, Protestantism, Catholicism, Daoism, and Buddhism are counted in China as the five officially recognized religions, with the interesting omission of Confucianism.[8] If sinification is understood as being more a matter of degree than essence, the distinction between Chinese Christianity and Islam on the one hand and Chinese Buddhism on the other is probably based on a different degree of symbiosis. That is, Buddhism seems to have formed stronger and more substantial links with Daoism and Confucianism than Christianity and Islam have done so far, although both

---

[4]Berling 1997, 41.

[5]See Ching 2002, 153–69.

[6]Yao and Zhao 2010, 8.

[7]Ibid., 9.

[8]By then Confucianism became a victim of the anti-imperial republican politics and was deemed as superstition (see Goossaert and Palmer 2011, 50–61). Under communist rule, Confucianism was seen as either "a purely secular humanist philosophy" or "feudal and reactionary ideology" (ibid., 152).

traditions had their own periods of approximation to Confucianism.[9] There is a long tradition in China of comprehending Confucianism, Daoism, and Buddhism as an inner unity, which found its expression in the concept of the "harmony of the three teachings" (*sanjiao heyi*). Only in the twentieth century, some religious groups expanded this concept to "five teachings," which then included Islam and Christianity.[10] Presumably, it is these strong inner links between Confucianism, Daoism, and Buddhism that lead to the perception of Buddhism as "indigenous," in contrast to Christianity or Islam. Along those lines, scholars like Xinzhong Yao and Yanxia Zhao have defined indigenous "Chinese religion as a single unit," which "contains both complementary and contrasting parts or elements" and is primarily composed of Confucianism, Daoism, Buddhism, and Chinese folk religion.[11]

Another attempt at looking at Chinese religions does not operate with the concept of one, three, four, or more of them, but suggests a simple binary structure of officially recognized and popular religion. "Official religion" is marked by its public institutional dimension and the close connection of these institutions with the state, which involves official support and control but also the religion's converse duty of loyalty to the state. "Popular religion" has no such privileges. This makes it "freer" in the sense of being comparatively less regulated or, better, less controllable by the state,[12] but also more vulnerable if some of its manifestations do become the target of official sanctions. As we will see, this constellation is also of considerable relevance regarding Chinese approaches to religious pluralism. It is obviously related to the fact that religious diversity has not always been that harmonious but was often a source of rivalry and at some occasions of open and violent conflict, which required public regulation.

The history of interrelationships among Confucianism, Daoism, and Buddhism is as replete with mutual borrowing as with reciprocal polemics and criticism. Particularly heated were the quarrels and disputes between Daoists and Buddhists as they recurred between the second and seventh centuries and even beyond.[13] Daoists claimed that the Buddha had been no one else than Laozi who left China for India in order to convert the Indian "barbarians." Buddhists retaliated by arguing that Laozi had in fact been Kāśyapa, a disciple of the Buddha, whom the Buddha sent to China for teaching the Chinese an adapted version of Buddhism. This legend and

---

[9]On Muslim Confucianism see Murata 2000; on Christian Confucianism see Gernet 1985. On Nestorian adaptations to Chinese religions see Tang 2002; Nicolini-Zani 2013.

[10]Goossaert and Palmer 2011, 93, 120–21. Before this, recognition of Christianity or Islam was confined to some exceptional cases. See Gentz 2013b, 126–27.

[11]Yao and Zhao, 10 and 2.

[12]See ibid., 17–19.

[13]For an excellent overview see Kohn 2008, 3–45. See also Zürcher 2007, 288–320.

counterlegend are symbolic of the reciprocal superiority claims of both traditions; both versions continued to be told until they were finally banned during the Yuan dynasty (1279–1368). Daoist-Buddhist rivalry often took the form of harsh doctrinal debates, which were usually fought in order to secure imperial support for the victorious side.[14] Sometimes official patronage of Buddhism resulted in the suppression of Daoism, as under the reign of Emperor Wudi (502–49) of the Southern Liang dynasty.[15] At other times Buddhism became the victim of public repression inspired by its Confucian and Daoist opponents, as in the case of its persecution between 446 and 453 under Emperor Wudi of the Northern Wei dynasty.[16] About a century later, public debates between Confucians, Daoists, and Buddhists, in which Confucians were declared as victors by Emperor Wudi (561–77) of the Northern Zhou dynasty, resulted in the suppression of both Buddhism and Daoism (574–77). After Empress Wu Zhao (or Wu Zetian), by the end of the seventh century, had given priority and massive support to Buddhism, to the disadvantage of Confucianism and Daoism, the subsequent decades saw again a strong rise in anti-Buddhist sentiments. Between 843 and 845 Emperor Wuzong carried out the largest persecution of Buddhism ever, which, as mentioned above, also included other "foreign" religions as Manichaeism, Zoroastrianism, and Christianity. Although this persecution significantly reduced the economic power of Buddhist institutions, it did not aim at the complete destruction of Buddhism, so that subsequently it was able to recover.[17] Toward the end of the Tang Dynasty (618–906) and during the Song Dynasty (960–1279), Confucianism experienced a vibrant revival. Some Neo-Confucians sharpened their attacks against Daoism and, even more so, Buddhism, despite the fact that they were considerably influenced by both. During the first half of the thirteenth century, the Daoists were privileged by the Mongol rulers and, during the second half of the same century, Buddhism became the favored religion. In both periods, Daoist and Buddhists respectively used their official support to massively subdue the other.[18] In between the fourteenth and sixteenth centuries, China was stricken by various rebellions and insurrections, often motivated by chiliastic expectations of a Buddhist and syncretistic nature. Thus, China's long experience of religious diversity included a strong dose of confrontations and conflicts with a religious dimension. This strengthened the conviction that religious diversity needs to be regulated and religious harmony to be promoted.

---

[14] See Gentz 2013b, 126.
[15] Ch'en 1973, 124.
[16] Ibid., 147–51.
[17] See ibid., 226–33; Eichhorn 1973, 249–51, 255–60.
[18] See Eichhorn 1973, 305–7.

DAOIST AND CONFUCIAN ATTITUDES
TOWARD RELIGIOUS DIVERSITY

In the words of Joachim Gentz, "Daoism is the most complex and indefinable of the great religious traditions in China."[19] That is, Daoism itself comprises an enormous diversity, as, for example, a range of different scriptures, concepts, rituals, practices, and groups. There are numerous "ingredients," but hardly any uniform systematic structures. Much circles around the goal of "immortality," which is itself rather differently interpreted, and the veneration of "Lord Lao," the deified figure of Laozi, considered as the author of the *Daode jing* and as an emanation of the *Dao*. The *Dao* is understood as a transcendent-immanent force, the origin and governing principle of the universe. Hence, another central motif of Daoism is to live in accordance with *qi*, the vital energy as which the unfathomable *Dao* is manifest in life. As with any other ideal, people often do not live up to it. That is, the force of life is thought to be strong and its flow can certainly be unimpeded, but it can also be disturbed and disrupted. This is the point where diversity comes into play. There is nothing wrong with diversity as such, including a diversity of "religious" teachings. The *Dao* and its energy become manifest in the diversity of the "ten thousand things." But everything needs to be in its proper place so that diversity leads to harmony instead of disharmony.

Different religions can, therefore, be either useful or harmful, depending on whether they function in accordance with the *Dao*. However, being in accordance with the *Dao* does not mean exactly the same thing to all people. Different people living in different parts of the world and at different times are in need of different means that keep them in the right place of the cosmic order. That is, the *Dao*, through the celestial figure of Lord Lao, has supplied them with different teachings and different practices fitting their inner dispositions. Different sages and teachers who lived at different times in various parts of the world are seen as manifestations of the archetypical Lord Lao who appears in the form of these sages in order to guide people in ways adapted to their particular temperaments. Buddhism was seen as one of those particular means designed for the people in the "barbarian" countries. In his appearance as the Buddha, Lord Lao taught harsh rules and ascetic practices that were required for taming people of a savage and obstinate nature.[20] But such means would not be equally appropriate to other people. Moreover, not all teachings and practices were regarded as useful means. Some teachings and practices were classified as harmful under any condition.

---

[19]Gentz 2013a, 70.
[20]See Kohn 2013, 56, 60.

This conception implies two basic possibilities of how other religions may be seen as dysfunctional. On the one hand, they contain the right means but apply them to the wrong people. That is, what would be a suitable practice for Indians must not be similarly wholesome for the Chinese. Or, on the other hand, they contain means that are harmful as such. This turns them into "heretical practices," which obstruct the flow of *qi* under any circumstances and are criticized and combated by the true sages, the different manifestations of Lord Lao. The Daoist superiority claim is therefore primarily rooted in the conviction that it knows the rules and standards by which all the different peoples are to be guided and governed.[21] That is, to the Daoists, Daoism was not just one teaching among others, but at the same time it "represented the totality of all teachings."[22]

Confucian attitudes to religious diversity have been described as alternating between flexibility and dogmatism.[23] As in Daoism, the ideal of harmony plays an important role in Confucianism. Here too harmony was, in principle, extended to religious diversity. In its commentarial section, the *Book of Changes* (*Yijing*) states that "different paths lead to the same goal,"[24] and Confucius was traditionally regarded as the author of this commentary. A further important principle is directly related to Confucius, the maxim of "seeking harmony but not conformity," which is found in the sayings of Confucius (see *Analects* 13:23). According to Xinzhong Yao, this has functioned as the overall guideline in Confucian approaches to religious diversity, that is, harmony within diversity should not be aspired to at the expense of losing one's identity. The ideal consists in finding a healthy balance, the "mean" or "middle way," between the necessary accommodation to others, for the sake of harmony, and the preservation of one's own interests and integrity, for the sake of avoiding conformity. While the longing for harmony fostered a certain openness toward syncretistic adaptations, the frequent merger of Confucianism with political power often led to a loss of "the mean" and turned the principle of retaining one's identity into harsh and intolerant dogmatism. Both tendencies are found in Confucian attitudes toward Daoism and Buddhism, which were perceived and in fact presented themselves to Confucians as rivals in vying for imperial patronage. Confucians usually regarded themselves as those who possess the right ethical norms and values on which alone the state could establish religious harmony. Their claim to this role was exclusive and did not permit any competitor.

A recurrent point of conflict was the Buddhist idea of the monastic order

---

[21]See ibid., 61.
[22]Kohn 2008, 41.
[23]See Yao 2013.
[24]Gentz 2013b, 124.

as a community beyond this world, which would not be obliged to paying homage to the emperor, who—from a Buddhist perspective—was seen as a layman ranked below a monk. Confucians took this as an intolerable attitude. From their point of view, no one was allowed to claim autonomy from the imperial government and exemption from state supervision. For this reason, Confucians often perceived Buddhism as a threat to social security and stability.[25] Yet Confucian and Daoist criticism of Buddhism went further:

> It was a foreign creed, absent during the idyllic age of high antiquity. Its tenets encouraged an irresponsible attitude toward the practical realities of everyday life. Its practices violated classical prescriptions of filial piety and modesty, leading the Chinese into disruptive displays of extravagance and passion. Its clergy contributed nothing to the empire's welfare and drained the nation's resources. Its various privileges attracted ne'er-do-wells and tricksters.[26]

When toward the end of the Tang dynasty Confucianism regained new strength and influence, some Confucian scholars, for example, Han Yu (768–824), denounced Buddhism "as a foreign excrescence and called for its immediate removal from Chinese society."[27] Ouyang Xiu (1007–72) compared Buddhism to a disease that had infected the body of China. But he commended an alternative cure: the cultivation of the traditional Confucian values that would automatically make Buddhism redundant.[28] Other Confucians, during the same period, defended Buddhism against such attacks.[29] Some Neo-Confucians of the Song dynasty, like Lü Benzhong (1084–1145), held "that the Buddhist theories are no different from [those of] Confucius,"[30] while others, like Lü's younger contemporary Zhu Xi (1130–1200), argued for the contrary, namely that the two traditions are "similar in appearance, but different in spirit, or appearing to be so but actually not."[31]

As we saw in chapter 6, Chinese Buddhists generally abided by their version of superiority claims. If at all, they were in disagreement about how far Buddhism would surmount Daoism and Confucianism, that is, whether these Chinese teachings were of any value whatsoever, or whether their value was confined to worldly affairs or whether they might perhaps constitute a preparation for entering the higher path of the Buddha.[32] However, as we also

---

[25] See Zürcher 2007, 256–62.
[26] Halperin 2006, 60–61. See also ibid., 160–74; Zürcher 2007, 254–85.
[27] Halperin 2006, 30.
[28] Ibid., 161.
[29] Ibid., 31, 44–52.
[30] Ibid., 103.
[31] Yao 2013, 72.
[32] See chapter 6.

saw, Buddhism, Daoism, and Confucianism harbor ideas that value diversity and can serve as foundations for the development of a pluralist approach. Yet in traditional China, all three religions have been as much convinced of their own superiority as the religions in the West or the Middle East.[33] "That they rarely conducted war against each other was mainly due to their weak positions of power *vis à vis* the Chinese state. They were not allowed to do so."[34] During the second millennium, it was in particular the state that promoted the idea of understanding religious diversity as a "harmony of the three teachings" and used it as an ideological tool to ban religious wars.

REGULATED PLURALISM
AND MULTIPLE PARTICIPATION

The term *sanjiao heyi* ("the three teachings combine into one" or "harmony of the three teachings") was coined during the later Ming dynasty (1368–1644).[35] Its antecedents stretch back as far as to the fourth century. In the fifth century *sanjiao* ("three teachings") had become a new category, which soon attracted the interest of the state.[36] It was, however, only during the second millennium CE that the concept acquired its central significance. In 1181 Emperor Xiazong of the Song Dynasty wrote an essay in which he emphasized the idea of an inner unity and harmony among the three teachings. Like the four seasons, they can be distinguished but not ripped apart. They are different but they all belong together.[37] In the fourteenth century, the first emperor of the Ming Dynasty, Zhu Yuanzhang, also dedicated an essay to the three teachings, and subsequently this text "served as a political discursive guideline with normative character."[38] At the same time, Confucianism became the solid foundation of state orthodoxy and provided the guiding pattern for the integration of the three teachings,[39] which was one of "a structured hierarchical unity."[40]

Among the various images, metaphors, and analogies that were used as illustrations for the relation between the three teachings, two major types can be discerned, which often appeared in conjunction: One type depicts the three religions as more or less identical. This identity could be understood as one of their divine origin or of their goal or of their true essence. The

---

[33]Gentz 2013a, 21–24.
[34]Ibid., 22.
[35]See Brook 2013, 293–95. The first translation is by Brook, the second by Gentz.
[36]See Gentz 2013b, 126.
[37]See ibid., 127–28.
[38]Ibid., 129.
[39]Yao 2013, 73.
[40]Ibid., 71.

other type operates with the ideas of complementarity and compartmental-
ism or "division of labor."[41] Both types of conceiving unity and harmony
were used by Confucians, Daoists, and Buddhists, but they were hardly ever
employed in a fully egalitarian sense. One's own tradition was always given
supremacy, either explicitly or in concealed ways.[42] One famous metaphor,
for example, compares the essential identity of the three traditions to that of
light, but the use of this image leaves no doubt about the hierarchical order:
"Buddhism is like the sun, Daoism like the moon and Confucianism like
the five planets."[43] Hence, they are identical in that they all emit light, but
they do so to significantly different degrees. Similarly, another Buddhist
scholar stated that "Buddhism and Confucianism share the same substance.
However, having evolved in different lands, they manifest differences in
doctrine and depth of understanding."[44]

The complementarity type of conceiving harmony usually presupposes
a functional division. In his influential essay of 1181 Emperor Xiazong famously declared: "With Buddhism one cultivates one's mind, with Daoism
one regulates one's body, and with Confucianism one governs the world."[45]
The phrase suggests that all three religions have their specific areas of
expertise, which was again stated in an edict written in 1733 by the Yong-
zheng emperor: "each has its specialties, its strengths, and also its areas of
inadequacy."[46] This idea also implied that all three religions are needed for
the well-being of the nation and its people. The three teachings were often
compared to a tripod which could not stand if one of its legs was missing.[47]
Yet even this metaphor may connote a hierarchical structure depending on
which of the three different functions is ranked as most important. In this
respect each of the three traditions regarded its own teachings not only as the
most significant but usually also as the most comprehensive ones. The concept of the "harmony of the three teachings" did not remove the competition
between the three "but transformed [it] into a struggle of preeminence."[48]
Above all, it served the interests of a unified state and centralized empire.[49]
The rulers were presumably less interested in theological issues; their aim
was rather pragmatic, that is, "to impose conciliation."[50]

The concept of the "harmony of the three teachings" did have its impact

---

[41]Gentz 2013b, 130–31; Yao 2013, 73.
[42]Gentz 2013b, 133–34. See also Brook 2013, 298–301.
[43]Gentz 2013b, 137n32.
[44]Yao 2013, 76.
[45]Gentz 2013b, 128.
[46]Brook 2013, 301.
[47]Gentz 2013b, 128; Yao 2013, 73.
[48]Gentz 2013a, 21.
[49]Ibid., 26.
[50]Brook 2013, 301.

on the religions in China. It clearly encouraged, fostered, and deepened the interaction and reciprocal influence among them. For example, between the fifteenth and seventeenth centuries, it became increasingly common that scholars of all three traditions wrote commentaries on each other's canonical scriptures or drew on canonical texts of the others in order to arrive at a new understanding of their own sacred texts. Such "attempts to read the different teachings in an interrelated way"[51] anticipate the contemporary efforts of comparative theology, in which interreligious reading and interreligious commentary play a significant role.[52]

Moreover, as has been shown by Timothy Brook, the efforts of the scholars to give the relations between their traditions an adequate intellectual expression were accompanied by a much less sophisticated interpretation in the practice of ordinary people.[53] At this level, one could find a growing practice of jointly venerating Confucius, Laozi, and the Buddha, for which, from the sixteenth to the eighteenth centuries, particular shrines, that is, "Three Teaching Halls," were constructed. Although such "joint worship offended magisterial expectations about the good order of religious institutions,"[54] public measures to suppress the practice remained comparatively weak or inefficient. In this type of syncretistic worship, no religion was given supremacy. Joint worship was rather seen as "a matter of improving efficacy, increasing human odds against the universe."[55] This approach ties in with what has often been described as an especially characteristic feature of Chinese religiosity, the phenomenon of "multiple religious participation."[56] This participation can assume the form of accumulation, as for example in placing symbols and deities of several religious traditions on the domestic altar together with the tablets of one's ancestors,[57] or it may take—as a variant of the complementarity pattern—the form of approaching the best "ritual service provider" for different purposes:

> For finding the best site for houses and graves one needs a *fengshui* master; for divining one's luck and fortune one consults a fortune-teller; for exorcising evil spirits one can hire a spirit medium or an exorcist; for a funeral one hires a troupe of Daoist or Buddhist priests. . . . To the majority of the Chinese, it is the efficacy of the rituals (and the ritualists) that matters, not one's religious identity (if that is even discernible).[58]

---

[51]Gentz 2013b, 129.
[52]See Clooney 2010, 57–68; Cornille 2014.
[53]See Brook 2013, 301–10.
[54]Ibid., 307.
[55]Ibid., 311.
[56]Berling 2013, 33. See also Berling 1997, 8–10; Berthrong 1994, 165–87.
[57]Chau 2013, 146.
[58]Ibid., 149.

Although such behavior is widespread, multiple religious participation cannot be reduced to the consumption—and purchase—of ritual services. It also extends to methods of personal cultivation such as various types of meditation, bodily exercises, regulations of one's day-to-day life and seeking the guidance of a spiritual master. It is, however, somewhat misleading to understand this attitude as dual or multiple religious "belonging." It might be better characterized as an expression of multireligious identity and/or multireligious practice. As such, it is very much in line with Chinese popular religion and could therefore also be understood as the standard type of identity and practice of all those belonging to this strand of Chinese religion(s). But "Chinese popular religion" is neither an institution nor a self-designation. The term was coined by Western scholars.[59] And after all, "Daoism, Buddhism and Confucianism have generated and influenced the development of diverse forms of popular religion . . . and have in turn also been influenced by them in their local forms."[60] That is, the phenomenon of popular religion with its multireligious facets is deeply interwoven with the interrelatedness of the "three teachings." Multiple religious participation seems to be a rather unambiguous expression of the inner conviction of ordinary believers that there is in fact a deep unity between different religious traditions. All these different aspects of traditional attitudes to religious diversity create the heritage and background against which the contemporary discourse about pluralist approaches needs to be seen.

CONTEMPORARY DISCOURSES

In their impressive study *The Religious Question in Modern China*, Vincent Goossaert and David A. Palmer describe the contemporary situation thus:

> China has . . . become a huge religious laboratory, in which all kinds of spirituality and religiosity—traditional, modern, and postmodern, old and invented, indigenous and imported, and all combinations between them—have become possible in a massive cauldron.[61]

Part of this picture is also the rise of a debate about the suitability of Western pluralist theologies as instruments for the understanding of religious diversity in China and promotion of interfaith dialogue. As has been said, it is obvious that there are significant inclinations toward religious pluralism

---

[59]Gentz 2013a, 112.
[60]Ibid., 114.
[61]Goossaert and Palmer 2011, 400.

in traditional Chinese discourses. But altogether the traditional scheme of religious harmony remains embedded in reciprocal superiority claims. Thus, one possible function of Western pluralist theologies could be to serve as catalysts in critically assessing the traditional arrangements of "regulated pluralism," that is, in discerning and challenging the open or concealed hierarchies, but also in strengthening the pluralist leanings. Moreover, it might help to extend the discussion by including other and more than the traditional "three teachings."

In recent years, a number of writings by Christian pluralists such as Wilfred Cantwell Smith, Raimon Panikkar, and Paul Knitter have been translated into Chinese. Most influential has become the work of John Hick. So far, ten of his books are available in translation.[62] The presence of Hick's ideas in contemporary Chinese discourses has become so strong that by now "for any scholar concerned with the philosophy of religion, the relationships among religions and religious dialogue, it is impossible to avoid Hick. Whether they take an attitude of affirming or opposing his ideas, Hick's thoughts have become a part of Chinese academia."[63] Among Chinese Christian theologians, Hick has provoked similar debates as in the West. There is, however, a difference insofar as Chinese theologians also argue over the question of whether religious pluralism might be helpful in developing a sinicized theology, which would allow Chinese Christians to accommodate the Christian tradition as well as their Chinese religious heritage.[64] Yet the debate about religious pluralism extends beyond Christian circles. Zhicheng Wang from the Zhejiang University in Hangzhou, one of the key translators and advocates of John Hick, understands Sino-theology as just one element of a broader picture. He is primarily interested in a "dialogue theology" that would be relevant to all religious believers in China and also to those of no religious affiliation.[65] According to Wang, religious pluralism, in particular the work of John Hick, is expressing and encouraging "the emerging spirit of humanity in the global new times."[66] With this broader perspective in mind, religious pluralism is thus also fruitful in that it "is helping people to more systematically explore and excavate the resources of religious pluralism in Chinese traditional culture."[67]

So far, Zhicheng Wang's view has been met with only partial approval. Some comparatively early voices such as those of Yu Wang or Guoxiang

---

[62]For a detailed overview see Zhicheng Wang 2012.
[63]Zhicheng Wang 2012, 250.
[64]See Lai 2008; 2013.
[65]See Zhicheng Wang 2013, 210.
[66]Ibid., 209.
[67]Zhicheng Wang 2012, 251.

Peng apparently agreed.[68] This is also true for Chenyang Li, who now teaches at the Nanyang Technological University of Singapore. As early as 1994, Li suggested that John Hick's position, according to which no single religious teaching can exhaust ultimate truth, is in fundamental agreement with traditional Chinese attitudes and would substantiate the widespread Chinese practice of multireligious participation.[69]

Serious doubts and even strong objections have been expressed by two PhD theses that were both submitted at the University of Birmingham in 2011. Wai Yip Wong accuses Hick of being unable to concede equal validity to Chinese folk religion. His main target is Hick's normative stance as expressed in his soteriological and ethical criteria. According to Wong, Chinese folk religion is unable to meet Hick's criteriological standards because, says Wong, it serves self-centered interests instead of promoting selflessness and does not ascribe any central value to the Golden Rule nor to universal compassion.[70] Wong criticizes Hick for not accepting a religious aim like "the pursuit of earthly fortunes" as an "equally legitimate conception of salvation."[71] At the end of the day, Wong demands an interpretation of religious diversity that abstains from any normative judgment, one that has to "remain completely neutral and accept all differences."[72] Somewhat surprisingly, he blames Hick's normative stance as "neither fair nor pluralistic,"[73] a criticism that, one might argue, seems itself to presuppose "fairness" as a moral norm or "Golden Rule."

Critical of Hick's normative approach is also the thesis submitted by Yen-Yi Lee of Taiwan. Taking the transformation from self-centeredness to Reality-centeredness as normative in discerning a true religion[74] contradicts, according to Lee, a genuinely pluralistic approach.[75] Yet his main point of critique is a different one. Per Lee, Hick's concept of "the Real *an sich*" is still too close to monotheism. Although the Real is not a personal God, it nevertheless refers to a transcendent Reality as different from the universe. This, says Lee, does not do justice to the understanding of Chinese religions, which strongly emphasize the immanence of ultimate Reality.[76] A pluralist approach constructed from within the Chinese religions would have to be built on a concept of "the Real that is this world itself rather than something

---

[68]See ibid., 246.

[69]See Li 1996. The publication is based on a paper read in 1994 (see ibid., n. 44).

[70]Wong 2012, 285–304. Wong understands Chinese folk religion as largely independent from the three major religions. For a brief summary of his views see Wong 2013.

[71]Wong 2012, 383.

[72]Ibid., 390.

[73]Ibid., 391.

[74]See chapter 2.

[75]Lee 2012, 222–23.

[76]Ibid., 235–37.

that is higher and above human beings."[77] What qualifies religions as "religious" is, per Lee, not belief in transcendence, but the search for the meaning of life, which finds tentative answers within the various existent religions. In the first phase of developing his pluralist position, Hick had compared the transition from Christian exclusivism and inclusivism to pluralism with the Copernican revolution. Similar to the replacement of a geocentric worldview by a heliocentric one, Hick had asked for the replacement of an ecclesiocentric or Christocentric theology of religions by a theocentric model. That is, neither the church nor Christ would be at the center of the religions but the Divine Reality around which all religions circle, like the planets revolving around the sun.[78] Lee suggests that this Copernican move is incomplete. Genuine pluralism would rather be comparable to the cosmological insight that there is not just one solar system with one sun at its center, but innumerable systems, which may differ considerably in that, for example, they have more than one focal star. All systems, however, are kept going by one single force, which is gravitation. Among the religions, this force can be interpreted as the Confucian *Li* or the Daoist *Dao* if this is interpreted as the human inclination, shared by all religions, to look for the meaning of life.[79]

The critique of Hick's insufficient neutrality seems to arise from a different understanding of the intellectual nature of "religious pluralism." This critique only makes sense if Hick's position is taken as an interpretation of religious diversity in the mode of a putatively "neutral" religious studies approach. Hick does certainly not wish to be "unfair," but as has been explained above, he is not pursuing a distanced and non-normative attitude, but rather claims that his suggestion is basically compatible with the normative perspective of the major religious traditions.[80] Especially in the case of Wong, one might speculate whether the context of such criticism may also be a very different one, namely the lack of official recognition of Chinese folk religions by the current political authorities, because of a supposedly inferior nature of this type of religiosity.[81]

Yen-Yi Lee's critique of Hick has a different thrust. It draws attention to the crucial issue of the concept of Ultimate Reality in Chinese religions. This issue is at the center of those Chinese pluralists who follow the ideas

---

[77]Ibid., 238.

[78]Hick 1973.

[79]See Lee 2012, 237–38, 327–32.

[80]See chapter 1.

[81]Unfortunately, Wong 2013 does not provide any greater clarity on this point. On the one hand, he still suggests a purely descriptive understanding of "religious pluralism" (ibid., 184); on the other hand, he does not deny "that it is meaningful and preferable to persuade and transform the followers of 'evil' traditions" (ibid., 187). His goal, he says, is not to exclude such traditions from dialogue.

of process philosophy and theology.[82] In accordance with John Cobb and David Griffin they hold that monocentric versions of pluralism do not pay sufficient attention to religious differences and particulars. Hence they give preference to a pluralism based on the idea of "different but complementary ultimates around which different religions are centered."[83] Zhihe Wang, now teaching at the Harbin Institute of Technology, like Zhejiang one of the elite universities in mainland China, and Chung-ying Cheng, professor of philosophy at the University of Hawai'i, establish their versions of religious pluralism on process philosophy/theology, which both of them see as in deep congruence with the traditional "harmony of the three teachings" discourse.[84] They both suggest that questions like the immanent or transcendent, impersonal or personal nature of Ultimate Reality can be solved more adequately, and more in line with traditional Chinese religions, if they are related to different ultimates or different aspects of a more complex Ultimate Reality.[85] Like John Cobb, they sometimes speak of different ultimates, but at other times, the personal God and the impersonal force of creativity are treated as inseparable in that, per Cheng, God is "the embodiment of creativity,"[86] or, in the words of Zhihe Wang, "the Tao is both Creativity as such and the supreme embodiment of Creativity."[87]

What both are most keen to highlight is that religious pluralism needs to develop an understanding of seemingly conflicting differences as complementary. If religions understand their differences as complementary instead of mutually exclusive, the differences become productive and inspiring. That is, religions can learn from each other in their respective strengths and weaknesses. In the tradition of the Ming dynasty,[88] Cheng recommends the practice of transreligious commentarial writings as a suitable tool of such reciprocal learning: "Theoretically there is no reason why there could not be mutual and equal interpretation of ancient texts in different religious schools."[89] That this is not without resonance can be seen in the 2013 launch of the multilingual *Journal of Comparative Scripture* by the Minzu University of China; the journal is explicitly dedicated to the aim of interreligious learning through interreligious reading.

Zhihe Wang quotes, without mentioning his source, Heschel's prophetic

---

[82]See chapters 2, 8, and 14.

[83]Zhihe Wang 2012.

[84]C. Cheng 2005; Zhihe Wang 2012, 161–76.

[85]Note that Cheng, although subscribing to the idea of several ultimates, also speaks of Ultimate Reality in the singular, as, for example, in explaining pluralism as being "based on new insights into the Ultimate Reality." C. Cheng 2005, 221; similarly in ibid., 218.

[86]C. Cheng 2005, 214.

[87]Zhihe Wang 2012, 193.

[88]See above in this chapter.

[89]C. Cheng 2005, 224.

word, "No religion is an island," and explains: "each religion can be enriched by insights from other religions and thus can assimilate these insights into its own nature."[90] According to Cheng, the reciprocal transformation of Confucianism, Daoism, and Buddhism in the course of their sustained interaction throughout Chinese history provides a perfect example of such mutual learning and transformation.[91] Both Cheng and Zhihe Wang are interested in broadening the horizon of the traditional discourse by assuming a global perspective. They are convinced that China's traditional idea of interreligious harmony can serve as an example for the religious future of our planet.[92] It is, to Zhihe Wang, "one of China's most important gifts to the rest of the world, even if it is also a gift that the Chinese must themselves remember and relearn."[93] Interestingly, he adds, that this suggestion "is in the spirit of Gandhi."[94]

However, in their recommendation of the traditional model, Zhihe Wang and Chung-ying Cheng both seem to turn a blind eye to two of its interrelated side aspects. They keep silent first about the hardly disputable fact that in the past "the harmony of the three teachings" was generally understood as a hierarchical unity, so that the scheme did not remove the religions' reciprocal, and conflicting, superiority claims.[95] And second, they don't touch on the issues of the political interest behind, and imposed character of, the traditional scheme. This, however, is by no means a matter of the past. Under the heading of "religious ecology," some Chinese scholars demand a religious policy that echoes the stance of the later imperial dynasties.[96] Harmonious relations between the Chinese religions are presented as a precious heritage that needs to be protected against the rapid expansion of Christianity. Christianity is perceived as a danger because of Christianity's intolerant and exclusivist nature, which threatens the harmonious "ecological" balance between Chinese religions instead of integrating itself into it. Being beneficial not just for China but for the future of humanity, it is important to keep religious harmony intact by controlling, and, if necessary, interfering with, those religions that refuse and evade harmonious integration.[97] In the light of this aspect of the contemporary Chinese discourse, Zhihe Wang's

---

[90]Ibid., 172; for Heschel see chapter 3.

[91]C. Cheng 2005, 220–21.

[92]See ibid., 225; Zhihe Wang 2012, 172.

[93]Zhihe Wang, 2012, 168.

[94]Ibid., 168, 169.

[95]Wang, for example, quotes the famous subordination of Daoism and Confucianism under Buddhism by Zongmi (Tsung-mi) (see chapter 6) as an example of "equal regard" without addressing this obvious inconsistency. C. Cheng (2011, 356) admits that "there are various forms of competition and currying favor between Daoism and Buddhism" but reduces these to "the political level." Serious clashes, according to Cheng, "were manipulated by the imperial power of the court" (ibid.).

[96]See Clart 2013, 192.

[97]See ibid., 188–92.

reference to the spirit of Gandhi may—wittingly or unwittingly—evoke associations with the argumentation of the Hindutva movement, which similarly justifies a fairly restrictive religious policy by the argument of protecting a model of religious harmony for the benefit of all humankind.[98] Cheng and Zhihe Wang both refer to the Confucian principle of "harmony but not conformity" as a regulative ideal,[99] and it is exactly this ideal that, according to the proponents of "religious ecology," needs public protection.[100] The notion of "regulated pluralism" is clearly in the air.[101]

As in the case of the other religious traditions covered by this survey, Chinese religions too have their potential for developing a pluralist understanding of religious diversity and have, in fact, come close to it at some stages in the past. As in other contexts too, contemporary Chinese discourses on religious pluralism confirm that a pluralist interpretation can persuade only if the differences between religions are fully taken into account and shown to be complementary instead of contradictory. No doubt, this is, ultimately, a question of interpretation. But on the credibility of this interpretation hinges the credibility of the pluralist approach. "Credibility" is not an abstract property. It must be credible *to someone*. A religious interpretation is credible only if it gains credit among religious people and religious communities. Religious pluralism therefore depends on interreligious dialogue. Its promise is to make this dialogue rewarding and transformative, that is, its promise lies in its potential to bring about an interreligious theology. One of pluralism's presuppositions is therefore something like mutual receptivity. Complementarity seems to presume some form of adaptivity. Zhihe Wang sees this illustrated in the well-known Chinese symbol of *yin* and *yang*: ☯. The two different principles can enter into a relation of dynamic complementarity because there is already something of *yin* inside *yang* and something of *yang* inside *yin*. "I see something of you in me and me in you."[102] Religions can complement each other if their mutual affinity is already given.

---

[98]See chapter 5.
[99]C. Cheng 2005, 212; Zhihe Wang 2012, 189.
[100]See Clart 2013, 190.
[101]See also the critical remarks by John Cobb (Cobb 2012) in his foreword to Zhihe Wang 2012.
[102]Zhihe Wang 2012, 188.

PART TWO

INTERRELIGIOUS THEOLOGY

8

From Religious Pluralism to Interreligious Theology

PLURALISMS ACROSS RELIGIOUS TRADITIONS

When we compare the development of pluralist approaches in the six religious traditions, it seems that in Christianity, Judaism, and Islam pluralist positions are not only proposed more often, in terms of numbers of theologians endorsing them, but also more consistently, in terms of inner determination. This finding may come as a surprise, given the widespread cliché of Eastern religions as naturally pluralist.[1] As this survey has shown, semipluralist images and motifs are indeed more widespread in Eastern religions than in the religions of Abrahamic descent. However, as has also been shown, Hinduism, Buddhism, and Chinese religions often stop short of a fully pluralist position and end up in their own specific versions of superiority claims. It is probably fair to say that in the Abrahamic religions, the point of departure is further removed from the goal of religious pluralism than it is in the Eastern religions. Although one should not underestimate the extent to which exclusivist positions existed and still exist in Hinduism and Buddhism, both religions had a stronger and more continuous inclusivist tradition than can be found in the Abrahamic faiths. However, in terms of the point of destination, many contemporary theologians in the Abrahamic religions seem to have come significantly closer to the pluralist end than their counterparts in the East.

If this picture is somewhat right, one of its implications is that pluralists in the Abrahamic religions are further ahead of (or further remote from) the religious mainstream than is apparently the case with the often quasi-pluralist approaches of the Eastern faiths. Accordingly, we do not find in the East the kind of severe condemnation of religious pluralism that pluralists

---

[1] John Hick too was convinced that "the pluralistic idea has a more familiar and accepted status in India and further east" (Hick 1999, 78–79).

109

in the Abrahamic religions are confronted with. This is most obvious when we compare, for example, the harsh rejection of religious pluralism in the Vatican's document *Dominus Iesus* (and the subsequent sanctions against Roman Catholic pluralists) or Muslim antipluralist fatwas with the decision of the Indian High Court about the acceptance of different paths of salvation as an essential feature of Hinduism. One major reason for this difference between East and West seems to be the doctrine of reincarnation, which in Hinduism and Buddhism enables a limited appreciation of religious diversity as serving in different degrees the needs of those who in their long, spiritual pilgrimage, encompassing many lives, have not yet arrived at the ultimate goal and the corresponding ultimate religion. This version of inclusivism has not been available to most parts of the Abrahamic religions.[2] If theologians of the Abrahamic religions wish to appreciate religious diversity they have to be more radical than their counterparts in the Eastern religions and understand the legitimacy of religious diversity not only as a diversity of degrees along a hierarchically structured religious continuum. They have to be serious about the possibility of finding a diversity at the top of the scale.

The scenario seems to be once more somewhat different in China. Although in Chinese Buddhism the attitude toward other religions remained more or less faithful to its Indian roots, Daoism and Confucianism pursued their own rationales in understanding religious diversity. In their original form, they don't believe in reincarnation; only later on, some of their branches adopted this belief under Buddhist influence. Their fundamental attitude to other religions is less shaped by a pattern of spiritual progress than by their concepts of harmony, which in Confucianism is primarily understood in terms of social intelligence or wisdom and in Daoism as part of the overall symphony of nature. On these foundations, Confucians and Daoists were also able to accommodate a diversity of religions, while claiming that their own ideas provide the best foundation for understanding this diversity. They see their own religion as a part of this diversity, but one that exceeds all other parts, in that it best understands the rules and structures of the whole. This type of primus-inter-pares pluralism is in the end another form of inclusivism, which much resembles the attitude to religious pluralism as found among some representatives of Neo-Hinduism.

As to the theoretical foundations of religious pluralism, it seems to be possible to identify two broad commonalities across the religion-specific particularities. First, the affirmation that ultimate reality transcends human words and concepts. This is also true for Daoism and Confucianism.

---

[2]Belief in reincarnation is not entirely absent from all three Abrahamic religions, but found in only some of its smaller branches (as among the Druses, Alawites, some ultra-orthodox Jews, and gnostic or esoteric forms of Christianity).

Even if they emphasize the immanence of ultimate reality, both, *Dao* and *Tian* ("Heaven"), remain beyond the scope of definitive verbalization and conceptualization. The transcategoriality of the ultimate is not an invention of religious pluralists, as purported by some critics, but a traditional conviction that is well testified in all major religions. Pluralists infer from this conviction the fundamental need of religious self-relativization, that is, of relativizing any absolutist doctrinal positions claiming to possess the whole truth. Second, pluralists widely agree that religious pluralism suggests itself if one wishes doing sufficient justice to the actual reality of the religious other as encountered today. This includes an explicit or implicit critique of the exclusivist and inclusivist attitudes or their respective traditions, which are seen as being less well compatible with the concrete experience of the religious other. This criticism of exclusivist and inclusivist approaches, however, is more explicit among pluralists in the Abrahamic religions than among those of the Eastern religions.

From this second commonality emerges a highly significant observation. Pluralists of different religious backgrounds can all agree—at least in principle—on a pluralist interpretation of religious diversity, even if the specific features of this pluralist view inevitably vary because of their tradition-specific nature. In this respect, religious pluralism differs decisively from exclusivism and inclusivism. An exclusivist or an inclusivist of a particular religion could never agree, not even in principle, with the exclusivist or inclusivist claims of another faith, though he or she may readily accept, as a matter of fact, that such claims are made, and may even understand why, in analogy to the structure of his or her own theology, the religious other is raising such claims. The reason for this is of a logical nature. It is logically impossible for two different religions to be exclusively true or uniquely superior in the same respect, just as it is impossible for two different people to each be one year older than the other.[3] In contrast, there is no such logical reason why a religious pluralist of one religion should a priori reject the possible truth of a pluralist position formulated within the conceptual framework of another religion. A Christian who claims the unique superiority of the Christian faith will, for logical reasons, be unable to accept that the claim to the unique superiority of, for example, a Vaishnava Hindu is true. A Christian pluralist and a Vaishnava pluralist, however, are not necessarily bound by logic to reject each other's position, even if some features of their pluralisms will differ. Hence it is, in principle, possible that Jewish,

---

[3]Strictly speaking, here too we would have to add the qualification "in the same respect." Modern medicine makes it possible that one person would be one year older in terms of birth, while the other might be one year older in terms of conception (e.g., when the fertilized egg was kept frozen for a year before its implantation).

Christian, Muslim, Hindu, Buddhist, Confucian, Daoist, Jain, Sikh, and other pluralists[4] would all agree on a pluralist interpretation of religious diversity, even if this interpretation is expressed in a diversity of forms.

The significance of this observation will become clearer when we dare to look at the possible future of religion on this planet. On the one hand, it seems to be rather unlikely that in the long run any one of the tradition-specific versions of an exclusivist or inclusivist interpretation of religious diversity, for example, of a Christian, Muslim, or Buddhist brand, would ever become the globally dominant and more or less generally accepted view. For this would imply that a particular religion would prove to be the overall most convincing one and would develop into the one and only religion of humankind. On the other hand, an ongoing rivalry of conflicting mutual superiority claims would further undermine the credibility of each and all religions. A multireligious acceptance of religious pluralism thus offers a feasible alternative to both scenarios. Different religions could co-exist without raising any exclusivist or inclusivist superiority claims, and agree, though in different, tradition-specific ways, on the legitimacy of religious diversity. That is, they would understand their home traditions as parts of a larger overarching religious reality, of which they represent equally valid components. Their still differing identities would be seen by all of them as diverse individualities within an all-embracing "we"-consciousness. The rise of pluralist approaches in all major religions may thus eventually turn out to be the initial evidence of a gradual and significant transformation in the religions' self-understanding, as the sociologist Thomas McFaul has prognosticated.[5]

If religious pluralism is understood not as a theory above and beyond the religions but as an interpretation of religious diversity that can and needs to be developed from within each of the religions in religion-specific ways, an interreligious consensus appears feasible but is not automatically guaranteed. The reasons for pluralism, as produced within the different religions, will partly differ because of the specific ways by which a pluralist interpretation is achieved within each of them. Reasons that may persuade Muslims of the truth of religious pluralism, for example, may not necessarily persuade Daoists or Hindus or others and vice versa. The religion-specific version of religious pluralism will become reciprocally consensual only if the different religions learn to mutually understand and make sense of their different ways of thinking and reasoning.

Religious pluralism, if constructed from tradition-specific perspectives,

---

[4]For possible foundations of a Jain form of religious pluralism see Jain 1989 and Long 2014; for possible pluralist foundations in Sikhism see Singh 1989 and Cole 2004, 127–39.

[5]See McFaul 2011, 159–74.

involves a value judgment: From the point of view of one religion some other religions are assessed as being equally valid, despite their being different. But this in itself does not yet imply that the reasons why one tradition might regard another tradition as equally valid are also acceptable to this other tradition. It is possible, but not obvious that, for example, the reasons that might motivate a Buddhist pluralist to assess Christianity as equally liberating as Buddhism are also approved by a Christian pluralist. Or, for example, whether the reasons that persuade a Muslim pluralist to accept Buddhism as an equally valid religion are also acceptable to a Buddhist pluralist. In order to increase the overall plausibility of religious pluralisms, it is necessary to transform the possibility of their interreligious acceptance into actuality. Religious pluralisms of different religious brands need to be subject to interreligious dialogue in order to test their compatibility. The step toward a pluralist approach within each specific religion means to understand other religions as compatible and equally valid *from the perspective of this particular religion*. This, however, is not enough. The next step is to understand and endorse the analogous pluralist moves in those other religions. The first step can be called a pluralist integration of different *religions*. The second step is the joint and reciprocal integration of different *religion-specific pluralisms* within a process of multiperspectival exchange. Only the second step will confirm the validity of the first step and will prevent it from degenerating into the quasi-pluralism of the primus-inter-pares position. It is, therefore, the second step that significantly increases the plausibility of religious pluralism. And this second step can be taken only within the broader context of interreligious theology.

Testing the compatibility of pluralisms from different religions is certainly not the only task of interreligious theology. As has been explained in chapter 1, interreligious theology is primarily defined as that type of doing theology which reflects on the major issues of human life by drawing on insights from more than one religious tradition.[6] However, the question of why humanity has not just one religion but a bewildering diversity of them *is* one of those major issues. And the more this diversity becomes vividly present within each continent, nation, and town, the more the pressing nature of this question is felt by an increasing number of people. Interreligious theology therefore also involves an interreligious reflection on different understandings of religious diversity and their possible compatibility. In a sense, the relationship between religious pluralism and interreligious theology is that of a hermeneutical circle. On the one hand, religious pluralism provides each religion with the strongest foundation and encouragement to practice interreligious theology. For why should one be inclined to draw for

---

[6]See chapter 1.

the reflection of theological issues on other religious traditions if this is not motivated by the reasonable expectation to find in them illuminating and enriching perspectives? On the other hand, it is only in and through inter-religious theology that the pluralist assumptions might find their own con-firmation. Both religious pluralism and interreligious theology are closely related. It is therefore not surprising that influential pioneers of religious pluralism also presented the vision of an interreligious or global theology.

RELIGIOUS PLURALISM AND THE VISION OF A GLOBAL THEOLOGY

Toward the end of his life, Paul Tillich (1886–1965) arrived at a theological vision in which we can see, retrospectively, the nascent concept of interreli-gious theology. In the last of his four Bampton Lectures, delivered in 1961, he unfolded his view that "the present encounter of the world religions" requires of Christianity, as of any other religion, that "it breaks through its own particularity."[7] And he concluded with the following remarkable statement:

> In the depth of every living religion there is a point at which the religion itself loses its importance, and that to which it points breaks through its particularity, elevating it to spiritual freedom and with it to a vision of the spiritual presence in other expressions of the ultimate meaning of man's existence.[8]

He reverted to this topic in the very last lecture of his life, delivered on October 12, 1965, ten days before his death. He suggested that each religion contains, with different forms of emphasis, three interrelated elements of the experience of "the Holy": first, the *sacramental* element, that is, the appearance of the Holy in a finite and hence specific form; second, the *mystical* element, pointing to the fact that the ultimate nature of the Holy "lies beyond any of its embodiments"; and third, the *ethical* or *prophetic* element, which is the self-critique of religion in the name of what "ought to be."[9] He calls the unity or balance of these three elements "the Religion of the Concrete Spirit," and it is found "in a fragmentary way in many moments in the history of religions."[10] According to Tillich, achieving this unity is the telos, the "inner aim," of "the otherwise extremely chaotic, or

---

[7] Tillich [1963] 1964, 95, 97.
[8] Ibid., 97
[9] Tillich 1966, 87.
[10] Ibid., 88.

at least seemingly chaotic, history of religions."[11] As a result, he expressed his hope that "the future of theology" might lie in the interpenetration of the religions, or in his words: "the structure of religious thought might develop in connection with another or different fragmentary manifestation . . . of the Religion of the Concrete Spirit."[12]

In 1961, the same year that Tillich gave his Bampton Lectures, Wilfred Cantwell Smith had criticized Tillich as one who "probably . . . belongs to the last generation of theologians who can formulate their conceptual system as religiously isolationist."[13] Subsequently, Smith was delighted when the publication of Tillich's Bampton Lectures indicated this significant change in Tillich's mind.[14] Two years before, in 1959, Smith had published his famous essay: "Comparative Religion: Whither—and Why?"[15] The essay was well ahead of its time. It was not written from the perspective of a Christian theologian, but from that of a scholar of comparative religion who reflects on the methodology of his discipline. Smith exposed the constrictions of the phenomenology of religion of his day and pointed out what a significantly transformed version of comparative religion could look like. First, the discipline, or more precisely the "object" and the "subject" of its investigations, should become personalized. Its object, the "religions," are not to be seen as stiff and abstract entities, but as living traditions of real persons. The investigator too should not be mistaken as a neutral, objective, or blank intellect but as a concrete person, as someone carrying out his or her studies from a specific background and perspective, which among other things, may be shaped by whether the scholar is a religious person or not. This implies that theologians from different religious backgrounds can and should be admitted to the discipline.[16] Second, as a result of this personalization, the discipline needs to become dialogical. To the extent that the other religion is perceived as in fact the religion of others, that is, of real people who have their own views on the investigator's religious or nonreligious perspective, the study of religion needs to assume a dialogical form. "What had been a description is therefore in process of becoming a dialogue."[17] And third, despite the full acknowledgment of the perspectival nature of comparative religion, its overall scope should remain global, that is, a global exchange of perspectives. It is worth quoting Smith's own summary of how these three points could change the nature of the discipline:

---

[11]Ibid.
[12]Ibid., 91.
[13]Smith 1963, 121. This chapter of Smith 1963 is a lecture delivered by Smith in 1961.
[14]Ibid., 122n4.
[15]Smith 1959.
[16]Ibid., 45–46, 49–50.
[17]Ibid., 47.

The traditional form of Western scholarship in the study of other men's religions was that of an impersonal presentation of an "it." The first great innovation in recent times has been the personalization of the faiths observed, so that one finds a discussion of a "they." Presently the observer becomes personally involved, so that the situation is one of a "we" talking about a "they." The next step is a dialogue, where "we" talk to "you." If there is listening and mutuality, this may become that "we" talk *with* "you." The culmination of this progress is when "we all" are talking *with* each other about "us."[18]

What Smith, at the end of the 1950s, called the personalization of comparative religion has by now become almost standard. In particular a wave of "postcolonial studies" has produced plenty of evidence that substantiates Smith's early critique of the image of the religious scholar as a neutral and objective spirit. And seeing religions as multifaceted, changeable, and living traditions of concrete people is no longer a matter of any serious dispute. However, the transformation of descriptive comparison into dialogue has not gained the kind of general acceptance that Smith prognosticated. In this respect, the past decades have been marked by a serious split. While in religious studies the development led to a widespread dismissal of comparative investigations in favor of localized studies focusing almost entirely on the particular, interreligious dialogue has indeed turned into a major branch of academic theology. In the course of an increasing systematization of dialogical studies a "new comparative theology" has emerged, which may influence religious studies and possibly support the efforts to revive comparative investigations beyond theology.[19]

To a significant degree the new comparative theology implements parts of Smith's vision. But some of its proponents differ from Smith in that they tend to see comparative theology as a rather one-sided enterprise, where "the theological impulse and focus . . . lie primarily within one's own tradition."[20] Comparison is done with the prime interest of gaining a renewed understanding of one's own faith. In this concept, the dialogical aspect becomes asymmetrical, tending to use the religious other as a means of fostering intrareligious reflection. Other scholars propose an alternative understanding of comparative theology "that engages different religious traditions around common questions, each tradition contributing to a deeper or higher understanding of the particular quest," an idea that is rejected by

---

[18]Ibid., 34.
[19]See on this the essays in Schmidt-Leukel and Nehring 2016.
[20]Cornille 2014, 14.

proponents of the first concept.[21] One could say that the first concept focuses on the aspect of "taking," while the later understanding of dialogical comparison emphasizes a "give-and-take" approach. The latter is clearly nearer to Smith's vision of a future state "when 'we all' are talking *with* each other about 'us.'"

About a decade after his visionary essay, Smith introduced the term "world theology" as a new label for what he had in mind.[22] He described the work of this theology as a "process . . . where we human beings learn, through critical analysis, empirical inquiry, and collaborative discourse, to conceptualise a world in which some of us are Christians, some of us are Muslims, some of us are Hindus, some of us are Jews, some of us are sceptics."[23] This endeavor, according to Smith, could be rightly called a "theology of religions," but in the sense "of a subjective genitive: a theology for which 'the religions' are the subject, not the object."[24] In other words, "world theology" is carried out jointly by the religions. Its object, says Smith, is "faith in its many forms":[25]

> Theology is critical intellectualisation of (and for) faith, and of the world as known in faith; and what we seek is a theology that will interpret the history of our race in a way that will give intellectual expression to our faith, the faith of all of us, and to our modern perception of the world.[26]

Given the interreligious nature of this new type of theology, I prefer the term "interreligious theology" over Smith's own "world theology." "Theology" is to be understood in the broad sense of the disciplined self-reflection as it is found in each of the major religious traditions, no matter whether they are predominantly theistic or nontheistic.[27] Ideally, the whole history of religions constitutes the material to be taken into account by interreligious theology.[28] In essence, I think, Smith's vision has lost nothing of its validity. One might contest whether he was right in seeing interreligious theology as the future shape of all religious studies, but I suggest that it definitely

---

[21]Ibid., 10.

[22]See Smith [1981] 1989. The book, which first appeared in 1981, is a revised version of the Edward Cadbury Lectures, which, according to the records of Birmingham University, were given in 1971 (as stated in an e-mail by Edmond Tang from January 18, 2011).

[23]Smith 1989, 101.

[24]Ibid., 124.

[25]Ibid.

[26]Ibid., 125.

[27]See chapter 1.

[28]"Henceforth the data for theology must be the data of the history of religions." Smith 1989, 126.

and inevitably characterizes the future shape of any theology. Certainly, religious pluralism cannot do without it.

Smith's book *Towards a World Theology* is based on his Cadbury Lectures, which he had given in 1971 in Birmingham at the invitation of John Hick.[29] At that time, Hick was already working on his largest book ever, *Death and Eternal Life*, which first appeared in 1976. In this work, Hick treated questions of possible life after death on a broad range of data from several religious traditions, but with an unambiguous theological interest. Hick characterized this study explicitly as a contribution to "global theology." At the same time he related it to his parallel efforts of developing a new theology of religions (which he later called "religious pluralism") that seeks to overcome the older "ptolemaic"[30] views because of the "solipsistic" inability to recognize significant truth beyond the borders of one's own faith.[31] In an article dating from 1977, Hick wrote:

> [I]nter-religious dialogue undertaken just like that, as two (or more) people bearing mutual witness to their own faiths, each in the firm conviction that his is the final truth and in hope of converting the other, can only result either in conversion or in a hardening of differences—occasionally the former but more often the latter. In order for dialogue to be mutually fruitful, lesser changes than total conversion must be possible and must be hoped for on both (or all) sides.[32]

Hick specified the latter as a

> truth-seeking dialogue in which each is conscious that the Transcendent Being is infinitely greater than his own limited vision of it, and in which they accordingly seek to share their visions in the hope that each may be helped towards a fuller awareness of the Divine Reality before which they both stand.[33]

In this sense, Hick affirmed in 1984 that

> we need a pluralistic theory which enables us to recognize and be fascinated by the manifold differences between the religious traditions, with their different conceptualizations, their different modes

---

[29]See note 22 above.

[30]The image is connected to Hick's early comparison of theocentric religious pluralism with a Copernican revolution. The religions are like planets circling around God as their "sun." See also chapter 7.

[31]See Hick [1976] 1985b, 29–34.

[32]Hick 1980, 85.

[33]Ibid., 81.

of religious experience, and their different forms of individual and social response to the divine.[34]

As these quotations unambiguously show, Hick as much as Smith saw his pluralist theology not as an aim in itself, especially not as an instrument for avoiding the painstaking dialogical engagement with the religious other, but on the contrary as a foundation on which such dialogical and comparative efforts could bear their fruits in terms of a "global" or "world theology." Hick's *Death and Eternal Life*[35] or Smith's comparative studies *Faith and Belief*[36] and *What Is Scripture?*[37] are milestones of comparative theology, which can easily compete with those comparative studies that were produced two or three decades later by the "new comparative theologians." It is simply wrong and ignorant to accuse Hick and Smith of a theological approach, which would be entirely different from or even opposed to the concerns of comparative theology.[38] Nevertheless, such criticism has been raised and will now be discussed.[39]

RELIGIOUS PLURALISM VERSUS RELIGIOUS DIVERSITY?

Religious pluralists are confronted with various types of criticism from different camps. One set of critical objections circles around the accusation that religious pluralism, or at least the monocentric type of pluralism held by John Hick and Wilfred Cantwell Smith, is unable to do sufficient justice to religious diversity as it really is. Let me quote Hugh Nicholson as one example of the many voices which have criticized religious pluralism along those lines.[40] He builds his critique mainly on James Fredericks but gives it a succinct expression. Theology of religions in general and religious pluralism in particular, first, "work(s) out a stance toward other traditions independently of an empirical study of those traditions." Second, it assumes "a global, totalizing perspective on the religions," which "implies a presumption to know other religions better than their own adherents." Third, this "has the effect of obviating a serious and open engagement with other

---

[34]Hick 1984, 158.

[35]Hick [1976] 1985b.

[36]Smith 1979.

[37]Smith 1993.

[38]See, e.g., Nicholson's adventurous assertion that comparative theology represents the "antithesis of the theology of religions" (Nicholson 2009, 620).

[39]For the remainder of this chapter, I further elaborate some of the arguments presented in Schmidt-Leukel 2012.

[40]For summaries and discussions of similar critics see Hedges 2008 and Hedges 2010, 146–96.

religious traditions." All of this entails, fourth, "to disregard the specific claims of the religious other."[41] That is: "The pluralist presupposition that all religions are fundamentally saying the same thing betrays an incapacity truly to respect religious difference, to respect the religious other *qua* other."[42]

Though often repeated, the first of Nicholson's objections is obviously unjustified. Whereas it is in fact well known that some of the major models of exclusivism and inclusivism were admittedly derived entirely from inner-Christian doctrinal assumptions, as for example in the case of Karl Barth[43] and Karl Rahner,[44] this is not at all true of the major pioneering pluralist theologians:[45] Raimon Panikkar turned his earlier inclusivist theology into pluralism under the impact of his deepened understanding of Hinduism.[46] Wilfred Cantwell Smith abandoned his earlier exclusivist attitude and embraced pluralism precisely because of his encounter with people of other faiths and his intensive empirical studies.[47] Smith's expertise in Islamic studies and a good deal of other religions stands unquestioned. John Hick, too, moved from his earlier exclusivism to pluralism because of his experience of other faiths.[48] Moreover, he has demonstrated more than once a sound knowledge of other religious traditions, particularly of Hinduism and Buddhism. Many more pluralists have in fact not developed "their stance toward other traditions independently of an empirical study of those traditions," as Nicholson and others impute, but, on the contrary, they developed pluralism as a result of their serious exposure to other religions. It would be helpful if critics of religious pluralism could take notice of this undeniable fact.

The second objection according to which pluralists claim to know other religions better than their adherents do, ignores that pluralist interpretations can be and are actually developed from within a broad range of different religious traditions. To uphold their objection in the light of this observation, Nicholson and other proponents would have to claim that any plural-

---

[41]All quotations from Nicholson 2009, 619.

[42]Nicholson 2010, 45, referring approvingly to Tanner 1993.

[43]Famously stated by Barth when he affirmed in conversation with D. T. Niles that he doesn't need to know Hindus in order to know that Hinduism is unbelief. See Niles 1969.

[44]See Rahner 1978, 312–13. Yet Rahner demanded that the aprioristic arguments of the Christian systematic theologian need to be—as far as possible—confirmed by the historian of religions (ibid.).

[45]Nor is this true of all exclusivist or inclusivist theologies. Hendrik Kraemer, Harold Netland, or the early Panikkar, for example, tried (or still try) to support their exclusivist or inclusivist positions by evidence derived from specific interreligious comparisons.

[46]Panikkar's change from his earlier inclusivist to a pluralist position is particularly evident in the comparison of the first edition of his *The Unknown Christ of Hinduism* with the second revised edition (see Panikkar 1964 and 1981).

[47]See, for example, Smith 1987, 63: "Mind you, I did not start my studies with the conviction that other communities' lives were lived in God's grace. I have come to this recognition only slowly, as I got to know the people and carefully studied their history."

[48]See Hick 2002, 159–226.

ists, from whatever religion, illegitimately claim to understand their own and other faiths, simply because of holding a pluralist interpretation. This criticism would be truly presumptuous and, above all, hyperdogmatist. For it amounts to the prohibition for followers of every religion to develop a pluralist understanding of their religion's place among other religions.

The third and the fourth objection are ambivalent. Pluralists are certainly critical of religious claims to an exclusivist or inclusivist understanding of religious diversity. This critical attitude applies not just to other religions but also to the home religions of the pluralists. As far as such claims are concerned, pluralists are not "obviating a serious and open engagement"; on the contrary, they are engaging them openly and critically. In rejecting exclusivist and inclusivist interpretations of other faiths, pluralists are not different from exclusivists and inclusivists of their own tradition. Yet exclusivists and inclusivists reject the claims of other religions in any possible form, which pluralists don't do. As has been shown above, only pluralism implies the possibility of some form of interreligious agreement. So who would be more guilty of not respecting the other?

Thus what remains is the objection that pluralism, especially the monocentric form of pluralism as advocated by Smith and Hick, disregards the particularities of religious diversity, that it "betrays an incapacity truly to respect religious difference, to respect the religious other *qua* other." What could it mean that pluralism is incapable of respecting religious difference, if it does not mean any of the three previous objections? Is it really the case that according to pluralism all religions "are fundamentally saying the same thing"?

As has been stated before,[49] a monocentric pluralism suggests that there is only one ultimate reality to which all the major religions are related in such a way that they can orient the lives of their adherents in different though equally valid and efficient ways toward this reality. The critique of this position in the name of religious diversity can be of three major types, depending on the respective background assumptions. The first type assumes, in accordance with monocentric pluralism, that there is indeed just one ultimate reality. The second type denies that there is any ultimate reality at all. And the third type assumes that there is more than one ultimate reality. In this regard, no other assumption is left. The critique of religious pluralism or monocentric pluralism in the name of religious diversity differs significantly with each of the three types. Let us look at them one by one.

If the critic assumes that there is only one ultimate reality, the "real" difference between the religions may be understood in the sense that merely one among the different religions is right in claiming a salvific relation to

---

[49]On the distinction between monocentric and polycentric pluralism see chapter 2.

ultimate reality, whereas the rest are all wrong. The divergences of their concepts of the ultimate from the concepts of that religion which is uniquely true is seen as evidence of their falsity. In this case, the rejection of pluralism is not that much in the name of religious diversity as such but in the name of religious exclusivism, which at the outset excludes the possibility of more than one true faith. Or, more precisely, which takes every divergence from the supposedly uniquely true religion as an indication of falsity. If the accusation of pluralism as not doing justice to religious differences emerges from this background, the implicit presupposition is that religious diversity is taken seriously only if every divergence among religions is understood as a sign of falsity. This presupposition, however, has hardly any persuasive force. In the end, its proponents will also have difficulties in accommodating the diversity within the supposedly uniquely true religion and hence be strongly bent toward sectarianism.

This first type of the objection may also be forwarded from an inclusivist background. Again, the assumption is that ultimate reality is single. It is further assumed that different religions are salvifically related toward this one ultimate, but not to the same degree. The differences between the religions are then interpreted not as evidence of falsity but as evidence of inferiority, which varies to the degree of their being different. One religion is seen as having the most accurate understanding of the ultimate, and hence the degree of accuracy of all the others depends on their similarity or dissimilarity to this one most adequate idea. The accusation that pluralism is not taking diversity seriously would then imply that religious diversity is taken seriously only if every difference between religions is understood along that spectrum of being closer to or remoter from the truth. This presupposition thus holds that it is impossible in matters of religious truth to combine diversity with equality. All who contradict and dare to make precisely this combination are hence blamed as not taking diversity seriously.

The second type of the said objection simply assumes that the religions' claims are essentially all wrong. If there is no ultimate reality, then the belief to be related to an ultimate reality must be false no matter which form it takes. The only way of doing justice to religious diversity is seeing it as a diversity of lies, deception, and errors. This is the position of the naturalist. But from this perspective religious pluralism is less often criticized, at least not with the argument that it would do insufficient justice to religious diversity. Like an exclusivist, the naturalist tends to assume that diversity can exist only as a diversity of falsities, but denies the possibility that truth may also exist in a diversity of forms.[50]

---

[50]See, for example, Bertrand Russell, who held that "all the great religions are untrue," but also: "It is evident as a matter of logic that, since they disagree, not more than one of them can be true" (Russell

The third type of this objection is based on the assumption that there can be and in fact are several ultimates. As we have seen, this position is closely linked to process philosophy or process theology.[51] The diversity among the religions, especially the diversity of different concepts of the ultimate, is—at least in part—explained by the presumption that these concepts do not reflect different human experiences of the same ultimate reality but different experiences of different ultimate realities. John Cobb, for example, suggests that there are three ultimate realities: the theistic God, Being as such or Creativity, and the Cosmos.[52] The problem with this version of the objection is, as already mentioned, the assumption that there could be more than one ultimate reality. When facing this problem, defenders of a "several ultimates" approach usually get less strict and tend to modify their assumption by speaking of different "aspects" or "features" of one complex ultimate.[53]

This raises an important question: To what extent does the talk of different "aspects" of the ultimate differ from the talk of "different human experiences" of the ultimate? Or, to be more specific: To what extent, if at all, is John Cobb's talk of three ultimates, which "are distinct" but "not separate from one another,"[54] and which are each related to a specific form of religious experience,[55] different from John Hick's talk of the different *personae* and *impersonae* of the one Ultimate, which exist as distinct manifestations of the ultimate in different forms of human religious experiences?[56] In short, what is the difference between such "aspects" and "manifestations," given that both exist in human experience? Cobb even admits that speaking "of a plurality of 'ultimate realities' . . . is misleading," if it "gives the impression that the three have analogous ultimate status."[57] Obviously this implies that not all three are "ultimate" in the same sense. If God, Creativity/Being, and Cosmos are "not separate," the metaphysical issue seems to be primarily how to understand the relation between divine immanence and transcendence and between its personal and impersonal dimensions. Cobb gives the illuminating analogy of the different concepts of the human body that we find in traditional Indian, traditional Chinese, and modern Western medicine. It is one complex human organism—not three. But each of the three concepts may have its valid insights without

---

[1967] 1992, 9). On atheist/naturalist arguments based on religious diversity see also Davis 1989, 166–92.

[51]See chapter 2.

[52]See on this also Griffin 2005c.

[53]Cobb 1999, 74, 135.

[54]Ibid., 123, 185.

[55]See ibid., 117–19. See also chapter 14.

[56]See Hick 1989, 252–96.

[57]Cobb 1999, 122.

possessing an exhaustive understanding of the body.[58] If one accepts this analogy, the difference between the polycentric pluralism of process theology and a monocentric pluralism as proposed by Hick and Smith seems to become marginal. Comparing Hick and Cobb, the difference might even boil down to the extent of the ultimate's inexhaustibility, with Hick opting for a stronger and Cobb for a lesser degree.[59] In any way, the accusation of not doing sufficient justice to religious diversity can hardly be targeted on monocentric pluralism as such. The critique would have a much stronger point if monocentric pluralists would also claim that there is only one form of valid religious experience, which is the same in all true religions. But this is not what Hick or Smith and many other monocentric pluralists hold. The supposition that, in Nicholson's words, according to religious pluralism "all religions are fundamentally saying the same thing" is just another polemical distortion by the critics.

RELIGIOUS PLURALISM AND THE NEED
FOR AN ONGOING DIALOGUE

If the accusation that religious pluralism neglects, disregards, or even denies religious diversity turns out to be baseless, there is another—related—objection according to which religious pluralism might be in a sense too hasty, that its understanding of religious diversity as, in principle, a diversity of equals has been arrived at prematurely, thereby making any further interfaith dialogue, and hence any interreligious theology, superfluous.

This objection has been produced by theologians from different religious backgrounds. According to James Fredericks:

> The purpose of interreligious dialogue is hard to imagine from a pluralist perspective. Since religious differences are of no great religious or theological consequence, dialogue serves merely as an exercise in discerning how, in fact, we really are in agreement with one another, despite our differences. Since the end point of the encounter between religious traditions is safely under control, there is little danger that Christians will be taken by surprise.[60]

A similar critique has been expressed by the Pure-Land Buddhist Ryusei Takeda. According to Takeda, the pluralist position that all major religions

---

[58]See ibid., 116.
[59]See also chapter 14.
[60]Fredericks 1999, 115.

are salvifically related to the same ultimate reality could only be made as the outcome of a global interreligious dialogue "that has come to perfect fulfilment." If it is advanced, as in the case of John Hick, as a hypothetical presupposition, it might "limit and distort the dialogue itself." Moreover, if the hypothesis presupposes that the same ultimate Reality is salvifically present in each of the major traditions, "the dialogue itself is meaningless," for "it is, then, totally unnecessary to learn new things from other religious traditions."[61]

Takeda gives no further explanation of how or why a pluralist theology would have a limiting and distorting impact on interfaith dialogue. Particularly, if pluralism is not stated dogmatically but as a hypothesis, the proponent implies that the hypothesis might be false. John Hick, for example, has always been very clear about the religiously ambiguous character of the universe.[62] We can neither prove nor disprove the existence of an ultimate reality. Hence it might be possible that in the end atheism or naturalism is right while all "theologies" of any religion are false. Perhaps we are unable, under pre-eschatological conditions, to determine with infallible certainty which interpretation of religious diversity is right or wrong. Nevertheless, we can meaningfully discuss which of the basic models is more likely to be true in the sense of which accounts better for the data that we encounter in the history of religions.[63] In this sense Hick has claimed that the pluralist hypothesis is "considerably more probable" than its rivals,[64] while his opponents, like James Fredericks, see it as "a rather implausible assertion," given "a vast amount of concrete data suggesting the contrary."[65] These two rival expectations show exactly the kind of discourse within which the pluralist hypothesis and its competitors can be meaningfully discussed: How well or badly will they fare in interpreting the data of the religious history? Yet whether a Christian, Muslim, Hindu, Buddhist, or other version of exclusivism or inclusivism or a basically pluralist model is more capable of accounting for the data is something that might become clearer in and through an ongoing and theologically deeper-going dialogue.

In 1992 Schubert Ogden suggested that apart from exclusivism, inclusivism, and pluralism there would be a fourth option, which according to him is different from pluralism in that it does not claim "that there actually *are*

---

[61]Takeda 2004, 283.

[62]See Hick 1989, 73–125.

[63]When Fredericks (1999, 106–7) denies that Hick's version of pluralism is a genuine hypothesis (because there would be nothing to falsify it), he ignores the possibility of eschatological falsification. Pluralism would be falsified eschatologically if, for example, some form of religious exclusivism should turn out to be true; see Hick 1995, 74–75.

[64]Hick 1985a, 100.

[65]Fredericks 1999, 107.

many true religions, but only that there *can be*."[66] I do not agree with Ogden in that a "potential" or "possible pluralism" would constitute an additional option. Its content is not different from that of the pluralist option. It merely restates the pluralist position in a more cautious way, underlining the hypothetical nature of religious pluralism. However, what is important about Ogden's suggestion—something that has often been overlooked—is that Ogden presented his proposal as "a certain optimism about all the specific religions," which "gives one every reason to look for signs of the actuality of the pluralism."[67] Ogden's suggestion may thus be read as a suggestion to see interreligious dialogue as sort of long-term research program[68] with the potential to either confirm or disconfirm religious pluralism.

No religious person will enter interreligious dialogue without any presuppositions. Everybody will bring to it "some theological assumptions about the other." This, as Kristin Kiblinger rightly holds, "is not tantamount to saying that one's theological presuppositions are set in stone; rather, certainly they are revisable, in light of the findings."[69] Perhaps we cannot expect that these "findings" will provide too many knockdown arguments that would have the force of ruling out some options entirely. But it might become clearer which price the various models of exclusivism, inclusivism, or pluralism may have to pay in order to retain their consistency in the face of the data. And in some cases the price may be far too high, that is, the necessary modifications of the initial assumption may heavily reduce its overall plausibility. In any way, I cannot see how this discussion would limit or distort a multilateral interfaith dialogue. The opposite is the case: Interfaith dialogue becomes crucial in assessing the explanatory force of the pluralist hypothesis or any other rival theory. This may sound like hijacking dialogue for the purpose of testing the pluralist position. But let us be clear: Testing the pluralist position means to find out, in and through dialogue, whether what people from different religions believe and how they live is ultimately irreconcilable or whether it may be, in substantial respects, compatible or even complementary, so that they can learn from each other. This seems to be a rather noble and central task of interreligious dialogue.

But then, would pluralism not render interfaith learning "meaningless" because, as Takeda submits, learning something new from other religions appears to be irrelevant ("totally unnecessary") to our salvation? It is right that according to the pluralist position learning from other religions is not seen as indispensable to one's salvation. Saying the opposite, as Hick himself

---

[66]Ogden 1992, 83.

[67]Ibid., 103.

[68]An interpretation of the pluralist hypothesis as an invitation to a "research program" has also been suggested by Ingram 2012, 27–55.

[69]Kiblinger 2010, 25.

has pointed out, would amount to the old exclusivist theory that learning from "us" (whatever religious community that "us" may be) is indispensable for the salvation of them.[70] However, denying significance in this exclusivist sense is not the same as holding that interreligious learning is totally unnecessary. It is necessary and even indispensable for arriving at a fuller, that is, more truthful and more accurate understanding of the religious situation of humankind, of our neighbor's faith, and of our own one. This even touches on the soteriological dimension: If one dimension of the salvific process is how we relate to our neighbor (as not only Christianity holds), then being open to the possible truth in the testimony of our neighbors to the religious experience enshrined and enacted in their religious tradition is far from being totally unnecessary or redundant. Lacking in such openness may not completely prevent but also may not foster a salvific transformation. Especially from a religious perspective it would not seem desirable that religions cultivate a mentality marked by distrust against what is most important to the heart and mind of one's religious neighbor—particularly in the current context in which interfaith encounter is becoming a standard feature in the day-to-day life of ever more people. But "openness to other religious truths" would become empty words if this openness would prohibit the joint effort of integrating insights from different religions and shy away from the transformation of traditional superiority claims if the latter might be the outcome of such integration.

As can be seen from both the biographies of pluralist pioneers and, more important, from their theological arguments, pluralists understand their theologies as the fruit of their encounter with the religious other. They are far away from "sealing themselves off from the transformative power of non-Christian religions," as purported by Fredericks.[71] They hold that pluralism is the result of allowing one's theology to be transformed by the encounter with the religious other. Pluralism is the transformation of exclusivist and inclusivist claims into an interpretation of religious diversity that does justice to what has been learned from the encounter with other faiths. Pluralist theologies are often the fruit of such interreligious learning. One may thus wonder how serious Fredericks really is about the openness to the transformative power of the religious other. He reproaches, for example, Christian pluralists as having become unfaithful to the Christian tradition.[72] In the case of the Indian Christian pluralist Stanley Samartha (1920–2001), Fredericks is fully aware that Samartha's theology was the outcome of

---

[70]See Hick 1997, 81.
[71]Fredericks 1999, 110–11.
[72]E.g., ibid., 52–53, 120ff.; and Fredericks 2004, 12ff.

his substantial learning from Indian religions.[73] Nevertheless, Fredericks claims: "Pluralism does not ask Christians to think of these differences [i.e., between the religions] as opportunities to deepen their faith by revising their religious views."[74] This bluntly contradicts his other line of criticism according to which pluralists have revised and transformed Christian views far too much. His latter critique clearly implies that pluralist theologies do not prevent transformations triggered by an in-depth encounter with other religions; it is rather the outcome of this transformation that Fredericks is not happy with. If, at the end of the day, Fredericks suggests that one has to live with the unresolved tension "between our commitments to the Christian tradition" and "openness to other religious truths,"[75] the suspicion may easily arise that it is not pluralism but Fredericks's own verdict against pluralism that is destined to seal Christians off "from the transformative power of non-Christian religions."

AN INTERIM CONCLUSION

So far, the present study has suggested understanding religious pluralism not as a position above and beyond the actual religions but as a particular interpretation of religious diversity, which can be, needs to be, and is in fact developed from within each specific religion. These different pluralisms will find their confirmation only in their reciprocal acceptability. Reciprocal acceptability presupposes a compatibility that can be tested only within the larger framework of an interreligious theology. Interreligious theology implies that religions may learn from their differences. Pioneers of Christian pluralism, such as Wilfred Cantwell Smith and John Hick, have neither disregarded religious differences nor negated the possibility of interreligious learning. On the contrary, they understood religious pluralism both as the outcome of such learning and, at the same time, as the foundation that would make global or interreligious theology possible and desirable.

The prima facie impression that polycentric versions of pluralism, especially those inspired by process philosophy and theology, would take differences between the religions more seriously than monocentric versions is relativized if one considers the interrelatedness of supposedly plural "ultimates" in the sense of constituting different "aspects" of a single but complex reality and the phenomenological link between those aspects and different modes or types of religious experience. According to the monocentric plu-

---

[73]See Fredericks 1999, 89–99.
[74]Ibid., 114 (my interpolation).
[75]Ibid., 170.

ralism of John Hick, different religious concepts of ultimate reality are not related to different ultimates but to "*different* manifestations of the Real," that is, to different experiences of the ultimate, which, as Hick says, constitute "different phenomenal realities."[76] Both monocentric and polycentric models of religious pluralism thus allow and require further investigations into the relationship between such different aspects or manifestations of the ultimate in the context of human religious experience. In producing a better understanding of how these different manifestations of the ultimate in the actual religions relate to each other, interreligious theology enables mutual learning and would thus lead to a fuller understanding of the impact of ultimate reality on human life as a whole. Monocentric and polycentric models take the differences between the religions as an encouragement of mutual learning and transformation.

Pluralism, therefore, does not make interreligious dialogue redundant. It functions as a hypothetical basis for dialogue which hopes for its own confirmation in and through dialogue. That is, it invites and encourages "theologians" from all religious traditions to explore the possible compatibility of their different and often apparently irreconcilable beliefs and orientations in life. Although such dialogue has important practical and political implications, it is primarily of a speculative or—broadly speaking—"theological" nature. And since this theology needs to be done by the religions jointly, it is an interreligious theology. All of this amounts to the conclusion that the religious pluralisms of the different religions require actual concrete dealing with the religious other, or better, the dealing of different religions with each other in a form of dialogical exchange that can be called "interreligious theology." To me it seems rather likely that future theology will to a large extent take the form of "interreligious theology."[77]

While the next chapter will systematize key principles and methodological characteristics of interreligious theology, chapters 10 to 13 will illustrate these theoretical deliberations by presenting concrete examples of interreligious theology. The concluding chapter will introduce the theory that religious diversity exhibits a fractal structure. Interreligious theology not only helps uncover this structure but can also benefit from its recognition.

---

[76]Hick 1995, 43.

[77]See also the recent consultation process within the Ecumenical Association of Third World Theologians (EATWOT): *Toward a Planetary Theology* (Vigil 2010).

9

Interreligious Theology:
Principles and Methodology

FOUR KEY PRINCIPLES
OF INTERRELIGIOUS THEOLOGY

In proposing four key principles of interreligious theology, I use "principles" in the sense of starting points. Like any other theology, interreligious theology is based on certain premises. A theology that consciously and constructively draws on more than one religious tradition needs principles that, in one sense, are more demanding because they go beyond those of religion-specific theologies. In another sense, they need to be more modest, so that they may work for a range of different religious traditions. I suggest four such principles which I currently consider as key for doing interreligious theology: All four are theoretical in that they formulate cornerstones of a larger theory of interreligious theology. But their points of reference differ. The first pair refers to the minimal *metaphysical* foundation, while the second pair demarcates the *practical* nature, the style or mode, of a theology undertaken interreligiously. Interreligious theology is still a rather new concept. It may turn out that it needs more than these four principles. But I doubt that it can do with fewer than these.

A Theological Credit of Trust

Let me recall that the use of the term "theology" in this context is not confined to the intellectual reflection within theistic religions but also comprises analogical efforts in nontheistic traditions.[1] Interreligious theology is possible only if it proceeds from the assumption that theologically relevant truth is not confined to one's own religious tradition but is also found in other religions. Interreligious theology is not based on the "art of mistrust" or a

---

[1] See above chapter 1.

"hermeneutics of suspicion" but on the "benefit of doubt," or, as Andreas Grünschloß called it, a "principle of charity."[2] The *first principle* of inter-religious theology is therefore a *theological credit of trust*. Such theological confidence is expressed in various religion-specific ways by means of a range of different possible justifications.

In Christianity this credit of trust is grounded in the assumption that revelation in the sense of divine self-communication is not limited to the people of the Judeo-Christian tradition. This assumption is well supported by a number of theological arguments that have been developed over the past decades in the Christian "theology of religions." As has been said before, the main argument is of a soteriological nature: God's mercy is impartial.[3] God, as stated in 1 Timothy 2:4, "wants all people to be saved and to come to the knowledge of the truth." If that "knowledge of the truth" which is indispensable for salvation is nothing but the knowledge of God, divine self-communication or revelation cannot be confined to Christianity. Both inclusivist and pluralist approaches in the Christian theology of religions endorse this argument. According to the medieval concept of theology, all theology is based on revelation, either on "natural revelation" or on "special revelation," that is, either on what can be known of God through reason alone on the basis of creation or on what can be known of God on the basis of special communication through the biblical prophets and through Jesus Christ. That is, if there was any truth at all in other religions, it was there because of "natural revelation."[4] On this premise, it made sense to look at nonbiblical religions only in terms of "natural theology," which was not seen as theology proper, but at best as a kind of preparation for it. Yet if Christians may justly assume that "special revelation" too is not confined to just one section of humanity, it becomes obligatory to base theological reflection on all possible testimonies of divine revelation.

In Judaism the confidence that theologically relevant truth is not confined to one's own tradition is based on the belief in the creator's universal care and covenant with all human beings. In Islam it is based on the Qur'ānic assertion that the just and merciful God has sent messengers to every people in the world (Sūrah 16:36, and more often), while no created medium of revelation, including the Qur'ān itself, can ever exhaust the truth of God (31:27; see also 18:109). In Mahāyāna Buddhism such confidence may be grounded in the work of the supranatural Bodhisattvas who, out of their all-encompassing compassion, are redeemingly active in and through other

---

[2]Grünschloß 1999, 299ff.

[3]See above chapter 2.

[4]For a typical example see Marcus Dods's *Four Lectures on Natural and Revealed Religion* (Dods 1887).

faiths. Ultimately, and for all forms of Buddhism, such confidence is rooted in the belief in the original purity of the human mind or in the universal presence of the Buddha-Nature. For in both versions this belief entails that at least in principle the liberating truth of the eternal Dharma can be experienced and discerned by all human beings. In Hinduism, the same function can be fulfilled by the belief in the presence of the Divine at the bottom of everybody's heart as their true self (*ātman*).[5] In Chinese religions the concept of *tian-dao*, the "Dao of Heaven" or "Divine Way" can play the same role if it is understood as the way of *all* humans, discernible by everybody through one's own heart or mind (心 *xin*).

Thus, the "theological credit of trust" requires that those religions that engage in interreligious theology presuppose the existence of an ultimate reality that is constitutively linked to the path of salvation/liberation/right-living as taught in their own tradition. It further implies that these religions assume that at least in some other religions there is a genuine access to this ultimate reality, a kind of knowledge that is sufficient for giving one's life the right orientation. Exclusivisms of all sorts are therefore ruled out by the principle of a theological credit of trust, because exclusivism is defined precisely by not granting that credit. This has been frequently pointed out in the discussion about the relationship between theology of religions and comparative theology. Comparative theology, as one way of doing inter-religious theology, would be impossible on the basis of the exclusivist assumption that there are no theologically relevant insights in other religions. As Paul Hedges says: "unless we have decided that other religions are not completely Satanic or deluded human errors (exclusivisms), then the very venture . . . is untenable."[6] Therefore, comparative theology is feasible only on the basis of either an inclusivist or pluralist approach.[7] This shows once again that the theology of religions and comparative theology cannot be regarded as totally separate or even antithetical as has been claimed by some proponents of comparative theology.

Thus, while the first principle implies that the religions presuppose the existence of an ultimate reality that is salvifically relevant, it does not imply that the religions have more or less the same understanding of ultimate reality. Nor does it imply that they have the same understanding of salvation or liberation. What it implies is that different concepts of ultimate reality are possibly compatible and that different concepts of salvation are capable of being reciprocally recognized as salvific according to the standards of

---

[5] For some voices from different religions on the idea of an interreligious theology see Vigil 2010.
[6] Hedges 2010, 53.
[7] See, for example, Hedges 2010, 53–54; Kiblinger 2010, 32; Drew 2014, 73–78; Bernhardt 2014, 24–28; Winkler 2014, 13–14. For further examples see Kiblinger 2010, 24–25.

the respective religions. This leads us to the second key principle, which is about the understanding and evaluation of differences.

The Unity of Reality

If a theological credit of trust can be justified in different ways within the different religious traditions, the fundamental task of interreligious theology is to discern and identify theologically relevant truth as it may be testified to in other religious traditions. This process is guided by the conviction that ultimately, all truth—wherever and in whatever form it might be found—must be compatible. This follows from the fundamental intuition of the unity of reality.[8] Reliance on the *unity of reality* can thus be taken as the *second principle* of interreligious theology.

As Abdolkarim Soroush rightly stated, this principle requires "of every truth-seeking researcher to try to resolve any inconsistencies in the truth table and to adjust the geometry of cognition."[9] In practice, the task of interreligious theology is therefore not merely to identify possible truth in other faiths but to investigate the compatibility of different beliefs, in particular if they seem to be contradictory. For what at first sight appears to be an irreconcilable contradiction may turn out to be compatible, depending on how the differences are interpreted. In that sense Wilfred Cantwell Smith recommends seeing apparent contradictions as an "invitation to synthesis":[10] "To insist on seeing conflict whenever one finds, in fundamentally differing systems, two statements of which a person would not make both within one of those systems or in a third, is unduly embattled, beleaguered."[11]

In this respect, the Jain principle of *anekāntavāda* ("non-one-sidedness"/"many-sidedness") may be of particular significance for any form of interreligious theology. The belief that all things are multirelational and interdependent has led the Jains to the assumption that each thing can be seen under a hardly comprehensible multiplicity of aspects. Given that the truth of any statement is always relative to the respective aspect, one may always expect that apparent contradictions could derive from a difference in aspect and might therefore ultimately dissolve in a higher synthesis. Within Jainism the idea was often used to substantiate their own superiority claim, in the sense that their teachings are based on the omniscience acquired by Mahāvīra in his enlightenment.[12] To make the idea fruitful for

---

[8]See Von Brück 1991. This publication is itself an early example of interreligious theology, or as Von Brück calls it, "dialogical theology."

[9]Soroush 2009, 146.

[10]Smith 1975, 160.

[11]Ibid.

[12]See Dundas 2002, 229–33; Long 2009, 117–39.

interreligious theology, I suggest giving it a different twist in stressing its hermeneutical potential. Religious doctrines are not merely confined to one particular aspect. Therefore they can be and need to be complemented by other doctrines reflecting other aspects, as the traditional understanding of the *anekāntavāda* theory seems to submit. The religious doctrines themselves are also many-sided. *Anekāntavāda* can thus be taken as a hint that religions are not fixated on just one possible interpretation of their own beliefs. The history of religions demonstrates that religions have a broad hermeneutical latitude when it comes to the auto-interpretation and permanent reinterpretation of their own doctrines. By taking into account this hermeneutical latitude, interreligious theology can point out under which "aspects," that is, under which interpretative conditions, apparently contradictory doctrines from different religions would become compatible and under which conditions oppositions might even harden.

The question of the eventual compatibility of seemingly contradictory beliefs is above all what makes interreligious theology attractive and theologically significant. A better understanding of different religious perspectives can lead not only to the identification of compatibility but also of complementarity. That is, religions can learn from each other if they grasp how something that is regarded as important within their own tradition has been developed in perhaps broader, more intense, or just different ways in another tradition. Insights from different religions can be experienced as mutually enriching precisely because such insights are different. And any new understanding that is gained by assuming perspectives different from one's own is not only enriching but will also be transformative. Interreligious theology is therefore a truly creative enterprise. As Hasan Askari once stated, it may lead to "unforeseen religious developments upon our planet."[13]

Proponents of a polycentric version of pluralism are keen on an understanding of interreligious dialogue and exchange as an opportunity to discover that differences may in fact be complementary and can trigger processes of reciprocal transformation. As I argued in the preceding chapter, this view is not confined to polycentric pluralism. Monocentric pluralists do not ignore differences. They too are interested in finding out to what extent interreligious differences may be seen as compatible and even complementary. In polycentric approaches, this happens when different concepts and experiences of ultimate reality are interpreted as different ultimates in the sense of different aspects of one complex ultimate reality. In monocentric approaches different concepts and experiences of the ultimate are construed as referring to different phenomenal realities, which are interlinked

---

[13] Askari 1991, 40.

inasmuch as they constitute different manifestations of one ultimate reality within the variegated complex of human diversity. The extent to which such interreligious differences are seen as either reflecting different aspects of the ultimate in a quasi-objective sense that abstracts from human experience or as different impressions left by a transcategorial and ineffable ultimate on a human mind, which is shaped by different categories and concepts, may vary. But the latter option would by no means entail that there is nothing to learn from the mutual exploration of these different impressions. On this version of religious pluralism the phenomenal manifestations of the ultimate will be seen as focal points crystallizing the multifaceted meaning that ultimate reality actually has for our understanding of human existence.

Although, in principle, the idea of a unity of reality can certainly be affirmed by exclusivists, inclusivists, and pluralists alike, exclusivists cannot acknowledge a unity of reality if this unity implies a unity of religiously different relations to the same ultimate reality (or the same complex ultimate reality). In conjunction with the first principle the second principle therefore restricts interreligious theology to inclusivist or pluralist approaches. Moreover, it reveals a difference between inclusivisms and pluralisms regarding their receptivity to the religious other or capability of interreligious learning. It would be clearly wrong to say that inclusivism has no room at all for interreligious learning. But compared to pluralism, the scope seems to be significantly smaller. The reason is that inclusivism tends to treat religious difference as a sign of inferiority. If another religion would be completely identical to one's own religion, the inclusivist could no longer claim any superiority for his or her own tradition. The idea of difference in equality is excluded by definition. Any significant difference between one's own and the other religion will therefore have to count as a sign of either the other's superiority or inferiority. The latter is what inclusivism usually assumes. Yet it is difficult to see how one could learn from a different religion if this difference is assessed as a sign of inferiority. Learning would be possible if difference is regarded either as a new variant of something already known or even more so if difference is seen as a positive qualitative difference. An inclusivist may acknowledge that there are certain limited areas in which other religions might be superior to one's own religion, so that it is indeed possible to learn something really new from them. However, lest these areas compromise the claimed superiority of one's own tradition, they need to be restricted in terms of their theological significance. This is markedly different from pluralism. Though pluralism also implies some restrictions in that the pluralist option excludes that another religion is essentially superior to one's own or even exclusively true (two possibilities that are, of course, also excluded on exclusivist or inclusivist premises), it is still more open to the idea of learning in relation to areas of central religious significance than inclusivists. A Christian inclusivist, for example, may expect to learn insights from other religions, which will deepen his or her understanding of the central role of Jesus Christ. But, contrary to a pluralist, he or she will not be open to learn insights that seriously question the central role of Christ or lead to its transformation.

To be clear, all these considerations apply to the kind of interreligious learning possible within the framework of either exclusivist, inclusivist, or pluralist approaches. They do not affect the basic possibility that proponents of all three approaches might arrive, through interreligious dialogue, at the insight that their approach was wrong. This most radical kind of learning is always an option, and all those religious pluralists who embarked on the adventure of interreligious encounter as exclusivists or inclusivists have gone through this experience.

The issue of interreligious learning is crucial for the project of interreligious theology. It therefore raises the question of whether a further principle might be necessary, which affirms the overall possibility of religious learning as such. I guess that this is not the case because the concept of theology itself already presupposes the idea of a possible deepening of one's faith, and hence of a learning process, by means of theological work. The real issue is therefore not the possibility of theological learning as such, that is, the possibility of growth in understanding in matters of religious insight, but the possibility of gaining new insights by learning from other religions. This, however, seems to be sufficiently warranted by the first two principles. Although the two principles of a theological credit of trust and the unity of reality thus sufficiently describe the possibility and the task of interreligious theology, two additional principles are needed that relate primarily to the *practice*, style, or mode of interreligious theology.

Tied to Interreligious Discourse

Edmund Chia, who served for many years as executive secretary of interreligious dialogue to the Federation of Asian Bishops' Conferences (FABC) has raised the important question about the location of interreligious theology: Are the beliefs of the different religions not too disparate to be articulated in a single, all-encompassing theology? If so, what does the "inter" in interreligious theology mean? Will the space of the "inter" become a no-man's-land so that interreligious or interfaith theology is a "theology that seems to belong to all but at the same time belongs to none"?[14] Having raised this question, Chia, who supports the idea of an interreligious theol-

---

[14]Chia 2008, 112.

ogy, provides what I think to be the right answer: *"Interfaith Theology* has to be done in an interfaith fashion."[15] This constitutes the *third principle* of interreligious theology: it needs to be practiced interreligiously; it is *tied to the interreligious discourse.*

This principle does not imply that all future books in the field of interreligious theology have to be written in interreligious co-authorship, or that all theological reflection in that field has to be done by interreligious teams. Individuals will continue to write from the particular perspective of their own religious tradition and will still be able to make important contributions to interreligious theology. However, such individual contributions will always be dedicated to the overarching goal of integrating different perspectives. This does not put them in a theological or religious no-man's-land, but it does mean that these theologians deliberately cross religious borders. As Smith puts it, interreligious theology will still be recognizably Christian, Muslim, Buddhist, etc., but at the same time, it will be more: it will be, in his words, "Christian plus . . . ," "Muslim plus . . . ," "Buddhist plus. . . ."[16] This "plus" refers to the effort of mediating between the insights of one's own tradition and those derived from other religious perspectives.

The principle that interreligious theology needs to be practiced interreligiously implies mutuality. As indicated in the preceding chapter, it would be insufficient to draw on other religious traditions solely for the purpose of deepening the understanding of one's own faith.[17] As Wilfred Cantwell Smith argued in 1959, it is no longer possible to write books about another religion *solely* for one's own religious community, that is, as if no one else would take any notice of them. Such books will increasingly be read also by members of other religions, especially of those religions that are treated in such works.[18] This is presumably even more true if books would be written with the explicit aim of drawing on other religions in order to learn from them. The awareness that whatever one writes about the religious other could and probably would also be read by the religious other needs to have its impact on the writing itself. Any contribution to interreligious theology should be made in the implicit or explicit expectation of receiving also a response from other faiths. And increasingly they should be written with the intention of inviting such responses. This applies to any narrowly circumscribed theological questions treated in a comparative interreligious fashion as much as to large-scale theological theories about religious diversity. As I have argued before: Such a large-scale theory as religious pluralism will

---

[15]Ibid., 115.
[16]Smith [1981] 1989, 125.
[17]See chapter 8.
[18]See Smith 1959, 40–41.

find its confirmation only within the framework of an interreligious theology in the course of which theologians from various religious traditions enter into a discourse about the reciprocal acceptability of their tradition-specific versions of pluralism.[19]

The principle of doing interreligious theology interreligiously has another important implication, which concerns the interleaving of bilateral and multilateral theological discourses. For example, imagine that Christian theologians in dialogue with Hindus or Buddhists would tend to reinterpret the concept of divine incarnation in a way that allows for multiple incarnations, while other Christian theologians engaged in dialogue with Jews and Muslims would tend to downplay the whole concept of incarnation. The overall task of seeking compatibility, as expressed in the second principle, would then require further dialogical efforts in order to combine and reconnect those two divergent developments in Christological reflection. And from this perspective, it will be highly relevant to consider and involve what is said and thought in theological dialogues between, for example, Hindus and Jews or Buddhists and Muslims. That is, within the large field of interreligious theology any bilateral theological reflections are interwoven with multilateral developments. Although each participant in interreligious theology will still be located within a specific religious tradition, his or her interreligious reflections are to some extent influenced by some other interreligious reflections in which he or she is not actively involved, but which nevertheless need one's close attention.

An Open Process

No individual theologian will ever be able to synthesize all religious perspectives. It will therefore be impossible for any single person to produce something like a completed interreligious theology. Systematic accounts of interreligious theology will certainly be produced. However, they will never conclude the work of interreligious theology but rather be welcomed as further contributions to the ongoing process of interreligious theological reflection and discourse. Interreligious theology is therefore not only a dialogical and colloquial but also an unfinished process. Otherwise, its results would be not more than the dogmatics of a newly emerging syncretistic religion. I do not see any problems with syncretism as such. All great religions are, after all, the product of syncretistic processes.[20] But any new syncretistic religion that may arise in the future will itself need to be integrated into

---

[19]See chapter 8,
[20]See Schmidt-Leukel 2009, 67–89.

the ongoing process of interreligious theology and therefore cannot constitute its final goal. The process of integrating different perspectives, the acceptance of the invitation to synthesis, remains inevitably incomplete and open-ended. This does not devalue the process of interreligious theology. Natural science, I suggest, is also essentially incomplete. It is hard to imagine that it would ever achieve a state where all scientific questions are answered. Yet this incompleteness of science in no way devalues the idea of scientific progress. To quote Michael von Brück, intercultural theology takes place as an "interreligious process of truth-seeking," that, on the one hand, "allows for concrete commitment," while, on the other hand, it "never comes to a stand-still."[21] This *processual, essentially incomplete nature* of interreligious theology constitutes its *fourth principle.*

The fourth principle implies that interreligious theology is not so much a specific subject area of theology, but it has the potential of developing into the style or mode of all future theology in whatever religion. Slowly but increasingly it may become just natural that theological studies written by Jews, Christians, and Muslims, and comparable studies written by Hindus, Buddhists, or Confucians, touch on other faiths and whenever this suggests itself, also actively draw on them. In addition, there will be a growing number of future theological works that purposely and directly employ comparative theological thinking in their attempts to elucidate perennial questions of human life. Surely we will also see a rise in works jointly composed by authors from different religious backgrounds who put the principle of doing interreligious theology interreligiously immediately and visibly into practice. If theology wants to be taken seriously on a global level, it can simply no longer afford to neglect the contributions that relate to the same subject area but come from other religious traditions. Once more, interreligious theology is very likely to shape, in the long run, the style of all theology.

METHODOLOGICAL ISSUES

Having established the broad metaphysical and practical framework of interreligious theology by means of these four key principles, I would like to proceed to some of the methodological issues connected to this largely uncharted terrain. I will do so once more in four points, arguing that methodologically interreligious theology should be (1) *perspectival,* (2) *imaginative,* (3) *comparative,* and (4) *constructive.*

---

[21]Von Brück 1992, 261.

Perspectival: Facing the Confessional Dimension

On my understanding—following in the footsteps of Wilfred Cantwell Smith—interreligious theology is *perspectival* but in the sense of integrating several perspectives. How does this translate into methodology? First of all, it implies that, in contrast to the phenomenological school of comparative religion, the interreligious theologian does not try to bracket his or her personal religious convictions. On the contrary, as Keith Ward emphasized in his Gifford Lectures of 1993–94, the interreligious theologian will be fully aware that "there is no neutral vantage-point, without any beliefs at all, from which a dispassionate judgement might be made."[22] He or she will "accept that one stands within a given tradition and admit that all one's judgements will be made from that standpoint."[23] But this does not imply seeing "a tradition as an unchanging, fixed set of irreformable beliefs."[24] The interreligious theologian will therefore be "prepared to revise beliefs if and when it comes to seem necessary."[25]

These remarks by Keith Ward have triggered considerable debate about the question of the extent to which interreligious theologians are bound by the confessional limits set by their religious affiliation. In particular Roman Catholic theologians such as Catherine Cornille and James Fredericks have described the task of the interreligious theologian, or "comparative theologian" as they prefer to say, as keeping the right balance between openness to the religious other and commitment to one's own religious community.[26] This may easily mean that any kind of possible learning process is, right from the start, thoroughly restricted or even prevented by preset doctrinal standards considered sacrosanct. Yet the interreligious theologian must not ignore the crucial role that the confessional stance plays in all the religions. Religious beliefs are not merely expressions of intellectual convictions but also of confessional commitments, that is, they have not only cognitive content but, as emphasized by Klaus von Stosch, "express values and attitudes of religious believers."[27] Interreligious theology differs from intercultural philosophy in not losing sight of this confessional dimension.

If interreligious theology stays aware of its perspectival nature and bears in mind the confessional tinge of any religious perspective, does that mean that the idea of a *global* interreligious theology is ultimately impossible? This has indeed been suggested but for different reasons. One line

---

[22]Ward 1994, 42.
[23]Ibid.
[24]Ibid., 47.
[25]Ibid., 48.
[26]See Fredericks 1999, 169; Cornille 2008, 84.
[27]Von Stosch 2014, 33.

of argument, which we may label "postliberal," holds that it is perfectly fine to acknowledge and accept the perspectival nature of all religious or nonreligious worldviews but that it is nevertheless legitimate to affirm the superiority of one particular perspective,[28] which is, of course, the one represented by one's own creed. This argument takes for granted that the perspective of another religion is seriously limited, that it lacks "the kind and degree of intimacy with what it speaks of as necessarily possessed by" one's own religion.[29] On this premise, interreligious theology is possible only, if at all, in terms of a highly asymmetric relationship: What one may learn from other religions, says Paul Griffiths, will at best go "into the margins of the sacred page,"[30] which according to Griffiths is in the sole custody of one's own faith.

A different type of argument holds that no single perspective is able to integrate all other perspectives. From this, comparative theologians such as von Stosch conclude that the aim cannot be "a global theology that integrates as many world views as possible."[31] This objection, however, is clearly a non sequitur. If one cannot integrate *all* other perspectives, one could still aim at integrating as many other perspectives as possible. There is even a kind of epistemological duty to do so if one is obliged to approach the truth as closely as one can. The real challenge for an interreligious theology arises not from the question of how many other perspectives one may be able to understand, but from the peculiar nature of religious perspectives, that is, from the insight into the close interweaving of religious beliefs with confessional stances. What does it mean to integrate different perspectives within one's own, if each perspective is inseparably linked with a confessional attitude? Can one integrate different confessions, different religious commitments? Will the interreligious theologian have to serve more than one master? The answer to this challenge takes us to the next methodological point.

Imaginative: Seeing through the Eyes of the Other

It was Raimon Panikkar who strongly defended the view that understanding another religion is possible only if one is convinced of its truth: "I can never understand his position as he does—and this is the only real under-

---

[28]See the remark in Lindbeck 1984, 50: "It could be . . . that there is only one religion which has the concepts and categories that enable it to refer to the religious object, i.e. to whatever in fact is more important than everything else in the universe." Lindbeck calls this the "categorical form of the claim to unsurpassability" (ibid.).

[29]Griffiths 2014, 41.

[30]Ibid., 45.

[31]Von Stosch 2014, 34. Similarly Cornille 2014, 16.

standing between people—unless I share his view."[32] This would involve that the integration of more than one religious perspective amounts to a multireligious allegiance, as indeed Raimon Panikkar confessed of himself.[33] Yet Panikkar's argument is faulty. If understanding would inevitably involve belief in the truth of what one understands, a justified rejection of any view would become impossible. For I can justly reject a view only if I have understood it. In defending his own theory of understanding, Panikkar definitely rejects the opposite position. That is, he rejects the position that understanding a view is possible without sharing it. But how can Panikkar legitimately reject this position, if, according to his own premise, he would not have understood it? Hence, Panikkar's position becomes indefensible. Panikkar exaggerates a point, which is in fact important if presented in a more sober way. Doing so will provide an answer to the question of how it is possible to understand the confessional dimension of another religious perspective without necessarily sharing it.

This more sober solution has been suggested by Wilfred Cantwell Smith. According to Smith, understanding implies that one understands the *reasons* that motivate the other in his or her belief. It means to put oneself imaginatively into the other's shoes. "To understand any human behaviour, any human feeling, any human hope or vision, is to recognize that if you had been in that situation, you would have had that particular act or quality or value-judgement as one of your options."[34] Interreligious theology therefore needs to be *imaginative* in this sense. But this alone does not yet solve our problem. For within the multireligious setting of our age, putting oneself in the other's shoes is by no means only a hypothetical option. If understanding the other means to understand the reasons behind his or her beliefs, the immediate question will be whether I have any reason to reject or share his or her reasons. And this brings back the issue of multireligious allegiance.

At this point it is important to realize that the confessional dimension of religious beliefs is usually not based on only one reason but on several. That is, religious creeds are affirmed because of various causes and reasons. This insight opens up, at least in theory, the possibility of a partial sharing. That is, one may find oneself in agreement with one or some of the reasons that sustain the other's commitment, so that one can share to some extent in the confessional dimension. What would this imply for the religious identity of the interreligious theologian? This question takes us from the imaginative to the comparative aspect of interreligious methodology.

---

[32]Panikkar 1978, 9.

[33]"I 'left' as a Christian, I 'found' myself a Hindu and I 'return' a Buddhist, without having ceased to be a Christian." Ibid., 2.

[34]Smith 1997, 133–34.

Comparative: Seeking Reciprocal Illumination

More than once, Wilfred Cantwell Smith expressed the imaginative aspect of interreligious theology by stating that in order "to understand Buddhists . . . we must not look at something called Buddhism but at the world, so far as possible, through Buddhist eyes."[35] It will take long and sustained studies before one might become able to look at the world through the eyes of one's religious neighbor. But once one begins doing so, one of the things one is likely to see will be one's own religious tradition. This may be a painful but at the same time wholesome experience. I think that, after World War II, Christian theology has benefited tremendously from looking at Christianity through Jewish eyes. To what extent has Christian theology started to look at Christianity through Muslim eyes, Hindu eyes, or Buddhist eyes, for example? Analogously this also applies to the self-perception and partner-perception of all other religions. Have Buddhists begun to look at Buddhism through Hindu eyes or vice versa?

The effort of assuming reciprocal perspectives characterizes the *comparative* work as it needs to be done in interreligious theology. Interreligious theology is not undertaking the purportedly neutral and distanced comparison attempted by the phenomenological school.[36] It is rather a way of looking at one's own tradition through the eyes of another tradition and of helping others in their attempts to look at their tradition through our own eyes. In his classic *The Way of All the Earth*, John Dunne aptly described this shift in perspectives as the process of "passing over" and "coming back."[37]

If in the context of a global multireligious colloquium this shift of perspectives is carried out by all participants and with mutual assistance, interreligious comparison or comparative theology carries the promise of what Arvind Sharma recently called "reciprocal illumination."[38] Our self-understanding and the understanding of our own religious tradition may change if it is seen in the light of the religious other. This is what interreligious theology is hoping for. This is the expectation that governs and guides its comparative investigations. But it is reciprocal, not one-sided illumination.

---

[35]Smith [1981] 1989, 82. Similarly Smith 1978, 138.

[36]Over the past decade, the phenomenological method has become the subject of severe criticism. One objection refers to its alleged "neutrality" (see for example Panikkar 1978, 39–52; Heelas 1978). The difference between interreligious theology and the phenomenological school can be seen by comparing the treatment of the Prophet, the Son, and the Buddha in the subsequent chapters with the more recent phenomenological comparison of "Buddha, Jesus and Muḥammad" in Gwynne 2014. For further suggestions of how phenomenology could be brought back in a transformed way see below (chapter 14) and Schmidt-Leukel and Nehring 2016.

[37]Dunne 1972, ix.

[38]A. Sharma 2005.

Inasmuch as reciprocal illumination brings about changes in religious understanding, religion itself is transformed. A change in self-understanding is at the same time a transformation of the self. Changes in the understanding of our religious traditions may contribute to a historical process in which these traditions themselves will change. This is why interreligious theology is also creative, constructive, or transformative.

Constructive: Mutual Transformation

The idea that genuine interreligious dialogue will necessarily lead to the transformation of the dialogue partners has often been affirmed.[39] Leonard Swidler, in his famous "Decalogue for Dialogue," established as the first rule: "The primary purpose of dialogue is to learn, that is, to change and grow in the perception and understanding of reality and then to act accordingly."[40]

So far, however, only little reflection has been done about what kind of transformation and growth is meant and how transformation and growth would be brought about. One way is certainly the revision of traditional prejudices and misrepresentations of the religious other inasmuch as these have become part of one's own tradition. Traditional Christian images of Judaism and Islam are as much examples of this as traditional Buddhist images of Hinduism. Another, far more controversial, step would be the revision of particular traditional beliefs. This too is something that may become necessary in the light of what one learns from other faiths. Presumably such revisions may often take the form of a reinterpretation or reconstruction. Although religions tend to deny that such changes are possible, the history of religions testifies that religions did in fact revise their understanding of certain doctrines in order to adapt them to what they were learning from others, although this usually happened more or less unconsciously and only gradually over a longer period of time. One such example is the Buddhist reconstruction of the doctrine of Buddha Nature under Daoist influence. As a result, the Buddhist concept of Buddha Nature began to resemble strongly the upanishadic concept of the Self (*ātman*, in conjunction with *brahman*), which once had been a favorite target of anti-Hindu Buddhist polemics.[41] We may assume that such processes will take place more often, faster, and, in particular, more consciously within the emerging interreligious theology. Currently one of the biggest obstacles to

---

[39]E.g., Cobb 1999, 44–48; Abe 1995, 5.

[40]Swidler 1990.

[41]See Park 2012. The Chinese *Buddha Nature Treatise* (*Fo hsing lun*), for example, could state: "It is in accordance with the principle of Tao (*tao li* 道理) that all sentient beings aboriginally possess (*pen yu*) pure-Buddha-nature." Quoted in King 1997, 184.

the idea of conscious interreligious borrowing seems to be the widespread fear of syncretism. Yet this fear ignores the syncretistic nature of all major religious traditions: They originated from and further developed under the influence of various other religions.[42]

What then will be the ultimate objective of interreligious learning? Will interreligious theology lead us to a better understanding of ultimate reality itself? Will the reconstruction and reinterpretation of our beliefs under the influence of other religions lead us to a more adequate way of speaking about ultimate reality? The answer depends on how interreligious theologians from different religious backgrounds will position themselves to the strong apophatic tendencies within their respective traditions. If they are optimistic about the human mind's capacity to acquire a conceptual understanding of the ultimate, the answer will be affirmative. If not, the answer will be ambiguous: On the one hand, we will not learn more about the ultimate itself but less. The widespread apophatic traditions of different religions will mutually reinforce the conviction of the transcategorial nature of the ultimate. On the other hand, we will better understand the rich variety in which the human experience of ultimate divine reality has provided meaning to the understanding of human life. In short, we will learn less about the ultimate but more about "faith in its many forms." So once again I find myself in fundamental agreement with Wilfred Cantwell Smith's vision that the end of interreligious theology is to give a new and better expression to faith, the "faith of all of us."

Having dealt with the rationale and methodology of interreligious theology, I will now enter its practice. That is, the subsequent chapters will be an exercise in interreligious theology. I will focus on those three religions that explicitly "claim to have a message for the whole of humanity."[43] Every religion, of course, assumes that their fundamental beliefs are true and as such are universally valid. But this is not the same as claiming globality for one's message. The latter applies clearly to Buddhism, Christianity, and Islam.

In focusing on these three religions I will first concentrate on the confessional dimension within each one of them, a dimension finding its expression in the religious titles they give to their key figures: Muḥammad, the "Prophet"; Jesus, the "Son of God"; and Gautama, the "Buddha." In line with my third principle, this exercise in interreligious theology will not be purely speculative but will follow closely the actual developments in interfaith dialogue. I will then turn to a question that marks one of the most significant metaphysical differences in the religions' concepts of the

---

[42]See Schmidt-Leukel 2009, 67–89; Ruparell 2013.
[43]Nasr 1999, 157.

ultimate, the question of whether, and if so in which sense, ultimate reality could or should be understood as the creator of the world. This question can and actually should be treated in relation to a number of different religious traditions. I will concentrate on the Buddhist rejection and the Christian affirmation of a divine creator, hoping that what can be said here will also have some significance for a theological comparison of further theistic and nontheistic religions.

10

The Prophet and the Son

Taken together, Muslims and Christians make up more than half of humanity.[1] The question of how they relate to each other is thus by no means a marginal one. In 2007, *A Common Word Between Us and You,* the most important statement so far on Muslim-Christian relations from the Muslim side, was drafted and initially signed by 138 Muslim leaders from all over the world and various branches of Islam.[2] One of the major figures in the production of this document was Prince Ghazi bin Muḥammad of Jordan. On the motivation behind this initiative Prince Ghazi says:

> We wanted—and want—to avoid a greater worldwide conflict between Muslims and the West. . . . We wanted to stop the drumbeat of what we feared was a growing popular consensus (on both sides) for worldwide (and thus cataclysmic and perhaps apocalyptic) Muslim-Christian *jihad*/crusade.[3]

Given the long history of tension and conflict between Islam and Christianity, the apocalyptic scenario invoked by Prince Ghazi's statement is not completely unlikely. In past and present the political clashes between Christian nations and Muslim nations were and are often interwoven with religious antagonism. Muslim-Christian relations are therefore a prime example of Hans Küng's dictum that there will be no peace among the religions without a serious dialogue between them.[4]

If it is serious, interfaith dialogue will include those issues that are at the center of religious controversy. The vision of an interreligious theology gets particularly demanding and particularly important when it takes the

---

[1] Usually Christians are numbered as about 32 percent and Muslims as 23 percent of the world's population. See, for example, http://www.pewforum.org/2012/12/18/global-religious-landscape-exec/.

[2] For the list of the initial signatories see http://www.acommonword.com/signatories/.

[3] Ghazi 2010a, 8–9.

[4] See above chapter 1.

form of Muslims and Christians jointly theologizing about those questions of faith that set them apart. Such questions find their focus in the reciprocal understanding and assessment of their key figures, Muḥammad and Jesus, or better in the affirmation and veneration of Muḥammad as the Final Prophet and of Jesus as the Son of God. These predicates are largely understood as mutually exclusive. Given the concept of interreligious theology presented in the preceding chapter, the task will be to find out whether what appears to be an outright contradiction can nevertheless be understood as compatible.[5] This does not mean that there are no genuine contradictions. My argument is rather that there exists a considerable hermeneutical latitude on both sides in how to interpret the predicates "the Prophet" and "the Son." Among the range of possible and legitimate interpretations, we can discern some which are indeed complementary instead of contradictory. A crucial task will be to identify the reasons behind the incompatible and the compatible interpretations and ask to what extent the latter can be shared interreligiously. Thus following Wilfred Cantwell Smith, I take contradictions as an "invitation to synthesis."[6] Such synthesis would still involve challenges on both sides. Yet this is exactly what accounts for the creative or constructive element in interreligious theology.

At first sight, the opposition between Islam and Christianity seems to be undisputable and irreconcilable: Christians claim that Christ is the Son of God, whereas Muslims claim that God has no son. Muslims claim that Muḥammad is God's final prophet, whereas Christians claim that Muḥammad is a false prophet. Various other oppositions depend on these two, most prominently the Islamic critique of the Christian scriptures as deliberate corruptions of the original revelation, and the Christian accusation that the Qur'ān is merely the product of delusion and deceit. In what follows I first deal with the Islamic critique of the "Son" and then with the Christian critique of the "Prophet." In both cases, I identify what I consider to be legitimate points behind the criticism and will move on to an understanding that is able to cope with the criticism and may lead to a synthesis.

THE SON

The Critique of "the Son"

As is well known, the Qur'ān does not reject Jesus. What it emphatically rejects is his designation as the "Son of God." In Sūrah 9:30–31, we read:

---

[5]See chapter 9.
[6]See also ibid.

The Jews call 'Uzayr[7] a son
Of God, and the Christians
Call Christ the Son of God.
That is saying from their mouth;
(In this) they but imitate
What the Unbelievers of old
Used to say. Allah's curse
Be on them: how they are deluded
Away from the Truth!
They take their priests
And their anchorites to be
Their lords in derogation of Allah,
And (they take as their Lord)
Christ, the son of Mary;
Yet they were commanded
To worship but One God:
There is no god but He.
Praise and glory to Him:
(Far is He) from having
The partners they associate
(With Him).[8]

These two verses contain the two major Islamic objections against the designation of Jesus as *a* or *the* "Son of God": First, calling a human being "Son of God" is seen as an unacceptable deification. No created being should be put in the rank of God. Doing so is condemned as an act of idolatry, that is, it misses the transcendent nature of God. Second, the title "Son of God" suggests that there could be more than one God and thus conveys polytheism. Therefore, the association of a created being with the creator not only neglects divine transcendence; it also inhibits the recognition of God's uniqueness and oneness.

It is essential to recognize the inner logic behind these two objections. Throughout the Qur'ān God is praised as the one who is highly exalted above everything else, as the one to whom nothing can be equated (42:11; 112:4). This is an expression of God's unequaled, absolute transcendence. Absolute transcendence, however, implies that there can be only one such reality, only one who can truly be called "God." For, if there were two or more gods, two or more beings of equally divine status, the word "God" would no longer signify a reality that exceeds everything else. Hence the

---

[7]The biblical figure of Ezra.
[8]'Alī 1999, 446–47.

affirmation of God's uniqueness or oneness functions as an affirmation of God's transcendence, of God's status as that "greater than which nothing can be conceived."[9] To quote Hasan Askari: "'One' is not number but a form of awareness of God's Transcendence."[10] Idolatry and polytheism are both rejected because they miss God's transcendent nature and thereby God as such.

The fundamental critique that the predicate "Son of God" distorts and obscures divine oneness and transcendence, and hence the truly divine nature of God, is significantly enhanced by the Muslim concern that "sonship" might be taken in a literal, biological sense. When the Qur'ān proclaims about God, "He begetteth not, nor is he begotten" (112:3), the Hadith, and commentarial literature have frequently taken this as a rejection of the idea, widespread in the ancient Greek world, that God would beget a child together with a female human consort.[11] In contrast, the Qur'ān declares that God has not begotten Jesus, but that Jesus was miraculously created by the breath of God's spirit in the womb of the *virgin* Mary.[12]

The verses from Sūrah 9, quoted above, show clearly that the critique of the title "Son of God" is not directed exclusively against Christianity. It is rather directed against idolatry and polytheism as larger religious phenomena. The accusation against Christians is that in calling Jesus the "Son of God," "they but imitate what the unbelievers of old used to say." That is, they are accused of falling back into a religious attitude that misses God's true nature.[13] This suspicion is further substantiated by the predicate's proximity to classical ideas of divinely begotten demigods.

At this point it is crucial to note that a large majority of Christians shares the intention behind this Qur'ānic critique. Christians are likewise keen on maintaining God's transcendence and oneness, and Christians too are therefore opposed to idolatry and polytheism. That is, from a Christian perspective, the Qur'ānic critique can be accepted as legitimate insofar as it tries to preserve an understanding of God that is shared by Christians and inasmuch as it hits such possible concepts of "sonship" that would indeed distort the true nature of God.

In the long history of Christian-Muslim debates, one of those who un-ambiguously affirmed this consensus in motivation was Nicholas of Cusa (1401–64). According to Cusanus, Christians fully affirm God's absolute transcendence. Together with the Muslims, says Cusanus, Christians reject the idea that there could be several gods, because each among several gods

---

[9]This is the famous circumscription of God used by Anselm of Canterbury in his *Proslogion*, chap. 2.

[10]Askari 1991, 43.

[11]See Ayoub 2007, 117–33.

[12]Qur'ān 3:45–48; 21:90–91; 66:12.

[13]See also Ayoub 2007, 125.

would lack "supreme glory." Further, Christians do not recommend that a created being is worshiped alongside God or in the place of God, and they certainly reject an understanding of "sonship" in any literal, biological sense.[14] Cusanus therefore concludes that if the Trinity is interpreted in that particular way in which it appears in the Muslim, and Jewish, critique, its rejection is not only completely legitimate, but even obligatory. If properly understood, Cusanus holds, the doctrine of the Trinity is as much opposed to a plurality and association of gods as is Islam.[15] Cusanus's stance is clear evidence that it is possible for Christians to recognize the legitimate concerns in the Muslim critique of the predicate "Son of God" and to share the motivation behind such criticism. But how is it possible to understand the concepts of "sonship" and "trinity" in a way that escapes such criticism?

Understanding "the Son"

To begin with, there is no such thing as *the* Christian understanding of Jesus or the Trinity. In fact there are many. Already within the New Testament we find a number of different Christologies, and over the first five centuries of Christendom, Christological disputes were rampant, being fought out fiercely and at times violently.[16] Although the consensus formulae that emerged from the major ecumenical councils acquired confessional status for the majority of Christianity, they never found full endorsement by all Christians. Even among those who accepted the official Christological *Sprachregelung* of the ecumenical councils, the range of possible interpretations and theological debates about the correct understanding of the doctrinal formulae remained considerable. In modernity, Christology has taken a new direction insofar as it became increasingly dominated by a historical perspective seeking to reconstruct how and under what kind of impact the Christological doctrines had emerged. Seen from a historical perspective, the Council of Chalcedon was indisputably wrong when it claimed that its statement about the relation between the human and divine nature of Jesus is what "Jesus Christ Himself . . . taught us about Him."[17] In fact the Chalcedonian Christology does not *quote* the teaching or self-understanding of

---

[14]See Nicolaus Cusanus, *Cribatio Alkorani.* For a summary of his arguments see Volf 2011, 50–54.

[15]Nicolaus Cusanus, *De pace fidei* 26: ". . . ac quod admission trinitatis est negare deorum pluralitatem et consocialitatem. . . . Modo autem quo negant Arabes et Judaei trinitatem, certe ab omnibus negari debet." See Kues 2002, 74, 76. "that to confess the Trinity is to deny a plurality, and an association, of gods . . . in the manner in which Arabs and Jews deny the Trinity, assuredly it ought to be denied by all." Translation in Hopkins 1994, 646–47.

[16]I am not only referring to events like the violent clashes accompanying the synod of Ephesus in 449 but to the long theological and military confrontation between the followers of Arius and his opponents.

[17]Kelly 1977, 340.

Jesus but *interprets* the meaning of Jesus for his followers after centuries of intensive theological struggle.

There is consensus among biblical scholars that Jesus, to all historical probability, did not consider himself as the incarnation of the second person of a Trinitarian God. Nowhere did Jesus teach a Trinitarian doctrine. As one would expect from a pious Jewish rabbi, he believed in one God and strictly refused to be equated with God. He rejected the address "good master" with the words "No one is good but God alone" (Mk 10:18). Jesus saw himself as a divinely authorized messenger who proclaimed the beginning of the "kingdom" of God, that is, of God's merciful rule. Hence, it was most natural for his contemporaries to see Jesus as a prophet[18] and this, although not entirely sure, may also reflect his own self-understanding. According to Ed Sanders, Jesus can be called a "prophet" in the sense that he felt commissioned directly by God.[19]

Although it is highly unlikely that Jesus spoke of himself as "Son of God," the title is used in the New Testament but not yet in the later sense of referring to the second person of a divine Trinity. Nor is the New Testament usage based on the birth narratives with their idea of a virginal conception. The concept of literal "sonship" in the sense of Greek demigods was unacceptable to Jews, although later on it may have been understood along those lines by Greek converts to Christianity. A metaphorical reading of "sonship," however, was quite common within a Jewish context.[20] In the New Testament, the title "Son of God" may reflect in particular Jesus' confidence of standing in a close relationship to God whom he addressed as "father." In the Lord's Prayer Jesus taught his followers to do the same. For Paul "all who are led by the Spirit of God are Sons of God" (Rom 8:14). And this, of course, is what Jesus' followers believed about him: that Jesus indeed led his life under the inspiration of God's spirit, that Jesus—like a good son—fulfilled the will of God. It is this aspect of "sonship," not the virgin birth, which leads us to a more meaningful understanding of the concept of incarnation. Within the context of Muslim-Christian dialogue, this insight reveals that the narrative of the virgin birth plays a different role in the Qur'ān and the New Testament. While in the New Testament it is inclined to lead away from the perception of Jesus as a true human being, turning him into a demigod, it is told in the Qur'ān in order to reject any idea of a demigod but affirm his status as a created human being.

Jesus understood the "kingdom" that he proclaimed as the rule of a merciful God. God's kingdom comes, that is, God's rule becomes real and

---

[18]See Lk 7:16; 24:19; Mt 21:46; Acts 3:23; 7:37; Mk 6:4. See also Schreiber 2015, 56.
[19]Sanders 1995, 238–39.
[20]See ibid., 243–46.

efficient, to the extent that people fulfill God's good will. This, as Geza Vermes has held, presumably constitutes the inner link between the two lines of the Lord's Prayer: "Thy kingdom come. Thy will be done on earth as in heaven." Vermes comments: "It is in the surrender of the self to God's will that his sovereignty is realized on earth."[21] This is fully in line with the Muslim understanding that *islām*, meaning surrender to God, is the essence of religion.[22] On Jesus' understanding, God's will is marked by God's boundless mercy: the mercy of the one who gives the light of the sun and the water of the rain, that is, the two requirements of biological life, indiscriminately to the righteous and the unrighteous (Mt 5:43–48). Being perfect like God therefore implies imitating God's indiscriminate benevolence.[23] This is apparently how Jesus interpreted his own words and deeds: as imitation of divine mercy, as the obedience of the son who does the will of his good father. "The kind of perfection he had in mind," says E. P. Sanders, "was . . . the perfection of mercy and humility." And Jesus "displayed this by being gentle and loving towards others, including sinners."[24] This attitude makes Jesus, in the eyes of his followers, an example of what it means to live under God's rule. Jesus represents and incorporates God's good rule. One knows what the kingdom of God looks like if one looks at Jesus. And thereby one sees, in Jesus, how God relates to us.

This idea gives Jesus a twofold meaning. On the one hand, Jesus is the representation of the true human being, the model of how and what the creator wants humans to be like, the prime example of a life led by the spirit. This makes Jesus the new and true Adam. As the new Adam, he should not remain unique but become the firstborn among many brothers and sisters (Rom 8:29). On the other hand, Jesus is at the same time the true representation of God's will, the concrete embodiment of God's kingdom and thereby the manifestation or revelation of God's mercy or love. As it is summarized in the First Letter of John: It is the love of God that has been revealed to us through Jesus (1 Jn 4:7–12). From this perspective it makes sense if the prologue in the Gospel of John calls Jesus the "Word of God," in Greek the *logos*, that has become flesh (Jn 1:14). This does not refer to the idea of a supernatural birth but to the life of a human person which reflects the glory, grace, and truth of God. It refers to the life of the one who makes God known (Jn 1:18). In this sense it can be said that in seeing Jesus one sees the father (Jn 14:9), while the father is and remains greater than Jesus (Jn 14:28). Colossians 1:15 has expressed this in the paradoxical but highly appropriate formulation of

---

[21]Vermes 1981, 25.
[22]Qur'ān 3:19. See also chapter 4.
[23]See Vermes 1993, 157ff., 200ff.
[24]Sanders 1995, 204.

Jesus as "the image of the invisible God." This phrase confirms that God, being "invisible," cannot and must not be put into any image. Yet for what can be known of God's meaning for us through God's revelation within the human sphere, Jesus is indeed a fitting, beautiful, and challenging image.

If incarnational thinking is understood along those lines, it leaves room for the Chalcedonian notion of two natures. This notion must be understood strictly as referring to Jesus' revelatory role. The concept of Jesus as the image of the invisible God can be expressed in contemporary language by saying that Jesus is a symbol of God. As Roger Haight[25] pointed out, every symbol has in a sense two natures: the nature of the symbol itself and the nature of that which the symbol stands for. Without the latter a symbol would cease to function as a symbol. "A symbol is that through which something else is made present and known."[26] Applying this to Jesus implies that Jesus as a finite and genuine human being reveals in a symbolic manner a reality that is infinitely different from him, for "God is infinitely other than any finite object."[27] The divine and human nature are thus dialectically related: "Since God is both present to and transcendent of any finite symbol, the symbol both makes God present and points away from itself to a God who is other than itself."[28] The ontological possibility of such symbolic mediation or revelation of God is grounded in the conviction that "God's infinite transcendence is such that God is also immanent to all things that God holds in existence by creation."[29] Haight's understanding of incarnation as a function of revelation and as grounded in creation explicitly allows for the possibility that "there will be other historical mediations."[30]

Toward a Synthesis

To what extent would an understanding of the predicate "Son of God" along such lines be compatible with a Qur'ānic perspective? The Qur'ān repeatedly affirms Jesus as a divine prophet. In this respect there is a fundamental agreement between Qur'ānic Christology and the earliest form of Christian Christology, presumably even with Jesus' self-understanding. The Qur'ān speaks of Jesus not only as a prophet but also as a "servant of God." Although the relation between a servant and his master is surely different from the relation of a son to his father, there is nevertheless an important correspondence inasmuch as the New Testament presents Jesus

---

[25]Haight 1999. See also chapter 2.
[26]Haight 1992, 263.
[27]Ibid.
[28]Ibid.
[29]Ibid.
[30]Ibid., 281. See also Haight 2005, 164.

as the good son who, like a servant, is obedient and does what the father wants him to do. Mahmoud Ayoub has pointed out that there is a tradition in Islamic commentarial writings that is hospitable to the idea that the title "Son of God" was initially applied to Jesus metaphorically as an expression of "love and high honor" comparable to the metaphor "friend of God," which is widely used in Islam.[31]

Seeing Jesus as someone who in an exemplary way fulfills the will of God has become a typical understanding in Islamic mysticism. As for early Christians, for a number of Sufis Jesus is both a representation of the perfect man and as such someone who in his life displays divine attributes.[32] In Islam, however, this is true of all the major prophets. According to a well-attested Hadith, the "prophets are brothers in terms of their father; their mothers are different, but their religion is one."[33] This Hadith does not suggest that God is the father of the prophets. But the "one father" that makes them all brothers is their religion in terms of their inner attitude, that is, the essential sameness of their relation to God. On this metaphorical level, Islam can go even further. According to one of the Hadith Qudsi, that is, the "holy Hadith" that contain words of God, a loving relationship between God and his servants may reach the point of an identification. Here God speaks about his servant: "When I love him I am his hearing with which he hears, his seeing with which he sees, his hand with which he strikes, and his foot with which he walks."[34]

The Qur'ān itself has more to say about Jesus than just calling him a prophet and servant of God. These titles are further qualified in a very special way in that Jesus is also called a "Word of God" and "Spirit of God." Sūrah 4:171 reads:

> Christ Jesus the son of Mary
> Was [no more than]
> A Messenger of Allah,
> and His Word,
> Which He bestowed on Mary;
> And a Spirit proceeding
> From Him.[35]

If one ignores the translator's insertion in brackets, the verse comes across as a high praise. In fact, no other prophet is called "Word of God" and

---

[31] Ayoub 2007, 124.
[32] Leirvik 2010, 97–98.
[33] Al-Bukhārī, Anbīyā, 48; Al-Muslīm, Fażā'īl, 145. Quoted in Aydin 2007, 38.
[34] Al-Bukhārī. See Ibrahim and Johnson-Davis (n.d.), 118.
[35] 'Alī 1999, 239.

"Spirit of God" by the Qur'ān, which has triggered plenty of debate among traditional Muslim exegetes about the proper understanding of these epithets. Relating to these designations, Mona Siddiqui states "that alongside Qur'ānic praise and honour of Jesus, albeit mainly as a human prophet, there remains a certain mystery around the events of his life." The question of how to understand the epithets "Word of God" and "Spirit of God," says Siddiqui, "should be seen as a worthy and necessary exercise in interreligious theology and individual piety." And she adds: "Muslims may not fully agree with what Christians believe about Jesus, but the boundaries of prophecy are open to interpretation."[36]

Already in 1957, Wilfred Cantwell Smith pointed out that it might be somewhat misleading to draw theological parallels between Jesus and Muḥammad or between the Bible and the Qur'ān. In terms of revelation, the more appropriate parallel would have to be drawn between the Qur'ān and Jesus.[37] For these two are "the points at which the Christian and Muslim find Divinity to have taken the initiative to 'come down' into our mundane world."[38] Smith's suggestion of comparing "incarnation" with "inlibration"[39] has been taken up recently by Muhammad Legenhausen, though Legenhausen does not refer to Smith.

Legenhausen is a Shi'ite philosopher who teaches in Qom, the center of Shi'ite theology in Iran. In a paper from 2009, Legenhausen suggests a literal understanding of the Qur'ānic designation of Jesus as the "Word of God." According to Legenhausen, the epithet means "that the form in which the divine revelation was manifest to the prophets in the cases of Moses and Muḥammad was textual, while in the case of the gospel it was made manifest in the life of Jesus, Jesus himself is to be considered the word of God, just as the Torah and the Glorious Qur'ān are considered the word of God."[40] The Qur'ān, says Legenhausen, replaces the Christian title "Son of God," because of its suspicious connotations, with the title "Word of God."[41] Yet this implies that both titles function analogously in designating the medium of divine revelation.

I consider Legenhausen's suggestion as extremely helpful. As I have argued so far, the title "Son of God" requires an interpretation in a revelatory sense, which makes it indeed interchangeable with the title "Word of God." I have also argued that this opens up an understanding of incarnation as subservient to revelation—an understanding that would allow seeing

---

[36]M. Siddiqui 2013, 59.
[37]Smith 1957, 17n13.
[38]Smith 1981, 244. The quoted essay was originally published in 1959.
[39]The term "inlibration" seems to have been coined by Harry A. Wolfson (see Wolfson 1976).
[40]Legenhausen 2009, 17.
[41]Ibid., 9.

Jesus as a symbol of God. Legenhausen is fully aware that his or, better, the Qur'ānic suggestion itself raises the issue of incarnation. He accepts that seeing Jesus as the "Word of God" parallels the statement of John's Gospel that in Jesus the word became flesh. "It is precisely at this point that Christian theology brings in discussions of the Incarnation, and the standard Muslim interpretation also seems to say that something became incarnate, if not divinity itself, then at least the divine word."[42] But if the divine word can assume both the form of a text and the form of a concrete human being, the question of incarnation surfaces in both cases. What is the meaning of "God" in the composite "Word of God," if that "Word" assumes, in one or the other way, a finite form? How is such incarnation or inlibration of something divine within a finite medium possible? The question of whether the Word of God that became manifest in the Qur'ān is eternal or not, whether it is uncreated like God, or whether God's word is an act of God and hence already somehow created, has occupied Islamic debates for centuries and never led to a general consensus. Legenhausen admits that an understanding of God's word as eternal would indeed come close "to the Christian idea of an eternal logos." He himself prefers an understanding of God's word as a divine activity and hence as not being eternal.[43] The position of the Sunnis, however, tends toward the opposite. They regard the primordial Word of God, called the "mother of the books" (*Umm al-Kitāb*), as eternal and uncreated. And notably, the metaphor of being a "mother," implies that the revealed books, or any other media of revelation, are "sons."

There was a time when Christians were likewise divided over the question of whether the primordial word, the *logos*, should be regarded as uncreated or, as Arius held, as God's first creation. Perhaps there is some truth in both positions. Expressing oneself is, on the one hand, a creative act. But on the other hand, this creative act points beyond itself to the agent. To quote Fazlur Rahman: "Whatever the agency of Revelation, however, the true revealing subject always remains God, for it is He Who always speaks in the first person."[44] Incarnational thinking is thus subservient to an understanding of the dialectics of revelation, as has been so lucidly expressed by Roger Haight: Revelation always implies the tension between the finite medium and the infinite reality that the medium is meant to mediate. Hence, there is far more continuity and complementarity than contrast between the two categories of prophecy and incarnation.

If revelation inevitably implies some kind of divine immanence in a finite medium, both Muslims and Christians are confronted with the question of

---

[42]Ibid., 10.
[43]Ibid., 12–13.
[44]Rahman 2009, 99.

how to understand incarnation or inlibration. Christian Trinitarian thinking can be considered as one possible way of explicating divine oneness and transcendence in the act of revelation:[45] the "father" signifying the eternal transcendent source of revelation, the "son" referring to one form that revelation can take, and the "spirit" indicating that form of activity or presence of God that inspires both the prophetic message and the prophet or son and that enables the recipients to understand the revelation. This view allows for a new assessment of the traditional Muslim accusation that Christians have corrupted and falsified the revelation that was given to them. If this revelation has never been a text but the person of Jesus, the accusation of corruption would become contingent on whether Muslims can accept the designation of Jesus as the "Son of God" as a legitimate attempt of expressing the dynamics of revelation in that case in which revelation assumes the form of a person. That is, if the "Word of God" that became flesh instead of book can legitimately be called "Son of God," this would not yet constitute corruption. Corruption would begin if this understanding would develop into forms that abandon monotheism. This is a view that Christians and Muslims might be able to share.

Keeping this in mind, we now turn to the Christian understanding of Muḥammad as the prophet or "final prophet."

THE PROPHET

Understanding "the Prophet"

When the Qur'ān designates Muḥammad as a prophet (3:144; 33:40; 47:2; 48:29), he is put in a long line of prophetic figures beginning with Adam. Although all humans have been given the capacity to distinguish between good and evil, they need the encouragement by divine prophets or messengers reminding them of God's justice and mercy. God sent his messengers to all people, as is repeatedly affirmed in the Qur'ān (5:19; 5:48; 10:47; 14:4; 35:24). Although not all of the messengers bring a book and a codified law and although the proclamation of the messengers is always adapted to the peculiarities of the different people (14:4), in essence their message is the same (16:36), proclaiming the transcendence and oneness of God, God's justice and mercy in God's relation to us, and submission to God as the appropriate human response.

---

[45]For a related suggestion see Cragg 1985, 278–88. According to Cragg, the Trinity "is the Christian form of belief in a God who has real and meaningful relation with humanity and the temporal world" (ibid., 288).

In this respect, Muḥammad is not much different from other major prophets. But in Sūrah 33:40 the Qur'ān calls him the "Seal of the Prophets" (*khātam an-nabīyīn*), which singles him out in three specific ways: First, the message he brings functions as a confirmation of all former prophetic revelations. Like a seal (*khātam*), it guarantees their authenticity. Second, the Islamic tradition understood the metaphor "seal" also in the sense of concluding the sending of messengers. After Muḥammad there is no need for any further confirmation. Third, as the final confirmation of all preceding revelation, the "seal" also functions as a critical norm. That is, against the Qur'ān one can assess to what extent former revelations may have become distorted, so that their original and essential meaning is restored by the Qur'ān. Nevertheless, there remains an important ambiguity: Does the designation of Muḥammad as the "Seal of the Prophets" imply only the final confirmation and restoration of the essential message of all prophets? Or does it imply that the Qur'ān, in addition to confirmation and restoration, also fulfills and supersedes all former revelations? In the past, many Muslim theologians have been inclined toward the latter. But as we have seen, Muslim theologians who affirm religious pluralism reject a supersessionist understanding of Muḥammad's mission.[46] The question is crucial when it comes to the Christian assessment of Muḥammad's prophetic status.

The Critique of "the Prophet"

Apart from very few exceptions, the traditional Christian assessment of Muḥammad has been extremely negative. When Dante Alighieri (1265–1321) in his *Commedia Divina* depicted Muḥammad and Ali, who was Muḥammad's cousin and son-in-law and is the founding figure of Shi'ite Islam, as both suffering in the lowest hell, he was in line with Christianity's majority position. For centuries Christians had not perceived Islam as a religion in its own right, but as a Christian heresy. Far from being valued as a prophet, Muḥammad was seen as a heretic. And traditionally heretics were regarded as instruments of the devil. It is therefore not surprising that some Christians, like Nicetas of Byzantium (9th–10th c.) even accused Muḥammad of fostering devil worship. This harsh rejection of Muḥammad was frequently supported by a critique of his personal conduct, which, allegedly, would not show any signs of saintliness but the marks of greed for power and lust.[47]

If we ask for the theological motives behind this extremely negative

---

[46]See chapter 4.
[47]See Schmidt-Leukel 2005a, 354–59.

dismissal of Muḥammad's prophetic status, we can identify three major reasons. First of all, the critique of divine sonship and of the Trinity as found in the Qur'ān was for many Christians undisputable evidence that the Qur'ān could not be taken as the word of God. Second, there was the widespread conviction that Divine revelation had reached its fulfillment and conclusion in Jesus Christ: "In many and various ways God spoke of old to our fathers by the prophets; but in these last days he has spoken to us by a Son" (Heb 1:1–2). Prophecy could be genuine only if it either pointed to the coming of Christ or confirmed his advent. The Christian belief in the conclusion of revelation in Christ is thus similar to the Muslim interpretation of Muḥammad as the final prophet. Both are means of expressing the underlying conviction that with Jesus or with the Qur'ān divine revelation has reached its unsurpassable climax. And this is the third reason behind the Christian rejection of Muḥammad as a prophet. If in and through Jesus God has been revealed as love, as ultimately merciful, nothing can be revealed about God which would go above and beyond such revelation. That is, any further prophecy would either have to confirm God's revelation in Christ, or it would relapse behind the climax of revelation. That is, at best it would revert to a proclamation of God's law as a preparation for the final revelation of God's love.[48] If Muḥammad could be a prophet at all, then one of a pre-Christian format. But this was not easily applicable to a post-Christian figure who explicitly spoke about Christ. The third argument was further supported by what appears to be a denial of Christ's death in the Qur'ān (4:157–59). For many Christians, the crucifixion is the decisive revelation that God's loving grace is greater and stronger than the worst kind of human sin. So how could Muḥammad be a prophet, if this understanding of the cross finds no support in the Qur'ān?

In more recent times, Christian statements about Islam have become much friendlier. In particular the Second Vatican Council virtually affirmed in its declaration *Nostra Aetate* that Muslims believe in the same God as Christians although in a different way. However, as far as I am aware, no official ecclesial document so far has advanced to a recognition of Muḥammad as a genuine prophet. Muslims committed to dialogue with Christians have repeatedly and sadly noted the Christian reluctance to take this step.[49] Yet this step can only be taken if the three theological obstacles, which I just mentioned, have been successfully removed. For the remainder of this chapter I would like to indicate briefly how this appears to be possible.

---

[48]A further problem of this view is that it also implies an untenable understanding of Judaism. To Jews, the law is not a preparation, but itself a sign of God's love or grace.

[49]See A. Siddiqui 1997, 59; Aydin 2002, 30–31, 169–73.

Toward a Synthesis

A number of Christian theologians, such as Wilfred Cantwell Smith, Kenneth Cragg (1913–2012), David Kerr (1945–2008), Hendrik Vroom (1954–2014), Martin Bauschke, and Reinhard Leuze, have in fact acknowledged a prophetic role of Muḥammad.[50] The main argument has been stated by Hans Küng: If Christians accept that Muslims believe in the one true God, Muḥammad has to be regarded as a prophet in the sense that "he alone led the Muslims to the worship of the one God."[51] In the past, there were only very few voices, like that of the Nestorian Patriarch Timothy I (8th–9th c.), who affirmed that Muḥammad "walked in the path of the prophets." Timothy based his judgment on the view that Muḥammad taught the unity of God, that he inspired people to do good works, that he led them away from idolatry and polytheism, and that he "taught about God, His Word and His Spirit."[52] In particular the last point shows that Timothy regarded Muḥammad as a kind of implicit or anonymous Trinitarian. Timothy thus perceived Muḥammad's role as similar to that of the pre-Christian Jewish prophets. However, the true challenge in acknowledging Muḥammad's prophetic role lies in his status as a post-Christian prophet.

This challenge can be met, if we take into account the above deliberations on the understanding of the incarnation and the Trinity. If both teachings are seen as subservient to the inner dialectics of revelation in a way that has its obvious analogues in the Islamic debates about the primordial Qurʾān, and if both sides agree that the Word of God may not only assume the form of a text but also that of a human person, it will become possible for Christians to acknowledge Muḥammad as a post-Christian prophet. Christians could then accept Muḥammad—as suggested by Hans Küng—as "a prophetic corrective for Christians in the name of the one and only God."[53] That is, Muḥammad could indeed be taken as someone who legitimately warns Christians not to be misled by their Trinitarian speculations into distorting God's oneness and transcendence. The revelation received by Christians in the person of Jesus Christ is not corrupted, but it is, as highlighted by the Qurʾān, in danger of corruption.

The major remaining obstacle is the *claim to finality* on both sides. An important step toward a solution could be to see that this claim to finality is, in essence, not about the medium of revelation but about the meaning of the revelation. Jesus Christ is the final Word of God only in the sense

---

[50]For a critical overview that covers some of these plus other recent theologians regarding their views of Muḥammad's prophetic role see Beaumont 2015.

[51]Küng et al. 1993, 27. Similarly Küng 2007, 123–24.

[52]Quoted from M. Siddiqui 2013, 48.

[53]Küng et al. 1993, 129.

that nothing higher can be said about God's meaning for us than "God is love." Christ is unsurpassable only in the sense that *this* revelation is unsurpassable. Can the same be said about Muḥammad as the seal of the prophets? Can we interpret this also in the sense that the Qur'ān, the Word of God brought by Muḥammad, transmits a final, unsurpassable revelation of God's meaning for us? And if so, is this compatible with the meaning conveyed by the Gospel?

There is no doubt that God's mercy figures prominently in the Qur'ān.[54] All Sūrahs of the Qur'ān, with one exception,[55] begin with the words "In the name of God [Allah], the most gracious, the most merciful." God's mercy, so the Qur'ān, is indiscriminate. It "extendeth to all" (7:156), and this mercy is what God has "inscribed for himself" (6:12). Christians sometimes wondered whether the mercy of God, on Islamic understanding, does indeed also include the ungodly. As Miroslav Volf has recently shown in a detailed discussion of this question, the answer can indeed be affirmative.[56]

The denial of Jesus' death on the cross should not be mistaken as a counterargument. First, the pertinent passage in the Qur'ān is ambiguous and its translation leaves plenty of room for interpretation.[57] Second, and more important, there are strong theological arguments in Christianity against an understanding of the cross as the constitutive cause of salvation. If there is hope for the sinner, this hope is based on God's mercy. God's mercy, however, is not constituted by the cross—as if it did not exist without the crucifixion—but is represented by the cross.[58] The cross reveals that God's readiness to forgive embraces even the worst extremes of anti-godly behavior.[59] But God's love does not depend on the cross. And hence Christians don't need to object when Muslims such as Mona Siddiqui affirm: "The absence of the cross does not diminish divine love."[60] But is God's love truly unlimited? "What happens," asks Volf, when people "persistently spurn God's mercy?"[61] Can we assume that, compared to Islam, the cross has led to a stronger confidence in God's love? I don't think so, for it appears that

---

[54]See also Khorchide 2014.

[55]Sūrah 9.

[56]Volf 2011, 176.

[57]For example, the passage might also be understood in the sense that God delivered Jesus from death—antedating the Easter message. For a helpful discussion of various possible interpretations see Ayoub 2007, 156–83.

[58]For the distinction between "constitutive" and "representative" see Ogden, 1992, 92–98. See also chapter 2.

[59]This has been impressively shown by Kenneth Cragg in his interpretation of Pilate, Judas, Caiaphas, and the mob as representative of forces of human evil, of sin in political, personal, ecclesiastical, and social form. The cross thus represents the divine readiness to overcome evil of any kind through forgiveness (Cragg 1985, 269–72).

[60]M. Siddiqui 2013, 245.

[61]Volf 2011, 176.

the critique of eternal damnation in the name of God's mercy has at least been as strong in Islam as in Christianity.[62] A Hadith Qudsi says about the primordial Word of God, the heavenly Qur'ān, or the "mother of all books":

When Allah decreed the Creation He pledged Himself by writing in His book which is laid down with Him: My mercy prevails over My wrath.[63]

This Hadith is the "gospel," or as the Qur'ān says, "good tidings," in pure form. If this is the essence of the Qur'ānic revelation, it is indeed "unsurpassable." If we may interpret the finality of Muḥammad as referring to the finality of *this* message, there is no reason for Christians to object. This "seal" does not supersede but truly confirms the truth of preceding revelations, including that through the Son.

Would an acknowledgment of Muḥammad as the Prophet oblige Christians to adopt the Sharia, the law brought by Muḥammad? The answer, I think, is both "yes" and "no." The moral and spiritual values that express and are rooted in the message of God's justice and mercy are certainly to be accepted. The question of how these are to be spelled out legally is a different issue, one about which Muslims themselves are not unanimous. Behind this dispute lies the question of how to renegotiate legal regulations within different historical and cultural contexts. If revelation, that is, the incarnation of God's word in Jesus and in the Qur'ān, can both be understood in symbolic terms, Christians and Muslims are free to admit the historical nature of the respective symbols, which implies that there are historical limitations of the symbolic forms. From this perspective, the fact that the different Sūrahs of the Qur'ān were not revealed all at once but successively in relation to specific circumstances gains an important theological significance. It constitutes further evidence of the historical nature of revelation, which always needs to be considered in distinction from its transhistorical significance. From this perspective, the adaptation and transformation of Islamic law within a modern society is an open option. Moreover, the full awareness of the historical limitation of the media of revelation reminds us that both the textual and the personal icons of God's word are ultimately images of an invisible God. God remains transcendent even in the act of revelation. And no finite medium of revelation may exhaust God's transcendent infinity, not even the Qur'ān, as Sūrah 31:27 proclaims.[64]

[62]See Bauer 2011, 278; Khorchide 2014 (chap. 2.5).
[63]Ibrahim and Johnson-Davies, n.d., 40.
[64]See chapter 4.

11

The Son and the Buddha

BETWEEN DEMONIZATION AND SANCTIFICATION

Christian Perspectives

Comparing Jesus Christ with Gautama Buddha has been a favorite subject of comparative religion almost since the beginning of the discipline. One of the numerous books in this genre was published in 1898 by Winfried Philipp Englert, by then a professor of apologetics at the University of Bonn. In his brief preface, Englert explains that a comparison of Christ and Buddha would help the reader discern "the true dew of paradise from the poison spread by the snakes."[1] The image is unmistakable: Behind the fascination of Buddhism lurks the seductive force of the devil. The harshness of this judgment is rooted in Englert's interpretation of Buddhism as atheism. Buddhism, Englert states, "declares a personal God as a gigantic spook,"[2] whereas Christ is truly divine and the redeemer of the world.[3] Englert concludes his book with some remarks about the global political situation of his time. In his days, says Englert, European civilization is about to bring the light of mercy to those deprived nations who were sitting in the shadow of death, that is, in the darkness of Buddhism. According to him, once a nation had fallen so deep as these Buddhist cultures, it is a law of history that the cross can only be introduced if preceded by the sword.[4]

Though Englert was by no means alone in his views, there exists a rather different strand in the Christian perception of Buddhism, which sees the Buddha not as a demonic but on the contrary as a saintly figure. This may be best illustrated by the story of *Barlaam and Josaphat*, which was one

---

[1] Englert 1898, foreword: "Hier lässt sich der echte Thau des Paradieses von dem ausgespritzten Gifte der Schlangen sehr deutlich unterscheiden."
[2] Ibid., 9.
[3] Ibid., 17.
[4] Ibid., 123.

of the most popular readings in the European Middle Ages and exists in a number of different recensions.[5] The earliest manuscript existant is written in Greek and dates from the eleventh century. This version was ascribed to Saint John of Damascus (676–749), who is known, among other things, for his fierce critique of Muḥammad as an alleged heretic. John's authorship, however, is now seen as rather unlikely, and it appears far more probable that the Greek version is based on an earlier Georgian version dating from the ninth or tenth century.[6] The plot of the novel is set in India. The text begins by saying that Christianity had initially been brought to India by the apostle Thomas and was subsequently spread by Christian monks: "They spake of nothing save of Christ. They clearly taught all men how changeful and impermanent were all things present; how sure and incorruptible was the life to come. Hence many were rescued from the darkness of deceit, and walked in the pleasant light of the truth."[7]

At the center of the novel is the story of the young Prince Josaphat. His father, King Abenner, is presented as an idolater who persecuted Christianity. Josaphat renounced his kingdom and became, like his mentor Barlaam, a monk and stern ascetic. Shortly after Josaphat's birth, an astrologer prophesied that Josaphat would not become a powerful and wealthy king but would pursue a religious career and embrace Christianity. To prevent the prophecy from coming true, the father took care that his son should never leave the royal palace and was kept away from "the miseries of life; he was to know nothing about death, nor old age, nor sickness."[8] After Josaphat had grown up, he became curious about the outside world. The king took precautions that the streets of the city were cleared from all unpleasant sights. But when his son undertook his first excursion, it occurred that he met two ill people, one who was blind and the other who suffered from leprosy. At a second excursion, Josaphat met an old man, and through this encounter he learned about the inevitability of death. After these depressing experiences he encountered the Christian monk Barlaam, who secretly introduced him to the Christian creed and finally baptized him. Josaphat decided to leave the world and become a Christian monk. After his father became aware of this, he tried in various ways to change his son's mind. As one of his attempts he brought the most beautiful girls to his son that they should seduce him. When one of the women was about to succeed, Josaphat had a vision of heavenly bliss "and immediately the beauty of the shameless maiden and of all the rest appeared to him more disgusting than what was defiled and decayed."[9]

---

[5]See Lopez and McCracken 2014; Lang 1957; Peri 1959; Almond 1987; De Blois 2009.
[6]See Lopez and McCracken 2014, 90–143.
[7]From the abridged translation of the early Greek version in Berry [1890] 1997, 139.
[8]Ibid., 146.
[9]Ibid., 183.

It is easy to recognize that the story of Josaphat contains several features of the Buddha legend: His royal descent as an Indian prince; the prophecy shortly after his birth about his future religious career; his seclusion from all miseries in his father's palace; his encounter with disease, old age, and death through his excursions; finally the inability of female beauty to delude him about human decay. When after the Middle Ages Europe became slightly more familiar with Buddhism, the proximity of the Barlaam and Josaphat tale to the Buddha legend was realized. In the early seventeenth century the Portuguese Diogo de Couto (1542–1616) reported that in India Josaphat was erroneously venerated as the Buddha because his true Christian identity had passed into oblivion.[10] Modern research, however, demonstrated that it was just the other way around. The legend of Prince Siddhārtha, the future Buddha, had first been transformed into an Arabic tale and then adopted into the Christian West. The name "Josaphat" goes back to "Bodhisattva," which is the technical term for Prince Gautama before he became the Buddha. And "Barlaam" is perhaps a version of "Bhagavan," another title of the Buddha.

As the introduction to the Greek version of the legend shows, the story was meant to illustrate how India was converted to Christianity, namely by monks who taught the impermanence of all things and how to find rescue from "the darkness of deceit." Monasticism, the realization of life's transience, and enlightenment as the liberation from the darkness of deceit are all key elements of foundational Buddhist spirituality. That is, Buddhist spirituality, wrapped into Christian gowns, was taken as a sign of the successful Christianization of India. As Donald Lopez comments, it is an "ultimate irony" that the life of the Buddha, together with Buddhist spirituality, "is turned into a tale about the conversion of heathens."[11] Yet the irony gets bizarre when, a millennium later, in Englert's comparative study, the same figure is brought into close proximity to the devil and made responsible for the alleged depravity of Asia, which would even justify the use of force. This, I think, is paradigmatic of the intricate difficulties besetting Christianity when it tries to express in doctrinal or theological terms the inner affinity that it feels toward Buddhism on the spiritual level.

Part of that difficulty is that, as a religious category, the title "Buddha," the "Awakened One," is alien to Christianity. Is the veneration of Gautama as the Buddha compatible or is it antagonistic to the Christian veneration of Jesus as the "Son of God"? What does it mean in Christian terms if someone is venerated as "awakened," as *the* or a "Buddha"? The closest parallel was—and I suggest rightly—identified in the motif of finding rescue from "the darkness of deceit." From a Christian perspective, the problem was that

---

[10]Lopez 2014, xiii.
[11]Ibid., xiv.

in Buddhism this rescue was not seen as the redeeming work of God. Buddha could become a Christian saint only after the conversion of his figure into that of the theistic ascetic Josaphat. To the extent that Buddhism was perceived as atheism, all parallels with Christian spirituality were regarded as deceiving, as demonic. Denouncing parallels to Christianity in non-Christian religions as diabolic imitation has, after all, a long tradition in Christian theology.

Buddhist Perspectives

From a Buddhist perspective, the epithet "Son of God" could easily evoke associations with the notion of sometimes large families of gods in the theistic branches of Hinduism or with the Hindu concept of an *avatāra*, that is, the human incarnation or manifestation of a particular deity. For Buddhists, however, Hindu deities are not transcendent but transient, even if they are heavenly beings (*devatā*). Although their lives are very long, they are still subject to the *saṃsāra*, the cycle of constant rebirth and re-death. They are neither liberated themselves, nor can they provide liberation to others. In order to find rescue from "the darkness of deceit," turning to the deities would be useless or even counterproductive. In the various anti-Christian writings produced in seventeenth-century China, it is evident how Mahāyāna Buddhists felt unable to make sense of Christian concepts because the Christian talk of God neither reflected their own understanding of transcendence and liberation nor their understanding of deities as heavenly but still *saṃsāric* beings. In a statement by the famous Chan monk Yuanwu (1566–1642) this problem becomes fairly clear. In order to associate the Christian God with transcendence, God would have to be defined as a Buddha. If the Christian God lacks the insight of the Buddha, he would not be transcendent but a being still caught in "the three worlds," that is, in the *saṃsāra*. Yet if he were a Buddha, he could not be designated as a "God," nor could he be seen as unique. In that sense Yuanwu states about the "Lord of Heaven," the term that Christians used for "God":

> If the Lord of Heaven has no insight, he too is like a man thrown back and forth in the three worlds. . . . Yet if in the three worlds a man has insight, then nothing will prevent him from being the lord in his place and the chief in his circumstances. In heaven he guides the gods; among humans he guides the humans. He is neither a god nor a human.[12]

Being "neither a god nor a human" is a traditional characterization of the Buddha.[13] And the insight that according to Yuanwu makes someone a

---

[12]Kern 1992, 129 (my translation).
[13]E.g., Aṅguttaranikāya 4:61.

Buddha is the realization of true nature, characterized by Yuanwu as the "highest wonder" and as "unfathomable":

> It comprehends heaven and earth and penetrates past and present. . . .
> It rules over gods and men. It pervades birth and death, but birth and
> death cannot pervade it.[14]

It may have occurred at least to some Buddhists that the Christian concept of God does not point to a transient deity, that is, not to *a being* that is still in need of liberation, but to a reality which is both radically transcendent and radically immanent, like "Buddha Nature" or "true nature" in Chinese Mahāyāna Buddhism. This conclusion would have enabled Buddhists to understand Jesus in analogy to the Buddha, that is, as someone who also realized transcendent reality as his own true nature. The Chinese scholar monk Zhixu (1599–1655) indicates this possibility while also repudiating it:

> Is the Lord of Heaven, having been born down here, still in heaven with his original "body" [*shen*]? If his original body no longer exists, then there is no longer a lord in heaven. If, however, his original "body" still exists, then one is usurping the Buddhist teaching of the two "bodies," namely the "body" of truth [*zhen shen*] and the "body" of retribution [*ying shen*]. But one does not reach the wonderful radiance of the billions of "bodies" of transformations [*hua shen*].[15]

In this quotation Zhixu refers to the Mahāyāna Buddhist teaching of the "three bodies" of the Buddha, or better, the three levels of reality comprised by the Buddha: The "original body" or *dharmakāya* ("Dharma body") which signifies ultimate reality, his Buddha Nature or true nature; the "body of retribution" or *sambhogakāya*, signifying the Buddha as a celestial, supranatural being and finally the "body of transformation," or *nirmāṇakāya*, that is, the manifestation or incarnation of the Buddha as a human being, in physical and thus transitory form. At the levels of supranatural and human existence, the Buddha is not unique. There are several celestial Buddhas and many human Buddhas.[16] In principle, enlightenment is possible for all beings and basically means to realize transcendent Buddha Nature. Given that Christians did not teach the multitude of such manifestations of the Dharma body, Zhixu no longer pursues the possibility of understanding the Christian teachings along those lines.

---

[14]Kern 1992, 130 (my translation).

[15]Ibid., 229. English translation from Barker and Gregg 2010, 230.

[16]On the problem that human Buddhas, at least on a non-Mahāyāna understanding, do not exist at the same time, see chapter 2.

The alternative options were radical and sinister. Ideologically, Christianity was excluded from the idea of the "harmony of the three teachings," and Christians like Matteo Ricci sharply criticized the whole concept.[17] If the integration of Christianity within the wider range of true and compatible teachings, like the "three teachings," was regarded as impossible, the alternative was its demonization. In fact, Christian teachings were branded not just as "heresies" but also as the "teachings of devils," both in seventeenth-century China and Japan,[18] a view that was clearly fostered by the aggressive attitude of Christianity toward Buddhism.

The demonization of Christianity and Jesus is also found in the early encounter of Theravāda Buddhism with Christianity. A folktale from the eighteenth century in Sri Lanka presents Jesus, the "Carpenter-Demon," as a criminal impostor. According to this story, Jesus was in fact an emanation of Māra, an evil deity that functions in Buddhism as a kind of devil, as someone who persistently tries to obstruct the Buddha's work. Jesus, that is, the "son of Māra,"was conceived by a carpenter girl. Having grown up, he and his followers pretended to be *arahats*, that is, enlightened Buddhist monks. In fact, however, they were a band of thieves. At night they stole cattle, ate the meat, and drank liquor. Having been betrayed by one of his followers, Jesus was finally caught and executed because of his crimes. Yet after his execution, Māra and other demons falsely proclaimed his resurrection.[19] The characterization of Jesus and his followers as thieves who drink alcohol and eat meat certainly reflects Buddhists' impressions of Christian colonialism. The European Christians ate meat, drank alcohol, and robbed the country. This impression is combined with a negative assessment of Christianity's religious claims. Jesus and his followers pretend to be enlightened monks; in fact they are not. The Christian idea of divine incarnation is turned into the incarnation of an evil deity, Māra, the antagonist of the Buddha.[20]

The tendency to demonize the Christian God and Jesus did not disappear from Theravāda Buddhist writings. But at times there is also uncertainty about the question of whether Christian spirituality is altogether deceptive. A good example of such ambivalence is found in the writings of the influential Theravāda Buddhist reformer Anagārika Dharmapala (1864–1933). On the one hand, Dharmapala calls Jesus the "Nazarene Carpenter,"[21] evoking

---

[17]See Kern 1992, 38–41. See also chapter 7.

[18]See Kern 1992, 26–27; Elison 1991, 331, 388.

[19]See Young 2005. For various versions of the legend, see Young and Senanayaka 1998; for an excerpt, see Barker and Gregg 2010, 234–38.

[20]However, the demonization of the religious other was not a product of the reaction to colonialism. There is unmistakable evidence that it was already used in inner-Buddhist controversies, when, for example, Mahāyāna Buddhists had to defend themselves against the accusation that their teachings were inspired by Māra (see Schmidt-Leukel 2017a).

[21]Dharmapala 1965, 449.

associations with the motif of the "Carpenter-Demon," and assesses him as "an utter failure": "The few illiterate fisherman of Galilee followed him as he had promised to make them judges to rule over Israel."[22] On the other hand, Dharmapala also speaks of Jesus as "the gentle Nazarene,"[23] whose "pure teachings" would make him "a central figure in the universal church of truth."[24] With these "pure teachings" Dharmapala refers primarily to the Sermon on the Mount, which he regards as "of universal application."[25] Yet he finds it difficult to assume a genuine Christian or Jewish origin and hence postulates Buddhist influence: "'The Sermon on the Mount' alleged to be the teachings of Jesus contain the re-echoings of Buddhist suttas (. . .)."[26]

The faltering between demonization and sanctification that can be observed in Christian perceptions of the Gautama Buddha and in Buddhist perceptions of Jesus Christ has certainly a number of different reasons. One reason, I suggest, is the difficulty of integrating the key religious epithets into the respective doctrinal system. Although the Buddhists' category of "awakening" has its affinities to Christian understanding of illumination or rescue from the "darkness of deceit," a Christian acknowledgment of the Gautama as an "Awakened One" would have been incompatible with the alleged Buddhist atheism. Conversely, categories of divine "sonship" or "incarnation" were not totally alien to Buddhists either. But against the background of the Buddhist understanding of deities as *saṃsāric* beings, these categories did not per se entail any relationship to the sphere of liberation. The latter would require seeing Jesus as an incarnation or manifestation of the Buddha Nature, along the lines of the three bodies teaching. If this was excluded, there was the other option at hand to interpret Jesus as the incarnation of a deity. Given the gravity of tensions, the deity seen behind Jesus was identified as Māra, the Buddha's spiritual adversary. As the Buddhist scholar José Cabezón summarizes, "The problem lies not in the claim that Jesus is the incarnation or manifestation of a deity. What Buddhists find objectionable is . . . the Christian characterization of the deity whose manifestation Jesus is said to be."[27] The dialogue between Buddhists and Christians, as it evolved in the twentieth century, has begun to change the situation illustrated by my historical sidelights. That is, ways have emerged of how the ambivalence in previous reciprocal judgments may turn into deeper understanding, which may accommodate an acknowledgment and endorsement of the motives behind the confession of Gautama as the Buddha and of Jesus as the Son of God.

---

[22]Ibid., 475.
[23]Ibid., 445.
[24]Ibid.
[25]Ibid.
[26]Ibid., 26.
[27]Cabezón 2000, 24.

ACKNOWLEDGING THE BUDDHA

An Atheist Philosopher?

The religious epithet "Buddha," the "Awakened One," refers to someone who awakens from the world of dreams and intoxication to the clear understanding of reality. This awakening or insight is not of an intellectual nature. It is a transformative, liberative experience in which a Buddha realizes not only the nature of impermanence and the origin of suffering but also the reality of the "deathless," that is, *nirvāṇa*. It is only through this experience that Gautama became a "Buddha." According to the canonical record, the "cessation of suffering" had been seen by him "face to face" and he knew: "The emancipation of my mind cannot be lost."[28]

As has already become clear, a major difficulty for Christians in accepting the Buddhist veneration of Gautama as an "Awakened One" was, and still is, that there is no mentioning of God in the canonical records of this awakening. A number of Christians understood Buddhism as a form of atheism, and some continue to do so. But is the absence of the concept of "God" equivalent to the atheist denial of God? The scholar of Buddhism and former practicing Buddhist Paul Williams argues that this is indeed the case. For Christians the concept of "God" refers to a transcendent reality that is essential for human salvation or liberation. If Buddhism does not teach a God that is "necessary to final spiritual fulfilment," then, according to Williams, "it must hold that such a God does not exist." It is, therefore, by implication that "the God referred to by Christians is indeed being denied. From a Christian point of view Buddhism is clearly a form of atheism."[29] How then could Christians, or any followers of a theistic religion, ever consider Gautama as a fully "Awakened One," if this awakening would contain the error of atheism?

Paul Williams's argumentation ignores[30] that Buddhism knows very well that "final spiritual fulfilment" depends on the existence of a transcendent reality. In a famous passage that appears twice in the canonical scriptures[31] the Buddha declares:

> There is, bhikkhus, a not-born, a not-brought-to-being, a not-made, a not-conditioned. If, bhikkhus, there were no not-born, not-brought-to-being, not-made, not-conditioned, no escape would be discerned from what is born, brought-to-being, made, conditioned.[32]

---

[28]Mahāvagga 1:6:25, 29. Rhys Davids and Oldenberg 1996, 96–97.
[29]Williams 2002, 26.
[30]For my debate with Williams on this issue see May 2007, 67–88, 117–54.
[31]*Udāna* 8:3; *Itivuttaka* 43.
[32]Ireland 1997, 103, 180.

This utterance refers to the *nirvāṇa*. The message is that if the "not-conditioned" or "un-conditioned" reality of *nirvāṇa* would not exist, liberation from the conditioned world of *saṃsāra* would be impossible. In traditional Buddhism, *nirvāṇa* does not signify the *mental state* of enlightenment. *Nirvāṇa* is rather a *transcendent* (Sanskrit: *lokottara*) and *unconditioned* (*asaṃskṛta*) *reality*,[33] which, according to classical Buddhist manuals like the *Milindapañhā* or the *Visuddhimagga*, exists independently of whether someone attains to it or not.[34] Other Western and Christian interpreters of Buddhism have therefore taken Buddhism not as a form of atheism but of mysticism. That is, Buddhism acknowledges a transcendent reality and does indeed see it as the crucial condition of salvation. But Buddhism does not conceive transcendent reality as a personal creator God. So Buddhism is a-theistic in that it denies a theistic understanding of transcendent reality. It is not atheistic in the sense of Western atheism that denies transcendent reality in any form. The designation of Buddhism as a form of "mysticism" may have its own problems. Yet it is right inasmuch as it points out that the idea of a personal God is not the only form in which transcendent reality can be affirmed and that, like Buddhism, the mystical traditions within the Abrahamic religions often use nonpersonal or impersonal concepts when they refer to the ultimate.

In the past, Buddhists have repeatedly criticized and rejected Hindu concepts of a divine creator.[35] Given the crucial significance of this issue for all theistic religions, I will come back to it in chapter 13. But traditional Buddhism did not only criticize theism. It also rejected the teachings of the Indian Cārvākas who were genuine atheists and materialists, and to whom the true liberation was simply corporal death perceived as complete extinction.[36] Today, however, there are Buddhists who, under Western influence—I guess—have adopted an understanding of Buddhism that is not just critical of theism but presents Buddhism as a rejection of any form of the transcendent.[37] This modern reinterpretation of Buddhism would indeed turn the Buddha into an atheist philosopher in the full sense, but it is a view far from the more traditional understanding of the Buddha, as has been pointedly expressed by Bhikkhu Bodhi:

When the secular presuppositions of modernity clash with the basic principles of Right Understanding stressed by the Buddha, I maintain there is no question which of the two must be abandoned. *Saṃsāra* as the beginningless round of rebirths, kamma as its regulative law,

---

[33]See also Pandit 1993, 312–39; Collins 1998, 135–233.
[34]See Schmidt-Leukel 2006b, 48–50.
[35]For an overview see Schmidt-Leukel 2006a, 123–41, and chapter 13 below.
[36]Radhakrishnan and Moore 1989, 235.
[37]See, e.g., Batchelor 1998; 2011.

Nibbāna as a transcendent goal—surely these ideas will not get a rousing welcome from sceptical minds. . . . Yet, these are all so fundamental to the true Dhamma, so closely woven into its fabric, that to delete them is to risk nullifying its liberative power.[38]

If one acknowledges that transcendent reality is not denied in traditional Buddhism, the question arises whether Christians should see Gautama's awakening as an incomplete form of religious insight. Was he someone who glimpsed that reality which had been more fully revealed in Jesus? Was Buddha another precursor of the Son? In 1937 the Roman Catholic theologian Romano Guardini wrote that there is but one person "whom we might be inclined to compare with Jesus: Buddha."[39] So far, says Guardini, no one has been able to say what the Buddha and Nirvāṇa might mean for Christians.[40] However, the major difference between the Buddha and Jesus is, according to Guardini, that in Jesus "a mind from beyond the world" is expressing itself, whereas the Buddha represents someone who belongs to the world and tries to break through the world from within.[41] Guardini's view can be contested. There is strong evidence that the Buddha too can be and has been understood by Buddhists as a "mind from beyond." This discovery will also reveal that despite the Buddhist rejection of a personal image of God, personal qualities are by no means absent from the Buddhist discourse about transcendence. I will sketch the idea that a "mind from beyond" appeared in and through the Buddha in three successive steps which reflect the development of the intra-Buddhist interpretation of the Buddha.

A Mind from Beyond

1. Through his enlightenment Siddhārtha Gautama had achieved the perfection of "wisdom" (*prajñā*). This, however, is only half of the story. The existence of Buddhism as a tangible religion is not only founded on Buddha's enlightenment. From a Buddhist perspective, Buddhism came into existence because the Buddha decided to use his insight for the benefit of others. With his enlightenment the Buddha had achieved the fulfillment of all his personal goals: "What had to be done has been done," as is stated in the canonical formula. At the time of his enlightenment the Buddha was, according to the tradition, just thirty-five years old. The remaining forty-five

---

[38]Bodhi 1998, 20.
[39]Guardini 1996, 355.
[40]Ibid., 355–56.
[41]"Hier redet ein Bewußtsein von über der Welt her. Und nicht nur so, wie einer spricht, der sittlich oder religiös durchgestoßen ist." Guardini 1997, 369. Unfortunately E. C. Briefs's English translation omits the first of these two crucial sentences; see Guardini 1996, 356.

years of his life, he spent spreading his teachings, establishing the Buddhist order, and alleviating suffering where he was able to do so. According to the canonical scriptures, the Buddha's activities after his enlightenment were motivated entirely by compassion. This implies that through his enlightenment he had not only achieved perfection in wisdom but also the perfection of compassion and—what may appear as most remarkable—the skill of combining these two virtues. At the heart of the Buddhist wisdom is the inner detachment from everything that is impermanent. But it is out of altruistic love and commitment that such detachment is taught. Without the Buddha's compassionate decision to spread his wisdom there would be no Buddhism. And no Buddha either! For, according to the Buddhist tradition, what makes a Buddha a Buddha in the full sense is that he does not remain satisfied with his own liberation but establishes a community that is able to transmit his wisdom for the sake of gods and humans. The Buddha and Buddhism are born out of an intimate union of wisdom and compassion.

The truth that Buddhist teachings seek to convey was, according to Buddhist understanding, not invented by the Buddha but discovered—like someone who rediscovers an ancient city that had been forgotten and overgrown by the jungle.[42] The words of the Buddha convey an eternal truth, referred to as the *dharma*. Just as *nirvāna* does not signify the conditioned reality of a mental state that the Buddha brought about by his own performance, but rather an unconditioned and eternal reality to which he awoke, the *dharma* does not signify anything that the Buddha would have invented. It is not the Buddha who produces *nirvāna* and *dharma*. On the contrary, it is the existence of *nirvāna* and *dharma* that makes the appearance of a Buddha possible. The Buddha, through his words and deeds, is a human manifestation of *dharma* and *nirvāna*. "Seeing the *dharma* one sees me; seeing me one sees the *dharma*,"[43] is what the Buddha of the Buddhist canonical scriptures says about his identity. The invisible and incomparable *nirvāna* becomes visible in and through the lives of those who, like the Buddha, achieve enlightenment and live a life that is freed from the roots of all evil: greed, hatred, and delusion.[44] Insofar as *nirvāna* and *dharma* signify a transcendent reality, the Buddha's liberated mind bears the features of a "mind from beyond." This mind, finding its perfect expression in the Buddha's wisdom and compassion, constitutes, according to early Buddhism, the true nature of everybody's mind. Greed, hatred, and delusion and all the resulting evils are merely defilements of a mind whose true nature is

---

[42]Samyuttanikāya 12:65.
[43]Ibid., 3:120; Itivuttaka 92.
[44]Anguttaranikāya 3:54–56.

pure and luminous.[45] According to Buddhism, evil is not our deepest reality.

The Sri Lankan theologian Aloysius Pieris has therefore claimed that at the bottom of our heart we know about the complementarity between love and wisdom, so that "deep within each one of us there is a Buddhist and a Christian engaged in a profound encounter."[46] Pieris is not suggesting that Buddhism represents wisdom and Christianity love. The complementarity of love and wisdom is rather affirmed by both traditions. But Jesus and the Buddha represent different manifestations of this complementarity, because this complementarity is expressed in two different idioms. There is, says Pieris, "a *Christian gnosis* that is necessarily agapeic; and there is also a *Buddhist agape* that remains gnostic."[47]

2. If the Buddha may be acknowledged by Christians as someone who, as a result of his experience of transcendent reality, manifests a mind of wisdom and compassion, the Christian may raise a further question: Was transcendent reality passive in Buddha's awakening to it, or did it play some active role? This question has also been raised within the Buddhist tradition itself, and large parts of Mahāyāna Buddhism have answered it in the affirmative. It was the influential *Lotus-Sūtra* which first proclaimed that the human Buddha was in fact the manifestation of a celestial, supranatural Buddha who always proclaims the *dharma* in numerous ways adapted to the spiritual capacity of all the different living beings.

This concept was deepened and expanded by the teaching of the three Buddha bodies, which we encountered in the early Chinese Buddhist comments on Christianity. According to this doctrine, the Buddha as a human and as a supranatural being are both manifestations of the formless, unmanifest Dharma or "Dharma body" (*dharmakāya*). The three bodies, or levels of existence, of the Buddha can be viewed in both directions: from below, in the sense that a deeper understanding of the human Buddha leads to an understanding of his source, the supranatural, celestial Buddha. And a deeper understanding of both the human and the supranatural Buddha leads to the insight that they emerge from a reality that transcends all manifestations, a reality that is formless. Yet as a formless reality, the "Dharma body" does not exist beside the other two bodies, because this would automatically provide it with a form of its own. Being itself formless, it appears only in the form of the other two Buddha bodies. Therefore, the inner dynamics of the three bodies can also be viewed from above. That is, the ultimate reality of the *dharmakāya* manifests itself in the form of the supranatural Buddha, and the supranatural Buddha is manifest in his human emanations or incar-

---

[45]Harvey 1995, 166–76.
[46]Pieris 1988, 113.
[47]Ibid.

nations. So ultimately the wisdom and compassion that become visible in the human Buddha emerge from the ineffable reality of the *dharmakāya*.

In the context of the doctrine of the three Buddha bodies, a "mind from beyond" expresses itself in the Buddha as much as it does, according to Christianity, in Jesus. Lynn de Silva (1919–82), like Aloysius Pieris a Sri Lankan theologian and a pioneer of Buddhist-Christian dialogue, understood the doctrine of the three Buddha bodies as an attempt to integrate transcendence and immanence, or, as he said, "ultimacy and intimacy." In this respect de Silva regarded the Buddhist teaching of the three bodies as similar to the Christian doctrine of the Trinity. "*Dharmakāya* appears in human forms as Buddha, created by absolute compassion."[48] And in the human appearance of the Buddha, in the "body of transformation," de Silva recognized "an analogy to the manifestation of God in Christ, who for Christians is the incarnation of the absolute, the *dharmakāya*, the Godhead, the ultimate which became intimate by becoming man."[49]

3. A third step is taken when we raise the question of how this "mind from beyond" liberates. The Buddhist tradition has given various answers to this question. First of all, it encourages one to seek liberation from suffering, and this search receives significant direction through the teaching of the Buddha. From this perspective, the Buddha is perceived as the unsurpassed teacher who liberates through his teaching. Yet the example of the Buddha encourages one to strive not just for one's own liberation but for that of all others as well. The spirit of the Buddha evokes and fuels compassion for the suffering fellow beings and drives his followers to put the happiness of others in the first place. It teaches that "all those who are unhappy in the world are so as a result of their desire for their own happiness," while "all those who are happy in the world are so as a result of their desire for the happiness of others," as it is expressed in a classical Mahāyāna text.[50] Out of this motivation the spirit and example[51] of the Buddha inspires his followers, if necessary, to even sacrifice their own life for the liberation of others.[52] That is, it transforms people into each other's saviors. In Mahāyāna Buddhism, this mind or spirit is called the "spirit of enlightenment" (*bodhicitta*). Everybody who is moved by this spirit is a Bodhisattva, someone on the way to Buddhahood.

A Bodhisattva saves or liberates by many means, not by teaching alone. Primarily he saves through his compassionate pro-existence. Doctrinally

---

[48]De Silva 1982, 55.
[49]Ibid.
[50]*Bodhicaryāvatāra* 9:129; translation from Wallace and Wallace 1997, 106.
[51]According to the Buddhist tradition, the Buddha had often sacrificed his own life for the sake of others in his previous existences.
[52]See *Bodhicaryāvatāra* 9:105.

Mahāyāna Buddhism has expressed this in the idea of merit transfer. All the karmic merit that a Bodhisattva accumulates throughout innumerable lives is dedicated and transferred to those who lack in karmic merit. Superior Bodhisattvas become a source of permanent consolation and inspiration. Whenever there is despair about one's own shortcomings, one can turn to them, asking them for forgiveness, and rely on their merit, which they readily transfer out of their limitless compassion.[53]

The Buddha is understood as a perfect example of this spirit. He is seen as someone whose motivation to become a Buddha was marked by compassion from the start. He wanted to become a Buddha only because as a Buddha he could be of utmost assistance to all others. All religious merit he made was dedicated to the salvation of others. From a Mahāyāna perspective, compassion is therefore the root of all salvation: the salvation spent and the salvation received. In some strands of Mahāyāna Buddhism, the supranatural Buddha who mediates between the ineffable *dharmakāya* and Gautama Buddha, that is, the *saṃbhogakāya* Buddha who became manifest or incarnate in Buddha Gautama, is called Amitābha or, in Japanese, Amida. Amida Buddha represents boundless, all-encompassing compassion. Salvation is received, *in nuce*, by entrusting oneself entirely to the compassion as it is represented by Amida Buddha and has become manifest or embodied in the compassionate spirit of Buddha Gautama. In essence, salvation is thus received by faith alone.

When the Jesuit missionaries came to Japan in the sixteenth century and learned about Amida Buddhism (or Shin Buddhism), they reported back home that the devil had brought the Lutheran heresy to Japan before the advent of the true Catholic faith.[54] In the twentieth century it was Karl Barth who declared that Amida Buddhism is the closest pagan parallel to the Gospel.[55] According to Barth, however, it was not the devil who had devised it but God himself. Yet being devised by God does not make Amida Buddhism true. According to Barth, God created this closest parallel of the Gospel in order to teach us the important lesson that there is only one thing that accounts for all the difference between truth and falsehood ("Wahrheit und Lüge") in religion, which is but the name of Jesus Christ, in the "formal simplicity of this name."[56] Why, however, should God do so? Why should God make saving truth dependent on the formal simplicity of a name? And why does Barth believe that God would do this? If we presuppose, as I suggested above,[57] a hermeneutic of trust instead of a her-

---

[53]See, e.g., *Bodhicaryāvatāra* 2:27–66, 6:124.
[54]Valignano 1944, 161.
[55]Barth 1960, 372.
[56]Ibid., 376.
[57]See chapter 9.

meneutic of suspicion, it is far more plausible to assume that in the name
of the Buddha the redeeming power of the ultimate has reached people as
much as through the name of the Son, although in somewhat different ways.
Against Karl Barth's rejection of Amida Buddhism, John Cobb therefore
held "that what Christians have learned about grace through . . . Jesus,
Buddhists have learned in a different way."[58] According to Cobb, Buddhists
have experienced transformative and redemptive wisdom and compassion
through Amida and Christians through Christ.[59] In this respect, says Cobb,
"Amida is Christ."[60]

For Christians, this way of acknowledging the Buddha draws into question the uniqueness of Jesus as the only savior. Cobb felt this challenge, and
the way that he resisted it will take us to some of the more recent Buddhist
reactions to Jesus.

ACKNOWLEDGING THE SON

1. In 1982 John Cobb published his book *Beyond Dialogue: Toward a Mutual
Transformation of Christianity and Buddhism*, which belongs to the clas-
sics of modern Christian-Buddhist dialogue. In view of his recognition of
Amida as Christ and of Christ as Amida, which he presented in this book, he
also pointed to an important difference. From a historical perspective, Cobb
says, the story of Bodhisattva Dharmakara, who vowed to save all beings by
creating his Pure Land and who finally became Amida Buddha in fulfillment
of his vows, has to be assessed as a myth.[61] This, Cobb holds, is different
with Christ. In his case, "little doubt remains that there *is* an historical story
to tell and that its deepest meaning can be understood as just as supportive
of belief in the graciousness of God as the mythical story could have ever
been."[62] Accordingly, Cobb suggested to the followers of Amida Buddhism
that the only person who could provide a historical basis to the mythical story
of Amida Buddha and hence support their faith in the wisdom and unconditioned compassion of the ultimate would not be Gautama, the historical
Buddha, but the historical Jesus. Cobb argued that the teachings of Gautama
are too different to sustain the message of radical grace as expressed in the
teachings of Amida Buddhism. Therefore, Amida Buddhists who look for
a corroboration of their faith in history should learn to find this in Jesus.[63]

---

[58]Cobb 1997.
[59]Ibid.
[60]Cobb 1982, 128.
[61]Ibid., 137–39.
[62]Ibid., 139.
[63]Ibid., 139–40.

Responding to John Cobb's challenge, John Shunji Yokota agreed that Amida is a transhistorical, metaphorical expression of an existential confidence in the compassionate quality of ultimate reality. Moreover, Yokota acknowledged that ultimate reality, in being seen as compassionate, assumes a "personal quality."[64] But Yokota replied that Cobb underestimated the link between Amida Buddhism and Buddha Gautama. According to Yokota, Gautama does provide a historical basis to Amida Buddhism. This does not primarily consist in Gautama's teachings but in the compassionate nature of Gautama's decision to disseminate his insight and guide others on their way to liberation.[65] The reality expressed in the metaphorical figure of Amida was historically actualized in the compassion of Gautama:

> The act of Siddhārtha Gautama to rise from the seat of enlightenment and go forth to talk of his understanding of reality in order to help others to gain enlightenment is the primordial act of compassion in our tradition and can, I believe, be seen as the actualization into history of the compassionate, saving activity of Amida Buddha.[66]

Per Yokota, there is thus no need to incorporate Jesus into the Amida Buddhist tradition thinking that otherwise its faith would lack in historical foundation. The need to incorporate Jesus, is, according to Yokota, based on something else, that is, on the "need" in any "mature or real interreligious dialogue . . . to adopt elements of the dialogue partner's vision and enunciation of reality to complement and develop one's own understanding."[67] Thus, Jesus can, and indeed should, become part of Amida Buddhism as someone in whose person "the reality of Amida Buddha is fully actualized."[68] This integration would change and expand the tradition, as for example by "a recognition of the moral imperative that the image of Christ includes," which would lead to the development of a social ethics in Amida Buddhism.[69] John Yokota is certainly a Buddhist who goes rather far in accommodating Jesus as an incarnation or even "pivotal incarnation"[70] of the salvific power of ultimate reality. Yet his endorsement of Jesus is enabled and supported by the astonishing and undeniable similarity between the Protestant forms of Christianity and Amida Buddhism.

    2. If we look at Theravāda Buddhism, reservations against any form of

---

[64] Yokota 2000, 212.

[65] Yokota 2005, 96–97.

[66] Yokota 2004, 260. See Yokota's earlier treatment of this issue (published under the name John Ishihara) in Yokota 1986.

[67] Yokota 2005, 99, 97.

[68] Ibid., 100.

[69] Ibid., 101.

[70] Ibid.

Buddhist recognition of Jesus are considerably higher. As indicated before, the reasons for this are in part found in the negative experiences of various Theravāda countries with Western colonial rule. But they are also grounded in Theravāda exclusivism, which does not allow for the idea that there could be more than one Buddha at the same time, that is, a Buddha in the sense of someone who establishes a salvific community.[71] At best, Jesus is seen as someone whose teachings may lead his followers to a better rebirth but not to ultimate salvation.[72] As we saw, this was different with the Thai Theravāda Buddhist reformer Bhikkhu Buddhadāsa (1906–93).[73] He held that the Sermon on the Mount, if put into practice, contains more than enough to achieve liberation,[74] and therefore did not hesitate to regard Jesus as a Buddha.[75] According to Buddhadāsa, the "basic theme" in the Sermon on the Mount is nonattachment. He perceives the teachings of Jesus as a guide to act in a "nonegoistic way." In line with traditional Theravāda Buddhist thought, Buddhadāsa presents nonattachment and the abandonment of any idea of ego or self as the essence of the *dharma*. It "is the highest . . . truth, is something wonderful, valuable, and extraordinary. . . . If there is a God, he is to be found here."[76] Thus Buddhadāsa repudiates the idea of "God" as a *deva*, that is, as a deity still part of the cycle of reincarnation, but suggests that "God" should be taken as another term for what is called *dharma* in Buddhism.[77] This enables him to make sense of the Christian confession of Jesus as the "Son of God":

> What is known as "God" is neither physical nor spiritual in nature, it is bodiless, without mouth, without any faculty of speech that we know of, but it can cause a body to be formed, with a mouth and a voice to speak what God wishes him to speak. That speaker may therefore be called the son of God.[78]

Accordingly, the epithet "son of God" should be applied "to those who can lead the world to perfect understanding of the dhamma"[79] (i.e., *dharma*).

It is important to note that Buddhadāsa relates the epithet "Son of God" to an act of revelation. The formless reality that is called "God" or

---

[71]See chapter 6.

[72]See, e.g., Nyanaponika 1981, 2.

[73]See chapter 6.

[74]Buddhadāsa 1967, 29.

[75]Ibid., 105ff. See also 98, where he speaks of Jesus as a "victor" (*jina*), that is, using one of the titles of a Buddha.

[76]Buddhadāsa 1989, 152.

[77]Ibid., 133.

[78]Buddhadāsa 1967, 105.

[79]Ibid., 106.

"*dharma*" expresses itself through its manifestation in a human being who leads others to the realization of the ultimate. His argumentation, although developed within Theravāda Buddhism, is actually similar to the pattern of the Mahāyāna "three bodies" teaching. But one should not forget that one of the roots of the "three bodies" teaching is found in the pre-Mahāyāna and Theravāda designation of the Buddha as the visible *dharma*. Buddhadāsa is thus able to capture an important aspect of the Christian concept of incarnation. Yet in the same way that he equates "God" and "*dharma*," he conflates the titles "Buddha" and "Son of God." Is his acknowledgment of Jesus as the Son thus achieved at the expense of seriously altering its meaning? Let us recall that, as I argued in the preceding chapter, the root of the Christian affirmation of Jesus as the Son of God is to be seen in Jesus' revelatory function. This is in line with Buddhadāsa's perception. Jesus is the embodiment of God's word inasmuch as he is the embodiment of God's kingdom or rule through his imitation of divine mercy.[80] If this argument is correct, the answer to whether Buddhadāsa, from a Christian perspective, distorts the concept of sonship depends on whether Christians are prepared to accept that the Buddhist spiritual values of nonattachment and not-self are part of what it means to live a life under God's rule, that is, of manifesting God's kingdom.

3. Like John Yokota, Buddhadāsa is rather exceptional in his recognition of Jesus. A more moderate, though still very open approach is that of the current Dalai Lama. When asked about his understanding of Jesus, the Dalai Lama answered: "For me, as a Buddhist, . . . Jesus Christ . . . was either a fully enlightened being or a Bodhisattva of a very high spiritual realization."[81] This is an ambiguous answer. From a traditional Mahāyāna perspective "a fully enlightened being," that is, a "Buddha," is more perfect than a Bodhisattva who is still on his way to the realization of perfect Buddhahood. However, in many Mahāyāna scriptures the boundaries between Buddhas and Bodhisattvas get blurred when it comes to supreme Bodhisattvas, as, for example, Avalokiteśvara. Nonetheless, a Bodhisattva is someone who represents selfless compassion. The Dalai Lama sees the Christian cross as a "deeply inspiring" and "perfect example" of the Bodhisattva ideal.[82] What makes it nevertheless difficult for him to regard Jesus as a Buddha is the difference between the teachings of Gautama and Jesus. The Dalai Lama suggests that if Jesus were fully enlightened, he may have employed his teachings about a personal God as a skillful means adapted to the epistemic and existential conditions of his Jewish audience. What counts, according

---

[80]See chapter 9.
[81]Dalai Lama 2002, 83.
[82]Dalai Lama 2010, 57.

to the Dalai Lama, is the result: by his teachings Jesus helped and inspired people to become compassionate.[83] In addressing Jesus' designation as both human and divine, the Dalai Lama voices his reservations against the idea of God as an absolute *being*. But like Lynn de Silva, he refers to the Trinity and the teaching of the three Buddha bodies as two analogous attempts to contemplate the relationship between "the finite and the infinite, the temporal and the atemporal, the relative and the ultimate."[84]

Similar to John Yokota, the Dalai Lama feels that a Buddhist recognition of Jesus as a manifestation of ultimate reality would involve a significant message to Buddhists, teaching them the importance of social responsibility.[85] This thought has also been expressed by other Buddhists, as for example Masao Abe[86] and John Makransky. Makransky holds that "the ultimate reality that Christians engage in practice as 'God' is what Buddhists engage in practice as '*dharmakāya*', differently understood."[87] Part of that difference is to Makransky "the Christian concern with a God of justice, vividly embodied in Jesus."[88] This aspect of the Christian God provides a constructive challenge to Buddhists. Buddhists, says Makransky, can learn to understand that a Bodhisattva must not only confront the individual barriers that blockade the good potential in each human being, that is, the defilements of greed, hatred, and delusion, but also the "social inhibitions and structures that prevent us from responding fully to others with reverence and care."[89]

CONCLUSION

Through dialogue, some Christians and Buddhists have tried to achieve a better understanding of what the confession of Gautama as the Buddha and of Jesus as the Son of God might mean to them reciprocally. On both sides, these attempts seem to point to the awareness of a common theme: The awakening to ultimate reality that makes a Buddha a Buddha and the embodiment of God's mercy in Jesus' life and death that makes him the Son can both be interpreted in terms of the manifestation of an unmanifest or unlimited reality in the realm of finite experience. Roger Haight and Paul Knitter have summarized this "functional analogy" rather precisely:

---

[83]See Grünschloß 2008, 258.
[84]Dalai Lama 2010, 69–70.
[85]See Ibid., 62–64.
[86]See, e.g., Abe 1995, 16, 181.
[87]Makransky 2005, 195.
[88]Makransky 2011, 125.
[89]Ibid., 126. See also Makransky 2014.

"Ultimacy revealed itself within them. . . . Both Buddha and Jesus, as understood by their followers, represent ultimate reality or the really real as an all-encompassing ungrounded power of being immanent to all things."[90] Moreover, Buddhist-Christian dialogue has led to the awareness of a common polarity in the spiritual practice of both religions, a polarity that Aloysius Pieris aptly describes as the union of "gnostic detachment and agapeic involvement."[91] Both traditions know that it is important to cultivate both aspects, though their accentuations may differ, and to keep them together as complementary and mutually corrective.

Acknowledging the Buddha by Christians and the Son by Buddhists implies creative challenges on both sides. To Christians, acknowledging the Buddha is to accept that the Buddha too manifests a "mind from beyond." From a Christian perspective the Buddha appears as another instance of divine incarnation. As a result, the Christian doctrine of incarnation as something unique needs to be revised.[92] To Buddhists, acknowledging the Son implies taking seriously that ultimate reality can be envisioned and experienced in the form of a personal God without diminishing the ineffable nature of the ultimate. That is, Buddhists are challenged to accept that liberative insight may also assume theistic forms of expression, which set free further dimensions of liberation as, in particular, the liberative value of justice.

Buddhist-Christian dialogue has thus convinced some Buddhists and some Christians of the inner complementarity of both traditions. In a number of cases this conviction has triggered a spirituality that sees itself as both Buddhist and Christian.[93] A prominent Buddhist example is Thich Nhat Hanh. According to him, accepting Jesus as "both the Son of Man and the Son of God is not difficult for a Buddhist,"[94] which he himself does by seeing Buddha and Christ as manifestations of the *dharmakāya*.[95] He expresses his own allegiance to Buddha and Christ in terms of filial piety, seeing Buddha as his natural and Christ as his "adopted" ancestor:[96]

> Before I met Christianity, my only spiritual ancestor was the Buddha. But when I met beautiful men and women who are Christians, I came to know Jesus as a great teacher. Since that day, Jesus Christ has become one of my spiritual ancestors. . . . on the altar of my hermitage

---

[90]Knitter and Haight 2015, 74.
[91]Pieris 1988, 118.
[92]This is further developed in Schmidt-Leukel 2005c and 2016.
[93]See the groundbreaking study of Rose Drew (2011) and the discussion in D'Costa and Thompson 2016.
[94]Nhat Hanh [1988] 1996, 36.
[95]Ibid., 51.
[96]Nhat Hanh 2005, 38–39, 41.

in France, I have statues of Buddhas and Bodhisattvas and also an image of Jesus Christ. I do not feel any conflict within me. Instead I feel stronger because I have more than one root.[97]

As so many others, Thich Nhat Hanh discerns the spiritual basis for the compatibility of the Buddha and the Son in the complementarity of wisdom and love. According to Nhat Hanh, the central point in the message of Jesus is forgiveness, which becomes radical in the commandment of loving one's enemy. But this can be done only if one understands one's enemy. When one sees and understands why the other causes suffering, forgiving becomes easier or even natural. Forgiveness therefore requires wisdom and mindfulness. In order to become the "blessed peacemakers" of Jesus' Sermon on the Mount, one needs to be "at peace with the world." This is how Buddha and Christ complement each other.[98]

A prominent Christian example of combining Buddhist and Christian spirituality is Paul Knitter.[99] If the Buddha and Jesus are particular and different manifestations of ultimate reality, "then they are important not just for their own followers but also for the followers of each other."[100] Explicitly, Knitter draws on Aloysius Pieris's affirmation of the complementarity of wisdom and compassion, and on Thich Nhat Hanh's complementary distinction between "Being Peace" and "Making Peace," and concludes: "If Buddha provides the *ability* to make peace, Jesus clarifies how *to do* it."[101]

In expounding the implications of the third of my four principles of interreligious theology, I underlined the interweaving of bilateral and multilateral dialogical efforts.[102] Hence, if we look at Christian and Muslim efforts to make reciprocal sense of their affirmations of Jesus as the Son of God and Muḥammad as the final Prophet, and if we connect this with the Christian and Buddhist efforts to make reciprocal sense of their affirmations of the Son and the Buddha, it will also be of interest to Christians to follow and learn from Muslim and Buddhist efforts in their attempts to understand the Buddha and the Prophet, as much as Buddhist-Christian dialogue may be of interest to Muslims and Muslim-Christian dialogue to Buddhists.

---

[97]Nhat Hanh [1988] 1996, 99–100.
[98]Ibid., 74–86.
[99]See Knitter 2009; Knitter and Haight 2015.
[100]Knitter 2012, 24.
[101]Ibid., 25.
[102]See above chapter 9.

12

The Buddha and the Prophet

HISTORICAL PERSPECTIVES

Within less than 150 years after its inception Islam spread from Spain to China. In the course of Islam's expansion toward the East, Muslims and Buddhists met in a number of different regions, and various countries with flourishing Buddhist cultures came under Muslim rule. But the reverse was also true. Before Iran became a Muslim country in the seventh century, Buddhism had been present in its eastern parts. Under Islamic rule Buddhism gradually disappeared. But in the thirteenth century Iran was conquered by the Buddhist Mongols and Buddhism was reintroduced.[1] After the politically motivated conversion of the Mongol ruler Mahmud Ghazan to Islam in 1295, Buddhism once again disappeared from Iran. As historical research has shown, "the history of Buddhist-Muslim relations was not characterized solely by conflict" but also involved "social accommodation and cultural cross-fertilisation."[2] Buddhists and Muslims have been in contact for many centuries and in various cultures, and although Muslim-Buddhist dialogue is still in its infancy, it has an important prehistory. The past has set some crucial parameters for both religions' present and future theological encounter. This will become clearer when we look at some of the earliest attempts by Muslims and Buddhists to make sense of their respective key figures, the Buddha and the Prophet.

Early Muslim Views

Early Muslim reports about Buddhism show how their authors struggled with accommodating the Buddha doctrinally. One of the earliest Muslim accounts

---

[1] On the encounter between Buddhism and Islam in Iran see Foltz 2010 and Vaziri 2012.
[2] Obuse 2010a, 67. See also Scott 1995; Berzin 2007, 2008; Elverskog 2010.

of Buddhism,[3] going back to an Indian travel record by Ibn-Khālid from the eighth century, reports that some Buddhists revere the Buddha as "the likeness of the Creator," while others see him as "the likeness of his apostle (sent) to them."[4] This understanding was confirmed in the tenth century by the Muslim historian Ṭāhir al-Maqdisī who reported that "the Buddhists are divided into two factions, that which claims that the Buddha is a prophet charged with a mission, and that which claims that He is the Creator Himself who was manifested to man in that image."[5] Apparently Ibn-Khālid and al-Maqdisī both refer to the two major Buddhist branches of non-Mahāyāna and Mahāyāna Buddhism and to their respective concepts of the Buddha.

As we saw in the preceding chapter,[6] the non-Mahāyāna schools, of which today only Theravāda Buddhism is left, understood the Buddha primarily as an exceptional teacher who proclaimed and embodied his transcendent insight. In Mahāyāna Buddhism a concept of the Buddha developed which understood him as a manifestation of a celestial Buddha and ultimately of transcendent reality itself. In their accounts of these different Buddhologies the early Muslim writers did not use the religious terminology of the Buddhists but translated it into their own familiar categories. The non-Mahāyāna understanding of the Buddha was rendered as that of "a prophet charged with a mission," and the Mahāyāna conception was identified with the notion of divine incarnation. An understanding of the Buddha as a prophet was more acceptable to Islam than the interpretation of the Buddha as a divine incarnation, which conveyed negative associations with Christianity. Thus al-Maqdisī commented on the latter: "May God protect us from such teachings."[7] But both Buddhist conceptions were reinterpreted within a Muslim doctrinal framework, that is, within a theistic framework. Whether the Buddha is taken as a prophet with a divine mission or as an incarnation of the "Creator," in both cases the difference from the original Buddhist notions is marked by the Muslim understanding of the ultimate as a theistic Creator-God.

The Muslim impression that the Buddha was revered by one strand of Buddhism as a prophet was naturally accompanied by the question of whether Muslims could endorse this view and recognize him as a *true* prophet. In principle, this was possible because of the Qur'ānic teaching that God had sent his messengers to every people.[8] Muslims were divided over this issue. In early Muslim discourse we encounter the Buddha in a

---

[3]The travel account is a section of Ibn al-Nadim's *Kitāb al-Fihrist* composed in the tenth century. See Elverskog 2010, 61–62.

[4]Elverskog 2010, 70.

[5]J. Smith 2012, 134; Elverskog 2010, 87.

[6]See chapter 11.

[7]J. Smith 2012, 134.

[8]See chapter 4.

familiar figure. As mentioned in the preceding chapter, the story of Barlaam and Josaphat had reached Christianity via Islam. Today, the Muslim version of this story is preserved in three different Arab recensions, of which the earliest presumably dates from the eighth or ninth century.[9] In the Muslim adaptation of the Buddha legend, Barlaam is Bilawhar and Josaphat bears the name Būdhāsaf. Būdhāsaf is characterized as a defender of monotheism against polytheism, and toward the end of the story he is praised as a prophet and renewer of religion. There is no doubt that the story was popular and widespread in the Islamic word. Ibn-Khālid says in his just mentioned account of Buddhism that some Buddhists identify the Buddha with "Budasaf, the wise, who came to them from Allah."[10] This obviously implies that as early as the eighth century, the story about Būdhāsaf was already well known in certain Muslim areas. But Būdhāsaf's status as a prophet was not uncontested. In the tenth and eleventh centuries some Muslim scholars, for example ʿAbd al-Qāhir al-Baghdādī, called Būdhāsaf a false prophet.[11] One reason may have been that the strong ascetic spirituality conveyed by the Buddha legend, which resonated so well with Christian monasticism, was seen as more problematic within Islam. It certainly had its appeal to Sufi circles, but other Muslims perhaps perceived it as being too close to Manichaean spirituality, which made it appear heretical.[12]

Although Muslim authors such as Ibn-Khālid realized the similarity between the Buddha and Būdhāsaf, the story of Būdhāsaf was not told as a story about the Buddha. But not only Būdhāsaf but also the Buddhist Buddha was treated with suspicion. This was nourished by the widespread Buddhist practice of his veneration through images, which Muslims took as idolatry. The link of Buddhism with idolatry was so close that the word "Buddha," in form of the Persian word *but*, became equivalent to "idol."[13] However, the question of whether the Buddha was a true or false prophet was not strictly dependent on the accusation of idolatry. Muslims had often blamed Christians as idolaters, while they nevertheless accepted Jesus as a genuine prophet, who was seen as innocent regarding the later idolatrous developments. Some Muslim authors, however, held the Buddha himself as responsible for the allegedly idolatrous cult.[14]

Another issue in the Muslim theological assessment of the Buddha was the lack of a clear monotheistic message. Those among the classical Muslim

---

[9]Forster 2015 counts three versions, while others interpret the Halle manuscript and the text by Ibn Bābawayh as one version, so that they count altogether just two versions (see Almond 1987, 403–4; Lopez and McCracken 2014, 54–89).

[10]Elverskog 2010, 70.

[11]See Forster 2015; Lopez and McCracken 2014, 59–60.

[12]See Almond 1987, 403–4; Forster 2015.

[13]Scott 1995, 143–44.

[14]See J. Smith 2012, 134; Obuse 2010a, 76.

authors who were nevertheless inclined to accept a prophetic mission of the Buddha were primarily attracted by the high standard of Buddhist morality. In the twelfth century, al-Sharastānī spoke favorably of the virtues of a Bodhisattva. He emphasized the rather peculiar nature of the Buddha as a religious figure, but compared him to the mysterious person of al-Khiḍr, who is widely revered in the Muslim tradition and often regarded as a prophet.[15] In the thirteenth century, the Persian author Juvaini praised Buddhist moral teachings as being "consonant with the law and faith of every prophet, urging men to avoid injury and oppression and the like, to return good for evil, and to refrain from the injuring of animals."[16]

An unambiguous acceptance of the Buddha as a true prophet is found in the work of Rashīd al-Dīn, a Muslim scholar of Jewish descent, who lived in the thirteenth and early fourteenth centuries and served in various high positions at the Mongol court in Iran. Al-Dīn was not only in immediate contact with the forms of Buddhism that the Mongol rulers had introduced to Iran but also witnessed the conversion of Mahmud Ghazan to Islam, which brought Buddhism into a dangerous situation. Ghazan's successor, Uljaytu (Öljeitü) Khan commissioned al-Dīn to write a sort of world history, the *Jāmi' al-Tavārīkh*. In its part on India this work includes a long section on the "Life and Teaching of Buddha."[17] Enjoying the support of the court, al-Dīn had access to a vast range of literature and was able to draw on the expertise of various foreign scholars. For the section on Buddhism he cooperated with the Buddhist monk Kamalaśrī from Kashmir and two Buddhists from China.[18]

Rashīd al-Dīn's account is without doubt "the most extensive and well-informed presentation of Buddhism in any Muslim source."[19] Theologically, al-Din pursued an inclusivist agenda. The relationship between Islam and Buddhism is not depicted as antagonistic but as continuous, with Islam as Buddhism's fulfillment. Given that al-Dīn wrote his work after Ghazan's conversion to Islam, this Muslim fulfillment theology may have also served Buddhist interests insofar as it granted Buddhism at least some kind of positive, although subordinate, place within the Muslim domain.[20]

Gautama Buddha, here referred to as Śākyamuni, is presented as the true prophet of India. In this respect he and his followers are distinguished from the followers of Śiva, Viṣṇu and Brahmā, and from the Jains and the

---

[15]See J. Smith 2012, 136–38. For a number of interesting parallels between the Muslim tradition about al-Khiḍr and Buddhist spirituality see S. H. Yusuf 2010.

[16]Boyle 1997, 60.

[17]For a complete German translation of this part see Jahn 1980.

[18]See Jahn 1965; Elverskog 2010, 145–62; Obuse 2010a, 85–87.

[19]Elverskog 2010, 149.

[20]For this sensible speculation see Obuse 2010a, 87.

Cārvākas, that is, the materialists. Hindus are, among other things, criticized for allegedly believing in a kind of trinity. And while their gods are accused of promoting evil, the Buddha is called a "prophet of mercy, compassion and kindness."[21] He and his followers are said to give guidance on "the straight path," which is a crucial Qur'ānic phrase to designate a true religion.[22] Like all major prophets, the Buddha is presented as having a book, whose content confirms the basic unity of all genuine prophets.[23] Much attention and approval is given to Buddhist morality and even more so to the Buddhist teaching according to which evil and good deeds will earn their respective results in the afterlife. However, belief in repeated rebirth is rejected.[24] One chapter contains a dialogue between the Buddha and a deity, here presented as an angel.[25] The text of this chapter follows closely a Buddhist original and functions as a summary of Buddhist spirituality. Nevertheless, al-Dīn gives the text a theistic tinge by characterizing Buddhist piety as the fear and search of God.[26] In this context, God is described by al-Dīn in typically Muslim ways as:

> A great Lord, without beginning and without end, truly and verily the maker of all works and (the Creator) of all creatures, vigilant, wise, indubitably without faults, knowing generally and specifically the cares of (all) creatures, without an equal and incomparable, nourisher of all, leader of all, guide of the willing and the unwilling . . . pardoning and rewarding.[27]

However, at another place, al-Dīn presents God in a way that emphasizes divine formlessness and seems to reflect some Buddhist influence:

> God, the Exalted, testified about himself that he was never born and never dies, that he has neither stature nor soul, nor scent nor colour. It is impossible for him to be seen by any eye on this Side or on the other Side. . . . He is the First and the Last of all things, infinite, without an abode, in need of nothing whereas he is needed by all.[28]

---

[21]Obuse 2010a, 85–86; see also Jahn 1965, xxxvi.

[22]See Obuse 2010a, 86; Jahn 1965, xxxvii.

[23]Jahn 1965, xxxvii–xxxviii.

[24]See Jahn 1980, 101.

[25]For a complete English translation of this chapter see Jahn 1965, lxi–lxiii. The Buddhist original has been identified as the *Devatasūtra*. See Mette 1981. For an English translation see https://www.reddit.com/r/Buddhism/comments/26inrv/the_sutra_of_the_questions_of_the_deva/.

[26]See also Schopen 1982. Apparently al-Dīn also replaced the Buddhist goal of *nirvāṇa* with the Muslim idea of paradise (see the differences between the original *Devatasūtra* and the text of al-Dīn in question 5 and in, the presumably inserted, question 8).

[27]Jahn 1965, lxiv.

[28]Ibid., lxxiv.

This, al-Dīn continues, is God as he had been known and praised by the Buddha. Indeed, attributes like "unborn," "deathless," and "formless" are typical Buddhist epithets of transcendent reality. Thus at least in rudimentary form al-Dīn tried to achieve both the application of the Muslim category of a "prophet" to the Buddha in order to express a fair degree of religious appreciation and the preservation of some features of genuine Buddhist spirituality within a Muslim doctrinal framework.

Of particular interest is how Rashīd al-Dīn dealt with the issue of idolatry. The Buddha taught, according to al-Dīn, that God himself had commanded him to build temples equipped with Buddha images as places where people should come to pray and where God would listen to their prayers.[29] According to al-Dīn, the inhabitants of Mecca and Medina had originally been Buddhists and venerated images of the Buddha in the Ka'ba before Muḥammad ordered these images to be destroyed,[30] an idea that even found artistic expression in later Persian art.[31] This idea is indicative of al-Dīn's view that the final prophet, Muḥammad, purified, excelled, and, to some extent, abrogated the religion that had been established by the earlier prophet Buddha.

Among the classical Muslim interpretations of the Buddha, al-Dīn's presentation is perhaps the most well-meaning one. However, large numbers of Muslims continued to simply regard the Buddha as a false prophet and his followers as idolaters. The third possibility, which early Muslim authors associated with Mahāyāna Buddhism, that is, the understanding of the Buddha as a divine incarnation, was, as far as I can see, not pursued by any early Muslim theologian as a serious theological option. Apparently, the negative connotations of this interpretation were far too strong to give it more theological attention. It is no surprise that a contemporary Muslim such as Imran Nazar Hosein, who is aware of the Mahāyāna understanding of the Buddha as an incarnation or manifestation of ultimate reality, puts this in parallel with Christian beliefs and rejects the first together with the latter as an unacceptable degradation of God.[32]

Early Buddhist Views

Although for centuries Buddhists and Muslims lived side by side, Buddhists have shown considerably less interest in Islam than vice versa. The very few Buddhist texts that mention Islam do so from a defensive perspective. That

---

[29]Ibid., lxxiv.
[30]Ibid., xl.
[31]See figure no. 4 in Elverskog 2010, 65.
[32]See Hosein [1972] 2014, 59, 132.

is, Islam was only taken into account when Buddhists felt threatened by it. Most of these texts belong to the literature associated with the influential Kālacakra Tantra.[33] The Kālacakra Tantra itself was presumably composed in North India in the eleventh century, when Buddhist areas had already experienced major attacks by the armies of Muslim rulers. The text assumes an apocalyptic perspective that it adopted from Vaishnava Hinduism.[34] Vaishnavism predicts the advent of Kalki, a future *avatāra* of Viṣṇu, who will bring the Golden Era of Truth (*satya yuga*). This bright future, however, can only begin after Kalki will have wiped out in a gigantic eschatological battle the non-Vedic religions of Jainism and Buddhism.[35] In the Buddhist adaptation of this narrative, Kalki appears as Kalkin Cakrin who is a manifestation of the Bodhisattva Mañjuśri. At the time of his arrival, all Hindus will have become Buddhists, and Kalkin Cakrin will lead the united forces of Buddhists and former Hindus, supported by major Hindu deities, against the true enemy, which is the "barbarian religion" of the Muslims. The decisive battle will be fought in the land of Mecca, and after the complete destruction of the barbarians the Golden Age will come, that is, "everyone on earth will be fulfilled with religion, pleasure, and prosperity."[36]

Muḥammad is introduced as "the teacher of the barbarian *Dharma*" and as the "guru and leader" of the barbarians.[37] Moreover, he is presented as belonging together with Adam, Noah, Abraham, Moses, Jesus, and the Mahdi to one "family of demonic snakes," that is, the Islamic prophets.[38] At the center of Muḥammad's "barbarian *Dharma*" is, according to the Kālacakra Tantra, the belief in a "mighty, merciless, demonic death-deity named *ar-Raḥmān*"[39]—an extremely sarcastic inversion of the term's original meaning of "the merciful," being one of the most prominent Qur'ānic names of God.[40] Muḥammad is not only presented as the teacher of this deity, he is also called a "demonic incarnation"[41] of *ar-Raḥmān*.[42] It is worth noting that the Kālacakra Tantra is not satisfied with presenting Muḥammad solely in those terms that are more in line with Muslim self-understanding, that is, as a religious teacher, a guru, or political leader, standing in the succession of other similar figures. In calling Muḥammad an incarnation, an *avatāra*, the Buddhist text applies a religious category that is familiar to Hinduism and

---

[33]For a detailed overview and analysis see Newman 1998.
[34]Schmidt-Leukel 2013d.
[35]This is depicted rather graphically in the Kalki Purāṇa. See Bhatt 1982.
[36]Newman 1995, 289.
[37]Newman 1998, 322, 337.
[38]Ibid., 288. Another figure in the list is the mysterious "white-clad one." See Newman 1998, 320ff.
[39]Ibid., 323.
[40]See also Obuse 2010a, 79.
[41]Newman 1995, 288; Newman 1998, 338.
[42]Newman 1998, 332–33.

Buddhism. And in depicting Muḥammad as the incarnation of a *demonic* deity, the text employs the category of incarnation as a means of complete religious rejection. The alternative would have been to see Muḥammad as the incarnation of the *dharmakāya*, the ultimate reality in a Buddhist sense, that is, as a Buddha. Yet such a positive religious assessment of the Prophet by Buddhists, which would match the positive evaluation of the Buddha as a prophet by Muslims, has so far not been detected in any classical Buddhist text—presumably because it does not exist.

In a later section of the Kālacakra Tantra, Kalkin's apocalyptic battle against Islam is reinterpreted as a metaphor for the inner spiritual struggle. Kalkin Cakrin is explained as a symbol of the true and luminous nature of one's own mind, and the "wicked barbarian lord" is a symbol for the "living beings' sin." His demon army stands for "malice, ill will, jealousy, and attachment and aversion," while Kalkin's forces consist of "love, compassion, sympathetic joy, and equanimity."[43] This spiritualization of the "external war" is reminiscent of the twofold meaning of *jihad* in Islam, which can also refer either to the inner spiritual struggle of following the way of God or to the external physical struggle of defending Islam against its enemies. In any event, the metaphorical reinterpretation in the Kālacakra Tantra, which associates Muḥammad and the Muslims with cardinal spiritual vices, is hardly suitable to put Islam in a better perspective than the literal interpretation found in the first part of the same text. In fact, a major Tibetan work from the eighteenth century repeats the prophecies of the Kālacakra Tantra in a very literal sense and relates them to concrete Muslim ethnicities. Their beliefs are, according to this text, based neither on logic nor meditative experience, but on "confusion, clinging, and ego-fixation" and are opposed to the true Dharma.[44] The Buddhist Uyghur *Insadi Sūtra*, dating perhaps from the fourteenth century, expresses the hope that in the future, with the coming of Buddha Maitreya, Islam and Christianity, here represented by the prophet Muḥammad, the "Lord Messiah" (i.e., Jesus) and Mother Mary, Baghdad and East-Rome, will turn toward Buddhism.[45]

Meanwhile, the Kalkin narrative underwent a further transformation among the Muslims of Baltistan. Baltistan is an area west of Tibet that used to be Buddhist before it came under Muslim rule during the fifteenth and sixteenth centuries. The people of Baltistan are of Tibetan descent and speak a Tibetan dialect. In their version of this apocalyptic story, the Buddhist Kalkin is identified as the *dajjāl*, who is an evil eschatological figure in Islam comparable to the anti-Christ in Christianity. In the final

---

[43]Newman 1995, 289.
[44]Jackson 2009, 382–84.
[45]See Tezcan 1974, 71–73.

battle between Buddhists and Muslims *dajjāl* alias Kalkin will be defeated through the power of Allah by the Mahdī, a messianic figure of Islam, who will be supported by the prophet Jesus. After Kalkin's defeat, the whole world will be converted to Islam.[46]

These glimpses into the past may illustrate that the hermeneutical question of how Buddhists and Muslims understand and make religious sense of their respective key figures has been, so far, closely intertwined with specific political constellations in combination with reciprocal superiority claims. For example, all three versions of the Kalkin narrative, the Hindu, the Buddhist, and the Muslim, have in common that the Golden Age will begin only after all other religions have been wiped out and all people have been converted to the one true faith. Under such presuppositions the chances of appreciating religious differences as an opportunity of theological learning are comparatively small. Has the beginning of contemporary Muslim-Buddhist dialogue revealed any potential to change this situation?

DIALOGICAL PERSPECTIVES

Tracking Down the Problem

During recent years Muslim Buddhist relations have unfortunately become very tense in several countries. In 2001 the Taliban destroyed the giant Buddha statues of Bamiyan, an act presented by the Taliban as directed against idolatry. However, it is rather likely that in this case Islamic iconoclasm was targeted more against the Western world than any Buddhists.[47] The times that there were Buddhists in Afghanistan venerating Buddha statues had been long gone. But in countries like Ladakh, Sri Lanka, Myanmar, and Thailand, Muslims and Buddhists live side by side. The recent tensions or even militant conflicts as in South Thailand are certainly complex and by no means only of a religious nature. Nevertheless, religion is part of the problem. As much as the accusation of idolatry is still present in anti-Buddhist Muslim propaganda, we still find evidence of the demonization of Islam on the Buddhist side. In South Thailand a mural painting from the nineteenth century depicts Muslims as the sons of Māra who are drowned and washed away by the floods coming from the earth goddess in defense of the Buddha.[48] To a considerable extent recent dialogues between Muslims and Buddhists were undertaken with the explicit goal of finding peaceful resolutions for

---

[46]For more details see Schmidt-Leukel 2013d.
[47]See Flood 2002; Obuse 2010a, 110–16.
[48]See the images in Keyes 2013, 59–62.

these conflict areas.[49] But apart from dealing with the particularities of local situations, it also emerged that Buddhist-Muslim relations need an overall improvement in terms of providing more accurate knowledge about each other and of deepening mutual understanding.

Given the historical parameters, the first and foremost goal of Buddhist-Muslim dialogue is certainly to overcome reciprocal misunderstandings and distortions. But can Buddhist-Muslim understanding also assume a deeper religious quality? Most of the recent Buddhist-Muslim dialogues focused on common moral values and excluded theological issues.[50] This is a significant step, though not without its own problems. The important document *Common Ground Between Islam and Buddhism*, to which I will return very soon, rightly states:

> [T]he simple affirmation of shared ethical and social values . . . can so easily go hand in hand with distrust, suspicion and condescension vis-à-vis the religion of the other. The religion of the other might be seen as generating positive ethical values despite the religion's falsity, rather than because of the religion's truth.[51]

As we have seen, Muslims, who expressed their *religious* appreciation of the Buddha in the past, did so by accepting the Buddha as a prophet. This, however, involves at least two problems: First the interpretation of the Buddha as a prophet may imply a subordination of Buddhism under Islam, if it is not accompanied by a pluralist attitude.[52] Second, it may risk simply ignoring the Buddhist understanding and meaning of the epithet "Buddha." Calling the Buddha a "prophet" may thus contradict the goal of deeper understanding. But if Muslims pay closer attention to the Buddhist conception, the question arises whether the Muslim category of prophethood can accommodate the category of buddhahood as understood by Buddhists. Is what it means to be a Prophet incompatible with what it means to be a Buddha? Can the notion of "prophethood" be expanded and transformed in such a way that it does full justice to Buddhist self-understandings? And what about those Mahāyāna Buddhist concepts that see the Buddha as an incarnation of ultimate reality? Will they have to remain excluded from any serious Muslim consideration?

Analogous questions arise for the Buddhist side: Buddhist assessments of the Prophet have been marked by demonizing him and by applying the

---

[49]For an overview see Obuse 2010a, 124–34. For Ladakh see Yi and Reis-Habito 2012.

[50]See, e.g., Ikeda and Tehranian 2004; Yi and Reis-Habito 2005. For a critical analysis see Schmidt-Leukel 2010a.

[51]Shah-Kazemi 2010a, 5.

[52]See chapter 4.

religious category of an "incarnation" or *avatāra* in a derogatory sense. While Muslims used the category of prophethood in positive and negative ways, by either categorizing the Buddha as a true or as a false prophet, Buddhists employed the category of incarnation only in the negative sense of a demonic incarnation—a characterization that, as we saw in the preceding chapter, was also applied to Jesus. It has only been since the twentieth century that Buddhists began to use the category positively, and that in relation to both figures.

In 1907, Daisetz T. Suzuki stated that Mahāyāna Buddhism perceives "an incarnation of the Dharmakāya in every spiritual leader regardless of his nationality and professed creed." Being an incarnation of the *dharmakāya* is, in classical Buddhist terminology, the designation of a human Buddha. And thus Suzuki continues that Mahāyāna Buddhists "recognise a Buddha in Socrates, Mohammed, Jesus, Francis of Assisi, Confucius, Laotze, and many others."[53] Per Suzuki, the *dharmakāya*, although not a Creator God, can nevertheless be called the "God . . . of Buddhism" because it is "a reality which transcends the limitations of phenomenality, but which is nevertheless immanent everywhere and manifests itself in its full glory,"[54] being "an inexhaustible fountainhead of love and compassion."[55] In 1985, Masao Abe suggested a similar understanding and listed Moses, Jesus, and Muḥammad, alongside Gautama Buddha, as incarnations of the *dharmakāya*. However, in contrast to Suzuki, Abe was more sensitive to the fact that Muslims do not regard Muḥammad as an incarnation of Allah, and Jews do not accept Moses as an incarnation of Yahweh.[56] Nonetheless Abe justified his interpretation by taking the *dharmakāya* as referring to an "ultimate ground" of reality expressing itself in a "boundless openness," which found historical embodiment in those figures.

Masao Abe's provisos show that Buddhist attempts at expressing a positive religious evaluation via the classical Buddhist concept of incarnation or buddhahood face similar problems as the Muslim application of prophethood to the Buddha. Can Buddhists do more justice to Muslim self-understanding and still express a religious appreciation? Can Buddhist religious categories be expanded and transformed so that they might accommodate the category of "prophethood"? If we recognize the similarity of the hermeneutical problems that surround the transreligious application of prophethood and buddhahood/incarnation, we will become aware that the underlying questions concern the inner relationship between all three categories of

---

[53]Suzuki [1907] 1977, 63.
[54]Ibid., 219.
[55]Ibid., 223.
[56]Abe 1985, 183.

prophethood, incarnation, and buddhahood. There are substantial similarities between Buddhist-Muslim dialogue, Muslim-Christian dialogue, and Christian-Buddhist dialogue. And these similarities have something to do with the logical or theological interrelations between the three confessional categories. That is, any progress that is achieved in understanding the relationship between prophethood, buddhahood, and incarnation in any of these different dialogues will have its repercussions on the other two. This once again illustrates how important it is for an interreligious theology to move beyond purely bilateral dialogues and combine multireligious perspectives.

Let me now specify these considerations and discuss whether Buddhist-Muslim dialogue has made any progress along the lines just sketched.

Acknowledging the Buddha

The question of whether Gautama Buddha can be regarded as a true prophet is still vital and controversial among contemporary Muslims.[57] In the twentieth century some Muslims suggested that the Buddha is mentioned in the Qur'ān under the name Dhul Kifl, interpreted as "the man from Kapilavastu" (21:85, 38:48). Or that the Buddha is indirectly referred to by the mentioning of a fig-tree in Sūrah 95:1, which is then associated with the Buddhist tree of enlightenment.[58] However, the by far most important and most impressive argument in support of understanding the Buddha as "one of the Messengers sent by God to humanity" has been presented in the document *Common Ground Between Islam and Buddhism*.[59] This text was published in 2010 on the initiative of Prince Ghazi of Jordan and supported by the current Dalai Lama. Prince Ghazi had also been the main initiator of the document *A Common Word Between Us and You*, which has become a milestone in Muslim-Christian dialogue.[60] The title *Common Ground Between Islam and Buddhism* deliberately indicates its connection with *A Common Word*. According to Prince Ghazi the hope is that *Common Ground* will have the same beneficial impact as *A Common Word*.[61]

Reza Shah-Kazemi was commissioned to draft *Common Ground*. He is a Muslim theologian and research associate at the Institute of Ismaili Studies in London. His theology is deeply influenced by Sufism and the interpretation of Sufism within the "perennialist" or "traditional school."[62] The most famous names associated with this school are Muslims like René Guénon

---

[57]See, e.g., Obuse 2010a; 2010b.
[58]See Obuse 2010b, 57–58.
[59]Shah-Kazemi 2010a.
[60]See chapter 10.
[61]Ghazi 2010b, x.
[62]See also chapter 4.

(1886–1951), Frithjof Schuon (1907–98), and Seyyed Hossein Nasr (b. 1933). Since its inception the school has had an interreligious orientation, so it has included Hindus, such as Ananda Coomaraswamy (1877–1947), Buddhists, such as Marco Pallis (1895–1989), and Christians, such as Huston Smith (b. 1919). Interreligious reflection as practiced and cultivated in the traditional school had a considerable impact on Shah-Kazemi and thus also influenced the argumentation found in *Common Ground*.

The explicit goal of the document is helping "Muslims to see Buddhism as a true religion or *dīn*, and Buddhists to see Islam as an authentic *Dharma*."[63] To achieve this goal the document deals with three major issues: First, the question of Buddhist nontheism; second, the issue of idolatry; and third, the compatibility of detachment and compassion in spiritual practice.

1. In line with a general conviction of the traditional school, the document defends the view that Buddhism is *nontheistic* but not atheistic. Buddhism does not deny ultimate reality but interprets it in a largely nontheistic way.[64] *Common Ground* further suggests that the Buddhist understanding of ultimate reality coincides with what Islamic theology calls the "essence" (*al-Dhāt*) of God.[65] This essence is understood as God's transcendent nature beyond all divine attributes. The Buddhist understanding of the unconditioned, ultimate reality is interpreted as a systematic abstention from the application of all divine attributes for the sake of divine transcendence.[66] According to the document, this does not only confirm but "can also deepen the Muslim's apprehension of the utter transcendence of God."[67] "No human conception of God—even if fashioned by ideas received through Revelation—can be identified with the transcendent reality of the divine Essence."[68] In Buddhism, divine oneness is implicitly affirmed in terms of nonduality. The Mahāyāna Buddhist analysis of all things as being empty of any self or substance can be understood as their non-dual dependence on the one ultimate and ineffable reality. Inasmuch as the ultimate is nondually manifest in the multiplicity of things, it is at the same time "infinite plenitude."[69] According to *Common Ground*, the Buddhist concept of nonduality can be adopted as a confirmation of the Qur'ānic teaching that everything is not existing in and of itself, but only as the "Face of God."[70]

2. Against this metaphysical background the document addresses the issue of *idolatry*. This issue arises in two different but interrelated ways, in

---

[63]Shah-Kazemi 2010a, 7.
[64]Ibid., 31. See, for example, Schuon 1993, 17–29.
[65]See Shah-Kazemi 2010a, 5.
[66]Ibid., 31.
[67]Ibid., 39.
[68]Ibid., 40.
[69]Ibid., 44–45.
[70]Ibid., 46–47.

terms of the veneration of Buddha images and, more profoundly, in terms of the veneration of the Buddha himself as an incarnation of the ultimate. It is remarkable that *Common Ground* does not envisage the issue of idolatry as a problem of Muslim-Buddhist controversy, that is, as something that sets Buddhism and Islam apart, but as a logical and ontological problem known within both traditions. Both traditions hold that the nature of ultimate reality will be missed if some finite reality is mistaken as the absolute. This generates the question of "how can the ultimate reality be 'embodied' in the form of a Buddha" without ceasing to be the ultimate?[71]

Common Ground suggests an answer that reflects the dialectical nature of the ultimate as, on the one hand, being totally empty of any attribution and, on the other hand, as being infinite plenitude as the ultimate ground of everything. That is, something can be accepted as an embodiment or manifestation of the ultimate to the extent that it is perceived as empty of itself and thus "transparent" to its ultimate ground.[72] In relation to religious figures this means: "The one who is most empty of his own self . . . is the one who is most full of the *Dharma*."[73] Or, in Islamic terms, the "Face of the Absolute shines through their individuality."[74] This implies that in a sense "God is seen or remembered 'through' such saintly beings."[75] On the existential level, selflessness is inseparably connected to the realization of particular traits of saintliness. Ultimate reality is the source of the qualities manifested by the selfless or transparent person. The Ultimate manifests itself through such spiritual qualities, and the one who perfects these qualities is "thus the most perfect mirror in which the utterly unknowable and eternally inaccessible Essence makes known and renders accessible Its own infinite perfections."[76] This can be observed in both the Buddha and the Prophet. The veneration of Buddha images has thus a function that is comparable to the Islamic practice of remembering God's names and attributes and of remembering the prophets. The contemplation of the Buddha by means of Buddha images can thus be taken as a "legitimate form of remembrance of God."[77]

These statements are astonishing in various ways. They allow Muslims to accept the Buddha as a prophet while doing justice to Buddhist concepts of the Buddha as an incarnation or manifestation of the *dharmakāya*. Moreover, this way of making space within Islamic theology for a synthesis of

---

[71] Ibid., 60.
[72] See ibid., 62
[73] Ibid., 72.
[74] Ibid., 71.
[75] Ibid.
[76] Ibid., 75.
[77] Ibid., 73.

prophethood and incarnation resonates with voices like that of Muhammad Legenhausen, who suggests, on sound Qur'ānic grounds, that Jesus can be accepted as someone in whom the word was made flesh, that is, in whom divine revelation assumed the form of a living person.[78] In fact, Shah-Kazemi, the drafter of *Common Ground Between Islam and Buddhism*, has also accepted that Jesus "is" or "constitutes" the Word of God.[79] Yet different from Legenhausen, *Common Ground* brings the figure of the Prophet himself into play. It does not exclusively focus on the inlibration of something ultimate (God's Word) in the Qur'ān. Via the idea of the Prophet as someone who perfectly embodies spiritual qualities rooted in the ultimate reality itself, an incarnational element is uncovered within the category of prophethood itself. This element allows for an expansion of prophethood that may also accommodate the category of the Buddha.

3. This solution is further substantiated by what *Common Ground* says about the key features of Buddhist and Muslim *spiritual practice*. It affirms that in both traditions, the cultivation of compassion/mercy in combination with detachment is regarded as essential. The particular emphasis on detachment in Buddhism reminds Muslims that being dominated by desire after worldly goods is a subtle but nevertheless vicious form of idolatry and polytheism. At this "level of spiritual insight into the human condition," Buddhist-Muslim dialogue can lead to genuine "mutual illumination."[80] As we saw in the preceding chapter, the insight into the spiritual complementarity of detachment and loving commitment also emerged from Christian-Buddhist dialogue.[81] And like the work of Aloysius Pieris, *Common Ground* does not merely describe this complementarity as one of detachment and compassion but also as that of "wisdom and love."[82] The resonance or consonance between progress in Muslim-Buddhist and Muslim-Christian dialogue is obvious.

Acknowledging the Prophet

So far, Buddhist efforts in making religious sense of the Muslim confession of Muhammad as the Prophet have been comparatively minimal. The Thai Buddhist reformer Bhikkhu Buddhadāsa regarded Islam as a valid religion together with Christianity, Hinduism, and Buddhism, and had no difficulty in applying the Qur'ānic concept of "messenger" or "apostle" to the Buddha.

---

[78]See chapter 10.
[79]Shah-Kazemi 2010b, 128–29.
[80]Shah-Kazemi 2010a, 84.
[81]See chapter 11.
[82]See Shah-Kazemi 2010a, 111.

To Buddhadāsa "apostle" means "a man of God who preaches the truth."[83] As has been shown in the preceding chapter, Buddhadāsa understood "God" as equivalent to Dharma in that both terms point to an ultimate reality that is experienced in radical selflessness.[84] While Buddhadāsa held that the essential message of all three religions—Christianity, Islam, and Buddhism—is identical, he explained their differences as adaptations of their joint truth to the differences in "environment, time, habits, mentality, temperament, etc. of people."[85] Wisdom, faith, and willpower are, to Buddhadāsa, three indispensable components of each valid religion, but they appear in different emphases. In Buddhism the dominant factor is wisdom, faith in Christianity, and willpower in Islam.[86] However, as far as I am aware, Buddhadāsa did not go into any further details.

Somewhat more specific has been the Dalai Lama in his recent writings about Islam. He points out various parallels on the level of religious practice: Like Islam, Buddhism has a kind of creed, that is, the triple refuge to the Buddha, Dharma, and Saṅgha (community). The Buddhist recitation of sūtras or mantras can be compared to Muslim ritual prayer, Muslim almsgiving to Buddhist generosity, Muslim fasting to food restrictions within the Buddhist order, and the pilgrimage to Mecca, the Hajj, to various forms of pilgrimage within Buddhism.[87] But the Dalai Lama also underlines the Islamic belief in God and a soul as something that sets Islam and Buddhism apart.[88] Nevertheless, he offers an interesting way of how he as a Buddhist can still make sense of Muḥammad's message. If the meaning of *islām* is "surrender" in the sense of submission to the will of God, and if "God is characterized as the Compassionate and the Merciful," the central point of Islam is "an absolute submission to the ideal of universal compassion."[89] This is certainly a spiritual attitude fully endorsed by Buddhism, which generates the question: Can Buddhists make sense of the Prophet as someone who calls to "submission" (*islām*) in the sense of calling to compassion?

Buddhadāsa's and the Dalai Lama's attempts to face Islam in its distinctiveness remain cautiously constructive, but altogether still vague. Although the Dalai Lama gives a sketch of the Muslim understanding of prophethood, he does not comment on it.[90] No doubt, the emphasis on the close relation between mercy and compassion is an important step in moving toward a Buddhist appreciation of the Prophet. However, a fuller account would

---

[83]Buddhadāsa 1967, 8.
[84]See chapters 6 and 11.
[85]Buddhadāsa 1967, 24–25.
[86]Ibid., 12–13.
[87]Dalai Lama 2010, 82–85.
[88]Ibid., 86.
[89]Ibid., 79.
[90]Ibid., 80–81.

have to take note of the inner link between mercy and justice in Muslim understanding. A move in this direction is found among Japanese Buddhists. One evident reason for this is seen in the similarities between the medieval Japanese reformer Nichiren Shōnin (1222–82) and Muḥammad. At the beginning of the twentieth century, Muḥammad was praised in Japanese Buddhist publications for manifesting a spirituality that is more this-worldly and realistic than the other-worldly and idealist spirituality of Buddha and Christ. This puts Muḥammad nearer to Nichiren. According to Hannosuke Ikemoto, both Muḥammad and Nichiren show the same "rebellious, passionate and revolutionary character." This enables both to be of benefit to society in the face of degenerate tendencies.[91] Similar statements are also found in contemporary Japanese Buddhist writings.[92] In 2000, Daisaku Ikeda, a leading Japanese Buddhist in the tradition of Nichiren, referred to Nichiren as "an outspoken prophet."[93] In his dialogue with Ikeda, the political scientist and Sufi Muslim Majid Tehranian (1937–2012) confirmed that the critical emphasis on the state of the present world is a "common feature of Islam and Nichiren Buddhism."[94] According to Tehranian, Nichiren's life resembles that of Muḥammad in many respects. "Their message will continue to be threatening to the ruling classes who prefer people to be submissive."[95] In the course of this dialogue, Ikeda specified his understanding of a prophet as a social and religious reformer. Prophets, according to Ikeda, criticize forms of social and religious degeneration.[96] And so did Nichiren: He "squarely confronted the established religions of his day that had become aristocratic and contemptuous of the ordinary folk."[97]

A prophetic spirituality as exemplified by Nichiren, that is, a spirituality that involves active social and religious criticism, is not absent from Buddhism but less strong and widespread than it is in Islam or Christianity, both of which inherited it from Judaism. Rita Gross (1943–2015), a scholar of religious studies and a practitioner of Tibetan Buddhism, thus argued that Buddhism should learn from the Abrahamic traditions by integrating their "prophetic voice."[98] According to Gross, "the Buddhist emphasis on compassion and the Christian prophetic emphasis on justice and righteousness . . . are subtly but significantly different from each other, and have a good bit to say to each other."[99] This assessment can be easily expanded to

---

[91]See Obuse 2010a, 177–78.
[92]See ibid., 225.
[93]Ikeda and Tehranian 2004, 31.
[94]Ibid., 25.
[95]Ibid., 32.
[96]Ibid., 30–31, 56–57.
[97]Ibid.
[98]Gross 1993, 132ff.
[99]Gross and Ruether 2001, 164.

the "prophetic voice" in Islam. In a notable speech at a Buddhist-Muslim dialogue in Bangkok in 2006, the Theravāda Buddhist monk Phra Paisan Visalo expressed a similar view when saying: "As a Buddhist, I think we can learn a lot from Muslim people, especially about cultivating a sense of justice."[100]

Nichiren's self-understanding was that of a Bodhisattva. The compassion that a Bodhisattva should cultivate involved, in his view, compassionate action for the benefit and social well-being of the people and the nation. This gave his spirituality its prophetic tinge. It is further evidence that the Bodhisattva ideal, or, more generally, the Buddhist practice of compassion, may enable Buddhists to make religious sense of the Muslim confession of Muḥammad as the prophet. At the same time it challenges Buddhists to expand and transform their understanding of compassionate practice by combining it with social criticism.

A Bodhisattva who has achieved perfection has become a Buddha. Or, conversely, a Buddha is a perfected Bodhisattva. Hence, if prophet-hood can be meaningfully connected to the ideal of a Bodhisattva, the category of prophethood is also interlinked with buddhahood. Nichiren's self-understanding as a Bodhisattva was strongly shaped by his belief in the Buddha Nature of all beings. A close connection between the Buddhist Bodhisattva ideal and its teaching of the universal Buddha Nature, on the one hand, and the Islamic understanding of prophethood, on the other hand, has been pointed out by Toshihiko Izutsu (1914–93). Izutsu was a Japanese Zen Buddhist and an outstanding scholar of Islam, with close links to the Traditional School. In an essay titled "A Buddhist View of Reality," Izutsu gave a brief account of how the Mahāyāna understanding of ultimate reality emerged from two lines of thinking: the radical apophatism, as expressed in the philosophy of emptiness, and the Buddha Nature teaching, which thematizes the ontological ground that makes the appearance of Buddhas possible. Through the merger of these two lines "emptiness" became "a plenitude of being," "a metaphysical storehouse of all ontological potenti-alities." Buddha Nature is thus emptiness in its "positive, ever-creative . . . aspect." According to Izutsu, Buddha Nature is therefore

> comparable . . . with the Islamic concept of *ḥaqīqah Muḥammadīyah* "Muḥammad-Reality" or the innermost reality of Muḥammad, indicat-ing in a similar way the universal, cosmic, and metaphysical reality of all things which is attributed to Muḥammad in that it found its most remarkable embodiment in Muḥammad, the prophet of Islam.[101]

---

[100]Visalo 2006, 20.
[101]All quotations in Izutsu 2008, 170–71.

The concept of "Muḥammad-Reality" is rooted in a branch of Islamic philosophy that is closely connected to the work of Ibn ʿArabī. Here the whole cosmos is understood as an expression and manifestation of God's names, that is, of God's revelation or manifestation in and through creation. Within this context, Muḥammad is seen as an example of human perfection, and as such he becomes the vessel of revelation.[102] This understanding provides indeed a solid link between the religious concepts of the Buddha and the Prophet. It is the same link that has been pointed out in *Common Ground*. Hence it is no surprise that this document also alludes to the concept of "the pre-human archetypal reality of the Prophetic substance," that is, the "Muḥammad Reality."[103] Moreover, in the context of Muslim-Christian dialogue, Shah-Kazemi, the drafter of *Common Ground*, argues that the notion of "Muḥammadan Reality" corresponds to the Christian understanding of the Logos.[104]

If we take all of this into account, we may conclude that prophethood, sonship, and buddhahood can be seen as different categories in which humanity has given expression to its confidence that human beings have the potential to become vehicles of divine revelation. They can be living promises of ultimate mercy in face of human guilt and failure, and mirrors, symbols, or images of those qualities and values of human life that ultimate reality elicits and sustains.[105] As in Christian-Muslim dialogue, Buddhist-Muslim dialogue will also highlight the complementarity of loving commitment and wise detachment as a central pair of those qualities. I think that the Muslim philosopher Tariq Ramadan has given this a remarkable expression:

> Loving life and watching it fade away, loving ourselves without any illusions about ourselves, loving one's loves in the knowledge that time will take them away, loving without idolatry, and loving with an awareness of the relativity of all things. That is the profound meaning of the loving compassion that must, in the Buddhist tradition, set us free. In the monotheist religions, the oneness of God has the same deep meaning. We must free ourselves from our illusions, from the false worship of our desires and idols of one's inner self if we wish to accede to a love-lucidity as we seek a proximity that can perceive the extent of distance in the absolute.[106]

---

[102]See Chittick 1994, 31–35.
[103]See Shah-Kazemi 2010a, 59–60, 72.
[104]See Shah-Kazemi 2010b, 124.
[105]For a similar suggestion see I. Yusuf 2005.
[106]Ramadan 2010, 205.

13

Toward an Interreligious Theology
of Creation

Any argument that allows Muslims, Christians, and Buddhists to make reciprocal sense of their confessional affirmations of the Prophet, the Son, and the Buddha presupposes that Islam, Christianity, and Buddhism are related, in different ways and through different concepts, to the same ultimate reality or at least (to bring in polycentric pluralism) to different but complementary aspects of a more complex ultimate. Among the strongest objections advanced against this line of interreligious thinking is that Muslim, Christian, and Buddhist concepts of the ultimate are incompatible because of the doctrine of creation. Whereas Islam and Christianity usually understand ultimate reality as a personal creator God, this concept seems to be unacceptable to Buddhism. Let me mention just three examples. From a Mahāyāna perspective, the Fourteenth Dalai Lama states:

> Now from the philosophical point of view, the theory that God is the creator, is almighty and permanent, is in contradiction to the Buddhist teaching. From this point of view there is disagreement. For Buddhists, the universe has no first cause and hence no creator, nor can there be such a thing as a permanent, primordially pure being.[1]

As we have seen, Buddhism does not deny ultimate reality as such.[2] But the ultimate is not conceptualized as *a* being, and in particular not as a personal creator God. Theravāda Buddhism affirms *nirvāṇa* (Pāli: *nibbāna*) as a transcendent, unconditioned, and imperishable reality, but not as a divine creator. Christopher Gowans makes this point very clear:

---

[1]Dalai Lama 1988, 12.
[2]See chapter 11.

Insofar as *Nibbāna* is portrayed as ultimate reality that is beyond change and conditioning, and that, when attained, enables us to overcome suffering, it might invite comparison with the God of the theistic traditions of Judaism, Christianity, and Islam. There are points of similarity. As we saw . . . *Nibbāna* is transcendent reality in the broad sense of the term: it is beyond the ordinary world of sense-experience and may be approached only via meditation. But the differences are quite significant. The most important are that, unlike God, *Nibbāna* is not the ultimate cause of the universe, and it is not a personal being, who is omnipotent, omniscient, and all-loving.[3]

Steven Collins, after a detailed account of the canonical statements about the transcendent and unconditioned nature of *nirvāṇa*, concludes:

> But a crucial difference between nirvāṇa and God(ess), the Hindu idea of brahman, the Chinese Tao, etc., is that nirvana is never said to be the origin or ground of the universe. . . . There is no ultimate beginning of things in Buddhism.[4]

In Buddhism, the relationship between ultimate reality and the world is not defined in terms of creation but of salvation or liberation. *Nirvāṇa* is not seen as the creative cause of the world, but as that reality that ensures liberation from conditioned existence. And this, apparently, also applies to Mahāyāna Buddhist concepts of the ultimate as Buddha Body (*dharmakāya*) or Buddha Nature (*tathāgatagarbha*) or as the True Reality beyond all concepts (*dharmadhatu, tattva, tathātā*, etc.).[5]

---

[3]Gowans 2003, 151.

[4]Collins 1998, 176–77.

[5]Some caution is advisable in interpreting "emptiness" (*śūnyatā*) as a Mahāyāna concept for ultimate reality. Initially, that is, in the philosophy of Nāgārjuna, "emptiness" is an epistemological or hermeneutical concept. Or better, it is an anticoncept that entails that all concepts are "empty" of what they signify. Concepts, or their content, are constructs, which receive their meaning not from reality but from a larger web of interdependent concepts, that is, through various forms of logical or grammatical determination and definition: A cause is "a cause" only in dependence on an effect and vice versa. Conceptual images of reality are unable to present reality as it truly is: " 'Not caused by something else,' 'peaceful,' 'not elaborated by discursive thought,' 'indeterminate,' 'undifferentiated': such are the characteristics of true reality (*tattva*)" (*Mūlamadhayamakakārikā* 18:9. Translation from Streng 1967, 204). "Emptiness" is therefore not a feature of a specific kind of reality, e.g., "ultimate reality." "Emptiness" is a feature of concepts, of *all* concepts, including itself (the "emptiness of emptiness"). According to the philosophy of emptiness, an ontological distinction between ultimate and nonultimate reality, e.g., between the unconditioned reality of *nirvāṇa* and the conditioned reality of *saṃsāra*, is only provisionally true. At the level of absolute (= nonconceptual) truth, both are indistinguishable, because no conceptual distinction applies to "true reality" (*Mūlamadhayamakakārikā* 25:19–24). In that negative sense, however, the understanding of "emptiness" refers to an insight that is, according to Nāgārjuna, constitutive for the attainment of *nirvāṇa* (*Mūlamadhayamakakārikā* 24:10). "Emptiness" may therefore

In this chapter, I will not deal with the question in what sense personal or impersonal qualities can be applied to ultimate reality. If there is a basic consensus between theistic and nontheistic religions that ultimate reality is, strictly speaking, ineffable or transcategorial and therefore beyond personal and impersonal categories, its designation via personal and impersonal attributes is probably best understood as referring to different modes of religious experience. That is, ultimate reality can be experienced in ways either shaped by personal or by impersonal concepts. It can be experienced as being like a merciful father or compassionate mother, or like a "cool place," a "deep ocean," a "safe city," and so on, to mention just a few of the prominent Buddhist impersonal analogies. Moreover, one must not forget that theistic religions also obtain over a range of impersonal concepts when they refer to ultimate reality, whereas a religion like Buddhism employs a paramount personal image: that of the Buddha. In early Buddhism, the Buddha is understood as the "visible *nirvāṇa*" or "visible *dharma*," and in Mahāyāna Buddhism ultimate reality is referred to as the essential "body" or nature of the Buddha. The question of whether the ultimate is creative or noncreative seems to be more intricate than the question of whether it is personal or impersonal. Although I will deal with the question of creation from a Christian perspective, some of my considerations may also be of interest to other theistic traditions.[6]

In line with the second principle of an interreligious theology and following Wilfred Cantwell Smith's recommendation, I take the apparent contradiction between the Buddhist denial and the Christian affirmation of a divine creator as an "invitation to synthesis."[7] The exploration of possible compatibilities in face of apparent incompatibilities is one of the most exciting and significant facets of interreligious theology. For it is here that we can really proceed to new insights that may challenge, enrich, and transform one's previous understanding. It is here that interreligious dialogue provides a genuine opportunity of theological learning.

---

indirectly refer to "ultimate reality." In later forms of Mahāyāna, the concepts of emptiness, true reality, and Buddha Nature all merged, which, at times, gave "emptiness" a more positive meaning, beyond its basic function as a critique of all concepts (see also Schmidt-Leukel 2006b, 105–26). Given the different connotations of "emptiness,," it could indeed be misleading to identify "emptiness" and "God," as John Cobb repeatedly argued. However, in some respect, as Cobb admits, "emptiness" resonates with the Neoplatonic strand of Christian theology (e.g., Cobb 1985, 154–60), especially if the ultimate nature of God is also understood as the "true reality" of, behind, or in everything. In that sense, "emptiness" could then be taken as indirectly referring to an ultimate reality that is obscured (but in a sense also revealed) by different conceptual manifestations (see Hick 1989, 291).

[6]For a more comprehensive presentation of the following argument see Schmidt-Leukel 2006a.

[7]Smith 1975, 160. See also chapter 9 above.

THE BUDDHIST CRITIQUE OF A DIVINE CREATOR

Buddhism looks back on a long tradition of critical intellectual engagement with theistic teachings, which were initially all of a Hindu provenience.[8] Buddhist objections are of three types: First, arguments directed against any attempts at demonstrating the existence of a divine creator; second, arguments that intend to disprove the existence of a divine creator; and third, arguments that criticize belief in a divine creator as spiritually detrimental or even harmful. Let us look briefly at these three types of objections.

1. Buddhist critiques of the first type are most frequently directed against teleological or cosmological theistic arguments. The teleological argument assumes that the world exhibits some form of intelligent design and concludes from this the existence of a divine designer. Against this argument Buddhist philosophers such as Dharmakīrti (7th c.) and Bhāvaviveka (6th c.) held that the intelligent or mental origin of the world does not necessarily have to be a single divine mind but could also be the mental karmic activity of the sentient beings. This objection is in line with the standard Buddhist belief in a beginningless chain of universes. After a long period, each universe will perish and, after a brief interval, a new universe will arise out of the collective karma of the sentient beings from the previous world. The diversity of these karmic tendencies is the reason for the structured diversity within the emerging new universe. That is, the karmic energies of those who deserve to be reborn as denizens of hells, as demons, as animals, as humans, or as deities are the cause for the emergence of a new world, which will contain the respective realms of reincarnation, that is, hells, demons, animals, human beings, and heavens.[9]

This belief is also behind the Buddhist refutation of cosmological arguments. Cosmological arguments assume that everything in the world has a cause of existence and conclude that, therefore, the world as such would also need a cause, which is the divine creator. The general objection is that if everything needs a cause, God too would need a cause. If, however, there is something that can exist without a cause, then this could also be the world as such. Buddhists support the first half of the argument: If everything needs a cause, God too would need a cause. A chain of infinite causes, however, would not need any further cause—outside of that chain—to explain its existence, because each member is explained by its preceding cause. That is, there is no need to postulate a divine creator of the whole line of karmic

---

[8]See Nyanaponika 1981; Lindtner 1999; Schmidt-Leukel 2006a; Patil 2009. For early modern and contemporary versions of Buddhist critiques of Christian concepts of God, see Elison 1991; Kern 1992; Dharmasiri 1988.

[9]*Abhidharmakośa* 4:1. See Pruden 1988–90, 2:551 (see also ibid., 2:477).

creators, that is, the sentient beings, which through their karmic tendencies cause each subsequent world to arise.[10] If a theist would admit that karma, or collective karma, is indeed a factor in the evolution of successive worlds, but would postulate God as an additional meta-cause, as some Hindu theists were inclined to do, this, according to the Buddhist critics, would represent an unnecessary and illegitimate multiplication of causes. Moreover, it would imply an unresolved tension between the sovereignty of the divine creator and the admitted sovereignty of the karmic agents: The divine creator would be sovereign but bound to act in accordance with the karma of the beings.[11]

2. Behind the Buddhist refutation of theistic arguments we thus find an alternative theory of creation: creation as a continuous process driven by collective karma. This is also relevant to the second type of traditional objections, which directly refute the existence of a divine creator. One such objection is based on the problem of evil: If God is good and almighty, why has he created a world full of suffering? This objection takes a specifically Buddhist form in its connection with what can be called the *argument from human responsibility*. The Buddhist view of creation by collective karma is based on the belief in just karmic retribution. Those who produced good karma will earn a good rebirth; those who accumulated evil karma will be reborn in a bad form of existence. On a cosmological scale, this presupposes that there is no first beginning to the chain of successive worlds, because each new world is believed to be the fair result of the karmic tendencies from the beings of the previous world.

Against this background, the belief in a divine creator would lead to a serious dilemma: If there is a first world in an absolute sense, that is, a world that is not the result of the collective karmic tendencies of a previous world, but one that has been created by a divine creator, this world should be good in every respect. If it contains the diverse realms of rebirth and the respective life forms, that is, denizens of hell, demons, animals, humans, and deities, the creator would be deeply unjust, because of creating beings of such different types without any fault of their own. Such a creator himself would deserve to be "roasted . . . in hell," as Bhāvaviveka puts it.[12] If, moreover, the creator would determine how sentient beings act and then punish or reward them according to their actions, things would not be any better. For this would negate any significant freedom and responsibility on the side of the sentient beings. Sentient beings would have no influence on their own moral and spiritual development, and, as a result, any religious pursuit would become meaningless. As it is stated in the *Shih-erh-men-lun*:

---

[10]Cf. *Shih-erh-men-lun* 10. See H. Cheng 1982, 97–99. See also Schmidt-Leukel 2006a, 125–27.
[11]See, e.g., Vasubandhu in his *Abhidharmakośabhāṣyam,* Pruden 1988, 1:307–8.
[12]*Tarkajvālā* on *Madhyamakahṛdaya* 3:222; 9:96. Lindtner 1999, 67, 69.

[I]f God were the maker, good, evil, suffering and happiness would come without being made (by man). But this would destroy the principle of the world (that men do good and obtain reward, and do evil and receive punishment). The practice of an ascetic life and Brahmanic deeds would be in vain.[13]

If, finally, sentient beings would have their own limited but nevertheless genuine freedom and responsibility and if a creator would create hells and heavens in accordance with karmic justice, there could be no first beginning. To postulate a divine creator would either become redundant or the concept of a "Creator God" would only be another term for "karma," as Bhāvaviveka suggests.[14]

From the traditional Buddhist perspective of creation by collective karma, the world is ambivalent: On the one hand, it is evil because it contains beings who are free to perform evil deeds that create suffering for themselves and for others. On the other hand, it is also good because freedom and responsibility are paired with cosmic justice in the form of karmic retribution and constitute a presupposition of the pursuit of ultimate liberation. Under the assumption of a divine creator, the world would also be a mix of good and evil, but this mix would be assigned and distributed entirely by the creator's sovereign will, so that there is no cosmic justice and no significant freedom and responsibility. Salvation could only be achieved as an arbitrary gift of God, while this God would not be good but a biased, unjust, and, in the end, evil being. If God were supposed to act justly, that is, in accordance with karma, then once more "God" would either be redundant or simply another word for what Buddhists mean by "karma."

Buddhists have developed further objections against the existence of a divine creator, which are not based on the problem of evil but on *ontological speculation*. Most prominent is the argument that if an eternal, immutable, simple being was the cause of the world, the world would have to display the same features as its cause. A world of internal diversification, dispersed over space and time, and intermittently arising and disappearing phenomena would contradict the alleged immutability and eternity of God. For a diverse and ever-changing world would entail changes and diversity within God, as, for example, the transition from not-causing (at some point in time) to causing (at another point in time), or from not-cognizing something to cognizing it, and so on.

Some Buddhists, for example, Bhāvaviveka, considered theistic counter-arguments. For example, theists might presuppose that God is not completely

---

[13]H. Cheng 1982, 98–99.
[14]*Tarkajvālā* on *Madhyamakahṛdaya* 9:103; Lindtner 1999, 70.

immutable, but immutable only in relation to God's essential nature. This would allow, to some extent, for changes in God, while God's essential characteristics would remain unaltered. But then, could God have any good reason to create a world like ours? Would it not contradict divine perfection to assume that God had to create a world in order to achieve some end or realize some wish, which would otherwise remain unfulfilled? In other words, the idea that God created the world in order to pursue certain aims seems to presuppose that God is not perfect, that God is lacking something and has unfulfilled wishes. This would contradict the idea of a perfect God. The Vedāntic answer that creation is a natural overflow of divine creativity, a kind of divine "play" or "game" (*līlā*) rather than the fulfillment of an unsatisfied wish, was met by Buddhists with mockery. How could God find his joy in a "game" that involves terrible suffering of sentient beings?[15] Yet what about the argument that God created the world out of love or compassion? This option was refuted by Śāntarakṣita (8th c.) with the argument that if the creator acts out of compassion, "then he should make the world absolutely happy."[16] But this is evidently not the case. Thus, in this version, the ontological antitheistic arguments merge with the argument from the problem of evil.

3. This leads to a third type of criticism, the accusation that belief in a divine creator is spiritually disadvantageous. To many Buddhists, past and present, it appears that the assumption of a divine creator is not merely unreasonable but also implies that the divine creator is an unjust, immoral being, allocating favor or misery arbitrarily. Worshipping such a dubious being would in itself be spiritually harmful. It could easily have a negative moral impact on the devotees, because they might no longer seek what is good, but just fearfully obey what they perceive as God's will, or fatefully accept what they perceive as divine predestination. Today, Gunapala Dharmasiri (d. 2015) has emphasized this objection: According to him, "the biggest and most dangerous problem of the concept of God is its authoritative implications. . . . This authoritarianism has done immense damage to humanity. One is . . . treating the religious dimension as superceding the moral dimension."[17] Moreover, "When the implications of theism are fully drawn, with the doctrines of predestination and grace etc., the ideas of finding means of salvation and spiritual struggle and therefore the idea of religion as a way of salvation loses all its meaning."[18] Similar critiques, though not always expressed as harshly as here, are also found in

---

[15]See Lindtner 1999, 71–72.
[16]*Tattva-Saṅgraha* 6:156. Jha 1986, 133.
[17]Dharmasiri 1988, 266–67.
[18]Ibid., 57.

the writings of Buddhists such as Anagarika Dharmapala, Masao Abe, and Shin'ichi Hisamatsu. The common motive is that theism cultivates a sense of heteronomy that deprives humans of their moral and spiritual autonomy.

There is another important aspect to Buddhist antitheistic arguments that needs to be considered. Among the traditional critics of a divine creator are a number of Buddhist masters who belong to the Madhyamaka School or its branches. To them, the critique of the idea of a divine creation is just one part of their overall criticism of any kind of causation, including Buddhist ideas of karmic causation. A good example is found in the *Shih-er-men-lun* which says:

> Since production cannot be established, origination, duration and de-struction cannot be established either. . . . Therefore you should know all things have no production; they are ultimately empty and tranquil.[19]

To the Mādhyamikas, the Buddhist idea of karmic creation is therefore not regarded as absolute truth but permitted as relative truth or skillful means. The same concession, however, was not always granted to the notion of divine creation. "Not even in a relative sense (*saṃvṛtitaḥ*) is it logical that God is the cause of the world, for he is only the cause of joy to some . . . those who believe in him," says Bhāvaviveka. Apparently the negative spiritual implications of theistic belief were assessed by some Buddhists as so negative that they were not prepared to accept theism as a relative truth.[20]

SOME IMPORTANT MODIFICATIONS

In the preceding paragraph I tried to give a fair characterization of some major Buddhist arguments against a divine creator and the motivation be-hind such criticism. One important aspect behind the Buddhist critique is that Buddhism has its own concept of creation, which identifies collective karma as the creative force.[21] In order to get a fuller idea of the Buddhist concept of creation, we need to look, first, more deeply into Buddhist ideas on karma. This will take us, second, to the question, by which forces karma itself may be driven. And this will lead to some important modifications regarding the overall picture of the Buddhist stance on creation.

---

[19]H. Cheng 1982, 107.

[20]See Lindtner 1999, 64. Nevertheless, Bhāvaviveka could also state that the Buddha assumes "the universal form of all the gods" as a skillful means in his compassionate attempt to draw people nearer to the goal of enlightenment. See Eckel 1992, 193.

[21]Although the doctrine of karmic creation is well attested in various classical Buddhist treatises, it is usually neglected in contemporary dialogues about creation, as, e.g., in Knitter and Haight 2015.

1. One of the earliest Buddhist texts that criticizes belief in a divine creator is found in *Aṅguttaranikāya* 3:61. The text rejects the view: "Whatever this person experiences—whether pleasure, pain, or neither-pain-nor-pleasure—all this is caused by God's creative activity."[22] If this view were true, then God would finally cause all moral evils. There would be no space for personal freedom and responsibility and hence no motivation to follow the path of salvation. This, as has already been said, is one of the standard Buddhist objections. But what is interesting here is that the same objection is also raised against a deterministic understanding of karma. If it were true, says this text, that "whatever this person experiences—whether pleasure, pain, or neither-pain-nor-pleasure—all this is caused by what was done in the past,"

> then it is due to past deeds that you might destroy life, take what is not given, indulge in sexual activity, speak falsehood, utter divisive speech, speak harshly, indulge in idle chatter; that you might be full of longing, have a mind of ill will, and hold wrong view. . . . Those who fall back on past deeds as the essential truth have no desire (to do) what should be done and (to avoid doing) what should not be done, nor do they make an effort in this respect. . . . [t]hey are muddle-minded, they do not guard themselves, and even the personal designation "ascetic" could not be legitimately applied to them.[23]

The very same charges are raised against those who believe that everything is caused by a divine creator. This clearly shows that the real target of the Buddhist critique is any view that denies human freedom and responsibility, regardless of whether the determinism is of a theistic nature or based on a deterministic understanding of karma.

Another classical text, the *Milindapañha,* also rejects the view that all good or bad events are caused by karma: "It is not all suffering that has its root in Karma."[24] According to this text, karma is just one factor alongside purely natural causes and causation by free agents.[25] In rejecting a deterministic understanding of karma, Buddhism defends human freedom and responsibility as a crucial condition of its own path of salvation. This is why karma must not be understood in any deterministic sense. Some Buddhist texts suggest that the mechanism of karma is dispositional,[26] that is, that one's deeds (in thought, word, and action) have a serious impact on the

---

[22]Bodhi 2012, 267.
[23]Ibid., 266–67.
[24]Rhys Davids 1894, 191.
[25]See *Milindapañha* IV 1:62–66; IV 3:27–30. See Rhys Davids 1894, 191–92, 249.
[26]E.g., *Aṅguttaranikāya* 3:100; see Bodhi 2012, 331–35.

state of one's own mind, hence on the course of one's spiritual development and—as a result of this—also on the type of future rebirth.

The Buddhist defense of freedom and responsibility and the rejection of a deterministic karma teaching implies that a perfectly just world is impossible. If there are genuinely free agents and autonomously operating natural laws, as is explicitly taught in the *Milindapañha*, these two will always cause a whole range of pleasant or painful events that cannot in any sense be seen as karmic retribution. If, for example, a large number of people is hit by a natural disaster, this cannot be interpreted as a result of their collective bad karma, if one assumes the autonomy of natural laws. The same applies to the situation in which someone becomes the victim of the evil decisions and deeds of someone else. Therefore, the *Milindapañha* declares that when the Buddha was hit and injured by a splinter of a rock that Devadatta had thrown at the Buddha, the reason was not any negative karma of the Buddha. That the splinter hit the Buddha's foot happened "by chance," and "the real cause . . . was the sorrow-working deed of that ungrateful, wicked, Devadatta."[27]

This position has significant implications for the Buddhist criticism of divine creation: An environment in which genuine human freedom and responsibility are possible—that is, in which there is a real choice between "what should be done and . . . what should not be done"—is as incompatible with a deterministic understanding of divine action as it is with a deterministic understanding of karma. But it would not be incompatible with their respective nondeterministic versions. As much as a karma theory is possible, which understands the impact of karma in a dispositional sense, belief in a divine creator does not necessarily presuppose that the creator revokes all human freedom. The Buddhist argument from human responsibility becomes pointless, if one admits that a divine creator may not necessarily interfere with human freedom. The price, however, of rejecting determinism and defending freedom is that cosmic justice in the sense of a perfectly just world is impossible. Neither all suffering nor all happiness occurs as a just retribution for bad or good performance. Moreover, the whole idea of cosmic "justice" would also become meaningless if karmic or divine determination explains everything. The idea of "just" retribution presupposes freedom and responsibility. What is compatible with the assumption of freedom and responsibility is karmic recompense in the sense of the impact that one's deeds have not only on other beings but also on one's own spiritual development. This understanding of karma substantiates the view that there is a genuine responsibility both for others and for oneself.

Will such a dispositional, in contrast to deterministic, understanding of

---

[27]Rhys Davids 1894, 250–51.

karma leave any room for divine action or would the latter still contradict human responsibility? To put our question otherwise: Is there any room for "grace" in the Buddhist view of karma? Space does not permit a more thorough discussion of this question here.[28] But at least three brief remarks shall be made. First, the relation between grace and one's own effort is a much-debated issue within theistic systems. There are theistic positions that postulate something like a more or less complete divine determination or predestination and reject any spiritually significant freedom. These are certainly hit by the Buddhist criticism. But this is not the case with all forms of theism. There are theologies that understand divine grace as that which enables and sets free human freedom and responsibility. This is possible, if grace, as for example in the work of Karl Rahner, is seen not as something different from God but as God's nature in relation to us. Second, within Buddhism not everything depends on human effort. If it is taken seriously that *nirvāṇa* is an unconditioned and unproduced reality, it is not the product of any human effort. Quite the contrary, it is the humanly unearned existence of *nirvāṇa* itself that makes liberation possible. It thus represents some form of "grace." The sheer existence of *nirvāṇa* is grace, as much as the existence of God is seen as "grace." Third, the aspect of grace gets even clearer when we consider that according to Buddhism one usually follows the path of salvation with the help of teachers and spiritual friends. Those who have achieved final liberation, like the Buddha, teach the Dharma out of compassion, and so do the Bodhisattvas who follow his example, so that there is always some "other power" at work that ultimately results from the experienceable presence of *nirvāṇa*. In some forms of Pure Land Buddhism this is understood as a matter of principle: If liberation is, in the end, liberation from self-centeredness, it cannot be achieved by one's own effort. All spiritual effort, if valid, needs to be understood as a reaction to some prevalent "other power" or "grace."

2. Let us now move on to the question of whether Buddhism assumes some further forces behind the creative energies of karma. In presenting the Buddhist idea of karmic creation as an alternative to the notion of a creator God, Bhāvaviveka argues that karmic tendencies have their origin in ignorance/delusion (*avidyā*) and that therefore "*avidyā* is the 'God' that creates the *karma* of the *saṃskāras*,"[29] that is, of the "mental formations," such as will, inclinations, and character traits. But can this view also do justice to the positive aspects of the world that Buddhists acknowledge? Notwithstanding its transitoriness (*anitya*) and unsatisfactoriness (*duḥkha*), this world is also a place where the experience of *nirvāṇa* is possible, where

---

[28]See Schmidt-Leukel 2006a, 148–55.
[29]*Tarkajvālā* on *Madhyamakahṛdaya* 3:222. Lindtner 1999, 67.

Buddhas and Bodhisattvas arise, and where one can successfully follow the path of salvation. Can the existence of all these aspects be explained by *avidyā* as their ultimate cause, or does the presence of ultimate reality, *nirvāṇa*, also have its share in the creation of this world?

Mahāyāna Buddhism has developed at least three lines of thought that point in this direction. First, there is the idea that the Buddhas, out of the positive karmic merit that they earned during their past Bodhisattva careers, *manifest* or *create Buddha Lands* where the conditions are most advantageous for sentient beings to achieve the spiritual goal. Usually, these "Pure Lands" are presented as sort of Buddhist paradises, as, for example, in the case of Buddha Amitābha's Land "Sukhāvatī." But what about a world like ours? In the famous and influential *Vimalakīrti-Nirdeśa* (chapter 1) it is taught that our world is in fact a Buddha Land too, but because of ignorance, beings are unable to realize its true nature, a message that already appeared in the *Lotus-Sūtra* (chapter 16). In this case, the creative force is the positive energy of a Buddha, and *avidyā*, delusion, creates not the world but a false impression of it.

In its tenth chapter, the *Vimalakīrti-Nirdeśa* gives an interesting interpretation why a world so full of genuine hardship and evil is nevertheless in truth a Buddha Land: Only in a world like this is it possible to develop the Bodhisattva virtues: generosity, morality, tolerance, effort, concentration, and wisdom, that is:

> to win the poor by generosity; to win the immoral by morality; to win the hateful by means of tolerance; to win the lazy by means of effort; to win the mentally troubled by means of concentration, to win the falsely wise by means of wisdom.[30]

In a world without poverty, immorality, ill-will, mental pain, and so on, the Bodhisattva virtues would have no point and would never be cultivated. According to this understanding, it is not *avidyā* that is the ultimate creator of the world. *Avidyā* creates only an insufficient and distorted perception of the world. In fact the world results from the compassion and mercy of the Buddhas, who bring about the most adequate environment for the realization of the spiritual path. This insight significantly modifies not only Bhāvaviveka's polemic, but also Śāntarakṣita's dictum that a compassionate creator could create only a world that is entirely happy. On the contrary, a truly good world can be one in which the realization of the highest moral values becomes possible, which, according to the *Vimalakīrti-Nirdeśa*, was not the case in a paradisiacal world. According to José Cabezón, "it is not

---

[30]Thurman 1991, 83.

implausible for Mahāyānists to argue that all universes everywhere are the pure fields of enlightened beings."[31] If every world is in fact a Buddha Land created out of compassion, and if the compassion of a Buddha emerges from his experience of *nirvāṇa*, then ultimate reality itself is behind the creative process.

A second line of thought that indicates a creative role of the Ultimate within a Buddhist context can be identified in the *Tathāgatagarbha tradition*. Again, the argument takes off from the question of whether *avidyā* can be seen as the only or as the chief driving force in the karmic process. If the karmic dynamism also involves the possibility that ignorant/deluded beings turn into enlightened ones, its explanation merely in terms of *avidyā* is not very plausible. Therefore Theravāda Buddhism postulates the "originally pure mind" as a kind of counterforce against the karmic defilements. This "luminous," or "pure," mind has ontological priority over the karmic defilements, in that the pure mind, and not the defilement, constitutes the deepest level of human nature. The defilements remain accidental. Without this assumption, the transformation of a deluded being into an enlightened Buddha would not be feasible.

One strand of Mahāyāna Buddhism interpreted this pure mind as the Buddha Germ or Buddha Nature (*tathāgatagarbha*) inherent in every sentient being. Some texts of this tradition, as for example the *Ratnagotravibhāga*, argue that without the presence of the Buddha Germ it would be impossible for sentient beings to realize *saṃsāric* existence as something intrinsically unsatisfying. For this realization presupposes already some form of hidden or obscured knowledge of the ultimate as our true goal.[32] Buddha Nature, therefore, functions as the driving force that by its sheer presence makes sentient beings feel unsatisfied in this world and draws them toward the ultimate goal. Thus the presence of the Ultimate in the human mind, and an initial though obscured knowledge of it, causes people to pursue the Buddhist path. If this path leads through the Bodhisattva career to full Buddhahood, and if Buddhas are the creators of the true "Pure Land" behind every world, which is as much covered by *avidyā* as the Buddha Germ itself, then actually and ultimately the Buddha Germ is the true creator. It is the motionless "agent" that brings about Buddhas who bring about their Buddha Lands, which represent the deeper and truer nature of our world/worlds.

Along those lines a third motive developed which understands the Buddha Nature not only as the true nature of every sentient being but also as the *true nature of everything*. If everything is "empty" of its own essential nature, then no discrimination or distinction between beings can be ultimately

---

[31]Cabezón 2006, 40.

[32]*Ratnagotravibhāga* 1:40–41; see Hookham 1991, 209.

valid. If "emptiness" is understood as indicative of the *dharmakāya* as the ultimate "body" of the Buddha, then Buddha Nature becomes equivalent to *tathatā*, the "suchness" of everything, or the *dharmadhātu*, the true ground of everything. All worldly reality, whether in its perception as an impure world or a Pure Land, is just a manifestation of the Buddha Nature to the individual mind. In a Tantric text like the *Hevajra Tantra*, this Buddha-Nature, the primordial Buddha, can thus speak:

> The whole of existence arises in me,
> In me arises the threefold world,
> By me pervaded is this all,
> Of naught else does this world consist.[33]

As Toshihiko Izutsu rightly emphasized, ideas like these form a conspicuous analogy to the understanding of creation as a divine manifestation in the mystical traditions of various theistic religions.[34] This brings us close to a synthesizing view.

A SYNTHESIZING VIEW

Having looked at some major Buddhist objections against divine creation and some important modifying aspects, it is now possible to sketch how one may find truth on both sides, that is, on the side of those who deny and those who affirm divine creation, and how both might fit together.

1. From a contemporary Christian perspective, it may be granted to Buddhist critics that the existence of a divine creator cannot be conclusively demonstrated. As a result of the debates on various "arguments for the existence of God" during and after the European Enlightenment, one has to admit that an incontrovertible demonstration of God's existence is not possible. This, however, does not imply that God does not exist. It only implies that if a divine reality exists, our intellect is not able to produce unquestionable evidence for it. Thus when we speculate about the existence or nonexistence of a divine reality, we are talking about rational possibilities, none of which can be ruled out by definitive proof or refutation.

2. From a Christian perspective (as also for most other theistic faiths) the creator and the redeemer are identical. The existence of the world and the salvation of the world have the same divine source. This aspect is crucial for Christian-Buddhist relations. It entails that Christians can affirm together

---

[33] *Hevajra Tantra* 1:8:41. Snellgrove 1959, 77.
[34] See Izutsu 1994, 66–97, 141–73.

with Buddhists that this world, notwithstanding its being divinely created, is nevertheless in need of salvation/liberation. And it implies the question to Buddhists of whether their understanding of ultimate reality is exclusively in terms of liberation. As we saw, there are developments—especially within Mahāyāna Buddhism—that explicitly or implicitly affirm a constructive role of ultimate reality in the process of karmic creation.

But if God is both creator and redeemer, why would a good God create a world that needs to be saved? Should not a good God, right from the start, create a world that is "saved" or that is not in need of being "saved"? The answer, of course, depends on what precisely is understood by salvation. Some contemporary theologians, most prominently John Hick, have opted for a concept of salvation in terms of a process of gradual sanctification, thereby drawing on the ancient Christian tradition of deification (*theosis*).[35] Hick originally spoke of this as a "soul-making" or "person-making" process, but he later described it as the "transformation from self-centeredness to Reality-centeredness," whereby "Reality" signifies ultimate, transcendent reality. This process is possible only in a world that contains genuine evil and allows for morally significant free choices. The creation of such a world is therefore not in tension with the aim of salvation but forms an integral part of it. Salvation, in this sense, is the true goal of creation. This understanding is basically in line with some of the major concerns of Buddhism: It presupposes a metaphysical framework that guarantees genuine human freedom and responsibility, gives meaning to the idea of a path of salvation, and understands transcendent reality as the driving *movens* behind this process. Hick even admits that one may have to reckon with the possibility of repeated existences so that the salvific process remains a genuine possibility for everyone.[36]

3. The close connection between creation and salvation is also reflected in the understanding of *creatio ex nihilo* ("creation out of nothing") as found in the work of Thomas Aquinas. This leads us to a further important observation: "Creation out of nothing" expresses the total dependence of the world on God, but, contrary to a widespread misunderstanding, it does not mean, at least according to Aquinas, "creation *after* nothing" (*creatio post nihilum*).[37] In principle, God can be the ultimate cause of a world that has a beginning but also of a world that is beginningless. According to Aquinas, both are compatible with the notion of creation as absolute dependence.[38]

---

[35]See Hick 1989, 36–55; Hick [1966] 1990; Hick 1993a, 127–33. See also chapter 2 above.

[36]For John Hick's earlier understanding of repeated existences in different worlds see Hick [1976] 1985b. For his later view, which also allows for rebirth in this world, see Hick 2006, 191–200; Hick 2008, 53–64.

[37]Cf. *Summa Theologiae* I. 46:2 ad 2.

[38]Cf. *Summa Theologiae* I. 46:2. See also Schneider 1999.

"Creation" does not signify an act *in* time, because time itself is created. If God is called the "first cause" (*causa prima*), "first" does not refer to the beginning of a chronological sequence but indicates logical or ontological priority. The doctrine of creation does indeed respond to the question "Why is there something and not nothing?" But this "why?" needs to be properly understood in the sense of "to what end?" The world exists because God is its true goal, its telos. The *causa finalis*, the teleological cause, is according to Aquinas the most fundamental, that is, the primary cause. It is the basis of all other causes, including the efficient cause.[39] That is, in his understanding of creation Aquinas adopts Aristotle's concept of God as the "unmoved mover": God "creates" without doing anything. Everything exists (with or without beginning—in the case of Aristotle: the latter) because of being moved or attracted toward God as its ultimate goal.[40] In this way Aquinas does full justice to the theological notion that the creator is also the redeemer and that salvation is the ultimate goal, purpose, and cause of creation.

Aquinas's understanding of creation resonates with crucial Buddhist concerns. Ultimate Reality does not "act" like a causal factor within a temporal sequence of events. It "acts" or is effective by its sheer presence and unsurpassable attractiveness. The question of whether there is a divine creator, that is, a transcendent source-goal of the world, does not correspond to and is not logically dependent on whether the world has a first beginning or stretches back infinitely into the past. Both possibilities are compatible with an idea of divine creation as held by Aquinas. Aquinas opted for the view that the world has a beginning, not because of philosophical reasons but because he believed that this was revealed in the Bible. Most Buddhist thinkers opted for the concept of a beginningless world or series of worlds because of their understanding of comprehensive justice. But if the Bible can no longer be seen as literally revealed and if Buddhists have to admit that the idea of comprehensive justice would amount to the kind of determinism that they wish to avoid, the issue of whether the world has a beginning or not can be left unanswered, as the Buddha himself suggested (e.g., *Majjhimanikāya* 63, 72, and more often). In any event, what is important is that a decision about a beginning or not of the world does not answer the question of whether the world is divinely created. Many past and contemporary Buddhist thinkers apparently assume that the idea of a beginningless world (or chain of worlds) would rule out the idea of divine creation.[41] This may be true for some types of creation doctrines. But in

---

[39]Cf. *Summa Theologiae* I-II 1:2.

[40]Cf. *Summa contra Gentiles* I 37.

[41]Cabezón (2006, 34) summarizes this view as: "there is no point before which there was nothing. Because there is no absolute origin, there is no first cause, and it follows, of course, that no one being (for example, God) could therefore have been that first cause."

the sense of Aquinas, belief in divine creation does not entail any statement about the chronological beginning of the world but about its *end* in the sense of its *true purpose*. And this salvific end, as we have seen, can be described by Buddhists and Christians in quite analogous and compatible ways. Having a salvific end or purpose does also not necessarily imply an end in a chronological sense. The question of whether the world has a beginning or an end in any chronological sense can be left open. Perhaps, one day the progress of scientific insight may provide further evidence on this.[42] From a theological perspective it is safe to say that if God can create a beginningless world, God can also create an endless world or series of worlds. This would have no impact on the statement that God is the eternal goal of everything that exists and that it exists only because God is its eternal goal.

4. All of this still leaves us with the difference that Christians express their understanding of creation in personal terms as an "act of divine will" whereas Buddhists express their understanding of creation in the impersonal terms of a karmic mechanism. In this respect it may be helpful to keep in mind that the Mādhyamikas understand karmic origination merely as "relative truth," or "skillful means." In terms of "ultimate truth," that is, after the complete deconstruction of all our concepts as "empty," no concepts of causation, origination, or creation will be left. The world becomes as mysterious and ungraspable as the Ultimate and hence indistinguishable from it. Nevertheless, "relative truth" is admissible, even inevitable, in order to orient human existence in a valid way toward the Ultimate. This position finds a strong confirmation in the apophatic traditions of Christianity. According to Thomas Aquinas, God surpasses every human concept, so that—strictly speaking—"we cannot know what God is, but rather what God is not, we have no means for considering how God is, but rather what God is not."[43] Any positive description of God, that is, any proposition that says more than what God is not, is at best analogically true, but not univocally, which means it does not apply to God in a sense that we would understand.[44]

From this, I think, we may conclude that also in Christianity any concrete images of the Ultimate, for example, as a divine person creating the world by an act of "his" eternal will, are not to be misunderstood as literally true and correct descriptions but have the function of relating and orienting us toward the ineffable Ultimate in a valid way. Yet precisely this existential, life-orienting dimension within the Buddhist and the Christian ways of talking about the Ultimate and its relation to the world reveal their complemen-

---

[42]For the trialogue between Buddhism, Christianity, and modern science see, e.g., Ingram 2008; Numrich 2008; Yong 2012.

[43]*Summa Theologiae* I. 3, opening section. See also *Summa Contra Gentiles* 14.

[44]*Summa Theologiae* I. 13:5.

tarity: The Christian talk of the world as God's good creation could remind Buddhists of what they already know, that the world is not just a place of mischief but at the same time the true "Pure Land," the environment where human freedom and responsibility are possible and meaningful, and where the path and the goal of salvation are experienceable. The Buddhist concept of karmic creation can remind Christians of what they already know, that the "goodness" of God's creation should not be mistaken in any sentimental or kitschy sense. The world is a harsh and demanding place, which too often crushes people, but as such it is the place where we can grow spiritually. Its goodness rests not in itself—at least not on a surface level—but in the goodness of the Ultimate to which it provides a way, or better, many ways.

14

A Fractal Interpretation
of Religious Diversity

As mentioned in chapter 2, a decisive point in the history of pluralist theologies of religions was the so-called Rubicon Conference, which took place in 1986 in Claremont, California.[1] In his contribution to this conference, Raimon Panikkar (1918–2010) pointed—almost in passing—to "the fact that each religion may be a dimension of the other in a kind of Trinitarian *perichoresis* or *circumincessio*. Each one represents the whole of the human experience in a concrete way."[2] In his 1989 Gifford Lectures, which were published only in 2010, shortly before his death, Panikkar extended this idea over all reality: "There a *perichōrēsis* running through the entire reality."[3] It is a "cosmotheandric *perichōrēsis*,"[4] an interpenetration of World, God, and Man. In his further explanations, Panikkar did not only draw on Trinitarian terminology but also on the ancient Indian idea of a correspondence between micro- and macrocosms: "Man is a microcosm and divine icon, . . . what goes on in the universe at large has resonances in us. There is a universal correlation, *perichōrēsis*. . . . The relation of all with all is one of inter-in-dependence."[5] It is not my intention to go any deeper into the implications of Panikkar's "cosmotheandric" vision. But as I show in this chapter, his idea of 1986 that the relationship between religions, or better, that religious diversity as such exhibits a perichoretic structure insofar as each religion represents the whole of religious experience in a specific form, expresses a truly exciting and immensely fruitful insight.

We have come across similar ideas at several places in this study. Ephraim Meir, for example, speaks in relation to religious diversity of a "trans-difference," which involves and creates "an 'open' identity that has otherness

---

[1]See chapter 2.
[2]Panikkar 1987, 112.
[3]Panikkar 2010, 329.
[4]Ibid., 227.
[5]Ibid., 59.

in itself.["6] Quite similarly Hasan Askari spoke of an experience of religious diversity in which one understands the religious other "as an empty mirror into which one can see both oneself and the other,"[7] and Jerusha Tanner Lamptey suggests that the religious other is "never wholly other."[8] Swami Vivekananda famously presented Hinduism as a religion that contains each form of religion.[9] According to Bhikkhu Buddhadāsa, Christianity, Islam, and Buddhism represent three ways of liberation: the way of faith, willpower, and wisdom. But, Buddhadāsa says, all three components are parts of each way, although the emphasis varies.[10] Zhihe Wang recognizes in religious diversity a principle of co-inherence, which he describes by alluding to the symbol of yin-yang as "something of you in me and me in you."[11] Or to mention one more, particularly clear example: Paul Tillich presented in his very last lecture the idea that religious diversity is marked by the three features of the sacramental, the mystical, and the prophetic, which according to Tillich are all interrelated and appear in fragmentary form in every religion.[12]

These remarks point to a constellation within religious diversity, which probably may best be described with the help of Benoît Mandelbrot's theory of fractals. Significant observations from intercultural philosophy and from comparative religion suggest that fractal structures are found not only in nature but also in culture and religion. In this chapter, I argue that religious diversity can indeed be interpreted in a fractal way and that this understanding of religious diversity is highly significant for interreligious theology and perhaps for any future study of religious diversity.

THE THEORY OF FRACTALS

The mathematician Benoît Mandelbrot (1924–2010) introduced the term "fractal" in 1975. It refers to certain patterns, structures, or forms that display either a rough or strict self-similarity across various scales. That is, a component of the pattern or structure constitutes an identical or similar copy of the whole. Recursiveness and scale invariance are the two key elements of fractals. A well-known example of a fractal shape with strict self-similarity and scale invariance is the so-called Sierpinski triangle.

---

[6]See chapter 3.
[7]See chapter 4.
[8]Ibid.
[9]See chapter 5.
[10]See chapter 6.
[11]See chapter 7.
[12]See chapter 8 and below.

The triangle is composed of three smaller triangles which contain within themselves the same structure and composition of still smaller triangles, and so on (see figure 1).

Figure 1.

In his book *The Fractal Geometry of Nature*,[13] first published in 1982, Mandelbrot proposed that fractal structures with less strict and more irregular forms of self-similarity are found in a number of inorganic and organic natural phenomena. They "tend to be *scaling*, implying that the degree of their irregularity and/or fragmentation is identical at all scales."[14] Mandelbrot chose the term "fractal" because it suited particularly well the kind of irregular form of self-replication often found in nature:

> I coined *fractal* from the Latin adjective *fractus*. The corresponding Latin verb *frangere* means "to break": to create irregular fragments. It is therefore sensible—and how appropriate for our needs!—that, in addition to "fragmented" (as in *fraction* or *refraction*), *fractus* should also mean "irregular," both meanings being preserved in *fragment*.[15]

A prominent example of such nonstrict self-similarity or of self-similarity in irregularity are coastlines. If one zooms into a coastline, getting ever larger magnifications of ever smaller sections, one will notice self-similarity in the sense that one gets similarly fringed lines, with similar shapes such as bays, fiords, spits, and tongues. Other well-known examples from inorganic nature are certain rock formations and ice-crystals, composed of smaller sections that exhibit similar though irregular structures. A well-known organic example is a cauliflower composed of florets each of which resembles the cauliflower as a whole. The same applies to the structure of many trees or ferns (see figures 2 and 3). Given the pervasiveness of fractal phenomena,

---

[13]Mandelbrot 1983.
[14]Ibid., 1.
[15]Ibid., 4.

Figure 2.   **Figure 3.**

Mandelbrot emphasized "that the fractal approach is both effective and 'natural.' Not only should it not be resisted, but one ought to wonder how one could have gone so long without it."[16] His theory finally culminates in the thesis: "there is a fractal face to the geometry of nature."[17] Apparently, this does not only apply to nature. Intercultural philosophers have provided evidence that culture too shows a "fractal face."

OBSERVATIONS FROM INTERCULTURAL PHILOSOPHY

In 1975, Hajime Nakamura published his intercultural and comparative history of ideas.[18] According to Nakamura, the conclusion of this voluminous study confirmed the view that despite the differences between human cultures and traditions in all of them "more or less the same problems arise."[19] This, Nakamura holds, "means that human nature and human concerns are also vastly similar."[20] To a large extent, debates in contemporary intercultural philosophy oscillate between the two positions of a radical incommensurability of human cultures and that of their complete commensurability or even essential identity, trying to find a satisfactory middle path between the two extremes. As one such middle position, the Indian intercultural philosopher Ram Adhar Mall suggests his concept of intercultural overlapping. Without any overlapping structures, intercultural understanding and communication would be impossible.[21] Mall assumes that one of the sources of intercultural overlapping may be found in the "biological . . . arrangement of human nature."[22] In passing, he refers to genetic

---

[16]Ibid., 3.
[17]Ibid., 3.
[18]Nakamura [1975] 1992.
[19]Ibid., 565.
[20]Ibid.
[21]Mall 2000, 13–24.
[22]Ibid., 17.

findings that show that genetic variations as they exist between different races also exist among members of the same race.[23] This would clearly be itself a fractal structure, although Mall is not using this terminology. Mall remains rather vague in further characterizing the cultural phenomenon of "overlapping." But his idea that a certain feature of human genetics, which actually shows a fractal structure, provides one possible source of cultural overlapping, suggests that cultural overlapping would also follow a fractal pattern. This is confirmed by his statement that the intracultural field bears the features of the intercultural one.[24]

The German intercultural philosopher Bernhard Waldenfels goes one step further with his concept of intercultural "intersection" ("Verschränkung"), meaning that what is culturally known and what is alien "are more or less entangled with each other." The borderlines between cultures are fuzzy and are more about "accentuation, emphasis and statistic frequency than clear-cut differentiation."[25] Thus, in speaking of intercultural intersection, Waldenfels seeks to point out that one will find something of one's own culture in the alien one and something of the alien culture within one's own.[26] This is, *in nuce*, a fractal interpretation of cultural diversity, which Waldenfels finds substantiated by the work of the Swiss intercultural philosopher Elmar Holenstein.[27]

Holenstein, who taught at the Universities of Bochum, Zürich, Tokyo, and Hong Kong, bases his observations primarily on his comparative studies of Western and Far Eastern cultures. According to Holenstein, "it is possible to identify those structures, which are particularly strong in one culture also (at least in rudimentary form) in (nearly all) other cultures."[28] One of his examples is the rich variety of different degrees of politeness in the Japanese language. Idioms conveying various forms of politesse exist in all languages, but they are not everywhere as elaborate as in Japanese.[29] Assuming that one particular feature, or cluster of features, is exclusively present in one culture while totally absent from another would be misleading. Cultural differences, says Holenstein, are rather based on the cross-cultural distribution of various features, but with different hierarchies, emphases, or elaboration.[30] The variations *between* cultures are thus mirrored in the variations that we find *within* cultures or even within one individual:[31]

---

[23]Mall 1995, 47, referring to the work of Stephen Jay Gould.
[24]Ibid., 41.
[25]Both quotations in Waldenfels 1995, 54.
[26]Ibid., 56.
[27]Cf. ibid., 55.
[28]Holenstein 1985, 133 (my translation).
[29]Ibid.
[30]Ibid., 137ff.
[31]Ibid., 149ff.

[T]he same oppositions that are thought to be ascertainable between two cultures *(interculturally)* can often be detected in the same kind and degree within one and the same culture *(intraculturally)*, even within one and the same person *(intrasubjectively)* depending on age, surroundings, task or just on mood and humour.[32]

In this important thesis, Holenstein distinguishes three different levels of diversity: (1) the "intercultural" level—that is, the global level of cultural diversity; (2) the "intracultural" level—that is, the diversity found within each culture; and (3) the "intrasubjective" level—that is, the diversity found within the mental cosmos of individual persons. Thus, what he says implies that various patterns of cultural diversity replicate over these three levels or scales. The cultural diversity at the global level is reflected in the diversity within each culture and this again is, to some extent, reflected, on a still smaller scale, in the individual. Holenstein therefore rejects the idea of a radical difference between cultures in favor of a model of numerous variations of identical or analogous features accompanied by wide-ranging structural similarities. This is, although Holenstein himself does not use the term, a fractal interpretation of cultural diversity. Not just Bernhard Waldenfels but also other intercultural philosophers such as Franz Martin Wimmer[33] and Gregor Paul[34] approvingly adopted Holenstein's view.

OBSERVATIONS FROM COMPARATIVE RELIGION

The relation between culture and religion is a much debated issue. It may be safe to say that religion and culture can be distinguished but not separated. If cultural diversity exhibits a fractal structure, it is therefore likely to find that in religion too. Indeed, various findings of comparative religion clearly point in this direction.

In the early days of the academic study of religions, theories of the evolution of religion played an influential role. Most of these theories assumed a progressive historical succession of different types of religion, whereby "higher" types of religion superseded the "lower" or "primitive" types. When in the twentieth century the science of religion (*Religionswissenschaft*) developed into an autonomous academic discipline, evolutionary theories lost much of their earlier significance. The interest in defining different types of religions, however, remained more or less unbroken. Typologies

---

[32]Holenstein 2003, 46.
[33]See Wimmer 2004, 143–50.
[34]See Paul 2008, 20–21.

of religions were seen as important instruments in achieving a structured understanding of religious diversity. Typologization and classification became dominant procedures in the so-called phenomenology of religion. Simply put, comparative studies were meant to pursue two interrelated goals: First, at the interreligious level, developing typologies of different religions, and second, at the intrareligious level, developing typologies of different elements or components found within the religions. The second aim was not less governed by a comparative perspective than the first one, and the overall expectation was to find strong correspondences between specific types of religions and the respective "typical" elements. In 1924, Gerardus van der Leeuw (1890–1950) stated programmatically: "It is our goal to classify the material," and to this purpose we take "characteristic examples from the proper history of religions."[35] And his mentor, W. Brede Kristensen (1867–1953), explained the task of the phenomenologist as classifying religious phenomena "according to characteristics which correspond as far as possible to the essential and typical elements of religion."[36]

A well-known example of such typologization, which also became influential beyond the boundaries of religious studies, is the typological distinction between *prophetic* (Judaism, Christianity, Islam) and *mystical* religions (Hinduism, Buddhism). Initially supported and spread by Friedrich Heiler (1892–1967), it was later expanded into a tripolar typology by Hans Küng and Julia Ching (1934–2001), who added a third type, the *sapiential* religions (Confucianism, Daoism). All three types are marked by typical elements, for example, by different types of religious authorities, as the prophet, the mystic, and the sage.[37]

However, one problem with such classifications is that they are not inescapable. As early as in 1924, Joachim Wach complained about the more or less arbitrary character of some popular typological classifications of his time and suggested a strictly systematic approach. A classification, so Wach, should relate either to the *form* of a religion or to its *content*, and either to the *objective* appearance or the *subjective* dimension of a religion.[38] Probably the most interesting point behind Wach's suggestion is his observation that the kind of typology one will arrive at depends not only on the material but to a large extent on which classifying criterion or aspect is being used.

Typologies of religious elements had to face another kind of problem: the

---

[35]Van der Leeuw [1924] 1925, 3 (my translation).

[36]Kristensen 1960, 8.

[37]See Küng and Ching 1989.

[38]From this he concluded four different types of classifications: (1) objective with regard to form, (2) subjective with regard to form, (3) objective with regard to content, (4) subjective with regard to content. See Wach [1924] 1988, 68–69.

discovery of wide-ranging parallels among the religions.[39] In almost every religion one can find such elements as sacred places, sacred times, sacred objects, sacred animals, sacred humans, different versions of saints, authorities, communities, of rituals, cults, sounds, scriptures, and buildings—mythical, narrative, poetic, doctrinal, or philosophical elements; various types of religious feelings, emotions, volitions, valuations, altered states of consciousness, and so on. When phenomenologists investigated such elements of religious life and compared them across the religions, the impression grew that the distribution of these elements did not support any sharp typological profiles of the religions. The same features reappear in different types of religions, though sometimes with a different tinge.[40] Already at the time when he still defended the typological distinction of prophetic and mystical religions, Friedrich Heiler noticed that actual religious traditions often display a mixture and merger of elements of the prophetic and mystical type.[41]

As with Holenstein's observation regarding different cultures, it became increasingly clearer that almost no specific features or clusters of features are exclusively present in just one religion while being totally absent from another one. It was possible to distinguish different hierarchies, different degrees of emphasis, elaboration, or combination of such elements and features, but: "Completely unique phenomena hardly ever occur."[42] There are very few exceptions. Sacred scriptures, for example, do not exist in oral traditions. But even here we find parallels in the form of standardized, almost canonized, myths and narratives. And in "scriptural" religions one should not underestimate elements of orality such as sound and proper recitation. Some phenomenologists, for example Mircea Eliade, claimed the existence of wide-ranging structural similarities across all religions:

> The dialectic of the hierophany remains one, whether in an Australian *churinga* or in the incarnation of the Logos. In both cases we are faced with a manifestation, vastly different obviously, of the sacred in a fragment of the universe.[43]

Thus almost everything that is found in one of the major religious traditions seems to reappear in some way or another in other religions as well: "Seen more deeply, therefore, everything is held in common."[44] To return

---

[39]See, e.g., the long and impressive enumeration of parallel elements in the religions as given in Otto 1923, 205–18.

[40]See Heiler [1959] 1962, 47–50.

[41]Heiler [1919] 1921, 233–34.

[42]Kristensen 1960, 2.

[43]Eliade [1949] 1996, 463.

[44]Kristensen 1960, 9.

to the Küng and Ching typology: Prophetic religions also contain mystical and sapiential elements; mystical religions contain prophetic and sapiential elements; and sapiential religions contain elements of a prophetic and mystical nature, as has been admitted by Hans Küng himself.[45] Obviously, the typological efforts of comparative religion and, in particular, of the phenomenological school suggest that religious diversity is, as much as cultural diversity, marked by fractal structures.

One of the phenomenologists who came fairly close to a fractal understanding of religious diversity was Hilko Wiardo Schomerus (1879–1945). In a study from 1932, Schomerus distinguished four major types of religions: (1) religions of the *law* (e.g., Judaism), (2) *magical-sacramental* religions (e.g., "Indian mysticism"), (3) *gnostic* religions (e.g., Greek Gnosis and Buddhism), and (4) *devotional* religions (e.g. Hindu *bhakti*-traditions and some forms of Mahāyāna Buddhism).[46] Schomerus derives his typology from a traditional Hindu distinction of four different paths of salvation: The way of works (*karmamārga*), the way of meditation (*yogamārga*), the way of knowledge (*jñānamārga*), and the way of devotion (*bhaktimārga*).[47] However, according to Schomerus, the actual religious traditions cannot be allocated strictly to these four different types: "There are religious formations which comprise not only one of the said four major types but several or even all four of them, and this in a variegated mixture."[48] The fact that Hinduism includes all four types is thus only one example of a more general situation. Hence the distinction between the four types should be applied to the actual religions not vertically but horizontally, even if in some religions one of the four types may exert a dominant and formative influence. (Note the structual similarity with self-inverse fractals as in Poincaré-chains; see figure 4.)

Figure 4. Poincaré-chains (Mandelbrot 1983, 173).

---

[45]See Küng and Ching 1989, 15–17.
[46]Schomerus 1932, 22.
[47]This is an extended version of the "three ways" scheme. See chapter 5.
[48]Schomerus 1932, 22 (my translation).

How close Schomerus gets to a fractal interpretation of religious diversity is obvious when he states: "Religion as such is hypostasized in a few major types, which persistently recur and unfold everywhere in similar ways, bringing about in all places kindred forms and formations."[49] But then he introduces—for theological reasons—a crucial exception to his rule. Although he admits that all four types of religion are also present in Christianity, they constitute, in this case, only the external form, the "shell" or "gown" of Christianity, not its essence. The essence, says Schomerus, is Christ, and Christ alone makes Christianity unique.[50] And the essence is not without impact on the form. Through Christ the external form assumes "a totally different meaning."[51] The difference between Christianity and other religions is thus, according to Schomerus, not a difference in degree but one in essence.[52]

However, the uniqueness of Christ, as understood by Schomerus, is based not on the uniqueness of Jesus as a human personality, but on the interpretation of Christ as the sole mediator between God and humankind,[53] or, more precisely, on a rather specific interpretation of this mediation along the lines of Dialectical Theology.[54] Schomerus's argumentation thus implies that the essential difference of Christianity from all other religions hinges on a highly specific theological interpretation of Christ. This specific interpretation appeared within Christianity at a fairly late stage and was held among only a comparatively small group of Christian theologians. Even if one would accept this particular interpretation of Christ as true, it would be difficult to maintain that it is the occurrence of this interpretation that makes Christianity "essentially" different from all other religions, given all the other wide-ranging similarities. It is impossible to reduce Christianity to Dialectical Theology. Schomerus neglects that the different types of religion, which, as he admits, are all found within Christianity, also condition and trigger different interpretations of Christ. Christianity comprises not only different types of religion, it also includes different Christologies that are interlinked with the different types of religion. Forms of Christianity that Schomerus would characterize as "religion of law" will tend to see Christ primarily as divine lawgiver, ruler, and judge. Mystical types of Christianity will possibly see Christ as a reality within each one of us, signifying our nondual relationship with God. Gnostic forms of Christianity tend to see

---

[49]Ibid., 26 (my translation).
[50]See ibid., 33.
[51]Ibid., 38.
[52]Ibid., 48.
[53]Ibid., 36.
[54]See ibid., 41–42.

Christ as the manifestation of divine redeeming wisdom, and devotional forms worship him as the gracious savior.

Schomerus's attempts to protect Christian superiority claims against his own insight into the fractal structure of religious diversity indicate that a fractal interpretation is not without a strong impact on questions of religious pluralism and interreligious theology. As the application of his own analysis on the multiple images of Jesus Christ suggests, a fractal understanding of religious diversity provides interreligious theology with a crucial hermeneutical tool. It helps to understand the possibility and legitimacy of different religious perspectives within and across religious traditions. Let us now take a closer look at this.

INTERRELIGIOUS THEOLOGY AND THE FRACTAL INTERPRETATION OF RELIGIOUS DIVERSITY

The comparative study of religion had come close to a fractal interpretation of religious diversity. But with the growing rejection of the phenomenology of religion and the rise of alternative approaches in religious studies, shaped by various forms of postmodernism, comparative studies rapidly declined and the investigation of particularities moved to the center of the discipline. Kimberley Patton employs a drastic but not inadequate metaphor: "For a number of years, comparative method in the study of religion has been under fire so heavily that there are very few left standing."[55] At the same time, interreligious comparison began to gain increasingly more ground within Christian theology. It is not unlikely that comparative theology may continue where comparative religion stopped, that is, with the discernment of fractal patterns in religious diversity. But while the phenomenology of religion worked under the methodological premise of bracketing one's own convictions (*epoché*) in order to secure an objective and neutral approach to the materials under comparison, comparative theology makes the reflection of its own theological background position part of its comparative work and is therefore interested in precisely those questions of religious truth and value that the phenomenological school tried to exclude. This means that interreligious comparison becomes a way of doing interreligious theology.[56] It is in this context that the significance of a fractal interpretation of religious diversity will become obvious.

---

[55]Patton 2000, 153.
[56]See chapters 2 and 9.

The Basic Idea

In order to spell out the basic idea it is helpful to draw on the three levels or scales identified by Elmar Holenstein and transfer them from cultural to religious diversity. A fractal interpretation of religious diversity proposes that the differences that can be observed at the *interreligious level* are, to some extent, reflected at an *intrareligious level* in the internal differences discerned within the major religious tradition, and that they can be broken down at the *intrasubjective level* into different religious patterns and structures of the individual mind.

This way of looking at religious diversity entails that each religion comprises characteristic features of other religions. Each element or aspect of the religions seems to fit into some kind of fractal configuration. That is, religious diversity is "scaling": Its occurrence on the global level is replicated within each of the major religions. Religions resemble each other, but they resemble each other precisely in their diversity. In view of the intrasubjective level, the fractal configuration can be analyzed both transcendentally and psychologically. It was in particular Rudolf Otto (1869–1937) who concluded that the huge number of interreligious parallels should ultimately be explained by the "underlying congruent and common predisposition of humanity in general,"[57] which Otto understood as an innate feature of the human mind. Otto assumed a transcendental foundation that accounts for the possibility of religious experience. Accordingly, the most rudimental features of religious diversity would have a substratum in basic structures of the mind. Per Otto, "the holy" in both its rational and nonrational components "is a *purely a priori* category."[58] The assumption that basic patterns of religious diversity are rooted in common features and potentials of the human mind can also be interpreted in terms of religious psychology. An early proponent of this perspective was William James (1842–1910), who suggested a psychological correspondence between the diversity of religions and the diversity of different types of religious personalities as they are found within each religion.[59] But it is not only different personalities who, at the intrasubjective level, represent different forms of religion. There is also plenty of evidence that one and the same person may instantiate different forms of religion in the course of his or her own life, as has, for example, been shown by James Fowler (1940–2015)[60] and other psychologists.

---

[57]"die zugrundeliegende, einheitliche, gemeinsame Anlage der Menschheit überhaupt" (Otto 1923, 217); see also ibid., 222.

[58]Otto 1936, 116.

[59]James [1902] 1990, 436–38.

[60]This observation does not require one to accept the evolutionary and hierarchical model that Fowler proposed (see Fowler 1981).

Finally, there is not only the possibility that different religious options may co-inhabit the psyche of a single individual person successively; they can also do so simultaneously. This takes us to the phenomenon of multireligious identity and multireligious belonging. In one of the most profound studies of multireligious belonging, Rose Drew notes that individuals who consciously follow two different religions in fact often oscillate between the two different perspectives, which are not always easily synthesized.[61] This observation has been confirmed by another study on dual belonging, which describes the spiritual attitude of so-called "JuBus," that is, Jewish-Buddhists, as a "perpetually ongoing inner dialogue."[62] Drew concludes that in this kind of internalized spiritual dialogue dual belongers "become microcosms of the dialogue as a whole."[63] This connects the smallest scale with the largest one and corresponds to a fractal interpretation.

Multireligious identity is a possible feature not only of religious individuals. It is also a feature of individual religious traditions. Among historians of religion it is more or less agreed "that indeed every religion is syncretistic, since it constantly draws upon heterogeneous elements to the extent that it is often impossible for historians to unravel what comes from where."[64] Any major religious tradition can be said to have had its origin in syncretistic processes and continued developing through further forms of syncretistic amalgamations. Multireligious belonging and multireligious identities are just part of this larger scenario. The fact that the multireligious formation of religious identities is now an increasing phenomenon in the West may indicate that the fractal structure of religious diversity is intensifying in our present age. As we saw in chapters 10 to 12, figures who occupy a central place in a religion, such as Muḥammad, Jesus, and Gautama, are in the process of acquiring positive religious significance in other than their home traditions. None of them is the exclusive possession of just one religion.[65] This takes us back to the question of how a fractal theory of religious diversity ties in with the nature and goals of interreligious theology.

A fractal interpretation of religious diversity as proposed here is not confined to one particular set of fractal structures. I concur with Wach's caveat that different viewpoints trigger different classifications. My suggestion is therefore of a *heuristic nature*. Whenever comparative studies identify significant differences *between* two religions, one should investigate carefully whether similar or analogous differences can also be discerned *within* each of the two traditions. The fractal interpretation that I suggest is

[61]Drew 2011, 209ff.
[62]Niculescu 2012, 356.
[63]Drew 2011, 226.
[64]Veer 1994, 208.
[65]See Barker 2005.

thus primarily of *hermeneutical value*. A fractal interpretation presupposes that the religious other is never completely or wholly other. It assumes that central aspects of the other's religion have parallels in one's own tradition. In trying to make sense of the otherness of the religious other, one will be able to resort to some common ground found within the larger reservoir of one's own tradition. Given that the similarities are never strict and that there will always be irregularities and variations of all sorts, the fractal approach also allows for a clear discernment of differences. In gaining a more comprehensive understanding of how the perspective of the religious other is shaped by a different hierarchization, organization, combination, or evaluation of common elements, automatically some new light is cast on how these elements are varied, located, and perhaps differently integrated within one's own tradition. This is what happens in "reciprocal illumination."[66] The otherness of the religious other will thus be grasped in terms of a different emphasis and elaboration of certain features that are less developed or differently developed in one's own tradition. This enables one to sense that and how such features might also assume a new, altered, or heightened significance within one's own faith.

This can be illustrated by the exercises in interreligious theology presented in the last four chapters. The controversial issue of divine creation is seen in new light if one asks to what extent and in which ways ultimate reality is involved in the standard Buddhist doctrine of karmic creation. That is, if one asks whether ultimate reality is conceived in Buddhism only as the presupposition of salvation or liberation or whether it may also have some indirect creative function. Similarly, in theism the belief in a divine creator must not be treated separately from the fact that the creator is also the redeemer. If the inner relation between creation and salvation in theistic beliefs is compared with the inner relation between liberation and creation in nontheistic beliefs, similar patterns and fractal structures become visible: The theistic and the nontheistic concepts carry connotations which include aspects of both a liberating and a creative function, in rather different arrangements, but also with significant resonances.

The common theme of the revelatory presence of ultimate reality in, through, and among human beings together with a set of corresponding human qualities and spiritual values enables members of Islam, Christianity, and Buddhism to reciprocally understand, appreciate, and learn from the motives behind the religious categories of the Prophet, the Son, and the Buddha. Through interreligious theology Muslims can discover that and how prophethood also involves the dimensions of incarnation and of awakening. Buddhists could become more aware that the way to buddhahood may

---

[66]See chapter 9, and A. Sharma 2005.

also include the quality of a prophetic voice (as in the case of Nichiren) and that its incarnational dimension may assume theistic forms. Christians can recognize and appreciate the incarnational dimension of awakening and rediscover how incarnational thinking is rooted in prophetic revelation. If central religious categories like those of the Prophet, the Son, and the Buddha are interrelated, a fractal structure becomes apparent: Each contains in itself components of all three.

My analysis of the Prophet, the Son, and the Buddha shows some similarity with Tillich's triad of the prophetic, the sacramental, and the mystical elements.[67] The "sacramental" refers to "the experience of the Holy within the finite."[68] Tillich is here obviously influenced by Eliade's idea of "hierophany," which follows an incarnational paradigm.[69] The mystical and the prophetic elements function as critical correctives of the sacramental. The mystical element consists in the emphasis that the Holy is always "beyond any of its embodiments."[70] While the mystical element is directed against the danger of absolutizing the incarnational medium, the prophetic element defies the danger of demonizing the Holy, that is, "the denial of justice in the name of holiness."[71] A crucial implication is that all three elements are necessary and interdependent. It would, however, be too simplistic to identify the "Son" with the "sacramental," the "Buddha" with the "mystical," and the "Prophet" with the "prophetic." From the point of view of a fractal interpretation, it is important to realize that all three elements are present, though with different emphasis, in the categories of the Son, the Buddha, and the Prophet.

Tillich's concept illustrates that a fractal interpretation of religious diversity is not only of hermeneutical value but may also play an important role in *theological evaluation*. On the presupposition of a fractal theory of religious diversity, the reluctance or readiness to accept different religious perspectives as valid, enriching, and complementary has its parallel in one's attitude to other manifestations of and within one's own religious tradition. There is an analogy between intrareligious ecumenism and interreligious ecumenism. The diversity within one's own tradition can be deplored as an expression of mushrooming heresy or may be welcomed as a wealth of mutually enriching and corrective perspectives. The same alternative of rejection or appreciation is also applicable to interreligious diversity. According to a fractal understanding of religious diversity, there is an inner

---

[67]See chapter 8

[68]Tillich 1966, 86.

[69]See above page 229. Tillich himself acknowledges Eliade's strong influence on his later ideas (Tillich 1966, 91). See also Eliade 1966.

[70]Tillich 1966, 86.

[71]Ibid.

relationship between the intrareligious, that is, ecumenical, and the inter-religious attitude. There is, for example, a substantial connection between Martin Luther's rejection of Roman Catholicism and his hostile attitude toward Judaism and Islam, or between Alexandro Valignano's condemna-tion of the Lutheran "heresy" and his negative attitude toward Pure Land Buddhism,[72] as much as there is a connection between Thomas Merton's appreciation of Christian contemplative monasticism and his endorsement of monastic Buddhism.[73] A fractal interpretation of religious diversity can foster an appreciative attitude, a view that understands and assesses reli-gious diversity as complementary.[74] A fractal interpretation does not oblige one to accept all forms of diversity as good or even equally good. A fractal interpretation of religious diversity may also include the darker aspects of religion. But a fractal interpretation of religious diversity is not confined to the idea that diversity is always an expression of either falsity or inferiority, as is presupposed by exclusivism and inclusivism.[75] This is the reason why a fractal interpretation of religious diversity, if applied within the realm of the theology of religions, ultimately tends toward religious pluralism.

Hints at a Fractal Approach in Current Interreligious Theology

So far, interreligious theology has produced significant hints at a fractal interpretation of religious diversity. Various examples have been mentioned at the beginning of this chapter. Let me now add, as two further samples, John Cobb's and Mark Heim's typologies of concepts of the ultimate and the corresponding religious experiences.

Cobb distinguishes three different types of religions on the basis of three different types of concepts of ultimate reality: cosmic, acosmic, and theistic.[76] Each of these three types correlates with a specific set of religious experiences. Cosmic concepts of ultimate reality recognize a sacred nature of the cosmos itself, as, for example, in Daoism or Native American religions.[77] They correspond to experiences that suggest "a kind of belonging to the cosmos, or kinship with other creatures, about which ordinary experience does not inform us."[78] The Mahāyāna Buddhist concept of "emptiness" (*śūnyatā*) and the Advaita Vedāntic concept of "Brahman without attributes" (*nirguṇa brahman*) are taken by Cobb as examples of acosmic concepts of

---

[72]See chapter 11.
[73]See Thurston 2007.
[74]For a similar understanding of religious diversity within the context of his intercultural philosophy, see Holenstein 1998, 348–52.
[75]For the structural difficulties of exclusivism and inclusivism with religious diversity, see chapter 1.
[76]For an excellent account of Cobb's views, see Griffin 2005c.
[77]Griffin 2005c, 49.
[78]Cobb 1999, 117.

the ultimate.[79] They correspond to experiences of an "inward" nature, the "discovery of a 'depth' that is free from all the particularities of ordinary experience" or "a removal of all culturally and existentially determined barriers to openness to what is as it is."[80] Theistic concepts, finally, correspond to experiences of a personal presence, of communion, of guidance, of being called to a life of righteousness and love and of being released from guilt.[81]

According to Cobb these different concepts are not related to different experiences of one and the same ultimate reality, but refer to different ultimates or better to ontologically different, but still ultimate features of one complex reality. This represents a further development of Cobb's earlier view of two ultimates, which he derived from the process philosophy of Alfred North Whitehead: One of the two is variously defined as "being itself" or—closer to Whitehead—as "creativity" or "prime matter," while the other is the "supreme being," that is, God or the "creator" as in the philosophy of Whitehead. One reason for the assumption of two instead of one ultimate reality is the rejection of the doctrine of the "creation out of nothing" (*creatio ex nihilo*). The "creator" has no coercive but only persuasive power. Like a demiurge, God "creates" by giving order to the otherwise formless or chaotic "prime matter" (or "being itself" or "creativity"). Thus, according to Cobb, "being itself" is not God, but God is the supreme instantiation of "being" or "creativity." The idea of three "ultimates" derives from the thought that the totality of things constitutes another "ultimate," inasmuch as it is different both from the creator and from pure creativity.[82] The cosmos as the third ultimate bears the mark of multiplicity, while God, as a kind of "Worldsoul," represents "a unity of experience that contains all the multiplicity of events and interacts with them."[83] The acosmic reality of being itself unites God and cosmos. It bears the mark of absolute unity and is manifest in the creativity of both, God and the world.[84]

In Cobb's application of, at first, two and then three ultimates to the actual concepts and experiences of the ultimate in the religions, one can distinguish two phases. The initial interest came from Cobb's dialogue with Mahāyāna Buddhists, especially with Masao Abe. Cobb was keen on retaining a difference between the theistic God of the biblical tradition and the Buddhist understanding of "emptiness" (*śūnyatā*). He identified "emptiness" both with Whitehead's concept of "creativity" or "prime matter" and with the Platonic and particularly Neoplatonic understanding of "being itself" as

---

[79]Griffin 2005c, 47.
[80]Cobb 1999, 118.
[81]Ibid.
[82]Ibid., 183–84.
[83]Ibid., 122.
[84]Ibid., 121–23. See also Griffin 2005c, 44–51.

unstructured unity. Cobb is fully aware that there is a broad and influential line in the Christian theological tradition that identifies God with "being itself" and interprets this identification under the influence of Neoplatonism. According to Cobb, however, this identification is in strong tension with the biblical image of God. Interpreting God not only as "being itself" but now, in the context of Buddhist-Christian dialogue, as "emptiness," would, according to Cobb, "break" Christianity's "last ties to the Bible."[85] Cobb's alternative is to assume that the Buddhist "emptiness" refers to the same kind of ultimate reality as the Platonic concept of "being itself" and as Whitehead's "creativity,"[86] while the biblical God simply refers to a different reality, namely that of the "creator" or demiurge as understood by Whitehead.

The expansion of this concept into a metaphysics of three ultimates and its application to specific religions was driven not only by the inner dynamism of process philosophy but also by Cobb's theological interest in ecological concerns and his corresponding attention to primal religion.[87] It was then under the influence of John A. Hutchison that Cobb developed his classification of cosmic, acosmic, and theistic religions.[88] What is of particular interest is Cobb's remark that *"more than one of these types can be discerned in most of the great traditions."*[89] That is, Cobb uses his typology in both ways: to classify different religious traditions *and* to classify different manifestations within each of the religious traditions. In other words, Cobb applies a fractal interpretation of religious diversity, and he interprets major features of this diversity as complementary. His assessment of these features as complementary is rooted in his metaphysical conviction that the cosmic, acosmic, and theistic features relate to "distinct" but not "separable" ultimates or aspects of the ultimate. For, according to Cobb,

---

[85]Cobb 1985, 156.

[86]The identification of Buddhist "emptiness" with Whitehead's "creativity" is not without serious problems. Cobb knows that within Buddhism "emptiness" is initially meant to show that "every concept one forms of reality or self must be dissolved, because all conceptualizing is distorted" (Cobb 1985, 158). Yet his identification of "emptiness" with "creativity" is fostered by the Buddhist identification of "emptiness" with "dependent origination." "Dependent origination" is the hallmark of *saṃsāra*. So for Nāgārjuna the identification of "emptiness" with "dependent origination" is part of his paradoxical identification of *saṃsāra* and *nirvāṇa*: The close analysis of "dependent origination" reveals that there is nothing that originates, nor any origination, nor any dependency, apart from the logical interdependency of concepts (see also Schmidt-Leukel 2006b, 122–24). From this point of view, an identification of "emptiness" with "creativity" would be highly problematic. But this changed, when "emptiness" became identified with "Buddha Nature" and even more so, when the interpretation of "Buddha Nature" became influenced by Daoism, as happened in China.

[87]See Cobb 1999, 185.

[88]Ibid., 120 (Cobb refers to the second edition of Hutchison's *Paths of Faiths* of 1975). Hutchison, however, speaks of "cosmic," "acosmic," and "historical" religion and is influenced in his terminology by Eliade.

[89]Cobb 1999, 121 (italics are mine). This is also in line with Hutchison (1991, 17).

none of the three, neither the world, nor God, nor their acosmic unity, can exist without the other two.[90] If these three ultimate features are inseparably linked, it is not surprising to find their religious expressions both across and within the religions.

A similar observation can be made in relation to Mark Heim's interpretation of religious diversity. According to Heim, different religions create their followers in their own image. The spirituality of the adherents of a particular religion is shaped and oriented by its specific understanding of the eschatological end. Thus, a practicing Buddhist will become fit for *nirvāṇa* but not for eternal life in a Christian sense and vice versa. Heim entered the theology of religions debate with the startling suggestion that the different religious ends for which the religions prepare their adherents may all be real and coexistent. Initially, he used this idea to support Christian exclusivism in suggesting that God would indeed allow Buddhists to go to *nirvāṇa* but that, from a Christian point of view, *nirvāṇa* would not be much different from hell.[91] Later on, Heim modified his theory and acknowledged some limited value to the non-Christian religious ends.[92] Finally he suggested that the different religious ends can be explained as different modes and degrees of experiencing the Christian Trinity.[93]

The Trinity, so Heim, comprises three dimensions: an *impersonal* dimension, a personal or *iconic* dimension, and a *communion* dimension. At the same time, these three dimensions are also mirrored in different types of religions with their specific concepts of the ultimate and the corresponding religious ends. In relation to the Trinity, the impersonal dimension consists in the mutual indwelling of the three persons. That is, each person is completely one with the other two persons and therefore totally empty of itself. The latter aspect of this dimension is reflected in Buddhist "not-self" teachings and in concepts like *nirvāṇa* or "emptiness," while the former aspect of radical mutual indwelling is mirrored in nondual concepts of the ultimate, most clearly so in Advaita Vedānta. The personal or iconic dimension of the Trinity consists in that "the three constitute one will, one purpose, one love toward creation."[94] This dimension is at the center of monotheistic concepts of the ultimate. But it is also present in the perception of a divine law without a divine person as, per Heim, in Daoism or in classical Stoicism: "what is

---

[90]Cobb 1999, 121.

[91]"To a Christian, the Buddhist *nirvāṇa*, or the Hindu release from reincarnation into the oneness of the raindrop with the sea . . . is not noticeably different from hell" (Heim 1985, 146). Remnants of this view are still present in his later works, in which Heim sees non-Christian ends as partly beneficial but partly also as forms of "loss" because the full Christian end is missed. See Heim 1995, 163, 165; Heim 2003, 400.

[92]Heim 1995.

[93]Heim 2001.

[94]Heim 2003, 394.

apprehended in these cases is the external unity of the Trinity,"[95] appearing as one divine or heavenly will or law. The third dimension, that is, the communion dimension, underlies the other two dimensions. It combines unity and difference in that the three persons participate and share in each other,[96] comparable to human relationships of "deep love or intimate friendship."[97]

Insofar as all three dimensions are combined and integrated in the Christian concept of the Trinity, belief in a Trinitarian God enables Christians to see some truth in non-Christian concepts of the ultimate and to regard the corresponding religious paths as leading to religious ends of some limited value. For, on the basis of a Trinitarian concept of God, the eschatological ends of non-Christian religions can be interpreted as experiences of some limited aspects or dimensions of the Trinity. The "richest human end,"[98] however, is the full communion with the triune God—an end to which, says Heim, Christianity alone shows the way.

Heim, however, makes an interesting admission, which is apt to cast serious doubt on his Christian superiorism. According to Heim, "each great religious tradition in some measure recognizes the variety of dimensions we have described," and each grasps "the set of dimensions *through* one of them."[99] This obviously implies a fractal perspective, because here Heim suggests that the differences between various types of religions are also present within each one of them. He further admits that "formally" Christianity is not different from other religions.[100] That is, Christianity too apprehends all three dimensions through the lens of one dimension that is taken as dominant, in this case, the dimension of communion. But then he claims that in other religions the corresponding dimensions are dissolved into or superseded by the dominant one, whereas only in Christianity does the dominant dimension of communion preserve all three dimensions.[101]

This point of Heim's argument can be contested. It seems to reflect the apologetic cliché that in mystical spirituality the dimensions of moral obligation and communal love are left behind and ultimately negated. And the additional cliché that the mystical and interpersonal dimension are ignored in religions of the law. In contrast to Heim, I suggest that in all cases it is rather a question of emphasis and configuration. That there can be differences in emphasis is implicitly admitted by Heim, when he states that in relation to particular aspects of the three dimensions "the distinctive

---

[95]Ibid., 396.
[96]Ibid., 397.
[97]Ibid., 391.
[98]Ibid., 399.
[99]Ibid.
[100]Ibid.
[101]Ibid.

religious paths and truths of other traditions exhibit greater purity and power than are usually manifest in Christianity."[102] A closer look at actual religious diversity will presumably demonstrate that nowhere has the dominance of one dimension led to the complete dissolution of the other two. It rather seems that everywhere all dimensions are preserved, although in different ways and with different accentuation. Thus, Heim's interpretation of the Trinity provides *one* model of how one may understand the complementarity of the different religious dimensions that characterize religious diversity across and within the religions. But if Heim's interpretation is correct, it implies that it is neither the only nor necessarily the supreme model. This, of course, is a consequence that undermines Heim's inclusivism.

Cobb and Heim take us back to one of the most crucial questions of interreligious theology: What exactly are religious concepts of the ultimate telling us?[103] Both Cobb and Heim downplay one element that is shared by all the major religious traditions, namely the affirmation that ultimate reality transcends any human conceptualization.[104] From the point of view of this apophatic tradition, concepts of the ultimate should not be mistaken as literally true descriptions of the ultimate but rather as symbols, pointers, or guideposts. Instead of referring directly to the ineffable nature of the ultimate, they have their more immediate reference point in different human experiences of the ultimate.[105] What is particularly helpful in Cobb's and Heim's models is that they attempt to elucidate correlations between specific concepts of the ultimate, of types of concepts, and corresponding types of human experiences and attitudes. If we focus on this aspect, Cobb's and Heim's models help illustrate the variety but also the complementarity of religious experiences and religious ends. From Heim one can learn that selflessness, morality, and interpersonal love have their own value and identity, while they also complement each other. A similar lesson can be learned from Cobb in relation to the experience of the divine in nature, in states of nondual consciousness, and in a personal relationship with God. Thus both authors contribute to a broader understanding of the full spectrum of what faith in an ultimate reality has meant and continues to mean for many people. Cobb and Heim realize that the diversity constituted by the spectrum that they describe is found among the religions *and* within them, even if this insight remains somewhat peripheral to their thinking. Although they have

---

[102]Ibid.

[103]See chapter 9.

[104]Cobb is giving the apophatic motif a subordinate place by making it a feature of only one of his three "ultimates," that of "prime matter," or "being itself." And in identifying it with Whitehead's "creativity," he turns its "formlessness" almost into a cataphatic feature.

[105]This is the basic assumption of John Hick's religious hermeneutics (see Hick 1989).

not been aware of this, it is definitely possible to read their considerations as contributions to a fractal interpretation of religious diversity.

THE FRUITFULNESS OF THE THEORY

Despite the fact that there have been moves toward a fractal interpretation of religious diversity within the phenomenology of religion and, more recently, within the theology of religions and interreligious theology, a fractal theory of religious diversity is only in a nascent state. Nevertheless it seems obvious that it can introduce a number of fruitful perspectives.

First of all, a fractal interpretation of religious diversity is helpful in the transition of theology into interreligious theology. The theory implies that there are substantial connections between ecumenical theology and interreligious theology. If there is a strong correspondence between intrareligious diversity and interreligious diversity, there must be significant correlations between the theological reflection about the diversity within one's own religious tradition and the theological reflection on the diversity between the religious traditions. In my reflections on the Prophet, the Son, and the Buddha I tried to exemplify how the variety of perspectives within each tradition can help the dialogue between the traditions. In a sense, a fractal interpretation of religious diversity reduces the difference between tradition-specific theology and interreligious theology, making both more continuous. Issues that arise between the religions are likely to have their parallels in issues known from the theological debates within the religions. The religious stranger turns out to be less strange than initially assumed. But a fractal understanding of religious diversity may also turn out to be fruitful in a number of other lines of inquiry, which, by means of conclusion, I would like to point out briefly.

Thus, second, a fractal theory of religious diversity presents a meaningful alternative to theories of radical cultural and religious *incommensurability* that have become influential in the wake of postmodernist philosophies. A claim to radical incommensurability cannot be justified, *if* incommensurability is meant to imply mutual unintelligibility. For if religions were in fact reciprocally unintelligible, one could state only that one has not understood any other culture or religion apart from one's own. It would be inconsistent to claim that one has in fact understood other cultures or religions and therefore knows that they are radically incommensurable in the sense of being mutually unintelligible. A less radical version of incommensurability could hold that not everything in religions may be directly translatable into each other. But in order to be mutually intelligible there must at least be some field of common reference. If mutual understanding is possible, incommensurability can be only a limited or partial phenomenon. What appears as incommensurable, or actually turns out to be so, can then still be made intelligible on both sides on the basis of their commonalities.[106] A fractal theory suggests that what cultures and religions have in common is their diversity. The familiarity with the diversity within one's own religious or cultural environment offers a sound starting point for understanding larger forms of diversity, which despite all irregularity may display sufficient structural similarity in order to permit some understanding.

Third, a fractal theory of religious diversity implies that the *notion of "religion"* is not an empty concept.[107] The difficulty here is that the more the concept "religion" is filled with specific meaning, the smaller appears the range of actual religions to which it may be applied. Conversely, the broader the range of its applicability is set, the more "religion" is emptied of content. This dilemma is actually solved by a fractal interpretation of religion. A fractal theory ties in very well with, and in fact supports, definitions or, better, circumscriptions according to which the concept "religion" comprises a cluster of variable elements,[108] so that the "religions" do not share any strict identity but a type of family resemblance.[109] If we call something a "different religion," the term "religion" is meaningful in that it carries the expectation to find in it a significant, though not strict, similarity in relation to the diversity of phenomena included in one's "home religion."

Fourth, a fractal theory of religious diversity brings back the *phenomenology of religion*, albeit in a different configuration. In postulating both randomness and orderliness within and among the religions, a fractal theory recommends all kinds of comparative studies in order to explore more closely the familiarity and similarity between intra- and interreligious constellations. With the dismissal of the phenomenological school and the corresponding concentration on localized and narrowly defined objects of study, interreligious comparison has fallen into oblivion or even disrepute in large parts of religious studies. Yet more recently comparative studies have reemerged, especially in the form of comparative theology, which constitutes an important branch of interreligious theology.[110] A fractal theory reinvites phenomenology. But it suggests that comparisons should be done without the *epoché*, that is, without phenomenology's former principle of excluding the scholar's own background from the sphere of research. It is, I think, a lasting legacy of the critique of phenomenology that such

---

[106]See also the discussion in Hintersteiner 2001, 150–206.
[107]For an example of the opposite view see Alles 2010.
[108]See, e.g., Glock 1972; Whaling 1986; Smart 1998.
[109]See Hick 1989, 3–5.
[110]See also Schmidt-Leukel and Nehring 2016.

bracketing is ultimately illusory. As, in particular, postcolonial studies have shown, objectivity requires taking fully into account the subjectivity of the researcher. A fractal theory of religious diversity suggests that this will be a hermeneutical gain.

Fifth, although a fractal theory of religious diversity will be of great value for interreligious theology, it is not confined to a religious interpretation of religion. There is no reason why an *atheist* or a *naturalist interpretation of religion* may not also benefit from a fractal interpretation. The similarity between the interreligious, intrareligious, and subjective levels of religious diversity will appear to the atheist as a demarcation of the spectrum that delusion and deception can take. However, within a religious interpretation of religion, a fractal interpretation of religious diversity will work best in conjunction with a pluralist theology of religions, that is, with the assumption that there is a diversity of different but in principle equally valid ways of experiencing and relating to ultimate reality, a diversity that reflects the diverse nature of humanity.

Sixth, and finally, a fractal theory of religious diversity also allows for and in fact invites a number of studies that compare segments and particular features of religious diversity from sociological, psychological, aesthetical, and philosophical perspectives. Given the likely assumption, so strongly expressed by Rudolf Otto, that the root of religious diversity is found in the structures of the human mind, the perspective of the cognitive science of religion[111] needs to be complemented by that of transcendental philosophy. As part of a fractal interpretation of religious diversity, a transcendental analysis would have to inquire about the transcendental conditions that not only permit[112] but possibly even require the evolution of different manifestations of religion.

---

[111]A paradigmatic example is set by Rose 2016, who identifies similar patterns of contemplative mental processes across different religious traditions and ascribes these to both transcendental and neurophysiological structures. For an attempt to explain not religious diversity but the evolution of certain religious ideas and practices on the basis of fractal patterns, see Czachesz 2012.

[112]This has been attempted by Oberhammer 1987. See also the constructive suggestions in Völker 2016.

References

Abe, Masao. 1985. "A Dynamic Unity in Religious Pluralism: A Proposal from the *Buddhist* Point of View." In *The Experience of Religious Diversity*, edited by J. Hick and H. Askari, 163–90. Aldershot: Gower.

———. 1995. *Buddhism and Interfaith Dialogue*. Edited by Steven Heine. Basingstoke: Macmillan.

Akasoy, Anna. 2011. "The Buddha and the Straight Path: Rashīd al-Dīn's Life of the Buddha—Islamic Perspectives." In *Rashīd al-Dīn: Agent and Mediator of Cultural Exchanges in Ilkhanid Iran*, edited by A. Akasoy, C. Burnett, and R. Yoeli-Tlalim, 173–96. London: Warburg Institute.

Aleaz, K. P. 2005. "Pluralism Calls for Pluralistic Inclusivism." In *The Myth of Religious Superiority*, edited by P. Knitter, 162–75. Maryknoll, NY: Orbis Books.

'Alī, 'Abdullah Yūsuf. 1999. *The Meaning of the Holy Qur'ān*. New edition with Qur'ānic text (Arabic), revised translation, commentary, and newly compiled comprehensive index. Beltsville, MD: Amana Publications.

Ali, Syed. 2004. "India's Cultural Traditions: Hindu-Muslim Synthesis." In *Tolerance in Indian Culture*, edited by R. Balasubramanian, 71–88. Delhi: Indian Council of Philosophical Research.

Alles, Gregory D. 2010. "After the Naming Explosion: Joachim Wach's Unfinished Project." In *Hermeneutics, Politics, and the History of Religions: The Contested Legacies of Joachim Wach and Mircea Eliade*, edited by C. Wedemeyer and W. Doniger, 51–78. Oxford: Oxford University Press.

Almond, Philip. 1987. "The Buddha of Christendom: A Review of the Legend of Barlaam and Josaphat." *Religious Studies* 23:391–406.

Amirpur, Katajun. 2014. "'Straight Paths': Thoughts on a Theology of Dialogue." In *Religions and Dialogue: International Approaches*, edited by W. Weisse et al., 187–99. Münster: Waxmann.

Ariarajah, Wesley. 1985. *The Bible and People of Other Faiths*. Geneva: World Council of Churches.

Arkoun, Mohammed. 1989. "New Perspectives for Jewish-Christian-Muslim Dialogue." *Journal of Ecumenical Studies* 26:523–29.

———. 1998. "From Inter-Religious Dialogue to the Recognition of the Religious Phenomenon." *Diogenes* 46 (2): 123–51.

———. 2002. *The Unthought in Contemporary Islamic Thought*. London: Saqi Books.

Askari, Hasan. 1977. *Inter-Religion*. Aligarh: Printwell Publications.

———. 1985. "Within and Beyond the Experience of Religious Diversity." In *The Experience of Religious Diversity*, edited by J. Hick and H. Askari, 191–218. Aldershot: Gower.

———. 1991. *Spiritual Quest: An Inter-Religious Dimension*. Pudsey: Seven Mirrors.

Aslan, Adnan. 1998. *Religious Pluralism in Christian and Islamic Philosophy: The Thought of John Hick and Seyyed Hossein Nasr*. Richmond, UK: Curzon.

Assmann, Jan. 1997. *Moses the Egyptian: The Memory of Egypt in Western Monotheism*. Cambridge, MA: Harvard University Press.

Atay, Rifat. 2014. *Religious Pluralism and Islam: A Critical Reading of John Hick's Pluralistic Hypothesis*. Saarbrücken: Scholars Press.

Aydin, Mahmut. 2000. "Is There Only One Way to God? A Muslim View." *Studies in Interreligious Dialogue* 10:148–59.

———. 2001. "Religious Pluralism: A Challenge for Muslims—A Theological Evaluation." *Journal of Ecumenical Studies* 38:330–52.

———. 2002. *Modern Western Christian Theological Understandings of Muslims since the Second Vatican Council*. Washington, DC: Council for Research in Values and Philosophy.

———. 2005. "A Muslim Pluralist: Jalaluddin Rūmi." In *The Myth of Religious Superiority: Multifaith Explorations of Religious Pluralism*, edited by P. Knitter, 220–36. Maryknoll, NY: Orbis Books.

———. 2007. "Islam in a World of Diverse Faiths—A Muslim View." In *Islam and Inter-Faith Relations*, edited by L. Ridgeon and P. Schmidt-Leukel, 33–54. London: SCM Press.

———. 2014. "Islam and Interfaith Dialogue: Qur'ānic Teaching of the Religious Other." In *Religions and Dialogue: International Approaches*, edited by W. Weisse et al., 215–29. Münster: Waxmann.

Ayoub, Mahmoud. 1997. "Islam and Pluralism." *Encounters: Journal of Inter-Cultural Perspectives* 3:101–18.

———. 2004. "Christian-Muslim Dialogue: Goals and Obstacles." *Muslim World* 94:313–19.

———. 2007. *A Muslim View of Christianity: Essays on Dialogue*. Edited by Irfan A. Omar. Maryknoll, NY: Orbis Books.

Balasubramanian, R., ed. [1992] 2004. *Tolerance in Indian Culture*. Delhi: Indian Council of Philosophical Research.

Barker, Gregory, ed. 2005. *Jesus in the World's Faiths: Leading Thinkers from Five Religions Reflect on His Meaning*. Maryknoll, NY: Orbis Books.

Barker, Gregory A., and Stephen E. Gregg, eds. 2010. *Jesus beyond Christianity: The Classic Texts*. Oxford: Oxford University Press.

Barth, Karl. 1960. *Die Kirchliche Dogmatik*. I/2. Zollikon-Zürich: Evangelischer Verlag.

Basya, M. Hilaly. 2011. "The Concept of Religious Pluralism in Indonesia: A

Study of the MUI's Fatwa and the Debate among Muslim Scholars." *Indonesian Journal of Islam and Muslim Societies* 1 (1): 69–93.

Batchelor, Stephen. 1998. *Buddhism without Beliefs: A Contemporary Guide to Awakening*. London: Bloomsbury.

———. 2011. *Confessions of a Buddhist Atheist*. New York: Spiegel & Grau.

Bauer, Thomas. 2011. *Die Kultur der Ambiguität: Eine andere Geschichte des Islams*. Berlin: Verlag der Weltreligionen.

Beaumont, Mark. 2015. "Christian Views of Muḥammad since the Publication of Kenneth Cragg's *Muḥammad and the Christian: A Question of Response* in 1984." *Transformation: An International Journal of Holistic Mission Studies* 32:145–62.

Becker, Karl J., and Ilaria Morali, eds. 2010. *Catholic Engagement with World Religions*. Maryknoll, NY: Orbis Books.

Berger, Peter L. 2014. *The Many Altars of Modernity: Toward a Paradigm for Religion in a Pluralistic Age*. Boston: de Gruyter.

Berling, Judith A. 1997. *A Pilgrim in Chinese Culture: Negotiating Religious Diversity*. Maryknoll, NY: Orbis Books.

———. 2013. "Why Chinese Thought on Religious Diversity Is Important." In *Religious Diversity in Chinese Thought*, edited by P. Schmidt-Leukel and J. Gentz, 27–37. London: Palgrave Macmillan.

Bernhardt, Reinhold. 2014. "Comparative Theology: Between Theology and Religious Studies." In *European Perspectives on the New Comparative Theology*, edited by F. X. Clooney and J. Berthrong, 21–30. Basel: MDPI.

Berry, T. Sterling. [1890] 1997. *Christianity and Buddhism: A Comparison and Contrast*. New Delhi: Asian Educational Service .

Berthrong, John H. 1994. *All under Heaven: Transforming Paradigms in Confucian-Christian Dialogue*. Albany: State University of New York Press.

Berzin, Alexander. 2007. "A Buddhist View of Islam." In *Islam and Inter-Faith Relations*, edited by P. Schmidt-Leukel and L. Ridgeon, 225–51. London: SCM Press.

———. 2008. "Buddhist-Muslim Doctrinal Relations: Past, Present and Future." In *Buddhist Attitudes to Other Religions*, edited by P. Schmidt-Leukel, 212–36. St. Ottilien: EOS Verlag.

Bhatt, Murari. 1982. *Le Kalki-Purāna*. Translated by Jean Remy. Milan: Archè.

Bloom, Alfred. 2013. "Shin Buddhism in Encounter with a Religiously Plural World." *Pure Land*, n.s., 8–9 (1992): 17–31. Reprinted in *Buddhism and Religious Diversity,* vol. 4: *Religious Pluralism*, edited by P. Schmidt-Leukel, 197–306. London: Routledge.

Boase, Roger, ed. 2005. *Islam and Global Dialogue: Religious Pluralism and the Pursuit of Peace*. Aldershot: Ashgate.

Bodhi, Bhikkhu. 1998. "Review of: 'Buddhism without Beliefs: A Contemporary Guide to Awakening.' By Stephen Batchelor." *Journal of Buddhist Ethics* 5:14–21.

————. 2000. *The Connected Discourses of the Buddha: A Translation of the Saṃyutta Nikāya*. Boston: Wisdom Publications.

————. 2012. *The Numerical Discourses of the Buddha: A Translation of the Aṅguttara Nikāya*. Boston: Wisdom Publications.

Boyle, J. A. 1997. *Genghis Khan: The History of the World Conqueror, by 'Ala-ad-Din 'Ata-Malik Juvaini*. Manchester: Manchester University Press.

Bretfeld, Sven. 2001. *Das singhalesische Nationalepos von König Duṭṭhagāmaṇī Abhaya*. Berlin: Dietrich Reimer Verlag.

Brill, Alan. 2010. *Judaism and Other Religions: Models of Understanding*. New York: Palgrave Macmillan.

————. 2012. *Judaism and World Religions: Encountering Christianity, Islam, and Eastern Traditions*. New York: Palgrave Macmillan.

Brook, Timothy. 2013. "Rethinking Syncretism: The Unity of the Three Teachings and Their Joint Worship in Late-Imperial China." In *Buddhism and Religious Diversity*, vol. 1: *Eastern Religions*, edited by P. Schmidt-Leukel, 290–317. London: Routledge.

Buddhadāsa, Bhikkhu. 1967. *Christianity and Buddhism*. Sinclaire Thompson Memorial Lecture. Fifth series. Bangkok: Sublime Life Mission.

————. 1989. *Me and Mine: Selected Essays of Bhikkhu Buddhadāsa*. Edited by D. K. Swearer. Albany: State University of New York Press.

Burton, David. 2011. "A Buddhist Perspective." In *The Oxford Handbook of Religious Diversity*, edited by C. Meister, 321–36. Oxford: Oxford University Press.

Cabezón, José Ignacio. 2000. "A God, but Not a Savior." In *Buddhists Talk about Jesus: Christians Talk about the Buddha*, edited by R. Gross and T. Muck, 17–31. New York: Continuum.

————. 2006. "Three Buddhist Views of the Doctrines of Creation and Creator." In *Buddhism, Christianity and the Question of Creation: Karmic or Divine?* edited by P. Schmidt-Leukel, 33–45. Aldershot: Ashgate.

Carney, 'Abd al-Hakeem. 2008. "Twilight of the Idols? Pluralism and Mystical *Praxis* in Islam." *International Journal for Philosophy of Religion* 64:1–20.

Carter, John Ross, and Mahinda Palihawadana, trans. 2000. *The Dhammapada*. Oxford: Oxford University Press.

Chau, Adam Yuet. 2013. "A Different Kind of Religious Diversity: Ritual Service Providers and Consumers in China." In *Religious Diversity in Chinese Thought*, edited by P. Schmidt-Leukel and J. Gentz, 141–54. Basingstoke: Palgrave Macmillan.

Cheetham, David, Douglas Pratt, and David Thomas, eds. 2013. *Understanding Interreligious Relations*. Oxford: Oxford University Press.

Ch'en, Kenneth. 1973. *Buddhism in China: A Historical Survey*. Princeton: Princeton University Press.

Cheng, Chung-ying. 2005. "Toward an Integrative Religious Pluralism: Embodying Whitehead, Cobb, and the *Yijing*." In *Deep Religious Pluralism*, edited by D. R. Griffin, 210–25. Louisville: Westminster John Knox Press.

———. 2011. "A Chinese Religions Perspective." In *The Oxford Handbook of Religious Diversity*, edited by C. Meister, 353–64. Oxford: Oxford University Press.

Cheng, Hsueh-li. 1982. *Nāgārjuna's Twelve Gate Treatise (Shih-erh-men-lun)*. Dordrecht: D. Reidel.

Chia, Edmund K.-F. 2008. "Is Interfaith Theology Possible?" *Studies in Interreligious Dialogue* 18:112–17.

Ching, Julia. 2002. *Chinese Religions*. 7th printing. Maryknoll, NY: Orbis Books.

Chittick, William C. 1994. *Imaginal Worlds: Ibn al-'Arabī and the Problem of Religious Diversity*. Albany: State University of New York Press.

Chu, William. 2006. "Syncretism Reconsidered: The Four Eminent Monks and Their Syncretistic Styles." *Journal of the International Association of Buddhist Studies* 29 (1): 63–86.

Clart, Philip. 2013. " 'Religious Ecology' as a New Model for the Study of Religious Diversity in China." In *Religious Diversity in Chinese Thought*, edited by P. Schmidt-Leukel and J. Gentz, 187–99. London: Palgrave Macmillan.

Clooney, Francis. 1993. *Theology after Vedānta: An Experiment in Comparative Theology*. Albany: State University of New York Press.

———. 2001. *Hindu God, Christian God: How Reason Helps Break Down the Boundaries between Religions*. Oxford: Oxford University Press.

———. 2003. "Hindu Views of Religious Others: Implications for Christian Theology." *Theological Studies* 64:306–33.

———. 2010. *Comparative Theology: Deep Learning across Religious Borders*. Chichester: Wiley-Blackwell.

Clorfene, Chaim, and Yakov Rogalsky. 1987. *The Path of the Righteous Gentile: An Introduction to the Seven Laws of the Children of Noah*. Southfield, MI: Targum Press.

Cobb, John B. 1982. *Beyond Dialogue: Toward a Mutual Transformation of Christianity and Buddhism*. Philadelphia: Fortress Press.

———. 1985. "Christian Witness in a Plural World." In *The Experience of Religious Diversity*, edited by J. Hick and H. Askari, 144–62. Aldershot: Gower.

———. 1997. "Amida and Christ: Buddhism and Christianity." Paper delivered at Ryukoku University, Kyoto, Japan, July 1997. http://www.religion-online.org/showarticle.asp?title=147.

———. 1999. *Transforming Christianity and the World: A Way beyond Absolutism and Relativism*. Edited and introduced by Paul Knitter. Maryknoll, NY: Orbis Books.

———. 2012. Foreword to *Process and Pluralism: Chinese Thought on the Harmony of Diversity*, by Zhihe Wang, v–vii. Frankfurt a.M.: Ontos Verlag.

Cohn-Sherbok, Dan. 1994. *Judaism and Other Faiths*. New York: St. Martin's Press.

———. 2005. "Judaism and Other Faiths." In *The Myth of Religious Superi-*

ority: Multifaith Explorations of Religious Pluralism, edited by P. Knitter, 119–32. Maryknoll, NY: Orbis Books.

Cole, W. Owen. 2004. *Understanding Sikhism*. Edinburgh: Dunedin Academic Press.

Collins, Steven. 1998. *Nirvāṇa and Other Buddhist Felicities: Utopias of the Pali Imaginaire*. Cambridge: Cambridge University Press.

Compson, Jane. 1996. "The Dalai Lama and the World Religions: A False Friend?" *Religious Studies* 32:271–79.

Conze, Edward. 1995. *The Perfection of Wisdom in Eight Thousand Lines and Its Verse Summary*. 5th printing. San Francisco: Four Seasons Foundation.

Cornille, Catherine. 2008. *The Im-Possibility of Interreligious Dialogue*. New York: Crossroad.

———, ed. 2013. *The Wiley-Blackwell Companion to Inter-Religious Dialogue*. Chichester: Wiley Blackwell.

———. 2014. "The Confessional Nature of Comparative Theology." *Studies in Interreligious Dialogue* 24 (1): 9–17.

Coward, Harold G., ed. 1987a. *Modern Indian Responses to Religious Pluralism*. Albany: State University of New York Press.

———. 1987b. "The Response of the Arya Samaj." In *Modern Indian Responses to Religious Pluralism*, edited by H. G. Coward, 39–64. Albany: State University of New York Press.

Cragg, Kenneth. 1985. *The Call of the Minaret*. 2nd rev. ed. Maryknoll, NY: Orbis Books.

Czachesz, István. 2012. "God in the Fractals: Recursiveness as a Key to Religious Behaviour." *Method and Theory in the Study of Religion* 24:3–28.

Dalai Lama (Tenzin Gyatso). 1977. "Essence of Tantra." In Tsong-ka-pa, *Tantra in Tibet: The Great Exposition of Secret Mantra*, translated and edited by Jeffrey Hopkins, 13–79. London: Allen & Unwin.

———. 1988. *The Bodhgaya Interviews*. Edited by José Ignacio Cabezón. Ithaca, NY: Snow Lion Publications.

———. 1995. *Universal Responsibility and the Good Heart*. 4th ed. Dharamsala: Library of Tibetan Works and Archives.

———. 2002. *The Good Heart*. Edited by Robert Kiely. London: Ryder.

———. 2010. *Toward a True Kinship of Faiths: How the World's Religions Can Come Together*. London: Abacus.

Davis, Caroline Franks. 1989. *The Evidential Force of Religious Experience*. Oxford: Clarendon Press.

D'Costa, Gavin. 2000. *The Meeting of Religions and the Trinity*. Maryknoll, NY: Orbis Books.

D'Costa, Gavin, and Ross Thompson, eds. 2016. *Buddhist-Christian Dual Belonging: Affirmations, Objections, Explorations*. Farnham: Ashgate.

De Blois, François. 2009. "On the Sources of the Barlaam Romance." In *Literarische Stoffe und ihre Gestaltung in mitteliranischer Zeit: Kolloquium anlässlich des 70. Geburtstages von Werner Sundermann*, edited by D. Durkin-Meisterernst, C. Reck, and D. Weber, 7–26. Wiesbaden: Ludwig Reichert Verlag.

De Silva, Lynn. 1982. "Buddhism and Christianity Relativised." *Dialogue*, n.s., 9:43–72.

Dharmapala, Anagarika. 1965. *Return to Righteousness*. Edited by Ananda Guruge. Colombo: Government Press.

Dharmasiri, Gunapala. 1988. *A Buddhist Critique of the Christian Concept of God*. Antioch, CA: Golden Leaves.

Dods, Marcus. 1887. *Mohammed, Buddha, and Christ: Four Lectures on Natural and Revealed Religion*. London: Hodder and Stoughton.

Doniger, Wendy. 1981. *The Rig Veda: An Anthology*. London: Penguin.

Dorff, Elliott N. 1982. "The Covenant: How Jews Understand Themselves and Others." *Anglican Theological Review* 64 (4): 481–501.

————. 1996. "A Jewish Theology of Jewish Relations to Other Peoples." In *People of God, Peoples of God: A Jewish-Christian Conversation in Asia*, edited by H. Ucko, 46–66. Geneva: WCC Publications.

Drew, Rose. 2011. *Buddhist and Christian? An Exploration of Dual Belonging*. London: Routledge.

————. 2014. "Challenging Truths: Reflections on the Theological Dimension of Comparative Theology." In *European Perspectives on the New Comparative Theology*, edited by F. X. Clooney and J. Berthrong, 71–84. Basel: MDPI.

Dundas, Paul. 2002. *The Jainas*. 2nd ed. London: Routledge.

Dunne, John. 1972. *The Way of All the Earth: Experiments in Truth and Religion*. New York: Macmillan.

Dupuis, Jacques. 1997. *Toward a Christian Theology of Religious Pluralism*. Maryknoll, NY: Orbis Books.

Eckel, Malcolm David. 1992. *To See the Buddha: A Philosopher's Quest for the Meaning of Emptiness*. Princeton: Princeton University Press.

Eichhorn, Werner. 1973. *Die Religionen Chinas*. Stuttgart: Kohlhammer-Verlag.

Eliade, Mircea. 1966. "Paul Tillich and the History of Religions." In *The Future of Religions*, by P. Tillich, edited by J. C. Brauer, 31–36. New York: Harper and Row.

————. [1949] 1996. *Patterns in Comparative Religion*. Lincoln: University of Nebraska Press. (French original: *Traité d'histoire des religions*, 1949.)

Elison, George. 1991. *Deus Destroyed: The Image of Christianity in Early Modern Japan*. 3rd printing. Cambridge, MA: Harvard University Press.

Elverskog, Johan. 2010. *Buddhism and Islam on the Silk Road*. Philadelphia: University of Pennsylvania Press.

Engineer, Ashgar Ali. 2005. "Islam and Pluralism." In *The Myth of Religious Superiority: Multifaith Explorations of Religious Pluralism*, edited by P. Knitter, 211–19. Maryknoll, NY: Orbis Books.

————. 2007. *Islam in the Contemporary World*. New Delhi: New Dawn Press.

Englert, Winfried Philipp. 1898. *Christus und Buddha in ihrem himmlischen Vorleben*. Vienna: Verlag von Mayer.

Esack, Farid. 1997. *The Qur'ān, Liberation and Pluralism: An Islamic Perspective on Interreligious Solidarity against Oppression*. Oxford: Oneworld.

Fenton, Paul. 1981. Introduction to ʿObadyāh b. Abraham b. Moses Maimonides, *The Treatise of the Pool. Al-Maqāla al Ḥawḍiyya*, 1–71. London: Octagon Press.

———. 2012. "*The Banished Brother*: Islam in Jewish Thought and Faith." In *Jewish Theology and World Religions*, edited by A. Goshen-Gottstein and E. Korn, 235–61. Oxford: Littman Library of Jewish Civilization.

Firestone, Reuven. 2013. "Jewish-Muslim Dialogue." In *The Wiley-Blackwell Companion to Inter-Religious Dialogue*, edited by C. Cornille, 224–43. Chichester: Wiley Blackwell.

Flood, Finbarr Barry. 2002. "Between Cult and Culture: Bamiyan, Islamic Iconoclasm, and the Museum." *Art Bulletin* 84 (4): 641–59.

Foltz, Richard. 2010. "Buddhism in the Iranian World." *Muslim World* 100:204–14.

Forster, Regula. 2015. "Barlaam and Josaphat." In *Encyclopaedia of Islam*, 3rd ed. Edited by Kate Fleet, Gudrun Krämer, Denis Matringe, John Nawas, and Everett Rowson. Brill online: http://referenceworks.brillonline.com/entries/encyclopaedia-of-islam-3/barlaam-and-josaphat-COM_24301.

Fowler, James. 1981. *Stages of Faith: The Psychology of Human Development and the Quest for Meaning*. San Francisco: Harper & Row.

Fredericks, James. 1995. "A Universal Religious Experience? Comparative Theology as an Alternative to a Theology of Religions." *Horizons* 22:67–87.

———. 1999. *Faith among Faiths: Christian Theology and Non-Christian Religions*. New York: Paulist.

———. 2004. *Buddhists and Christians: Through Comparative Theology to Solidarity*. Maryknoll, NY: Orbis Books.

———. 2010. Introduction to *The New Comparative Theology: Interreligious Insights from the Next Generation*, edited by Francis X. Clooney, ix–xix. London: T&T Clark.

Fredriksen, Paula. 2014. "Paul, Practical Pluralism, and the Invention of Religious Persecution in Roman Antiquity." In *Understanding Religious Pluralism: Perspectives from Religious Studies and Theology*, edited by P. Phan and J. S. Ray, 87–113. Eugene, OR: Pickwick.

Frei, Fritz. 1996. "Religiöse Tradition als Rettung der Nation und der Welt." In *Christlicher Glaube in multireligiöser Gesellschaft*, edited by A. Peter, 170–86. Immensee: Supplementa NZW.

Gambhirananada, Swami, trans. 2004. *Brahma-Sūtra-Bhāṣya of Śrī Śaṅkarācārya*. Kolkata: Advaita Ashrama.

Gantke, Wolgang. 1998. "Probleme des Hindufundamentalismus im interkulturellen Kontext." In *Begegnung von Religionen und Kulturen: Festschrift for Norbert Klaes*, edited by D. Lüddeckens, 231–54. Dettelbach: J. H. Röll.

Gentz, Joachim. 2008. "Buddhism and Chinese Religions." In *Buddhist Attitudes to Other Religions*, edited by P. Schmidt-Leukel, 172–211. St. Ottilien: EOS.

———. 2013a. *Understanding Chinese Religions*. Edinburgh: Dunedin Academic Press.

———. 2013b. "Religious Diversity in the Three Teachings Discourses." In *Religious Diversity in Chinese Thought*, edited by P. Schmidt-Leukel and J. Gentz, 123–40. Basingstoke: Palgrave Macmillan.

Gernet, Jacques. 1985. *China and the Christian Impact: A Conflict of Cultures*. Cambridge: Cambridge University Press.

Gez, Yonatan N. 2011. "The Phenomenon of Jewish Buddhists in Light of the History of Jewish Suffering." *Nova Religio: The Journal of Alternative and Emergent Religions* 15:44–68.

Ghazi bin Muḥammad, Prince of Jordan. 2010a. "On 'A Common Word between Us and You.'" In *A Common Word: Muslims and Christians on Loving God and Neighbor*, edited by M. Volf, Ghazi bin Muḥammad, and M. Yarrington, 3–17. Grand Rapids, MI: Eerdmans.

———. 2010b. "Introduction." In Reza Shah-Kazemi, *Common Ground between Islam and Buddhism*, ix–xvi. Louisville: Fons Vitae.

Gilkey, Langdon. 1987. "Plurality and Its Theological Implications." In *The Myth of Christian Uniqueness: Toward a Pluralistic Theology of Religions*, edited by J. Hick and P. Knitter, 37–50. Maryknoll, NY: Orbis Books.

Gillespie, Piers. 2007. "Current Issues in Indonesian Islam: Analysing the 2005 Council of Indonesia Ulama Fatwa No. 7 Opposing Pluralism, Liberalism and Secularism." *Journal of Islamic Studies* 18 (2): 202–40.

Glock, Charles Y. 1972. "On the Study of Religious Commitment." In *Religion's Influence in Contemporary Society: Readings in the Sociology of Religion*, edited by J. E. Faulkner, 38–56. Columbus, OH: Charles E. Merrill.

Golwalkar, M. S. 1996. *Bunch of Thoughts*. 3rd ed., rev. and enl. Bangalore: Sahitya Sindhu Prakashana.

Gómez, Luis O. 1976. "Proto-Mādhyamika in the Pāli Canon." *Philosophy East and West* 26 (2): 137–65.

Goodall, Dominic. 1996. *Hindu Scriptures*. London: Phoenix.

Goossaert, Vincent, and David A. Palmer. 2011. *The Religious Question in Modern China*. Chicago: University of Chicago Press.

Goshen-Gottstein, Alon. 2007. "No Religion Is an Island: Following the Trail Blazer." *Shofar: An Interdisciplinary Journal of Jewish Studies* 26 (1): 72–111.

———. 2009. "Heschel and Interreligious Dialogue—Formulating the Questions." In *Abraham Joshua Heschel: Philosophy, Theology, and Interreligious Dialogue*, edited by S. Krajewski and A. Lipszyc, 161–67. Wiesbaden: Harrassowitz.

———. 2012a. "Encountering Hinduism: Thinking through *Avodah Zarah*." In *Jewish Theology and World Religions*, edited by A. Goshen-Gottstein and E. Korn, 263–98. Oxford: Littman Library of Jewish Civilization.

————. 2012b. "Concluding Reflections." In *Jewish Theology and World Religions*, edited by A. Goshen-Gottstein and E. Korn, 317–27. Oxford: Littman Library of Jewish Civilization.

Goshen-Gottstein, Alon, and Eugene Korn, eds. 2012. *Jewish Theology and World Religions*. Oxford: Littman Library of Jewish Civilization.

Gowans, Christopher W. 2003. *Philosophy of the Buddha*. London: Routledge.

Greenberg, Irving. 2000. "Judaism and Christianity: Covenants of Redemption." In *Christianity in Jewish Terms*, edited by T. Frymer-Kensky et al., 141–58. Boulder, CO: Westview Press.

————. 2004. *For the Sake of Heaven and Earth: The New Encounter between Judaism and Christianity*. Philadelphia: Jewish Publication Society.

————. 2006. "Theology after the Shoah: The Transformation of the Core Paradigm." *Modern Judaism* 26 (3): 213–39.

Griffin, David Ray, ed. 2005a. *Deep Religious Pluralism*. Louisville: Westminster John Knox Press.

————. 2005b. "Religious Pluralism: Generic, Identist, and Deep." In *Deep Religious Pluralism*, edited by D. Griffin, 3–38. Louisville: Westminster John Knox Press.

————. 2005c. "John Cobb's Whiteheadian Complementary Pluralism." In *Deep Religious Pluralism*, edited by D. Griffin, 39–66. Louisville: Westminster John Knox Press.

Griffiths, Paul. 2014. "What Are Catholic Theologians Doing When They Do Comparative Theology?" *Studies in Interreligious Dialogue* 24 (1): 40–45.

Gross, Rita M. 1993. *Buddhism after Patriarchy: A Feminist History, Analysis, and Reconstruction of Buddhism*. Albany: State University of New York Press.

————. 2005. "Excuse Me, but What's the Question? Isn't Religious Diversity Normal?" In *The Myth of Religious Superiority: Multifaith Explorations of Religious Pluralism*, edited by P. Knitter, 75–87. Maryknoll, NY: Orbis Books.

————. 2014. *Religious Diversity—What's the Problem? Buddhist Advice for Flourishing with Religious Diversity*. Eugene, OR: Cascade Books.

Gross, Rita M., and Rosemary Radford Ruether. 2001. *Religious Feminism and the Future of the Planet: A Buddhist-Christian Conversation*. London: Continuum.

Grünschloß, Andreas. 1999. *Der eigene und der fremde Glaube: Studien zur interreligiösen Fremdwahrnehmung in Islam, Hinduismus, Buddhismus und Christentum*. Tübingen: Mohr Siebeck.

————. 2008. "Buddhist-Christian Relations." In *Buddhist Attitudes to Other Religions*, edited by P. Schmidt-Leukel, 237–68. St. Ottilien: EOS-Verlag.

Guardini, Romano. 1996. *The Lord*. Washington, DC: Regnery.

————. 1997. *Der Herr*. Mainz: Matthias-Grünewald; Paderborn: Schöningh.

Guruge, Ananda, trans. 2005. *Mahāvaṃsa: The Great Chronicle of Sri Lanka*. 2nd rev. ed. Colombo: S. Godage & Brothers.

Gwynne, Paul. 2014. *Buddha, Jesus and Muḥammad: A Comparative Study*. Oxford: Wiley Blackwell.

Haight, Roger. 1992. "The Case for Spirit Christology." *Theological Studies* 53:257–87.

———. 1999. *Jesus Symbol of God*. Maryknoll, NY: Orbis Books.

———. 2005. *The Future of Christology*. London: Continuum.

Halbfass, Wilhelm. 1988. *India and Europe: An Essay in Understanding*. Albany: State University of New York Press.

———. 1991. *Tradition and Reflection: Explorations in Indian Thought*. Albany: State University of New York Press.

———. 1998. "Der Buddha und seine Lehre im Urteil des Hinduismus." In *Wer ist Buddha? Eine Gestalt und ihre Bedeutung für die Menschheit*, edited by P. Schmidt-Leukel, 176–94, 260–62. Munich: Diederichs Verlag.

Halperin, Mark. 2006. *Out of the Cloister: Literati Perspectives on Buddhism in Sung China, 960–1279*. Cambridge, MA: Harvard University Asia Center.

Harris, Elizabeth. 2013. "Buddhism and the Religious Other." In *Understanding Interreligious Relations*, edited by D. Cheetham, D. Pratt, and D. Thomas, 88–117. Oxford: Oxford University Press.

Harris, Elizabeth, Paul Hedges, and Shanthikumar Hettiarachchi, eds. 2016. *Twenty-First Century Theologies of Religions: Retrospection and Future Prospects*. Leiden: Brill.

Hartman, David. 1990. *Conflicting Visions: Spiritual Possibilities of Modern Israel*. New York: Schocken Books.

———. 2002. *A Heart of Many Rooms: Celebrating the Many Voices within Judaism*. Woodstock, VT: Jewish Lights.

Harvey, Peter. 1995. *The Selfless Mind: Personality, Consciousness and Nirvāṇa in Early Buddhism*. London: RoutledgeCurzon.

Hazra, Kanai Lal. 1995. *The Rise and Decline of Buddhism in India*. Delhi: Munshiram Manoharlal.

Hedges, Paul. 2008. "Particularities: Tradition-Specific Post-modern Perspectives." In *Christian Approaches to Other Faiths*, edited by P. Hedges and A. Race, 112–35. London: SCM Press.

———. 2010. *Controversies in Interreligious Dialogue and the Theology of Religions*. London: SCM Press.

———. 2014a. "The Old and New Comparative Theologies: Discourses on Religion, the Theology of Religions, Orientalism and the Boundaries of Traditions." In *European Perspectives on the New Comparative Theology*, edited by Francis X. Clooney and John Berthrong, 52–70. Basel: MDPI.

———. 2014b. "Why Are There Many Gods? Religious Diversity and Its Challenges." In *Controversies in Contemporary Religion: Education, Law, Politics, Society, and Spirituality*, vol. 1: *Theoretical and Academic Debates*, edited by P. Hedges, 191–218. Santa Barbara: Praeger.

Heelas, Paul. 1978. "Some Problems with Religious Studies." *Religion* 8:1–14.

Heiler, Friedrich. [1919] 1921. *Das Gebet: Eine religionsgeschichtliche und religionspsychologische Untersuchung.* 3rd ed. Munich: Verlag Ernst Reinhardt.

———. [1959] 1962. *Die Religionen der Menschheit in Vergangenheit und Gegenwart.* 2nd ed. Stuttgart: Recclam.

Heim, S. Mark. 1985. *Is Christ the Only Way? Christian Faith in a Pluralistic World.* Valley Forge, PA: Judson Press.

———. 1995. *Salvations: Truth and Difference in Religion.* Maryknoll, NY: Orbis Books.

———. 2001. *The Depth of the Riches: A Trinitarian Theology of Religious Ends.* Grand Rapids, MI: Eerdmans.

———. 2003. "The Depth of the Riches: Trinity and Religious Ends." In *Theology and the Religions: A Dialogue,* edited by V. Mortensen, 387–402. Grand Rapids, MI: Eerdmans.

Heschel, Abraham Joshua. 1991. "No Religion Is an Island." In *No Religion Is an Island: Abraham Joshua Heschel and Interreligious Dialogue,* edited by H. Kasimow and B. L. Sherwin, 3–22. Maryknoll, NY: Orbis Books.

Hick, John. 1968. *Christianity at the Centre.* Basingstoke: Macmillan.

———. 1973. *God and the Universe of Faiths.* Basingstoke: Macmillan.

———. 1975. "Conflicting Truth-Claims: A Rejoinder." In *Truth and Dialogue: The Relationship between World Religions,* edited by J. Hick, 156–62. London: Sheldon Press.

———. 1977. "Jesus and the World Religions." In *The Myth of God Incarnate,* ed. John Hick, 167–85. London: SCM Press.

———. 1980. *God Has Many Names: Britain's New Religious Pluralism.* Basingstoke: Macmillan.

———. 1982. *God Has Many Names.* Philadelphia: Westminster.

———. 1984. "Religious Pluralism." In *The World's Religious Traditions: Current Perspectives in Religious Studies: Essays in Honour of Wilfred Cantwell Smith,* edited by F. Whaling, 147–64. Edinburgh: T&T Clark.

———. 1985a. *Problems of Religious Pluralism.* Basingstoke: Macmillan.

———. [1976] 1985b. *Death and Eternal Life.* Basingstoke: Macmillan.

———. 1989. *An Interpretation of Religion: Human Responses to the Transcendent.* Basingstoke: Macmillan.

———. [1966] 1990. *Evil and the God of Love.* Basingstoke: Macmillan.

———. 1993a. *The Metaphor of God Incarnate.* London: SCM.

———. 1993b. *Disputed Questions in Theology and the Philosophy of Religions.* Basingstoke: Macmillan.

———. 1995. *The Rainbow of Faiths.* London: SCM.

———. 1997. "Five Misgivings." In *The Uniqueness of Jesus: A Dialogue with Paul Knitter,* edited by L. Swidler and P. Mojzes, 7–84. Maryknoll, NY: Orbis Books.

———. 1999. *The Fifth Dimension.* Oxford: Oneworld.

————. 2001. *Dialogues in the Philosophy of Religion.* Basingstoke: Palgrave.

————. 2002. *An Autobiography.* Oxford: Oneworld.

————. 2006. *The New Frontier of Religion and Science.* Basingstoke: Palgrave.

————. 2008. *Who or What Is God? And Other Investigations.* London: SCM Press.

————. 2010. *Between Faith and Doubt: Dialogues on Religion and Reason.* Basingstoke: Palgrave Macmillan.

Hick, John, and L. Hempel, eds. 1989. *Gandhi's Significance for Today.* New York: St. Martin's Press.

Hick, John, and Paul Knitter, eds. 1987. *The Myth of Christian Uniqueness: Toward a Pluralistic Theology of Religions.* Maryknoll, NY: Orbis Books.

Hintersteiner, Norbert. 2001. *Traditionen überschreiten: Angloamerikanische Beiträge zur interkulturellen Traditionshermeneutik.* Vienna: WUV-Universitätsverlag.

Hiremath, R. C. 1994. *Buddhism in Karnataka.* New Delhi: D. K. Printworld.

Hirota, Dennis, ed. 2000. *Toward a Contemporary Understanding of Pure Land Buddhism: Creating a Shin Buddhist Theology in a Religiously Plural World.* Albany: State University of New York Press.

Holdrege, Barbara A. 2013. "Hindu-Jewish Encounters." In *The Wiley-Blackwell Companion to Inter-Religious Dialogue,* edited by C. Cornille, 410–37. Chichester: Wiley Blackwell.

Holenstein, Elmar. 1985. *Menschliches Selbstverständnis: Ichbewußtsein—Intersubjective Verantwortung—Interkulturelle Verständigung.* Frankfurt a.M.: Suhrkamp.

————. 1998. *Kulturphilosophische Perspektiven.* Frankfurt a.M.: Suhrkamp.

————. 2003. "A Dozen Rules of Thumb for Avoiding Intercultural Misunderstandings." *Polylog.* http://them.polylog.org/4/ahe-en.htm.

Hookham, Shenpen K. 1991. *The Buddha Within.* Albany: State University of New York Press.

Hopkins, Jasper. 1994. *Nicholas of Cusa's* De Pace Fidei *and* Cribatio Alkorani: *Translation and Analysis.* 2nd ed. Minneapolis: Arthur J. Banning Press. http://jasper-hopkins.info/DePace12-2000.pdf.

Horne, Charles F. 1917. *The Sacred Books and Early Literature of the East,* vol. 12: *Medieval China.* New York: Parke, Austin, & Lipscomb.

Hosein, Imran N. [1972] 2014. *Islam and Buddhism in the Modern World.* Trinidad and Tobago: Imran N. Hosein Publications.

Hume, David. 2000. *Enquiries concerning Human Understanding and concerning the Principles of Morals.* Reprinted from the posthumous edition of 1777 and edited with introduction, comparative table of contents, and analytical index by L. A. Selby-Bigge. Reprint of the 3rd rev. ed. by P. H. Nidditsch. Oxford: Clarendon Press.

Hutchison, John A. 1991. *Paths of Faith*. 4th ed. Boston: McGraw-Hill.

Ibrahim, Ezzedin, and Denys Johnson-Davies. n.d. *An-Nawawī's Forty Hadith*. Jakarta: Dar al-ilm.

Ikeda, Daisaku, and Majid Tehranian. 2004. *Global Civilization: A Buddhist-Islamic Dialogue*. London: British Academic Press.

Ingram, Paul. 2008. *Buddhist-Christian Dialogue in an Age of Science*. Lanham, MD: Rowman & Littlefield.

———. 2012. *Theological Reflections at the Boundaries*. Eugene, OR: Cascade Books.

Ireland, John D. 1997. *The Udāna: Inspired Utterances of the Buddha and the Ittivuttaka: The Buddha's Sayings*. Kandy: Buddhist Publication Society.

Izutsu, Toshihiko. 1994. *Creation and the Timeless Order of Things*. Ashland, OR: White Cloud Press.

———. 2007. *The Concept of Reality and Existence*. Kuala Lumpur: Islamic Book Trust.

———. 2008. *The Structure of Oriental Philosophy: Collected Papers of the Eranos Conference*. Vol. 2. Tokyo: Keio University Press.

Jackson, Peter. 2003. *Buddhadāsa: Theravāda Buddhism and Modernist Reform in Thailand*. Chiang Mai: Silkworm Books.

Jackson, Roger, ed. 2009. *Thuken Losang Chökyi Nyima: The Crystal Mirror of Philosophical Systems*. Boston: Wisdom Publications.

Jackson, Roger, and John Makransky, eds. 2003. *Buddhist Theology: Critical Reflections by Contemporary Buddhist Scholars*. London: Routledge Curzon.

Jahn, Karl. 1965. *Rashīd Al-Dīn's History of India*. The Hague: Mouton.

———. 1980. *Die Indiengeschichte des Rašīd ad-Dīn*. Vienna: Verlag der Österreichischen Akademie der Wissenschaften.

Jain, Gokul Chandra. 1989. "Jainism—Its Resources for Interreligious Dialogue." In *Interreligious Dialogue: Voices from a New Frontier*, edited by M. D. Bryant and F. Flinn, 163–67. New York: Paragon House.

James, William. [1902] 1990. *The Varieties of Religious Experience*. Vintage Books: New York.

Jha, Ganganatha. 1986. *The Tattvasaṅgraha of Shāntarakṣita*. With the commentary of Kamalashīla. Translated into English by Ganganatha Jha. Vol. 1. Delhi: Motilal Banarsidass (repr.).

Jordans, J. F. T. 1987. "Gandhi and Religious Pluralism." In *Modern Indian Responses to Religious Pluralism*, edited by H. Coward, 3–17. Albany: State University of New York Press.

Joshi, Lal Mani. 1983. *Discerning the Buddha: A Study of Buddhism and of the Brahmanical Hindu Attitude to It*. New Delhi: Munshiram Manoharlal.

Jospe, Raphael. 2007. "Pluralism out of the Sources of Judaism: Religious Pluralism without Relativism." *Studies in Christian-Jewish Relations* 2 (2): 92–113 (e-journal).

———. 2012. "Pluralism out of the Sources of Judaism: The Quest for Religious

Pluralism without Relativism." In *Jewish Theology and World Religions*, edited by A. Goshen-Gottstein and E. Korn, 87–133. Oxford: Littman Library of Jewish Civilization.

Kalisch, Muḥammad (Sven). 2007. "A Muslim View of Judaism." In *Islam and Inter-Faith Relations*, edited by P. Schmidt-Leukel and L. Ridgeon, 67–83. Gerald Weisfeld Lectures 2006. London: SCM Press.

Kamenetz, Rodger. 1995. *The Jew in the Lotus: A Poet's Rediscovery of Jewish Identity in Buddhist India*. New York: HarperOne.

Kaplan, Stephen. 2002. *Different Paths, Different Summits: A Model for Religious Pluralism*. Lanham: Rowman & Littlefield.

Kasimow, Harold. 1991. "Heschel's Prophetic Vision of Religious Pluralism." In *No Religion Is an Island: Abraham Joshua Heschel and Interreligious Dialogue*, edited by H. Kasimow and B. L. Sherwin, 79–96. Maryknoll, NY: Orbis Books.

Kasimow, Harold, and Byron L. Sherwin, eds. 1991. *No Religion Is an Island: Abraham Joshua Heschel and Interreligious Dialogue*. Maryknoll, NY: Orbis Books.

Katz, Nathan. 2013. "Buddhist-Jewish Relations." In *The Wiley-Blackwell Companion to Inter-Religious Dialogue*, edited by C. Cornille, 394–409. Chichester: Wiley Blackwell.

Kelly, John Norman Davidson. 1977. *Early Christian Doctrines*. 5th rev. ed. London: Adam & Charles Black.

Kern, Iso. 1992. *Buddhistische Kritik am Christentum im China des 17. Jahrhunderts*. Bern: Peter Lang Verlag.

Keyes, Charles. 2013. "Muslim 'Others' in Buddhist Thailand." In *Buddhism and Religious Diversity,* vol. 3: *Islam and Judaism*, edited by P. Schmidt-Leukel, 59–80. London: Routledge.

Khalil, Mohammad Hassan, ed. 2013. *Between Heaven and Hell: Islam, Salvation, and the Fate of Others*. Oxford: Oxford University Press.

Khorchide, Mouhanad. 2014. *Islam Is Mercy: Essential Features of a Modern Religion*. Freiburg i.Br.: Herder.

Kiblinger, Kristin. 2005. *Buddhist Inclusivism: Attitudes towards Religious Others*. Aldershot: Ashgate.

———. 2010. "Relating Theology of Religions and Comparative Theology." In *The New Comparative Theology: Interreligious Insights from the Next Generation*, edited by Francis X. Clooney, 21–42. London: T&T Clark.

King, Sallie B. 1997. "The Doctrine of Buddha-Nature Is Impeccably Buddhist." In *Pruning the Bodhi Tree: The Storm over Critical Buddhism*, edited by J. Hubbard and P. L. Swanson, 172–92. Honolulu: University of Hawai'i Press.

Klostermaier, Klaus. 1979. "Hindu Views of Buddhism." In *Developments in Buddhist Thought: Canadian Contributions to Buddhist Studies*, edited by R. C. Amore, 60–82. Waterloo: Wilfred Laurier University Press.

———. 1989. *A Survey of Hinduism*. Albany: State University of New York Press.

————. 2000. *Hinduism: A Short Introduction*. Oxford: Oneworld.

Knitter, Paul. 1987. "Toward a Liberation Theology of Religions" In *The Myth of Christian Uniqueness: Toward a Pluralistic Theology of Religions*, edited by J. Hick and John; P. Knitter, 178–200. Maryknoll, NY: Orbis Books.

————. 1995. *One Earth, Many Religions: Multifaith Dialogue and Global Responsibility*. Maryknoll, NY: Orbis Books.

————. 1996. *Jesus and the Other Names: Christian Mission and Global Responsibility*. Maryknoll, NY: Orbis Books.

————. 1997. "Five Theses on the Uniqueness of Jesus." In *The Uniqueness of Jesus: A Dialogue with Paul F. Knitter*, edited by L. Swidler and P. Mojzes, 3–16. Maryknoll, NY: Orbis Books.

————. ed. 2005. *The Myth of Religious Superiority: Multifaith Explorations of Religious Pluralism*. Maryknoll, NY: Orbis Books.

————. 2009. *Without Buddha I Could Not Be a Christian*. Oxford: Oneworld.

————. 2012. "A '*Hypostatic Union*' of Two Practices but One Person?" *Buddhist-Christian Studies* 32:19–26.

Knitter, Paul, and Roger Haight. 2015. *Jesus and Buddha: Friends in Conversation*. Maryknoll, NY: Orbis Books.

Kogan, Michael S. 2005. "Toward a Pluralist Theology of Judaism." In *The Myth of Religious Superiority: Multifaith Explorations of Religious Pluralism*, edited by P. Knitter, 105–18. Maryknoll, NY: Orbis Books.

————. 2008. *Opening the Covenant: A Jewish Theology of Christianity*. Oxford: Oxford University Press.

Kohn, Livia. 2008. *Laughing at the Dao: Debates among Buddhists and Daoists in Medieval China*. Magdalena, NM: Three Pines Press.

————. 2013. "One Day—Many Ways: Daoist Approaches to Religious Diversity." In *Religious Diversity in Chinese Thought*, edited by P. Schmidt-Leukel and J. Gentz, 55–63. London: Palgrave Macmillan.

Kristensen, W. Brede. 1960. *The Meaning of Religion: Lectures in the Phenomenology of Religion*. The Hague: Martinus Nijhoff.

Kues, Nikolaus von. 2002. *Vom Frieden zwischen den Religionen (De Pace Fidei)*. Latin, German, edited and translated by Klaus Berger and Christiane Nord. Frankfurt a.M.: Insel Verlag.

Küng, Hans. 1991. *Global Responsibility: In Search of a New World Ethic*. London: SCM Press.

————. 2007. *Islam: Past, Present, and Future*. Oxford: Oneworld.

Küng, Hans, and Julia Ching. 1989. *Christianity and Chinese Religions*. New York: Doubleday.

Küng, Hans, Josef van Ess, Heinrich von Stietencron, and Heinz Bechert. 1993. *Christianity and the World Religions*. 2nd ed. London: SCM Press.

Lamptey, Jerusha Tanner. 2014a. *Never Wholly Other: A* Muslima *Theology of Religious Pluralism*. Oxford: Oxford University Press.

————. 2014b. "Lateral and Hierarchical Religious Difference in the Qur'ān:

Muslima Theology of Religious Pluralism." In *Understanding Religious Pluralism: Perspectives from Religious Studies and Theology*, edited by P. Phan and J. S. Ray, 209–22. Eugene, OR: Pickwick.

Lang, D. M. 1957. "The Life of the Blessed Iodasaph: A New Oriental Christian Version of the Barlaam and Ioasaph Romance (Jerusalem, Greek Patriarchal Library: Georgian MS 140)." *Bulletin of the School of Oriental and African Studies, University of London* 20:1–3 (Studies in Honour of Sir Ralph Turner, Director of the School of Oriental and African Studies, 1937–57): 389–407.

Langer, Ruth. 2003. "Jewish Understanding of the Religious Other." *Theological Studies* 64:255–77.

Lee, Yen-Yi. 2012. "One and Many: Rethinking John Hick's Pluralism." PhD dissertation, University of Birmingham. http://etheses.bham.ac.uk/3278/.

Legenhausen, Muhammad. 2005. "A Muslim's Non-Reductive Religious Pluralism." In *Islam and Global Dialogue: Religious Pluralism and the Pursuit of Peace*, edited by R. Boase, 51–73. Aldershot: Ashgate.

———. 2009. "Jesus as Kalimat Allah: The Word of God." https://www.academia.edu/2516415/_Jesus_as_Kalimat_Allah_the_Word_of_God.

Leirvik, Oddbjørn. 2010. *Images of Jesus Christ in Islam*. 2nd ed. London: Continuum.

Li, Chenyang. 1996. "How Can One Be a Taoist-Buddhist-Confucian? A Chinese Illustration of Multiple Religious Participation." *International Review of Chinese Religion & Philosophy* 1:29–66.

Lindbeck, George. 1984. *The Nature of Doctrine: Religion and Theology in a Postliberal Age*. Philadelphia: Westminster Press.

Lindtner, Christian. 1999. "Madhyamaka Causality." *Hōrin: Vergleichende Studien zur japanischen Kultur* 6:37–77.

Linzer, Judith. 1999. "Maurice Friedman and Zalman Schachter-Shalomi: Pilgrims to the East." *Shofar: An Interdisciplinary Journal of Jewish Studies* 17 (3): 85–92.

Lipner, Julius. 1998. *Hindus: Their Religious Beliefs and Practices*. London: Routledge.

Llewellyn, Jack E., ed. 2005. *Defining Hinduism: A Reader*. London: Equinox.

Long, Jeffery D. 2005. "Anekanta Vedānta: Toward a Deep Hindu Religious Pluralism." In *Deep Religious Pluralism*, edited by D. Griffin, 130–57. Louisville: Westminster John Knox Press.

———. 2007. *A Vision for Hinduism: Beyond Hindu Nationalism*. London: I. B. Tauris.

———. 2009. *Jainism: An Introduction*. London: I. B. Tauris.

———. 2013. "Hinduism and the Religious Other." In *Understanding Interreligious Relations*, edited by D. Cheetham, D. Pratt, and D. Thomas, 88–117. Oxford: Oxford University Press.

———. 2014. "Diversity as the Nature of Reality: A Jain-Informed Approach to the Variety of Worldviews." In *On World Religions: Diversity, Not Dis-*

sension, edited by A. N. Balslev, 17–32. New Delhi: Sage Publications.

Lopez, Donald S. 2014. Introduction to *Barlaam and Josaphat: A Christian Tale of the Buddha*, by Gui de Cambrai, vii–xx. New York: Penguin.

Lopez, Donald S., and Peggy McCracken. 2014. *In Search of the Christian Buddha: How an Asian Sage Became a Medieval Saint*. New York: W. W. Norton.

Lorenzen, David N. 1999. "Who Invented Hinduism?" *Comparative Studies in Society and History* 41:630–59.

Lubarsky, Sandra B. 1990. *Tolerance and Transformation: Jewish Approaches to Religious Pluralism*. Cincinnati: Hebrew Union College Press.

———. 2005. "Deep Religious Pluralism and Contemporary Jewish Thought." In *Deep Religious Pluralism*, edited by D. R. Griffin, 111–29. Louisville: Westminster John Knox Press.

Lüddeckens, Dorothea. 2001. *Das Weltparlament der Religionen von 1893: Strukturen der interreligiösen Begegnung im 19. Jahrhundert*. Berlin: Walter de Gruyter.

Makransky, John. 2003a. "Buddhist Perspectives on Truth in Other Religions: Past and Present." *Theological Studies* 64:334–61.

———. 2003b. "Historical Consciousness as an Offering to the Trans-Historical Buddha." In *Buddhist Theology*, edited by J. Makransky and R. Jackson, 111–35. London: RoutledgeCurzon.

———. 2005. "Buddha and Christ as Mediators of the Transcendent: A Buddhist Perspective." In *Buddhism and Christianity in Dialogue*, edited by P. Schmidt-Leukel, 176–99. The Gerald Weisfeld Lectures 2004. London: SCM Press.

———. 2008. "Buddhist Inclusivism." In *Buddhist Attitudes to Other Religions*, edited by P. Schmidt-Leukel, 47–84. St. Ottilien: EOS.

———. 2011. "Thoughts on Why, How and What Buddhists Can Learn from Christian Theologians." *Buddhist-Christian Studies* 31:119–33.

———. 2014. "What Christian Liberation Theology and Buddhism Need to Learn from Each Other." *Buddhist-Christian Studies* 34:117–34.

Malinar, Angelika. 2007. *The Bhagavadgītā: Doctrines and Contexts*. Cambridge: Cambridge University Press.

———. 2009. *Hinduismus*. Göttingen: Vandehoeck & Ruprecht.

Mall, Ram Adhar. 1995. *Philosophie im Vergleich der Kulturen: Interkulturelle Philosophie—eine neue Orientierung*. Darmstadt: Wissenschaftliche Buchgesellschaft.

———. 2000. *Intercultural Philosophy*. Lanham, MD: Rowman & Littlefield.

Mandelbrot, Benoît B. 1983. *The Fractal Geometry of Nature*. Updated and augmented. New York: W. H. Freeman.

May, John D'Arcy, ed. 2007. *Converging Ways? Conversion and Belonging in Buddhism and Christianity*. St. Ottilien: EOS Verlag.

McFaul, Thomas. 2011. *The Future of God in the Global Village: Spirituality in an Age of Terrorism and Beyond*. Bloomington, IN: Author House.

McLeod, W. H. 1984. *Textual Sources for the Study of Sikhism*. Totowa, NJ: Barnes & Noble Books.

Meir, Ephraim. 2013. *Dialogical Thought and Identity: Trans-Different Religiosity in Present-Day Societies*. Berlin: De Gruyter; Jerusalem: Magnes Press.

————. 2014. "Building Stones for an Interreligious Dialogue and Theology." In *Religions and Dialogue: International Approaches*, edited by W. Weisse et al., 125–35. Münster: Waxmann.

————. 2015. *Jewish Dialogical Thought and Interreligious Theology*. Berlin: De Gruyter; Jerusalem: Magnes Press.

Meister, Chad, ed. 2011.*The Oxford Handbook of Religious Diversity*. Oxford: Oxford University Press.

Mette, Adelheid. 1981. "Zwei kleine Fragmente aus Gilgit." *Studien zur Indologie und Iranistik* 7:133–51.

Michaels, Axel. 1998. *Der Hinduismus: Geschichte und Gegenwart*. Munich: C. H. Beck.

Michel, Thomas. 2014. "Religious Pluralism in Islam." In *Understanding Religious Pluralism: Perspectives from Religious Studies and Theology*, edited by P. Phan and J. S. Ray, 170–85. Eugene, OR: Pickwick.

Murata, Sachiko. 2000. *Chinese Gleams of Sufi Lights: Wang Tai-yü's* Great Learning of the Pure and Real *and Liu Chih's* Displaying the Concealment of the Real Realm. Albany: State University of New York Press.

Nakamura, Hajime. [1975] 1992. *A Comparative History of Ideas*. Rev. ed. London: Kegan Paul.

Ñāṇamoli, Bhikkhu, and Bhikkhu Bodhi. 2001. *The Middle Length Discourses of the Buddha: A Translation of the Majjhima Nikāya*. 2nd ed. Boston: Wisdom Publication.

Nasr, Seyyed Hossein, ed. 1991. *The Essential Writings of Frithjof Schuon*. Rockport, MA: Element.

————. 1989. *Knowledge and the Sacred*. Albany: State University of New York Press.

————. 1999. "Religion, Globality, and Universality." In *A Dome of Many Colors: Studies in Religious Pluralism, Identity, and Unity*, edited by A. Sharma and K. M. Dugan, 152–78. Harrisburg, PA: Trinity Press International.

Neufeldt, R. W. 1987. "The Response of the Ramakrishna Mission." In *Modern Indian Responses to Religious Pluralism*, edited by H. G. Coward, 65–84. Albany: State University of New York Press.

Neville, Robert Cummings. 1991. *Behind the Masks of God: An Essay toward Comparative Theology*. Albany: State University of New York Press.

Newman, John. 1995. "Eschatology in the Wheel of Time Tantra." In *Buddhism in Practice*, edited by D. S. Lopez Jr., 284–89. Princeton: Princeton University Press.

————. 1998. "Islam in the Kālacakra Tantra." *Journal of the International Association of Buddhist Studies* 21 (2): 311–71.

Nhat Hanh, Thich. [1988] 1996. *Living Buddha, Living Christ*. London: Rider.
————. 2005. "Jesus and Buddha as Brothers." In *Jesus in the World's Faiths: Leading Thinkers from Five Religions Reflect on His Meaning*, edited by G. A. Barker, 38–45. Maryknoll, NY: Orbis Books.

Nicholson, Hugh. 2009. "The Reunification of Theology and Comparison in the New Comparative Theology." *Journal of the American Academy of Religion* 77 (3): 609–46.
————. 2010. "The New Comparative Theology and the Problem of Theological Hegemonism." In *The New Comparative Theology: Interreligious Insights from the Next Generation*, edited by Francis X. Clooney, 43–62. London: T&T Clark.

Nicholson, Reynold A. 1911. *The Tarjumán Al-Ashwáq: A Collection of Mystical Odes by Muḥyi'ddín Ibn Al-'Arabí*. London: Royal Asiatic Society.

Nicolini-Zani, Matteo. 2013. "Christian Approaches to Religious Diversity in Premodern China." In *Religious Diversity in Chinese Thought*, edited by P. Schmidt-Leukel and J. Gentz. London: Palgrave Macmillan.

Niculescu, Mira. 2012. "I the Jew, I the Buddhist: Multi-Religious Belonging as Inner Dialogue." *Crosscurrents* 62 (3): 350–59.

Nikhilananda, Swami. 2005. *The Gospel of Sri Ramakrishna*. Abridged version. 7th printing. New York: Ramakrishna-Vivekananda Center.

Niles, D. T. 1969. "Karl Barth—A Personal Memory." *South East Asia Journal of Theology* 11:10–11.

Novak, David. 1983. *The Image of the Non-Jew in Judaism: An Historical and Constructive Study of the Noahide Laws*. Lewiston, NY: Edwin Mellen Press.
————. 1989. *Jewish-Christian Dialogue: A Jewish Justification*. New York: Oxford University Press.

Numrich, Paul D., ed. 2008. *The Boundaries of Knowledge in Buddhism, Christianity, and Science*. Göttingen: Vandehoeck & Ruprecht.

Nyanaponika, Thera. 1977. *Sutta-Nipāta: Früh-buddhistische Lehr-Dichtungen aus dem Pali-Kanon mit Azszügen aus den alten Kommentaren*. 2nd rev. ed. Konstanz: Christiani Verlag.
————. 1981. *Buddhism and the God-Idea: Selected Texts*. Kandy: BPS.

Oberhammer, Gerhard. 1987. *Versuch einer transzendentalen Hermeneutik religiöser Vielfalt*. Vienna: Publications of the De Nobili Research Library.

Obuse, Kieko. 2010a. "Doctrinal Accommodations in Buddhist-Muslim Relations: With Special Reference to Contemporary Japan." PhD dissertation. University of Oxford.
————. 2010b. "The Muslim Doctrine of Prophethood in the Context of Buddhist-Muslim Relations in Japan: Is the Buddha a Prophet?" *Muslim World* 100:215–32.

Ogden, Schubert M. 1992. *Is There Only One True Religion or Are There Many?* Dallas: Southern Methodist University Press.

Oldmeadow, Harry. 2010. *Frithjof Schuon and the Perennial Philosophy*. Bloomington, IN: World Wisdom.

Otto, Rudolf. 1923. *Vischnu-Nārāyana: Texte zur indischen Gottesmystik*. Jena: Eugen Diederichs.

———. 1936. *The Idea of the Holy*. Translated by John W. Harvey. Oxford: Oxford University Press.

Pandit, Moti Lal. 1993. *Being as Becoming: Studies in Early Buddhism*. New Delhi: Intercultural Publications.

Panikkar, Raimundo. 1964. *The Unknown Christ of Hinduism*. London: Darton, Longman & Todd.

———. 1978. *The Intrareligious Dialogue*. New York: Paulist Press.

———. 1981. *The Unknown Christ of Hinduism*. Completely revised and enlarged edition. Maryknoll, NY: Orbis Books.

———. 1987. "The Jordan, the Tiber, and the Ganges: Three Kairological Moments of Christian Self-Consciousness." In *Myth of Christian Uniqueness: Toward a Pluralistic Theology of Religions*, edited by J. Hick and P. Knitter, 89–116. Maryknoll, NY: Orbis Books.

———. 1993. *The Cosmotheandric Experience: Emerging Religious Consciousness*. Maryknoll, NY: Orbis Books.

———. 1995. *Invisible Harmony: Essays on Contemplation and Responsibility*. Minneapolis: Fortress.

———. 2010. *The Rhythm of Being: The Gifford Lectures*. Maryknoll, NY: Orbis Books.

Park, Jungnok. 2012. *How Buddhism Acquired a Soul on the Way to China*. Sheffield: Equinox.

Parrinder, Geoffrey. 1997. *Avatar and Incarnation: The Divine in Human Form in the World's Religions*. Oxford: Oneworld.

Patil, Parimal G. 2009. *Against a Hindu God: Buddhist Philosophy of Religion in India*. New York: Columbia University Press.

Patton, Kimberley C. 2000. "Juggling Torches: Why We Still Need Comparative Religion." In *A Magic Still Dwells: Comparative Religion in the Postmodern Age*, edited by K. C. Patton and B. C. Ray, 153–71. Berkeley: University of California Press.

Paul, Gregor. 2008. *Einführung in die Interkulturelle Philosophie*. Darmstadt: Wissenschaftliche Buchgesellschaft.

Peri (Pflaum), Hiram. 1959. *Der Religionsdisput der Barlaam-Legende, ein Motiv abendländischer Dichtung*. Untersuchung, ungedruckte Texte, Bibliographie der Legende (Acta Salamanticenssia 14:3). Salamanca: Universidad de Salamanca.

Pieris, Aloysius. 1988. *Love Meets Wisdom: A Christian Experience of Buddhism*. Maryknoll, NY: Orbis Books.

Plantinga, Richard J., ed. 1999. *Christianity and Plurality: Classic and Contemporary Readings*. Oxford: Blackwell.

Pruden, L. M. 1988–90. *Abhidharmakośabhāṣyam of Vasubandhu*. Translated into French by Louis de La Vallee Poussin. English version by Leo M. Pruden. 4 vols. Berkeley: Asian Humanity Press.

Race, Alan. 1983. *Christians and Religious Pluralism: Patterns in the Christian Theology of Religions*. London: SCM Press.

———. 1993. *Christians and Religious Pluralism*. 2nd enl. ed. London: SCM Press.

———. 2001. *Interfaith Encounter: The Twin Tracks of Theology and Dialogue*. London: SCM Press.

Race, Alan, and Paul Hedges, eds. 2008. *Christian Approaches to Other Faiths*. London: SCM Press.

Radhakrishnan, Sarvepalli. 1956. *Recovery of Faith*. London: Allen & Unwin.

———. [1927] 1974. *The Hindu View of Life*. 17th printing. London: Unwin Books.

Radhakrishnan, Sarvepalli, and Charles Moore, eds. 1989. *A Sourcebook in Indian Philosophy*. Princeton: Princeton University Press.

Raghavan, V. 1966. *The Great Integrators: The Saint-Singers of India*. Delhi: Ministry of Information and Broadcasting, Publication Division.

Rahman, Fazlur. 2009. *Major Themes of the Qur'ān*. 2nd ed. Chicago: University of Chicago Press.

Rahner, Karl. 1978. *Foundations of Christian Faith: An Introduction to the Idea of Christianity*. 3rd printing. New York: Seabury Press.

Rajkumar, Peniel Jesudason Rufus, ed. 2015. *Multiple Religious Belonging: Exploring Hybridity, Embracing Hospitality* (= *Current Dialogue* 57). Geneva: WCC.

Ramadan, Tariq. 2010. *The Quest for Meaning: Developing a Philosophy of Pluralism*. London: Alan Lane.

———. 2013. "Foreword: Salvation—The Known and the Unknown." In *Between Heaven and Hell: Islam, Salvation, and the Fate of Others*, edited by M. H. Khalil, ix–xiii. Oxford: Oxford University Press.

Rambachan, Anantanand. 1989. "Swami Vivekananda: A Hindu Model for Interreligious Dialogue." In *Interreligious Dialogue: Voices from a New Frontier*, edited by D. Bryant and F. Flinn, 9–19. New York: Paragon House.

———. 1992. *The Hindu Vision*. Delhi: Motilal Banarsidass.

———. 1999. "My God, Your God, Our God, No God?" *Current Dialogue* 33. http://wcc-coe.org/wcc/what/interreligious/cd33-13.html.

———. 2000a. "What Difference Does Religious Plurality Make?" *Current Dialogue* 34. http://wcc-coe.org/wcc/what/interreligious/cd34-09.html.

———. 2000b. "Hinduism and the Encounter with Other Faiths." *Global Dialogue* 2 (1): 1–9.

———. 2001. "The Significance of the Hindu Doctrine of Ishtadeva for Understanding Religious Pluralism." *Current Dialogue* 37. http://wcc-coe.org/wcc/what/interreligious/cd37-08.html.

———. 2006. *The Advaita Worldview: God, World, and Humanity*. Albany: State University of New York Press.

———. 2009. "One Goal, Many Paths? The Significance of Advaita Apologetic Norms for Interreligious Dialogue." In *Criteria of Discernment in Interreligious Dialogue*, edited by C. Cornille, 155–81. Eugene, OR: Cascade Books.

———. 2011. "Interreligious Relationships and Self-Understanding: Learning from Christianity and Hinduism." In *Theology beyond Neutrality: Essays to Honour Wesley Ariarajah*, edited by M. Fernando and R. Crusz, 137–47. Colombo, Sri Lanka: Ecumenical Institute for Study and Dialogue.

———. 2012. "The Ambiguities of Liberation and Oppression: Assuming Responsibility for One's Tradition." In *My Neighbor's Faith: Stories of Interreligious Encounter, Growth, and Transformation*, edited by J. H. Peace, O. N. Rose, and G. Mobley, 154–58. Maryknoll, NY: Orbis Books.

———. 2015. *A Hindu Theology of Liberation: Not-Two Is Not One*. Albany: State University of New York Press.

Ramey, Steven W. 2008. *Hindu, Sufi, or Sikh: Contested Practices and Identifications of Sindhi Hindus in India and Beyond*. Basingstoke: Palgrave Macmillan.

Ram-Prasad, Chakravarti. 2005. "Hindu Views of Jesus." In *Jesus in the World's Faith*, edited by G. Barker, 81–91. Maryknoll, NY: Orbis Books.

———. 2006. "Hindu Perspectives on Islam." In *Religions View Religions: Explorations in Pursuit of Understanding*, edited by J. D. Gort, H. Jansen, and H. M. Vroom, 177–96. Amsterdam: Rodopi.

———. 2007. "A Hindu View of Islam." In *Islam and Inter-Faith Relations*, edited by P. Schmidt-Leukel and L. Ridgeon, 180–201. London: SCM Press.

Randeria, Shalini. 1996. "Hindu-'Fundamentalismus': Zum Verhältnis von Religion, Geschichte und Identität im modernen Indien." In *Religion—Macht—Gewalt: Religiöser 'Fundamentalismus' und Hindu-Moslem-Konflikte in Südasien*, edited by C. Weiß et al., 26–56. Frankfurt a.M.: IKO—Verlag für Interkulturelle Kommunikation.

Rao, K. L. Seshagiri. 2005. "Mahatma Gandhi: A Prophet of Pluralism." In *The Myth of Religious Superiority: Multifaith Explorations of Religious Pluralism*, edited by P. Knitter, 45–55. Maryknoll, NY: Orbis Books.

Ratankul, Pinit. 2014. "The Buddhist Attitude to Religious Pluralism." In *ASEAN Religious Pluralism: The Challenges of Building a Socio-Cultural Community*, edited by I. Yusuf, 1–13. Bangkok: Konrad Adenauer Stiftung.

Ratzinger, Cardinal Joseph. 1996. "The Central Problem for Faith Today." http://www.ewtn.com/library/curia/ratzrela.htm.

———. 1997. *Salt of the Earth*. San Francisco: Ignatius Press.

Ravitzky, Aviezer. 2006. "Judaism Views Other Religions." In *Religions View Religion: Explorations in Pursuit of Understanding*, edited by J. D. Gort, H. Jansen, and H. M. Vroom, 75–107. Amsterdam: Rodopi.

Rhys Davids, T. W. 1890. *The Questions of King Milinda*. Part I (SBE 35). Oxford: Clarendon Press.

———. 1894. *The Questions of King Milinda*. Part II (SBE 36). Oxford: Clarendon Press.

Rhys Davids, T. W., and Hermann Oldenberg. [London, 1885] 1996. *Vinaya Texts*. Part I (SBE 13). Delhi: Motilal Banarsidass.

Richards, Glyn, ed. 1985. *A Source-Book of Modern Hinduism*. London: Curzon.

Ridgeon, Lloyd, ed. 2012. *Islam and Religious Diversity*. 4 vols. London: Routledge.

Ridgeon, Lloyd, and Perry Schmidt-Leukel, eds. 2007. *Islam and Inter-Faith Relations*. London: SCM Press.

Rocker, Simon. 2003. "Vive la difference." *Jewish Chronicle*, February 14, 27.

Rose, Kenneth. 2016. *Yoga, Meditation, and Mysticism. Contemplative Universals and Meditative Landmarks*. London: Bloomsbury Academics.

Rumi, Jalal Al-Din. 2013. *The Masnavi: Book Three*. Translated with an introduction and notes by Jawid Mojaddedi. Oxford: Oxford University Press.

Ruparell, Tinu. 2013. "Inter-Religious Dialogue and Interstitial Theology." In *The Wiley-Blackwell Companion to Inter-Religious Dialogue*, edited by C. Cornille, 117–32. Chichester: Wiley Blackwell.

Russell, Bertrand. [1967] 1992. *Why I Am Not a Christian and Other Essays on Relation and Related Subjects*. London: Routledge.

Sachedina, Abdulaziz. 2001. *The Islamic Roots of Democratic Pluralism*. Oxford: Oxford University Press.

Sacks, Jonathan. 2002. *The Dignity of Difference: How to Avoid the Clash of Civilizations*. London: Continuum.

———. 2003. *The Dignity of Difference: How to Avoid the Clash of Civilizations*. Rev. ed. with a new preface. London: Continuum.

Saddhatissa, H. 1985. *The Sutta-Nipāta*. London: Curzon Press.

Sanders, E. P. 1995. *The Historical Figure of Jesus*. London: Penguin.

Saraswati, Swami Dayananda. 1984. *Light of Truth (Satyarth Prakash)*. Translated by Chiranjiva Bharadwaja. New Delhi: Sarvadeshik Arya Pratinidhi Sabha.

Schachter-Shalomi, Zalman. 1977. "Bases and Boundaries of Jewish, Christian, and Moslem Dialogue." *Journal of Ecumenical Studies* 14:407–18.

———. 2003. "Interview, April 25, 2001." In *Beside Still Waters: Jews, Christians, and the Way of the Buddha*, edited by H. Kasimow, J. P. Keenan, and L. Klepinger Keenan, 85–97. Boston: Wisdom Publications.

Schilbrack, Kevin, ed. 2017. *The Wiley-Blackwell Companion to Religious Diversity*. New York: Wiley-Blackwell.

Schleiermacher, Friedrich. 1958. *On Religion: Speeches to Its Cultured Despisers*. New York: Harper & Row.

Schmidt-Leukel, Perry. 2005a. *Gott ohne Grenzen: Eine christliche und pluralistische Theologie der Religionen*. Gütersloh: Gütersloher Verlagshaus.

———. 2005b. "Exclusivism, Inclusivism, Pluralism: The Tripolar Typology—Clarified and Reaffirmed." In *The Myth of Religious Superiority: Multifaith Explorations of Religious Pluralism*, edited by P. Knitter, 13–27. Maryknoll, NY: Orbis Books.

———. 2005c. "Buddha and Christ as Mediators of the Transcendent: A Christian Perspective." In *Buddhism and Christianity in Dialogue: The Gerald Weisfeld Lectures 2014*, edited by P. Schmidt-Leukel, 151–75. London: SCM Press.

———. 2006a. "The Unbridgeable Gulf? Towards a Buddhist-Christian Theology of Creation." In *Buddhism, Christianity and the Question of Creation: Karmic or Divine?*, edited by P. Schmidt-Leukel, 111–78. Aldershot: Ashgate.

———. 2006b. *Understanding Buddhism*. Edinburgh: Dunedin Academic Press.

———, ed. 2008a. *Buddhist Attitudes to Other Religions*. St. Ottilien: EOS.

———. 2008b. "Pluralisms: How to Appreciate Religious Diversity Theologically." In *Christian Approaches to Other Faiths*, edited by A. Race and P. Hedges, 85–110. London: SCM.

———. 2008c. "Buddhist-Hindu Relations." In *Buddhist Attitudes to Other Religions*, edited by P. Schmidt-Leukel, 143–71. St. Ottilien: EOS.

———. 2009. *Transformation by Integration: How Inter-Faith Encounter Changes Christianity*. London: SCM.

———. 2010a. "Buddhist-Muslim Dialogue: Observations and Suggestions from a Christian Perspective." *Muslim World* 100:349–63.

———. 2010b. "Pluralist Theologies." *Expository Times* 122:54–72.

———. 2012. "Religious Pluralism and the Need for an Interreligious Theology." In *Religious Pluralism and the Modern World: An Ongoing Engagement with John Hick*, edited by S. Sugirtharajah, 19–33. Basingstoke: Palgrave Macmillan.

———, ed. 2013a. *Buddhism and Religious Diversity*. 4 vols. London: Routledge.

———. 2013b. "Christianity and the Religious Other." In *Understanding Interreligious Relations*, ed. D. Cheetham, D. Pratt, and D. Thomas, 118–47. Oxford: Oxford University Press.

———. 2013c. "Die Vorstellung einer universalen Offenbarung aus der Perspektive von Hinduismus und Buddhismus." In *Universale Offenbarung? Der eine Gott und die vielen Religionen*, edited by W. Zager, 45–64. Leipzig: Evangelische Verlagsanstalt.

———. 2013d. "Drei Kalkins und die Frage nach den Wurzeln religiöser Gewalt." *Zeitschrift für Missions- und Religionswissenschaft* 97:91–101.

———. 2014. "Intercultural Theology as Interreligious Theology." In *Religions and Dialogue: International Approaches*, edited by W. Weisse et al., 101–12. Münster: Waxmann.

———. 2016. "Christ as Bodhisattva: A Case of Reciprocal Illumination." In

Interreligious Comparisons in Religious Studies and Theology: Comparison Revisited, edited by P. Schmidt-Leukel and A. Nehring, 204–19. London: Bloomsbury.

———. 2017a. "Buddhist Accounts of Religious Diversity." In *The Wiley-Blackwell Companion to Religious Diversity*, edited by K. Schilbrack. New York: Wiley-Blackwell.

———. 2017b. *God beyond Boundaries: A Christian and Pluralistic Theology of Religions*. Muenster: Waxmann.

Schmidt-Leukel, Perry, and Joachim Gentz, eds. 2013. *Religious Diversity in Chinese Thought*. Basingstoke: Palgrave Macmillan.

Schmidt-Leukel, Perry, and Andreas Nehring, eds. 2016. *Interreligious Comparisons in Religious Studies and Theology: Comparison Revisited*. London: Bloomsbury.

Schneider, Jakob H. J. 1999. "The Eternity of the World: Thomas Aquinas and Boethius of Dacia." *Archives D'Histoire Doctrinale et Littéraire du Moyen Age* 66:121–41.

Schomerus, Hilko Wiardo. 1932. *Parallelen zum Christentum als religionsgeschichtliches und theologisches Problem*. Gütersloh: Bertelsmann.

Schopen, Gregory. 1982. "Hīnayāna Texts in a 14th-Century Persian Chronicle." *Central Asiatic Journal* 26:228–35.

Schreiber, Stefan. 2015. *Die Anfänge der Christologie: Deutungen Jesu im Neuen Testament*. Neukirchen-Vluyn: Neukirchner Verlagsgesellschaft.

Schuon, Frithjof. 1953. *The Transcendent Unity of Religions*. London: Faber & Faber.

———. 1963. *Understanding Islam*. London: Allen & Unwin.

———. 1993. *Treasures of Buddhism*. Bloomington, IN: World Wisdom Books.

Scott, David. 1995. "Buddhism and Islam: Past to Present Encounters and Interfaith Lessons." *Numen* 42:141–55.

Seager, Richard Hughes, ed. 1993. *The Dawn of Religious Pluralism: Voices from the World's Parliament of Religions, 1893*. Chicago: Open Court.

Shah-Kazemi, Reza. 2006a. *The Other in the Light of the One: The Universality of the Qur'ān and Interfaith Dialogue*. Cambridge: Islamic Text Society.

———. 2006b. *Paths to Transcendence according to Shankara, Ibn Arabi, and Meister Eckhart*. Bloomington, IN: World Wisdom.

———. 2010a. *Common Ground between Islam and Buddhism*. Louisville: Fons Vitae.

———. 2010b. "Light Upon Light? The Qur'ān and the Gospel of St. John." In *Interreligious Hermeneutics*, edited by C. Cornille and C. Conway, 116–48. Eugene, OR: Cascade Books.

———. 2012. *The Spirit of Tolerance in Islam*. London: I. B. Tauris.

———. 2013. "Beyond Polemics and Pluralism." In *Between Heaven and Hell: Islam, Salvation, and the Fate of Others*, edited by M. H. Khalil, 87–105. Oxford: Oxford University Press.

Sharma, Arvind. 1990. *A Hindu Perspective on the Philosophy of Religion.* New York: St. Martin's Press.

———. 2005. *Religious Studies and Comparative Methodology: The Case for Reciprocal Illumination.* Albany: State University of New York Press.

Sharma, Jyotirmaya. 2007. *Terrifying Vision: M. S. Golwalkar, the RSS and India.* New Delhi: Penguin/Viking.

Siddiqui, Ataullah. 1997. *Christian-Muslim Dialogue in the Twentieth Century.* Basingstoke: Palgrave Macmillan.

Siddiqui, Mona. 2013. *Christians, Muslims, and Jesus.* New Haven: Yale University Press.

Singh, Avtar. 1989. "Fences around God." In *Interreligious Dialogue: Voices from a New Frontier,* edited by M. D. Bryant and F. Flinn, 101–6. New York: Paragon House.

Sinn, Simone. 2014. *Religiöser Pluralismus im Werden: Religionspolitische Kontroversen und theologische Perspektiven von Christen und Muslimen in Indonesien.* Tübingen: Mohr Siebeck.

Smart, Ninian. 1998. *Dimensions of the Sacred: An Anatomy of the World's Beliefs.* Berkeley: University of California Press.

Smith, Jane I. 2012. "Early Muslim Accounts of Buddhism in India." In *Islam and Religious Diversity,* vol. 3: *Eastern Religions,* edited by L. Ridgeon, 130–40. London: Routledge.

Smith, Wilfred Cantwell. 1957. *Islam in Modern History.* Princeton: Princeton University Press.

———. 1959. "Comparative Religion: Whither—and Why?" In *The History of Religions: Essays in Methodology,* edited by M. Eliade and J. M. Kitagawa, 31–58. Chicago: University of Chicago Press.

———. 1963. *The Faith of Other Men.* New York: New American Library.

———. 1967. *Questions of Religious Truth.* London: Victor Gollancz.

———. 1975. "Conflicting Truth Claims: A Rejoinder." In *Truth and Dialogue: The Relationship between World Religions,* edited by J. Hick, 156–62. London: Sheldon Press.

———. 1977. *Belief and History.* Charlottesville: University Press of Virginia.

———. [1963] 1978. *The Meaning and End of Religion.* New York: Harper and Row.

———. 1979. *Faith and Belief.* Princeton: Princeton University Press.

———. 1981. *On Understanding Islam: Selected Studies.* The Hague: Mouton.

———. 1987. "Theology and the World's Religious History." In *Toward a Universal Theology of Religion,* edited by L. Swidler, 51–72. Maryknoll, NY: Orbis Books.

———. [1981] 1989. *Towards a World Theology: Faith and the Comparative History of Religion.* Maryknoll, NY: Orbis Books.

———. 1993. *What Is Scripture? A Comparative Approach.* London: SCM Press.

————. 1997. *Modern Culture from a Comparative Perspective*. Edited by J. W. Burbidge. Albany: State University of New York Press.

Snellgrove, D. L. 1959. *The Hevajra Tantra: A Critical Study*. Part I: Introduction and Translation. London: Oxford University Press.

Solomon, Norman. 1991. *Judaism and World Religion*. New York: St. Martin's Press.

————. 1996. "Faith in the Midst of Faiths: Traditional Jewish Attitudes." In *People of God, Peoples of God: A Jewish-Christian Conversation in Asia*, edited by H. Ucko, 84–99. Geneva: WCC Publications.

————. 2005. "Towards a Jewish Theology of Trilateral Dialogue." In *Islam and Global Dialogue: Religious Pluralism and the Pursuit of Peace*, edited by R. Boase, 203–14. Aldershot: Ashgate.

Soroush, Abdolkarim. 2000. *Reason, Freedom, and Democracy in Islam: Essential Writings of Abdolkarim Soroush*. Edited and translated by M. Sadri and A. Sadri. Oxford: Oxford University Press.

————. 2009. *The Expansion of Prophetic Experience: Essays on Historicity, Contingency and Plurality in Religion*. Leiden: Brill.

Streng, Frederick J. 1967. *Emptiness: A Study in Religious Meaning*. Nashville: Abingdon Press.

Sugirtharajah, Sharada. 2012. "The Mahatma and the Philosopher: Mohandas Gandhi and John Hick and Their Search for Truth." In *Religious Pluralism and the Modern World: An Ongoing Engagement with John Hick*, edited by S. Sugirtharajah, 121–33. Basingstoke: Palgrave Macmillan.

Suzuki, Daisetz Teitaro. [1907] 1977. *Outlines of Mahāyāna Buddhism*. New York: Schocken Books.

Swearer, Donald, ed. 1989. *Me and Mine: Selected Essays of Bhikkhu Buddhadāsa*. Albany: State University of New York Press.

Swidler, Leonard. 1990. *After the Absolute: The Dialogical Future of Religious Reflection*. Minneapolis: Fortress Press.

Takeda, Ryūsei. 2004 and 2013. "Mutual Transformation of Pure Land Buddhism and Christianity: Methodology and Possibilities in the Light of Shinran's Doctrine." In *Living in Amida's Vow: Essays in Shin Buddhism*, edited by A. Bloom, 255–87. Bloomington, IN: World Wisdom. Also reprinted in *Buddhism and Religious Diversity*, vol. 2: *Christianity*, edited by P. Schmidt-Leukel, 231–64. London: Routledge, 2013.

Tanaka, Kenneth. 2008. "Buddhist Pluralism: Can Buddhism Accept Other Religions as Equal Ways?" In *Buddhist Attitudes to Other Religions*, edited by P. Schmidt-Leukel, 69–84. St. Ottilien: EOS.

Tang, Li. 2002. *A Study of the History of Nestorian Christianity in China and Its Literature in Chinese*. Frankfurt a.M.: Peter Lang.

Tanner, Kathryn. 1993. "Respect for Other Religions: A Christian Antidote to Colonialist Discourse." *Modern Theology* 9:1–18.

Tezcan, Semih. 1974. *Das uigurische Insadi-Sūtra*. Berlin: Akademie Verlag.

Thurman, Robert A. F. 1991. *The Holy Teaching of Vimalakīrti: A Mahāyāna Scripture*. Delhi: Motilal Banarsidass.

Thurston, Bonnie B. 2007. "Unfolding of a New World: Thomas Merton and Buddhism." In *Merton and Buddhism: Wisdom, Emptiness, and Everyday Mind*, edited by B. B. Thurston, 15–27. Louisville: Fons Vitae.

Tillich, Paul. [1963] 1964. *Christianity and the Encounter of the World Religions*. New York: Columbia University Press.

———. 1966. "The Significance of the History of Religions for the Systematic Theologian." In *The Future of Religions*, by P. Tillich, edited by J. C. Brauer, 80–94. New York: Harper and Row.

Troeltsch, Ernst. [1923] 1980. "The Place of Christianity among World Religions." In *Christianity and Other Religions: Selected Readings*, edited by J. Hick and B. Hebblethwaite, 11–31. London: Fount Paperbacks.

Valignano, Alexandro. 1944. *Historia del principio y progresso de la Compañia de Jesús en las Indias Orientales (1542–64)*. Edited by Josef Wicki, S.J. Rome: Institutum Historicum S.J.

Van der Leeuw, Gerardus. [1924] 1925. *Einführung in die Phänomenologie der Religion*. Munich: Ernst Reinhardt.

Vaziri, Mostafa. 2012. *Buddhism in Iran: An Anthropological Approach to Traces and Influences*. London: Palgrave Macmillan.

Veer, Peter van der. 1994. "Syncretism, Multiculturalism, and the Discourse of Tolerance." In *Syncretism / Anti-Syncretism: The Politics of Religious Synthesis*, edited by C. Stewart and R. Shaw, 196–211. London: Routledge.

Vélez de Cea, J. Abraham. 2013. *The Buddha and Religious Diversity*. London: Routledge.

Vermes, Geza, 1981. *The Gospel of Jesus the Jew*. The Riddell Memorial Lectures. University of Newcastle upon Tyne.

———. 1993. *The Religion of Jesus the Jew*. London: SCM Press.

Vigil, José M. 2008. *Theology of Religious Pluralism*. Berlin: LIT Verlag.

———, ed. 2010. *Toward a Planetary Theology: Along the Many Paths of God*. Montreal: Dunamis.

Visalo, Phra Paisan. 2006. "On the Path toward Peace and Justice: Challenges Confronting Buddhists and Muslims." *Seeds of Peace* 22 (3): 15–20.

Vivekananda, Swami. 1989. *The Complete Works of Swami Vivekananda*. 8 vols. Mayavati Memorial Edition. Reprint, Calcutta: Advaita Ashrama, 1994.

Volf, Miroslav. 2011. *Allah: A Christian Response*. New York: HarperCollins.

Völker, Fabian. 2016. "On All-Embracing Mental Structures: Towards a Transcendental Hermeneutics of Religion." In *Interreligious Comparisons in Religious Studies and Theology: Comparison Revisited*, edited by P. Schmidt-Leukel and A. Nehring, 142–60. London: Bloomsbury.

Von Brück, Michael. 1991. *The Unity of Reality: God, God-Experience and*

Meditation in the Hindu-Christian Dialogue. New York: Paulist Press.

———. 1992. "Religionswissenschaft und interkulturelle Theologie." *Evangelische Theologie* 52:245–61.

Von Stosch, Klaus. 2014. "Comparative Theology as Liberal and Confessional Theology." In *European Perspectives on the New Comparative Theology*, edited by F. X. Clooney and J. Berthrong, 31–41. Basel: MDPI.

Waardenburg, Jacques. 2003. *Muslims and Others: Religions in Context*. Berlin: de Gruyter.

Wach, Joachim. [1924] 1988. *Introduction to the History of Religions*. Edited by J. Kitagawa and G. Alles. New York and London: Macmillan.

Waldenfels, Bernhard. 1995. "Verschränkung von Heimwelt und Fremdwelt." In *Philosophische Grundlagen der Interkulturalität*, edited by R. A. Mall and D. Lohmar, 53–65. Amsterdam: Rodopi.

Wallace, Vesna A., and B. Alan Wallace, trans. 1997. *A Guide to the Bodhisattva Way of Life (Bodhicaryāvatāra) by Śāntideva*. Ithaca, NY: Snow Lion Publications.

Wang, Zhicheng. 2012. "John Hick and Chinese Religious Studies." In *Religious Pluralism and the Modern World: An Ongoing Engagement with John Hick*, edited by S. Sugirtharajah, 241–52. Basingstoke: Palgrave Macmillan.

———. 2013. "Does China Need a Pluralist Theology of Religions?" In *Religious Diversity in Chinese Thought*, edited by P. Schmidt-Leukel and J. Gentz, 201–14. London: Palgrave Macmillan.

Wang, Zhihe. 2012. *Process and Pluralism: Chinese Thought on the Harmony of Diversity*. Frankfurt a.M.: Ontos Verlag.

Ward, Keith. 1994. *Religion and Revelation: A Theology of Revelation in the World's Religions*. Oxford: Clarendon Press.

Whaling, Frank. 1986. *Christian Theology and World Religions: A Global Approach*. Basingstoke: Marshall Pickering.

Wilke, Annette. 2006. "Gewaltlosigkeit und Gewaltausübung in Hinduismus und Buddhismus." In *Friede auf Erden? Die Weltreligionen zwischen Gewaltverzicht und Gewaltbereitschaft*, edited by A. Fürst, 83–150, 197–205. Freiburg i.Br.: Herder.

Williams, Paul. 1991. "Some Dimensions of the Recent Work of Raimundo Panikkar: A Buddhist Perspective." *Religious Studies* 27:511–21.

———. 2002. *The Unexpected Way: On Converting from Buddhism to Catholicism*. Edinburgh: T&T Clark.

Wimmer, Franz Martin. 2004. *Interkulturelle Philosophie*. Vienna: WUV Facultas.

Winkler, Ulrich. 2014. "Reasons for and Contexts of Deep Theological Engagement with Other Religious Traditions in Europe: Toward a Comparative Theology." In *European Perspectives on the New Comparative Theology*, edited by F. X. Clooney and J. Berthrong, 5–20. Basel: MDPI.

Wolfson, Harry A. 1976. *The Philosophy of the Kalam*. Cambridge, MA: Harvard University Press.

Wong, Wai Yip. 2012. "Reconstructing John Hick's Theory of Religious Plural-ism: A Chinese Folk Religion's Perspective." PhD dissertation, University of Birmingham. http://etheses.bham.ac.uk/3627/.

———. 2013. "Incompatibility between Chinese Folk Religion and John Hick's Criteriology." *Journal of Comparative Scripture* 2:153–88.

Yampolsky, Philip B. 1967. *The Platform Sūtra of the Sixth Patriarch: The Text of the Tun-Huang Manuscript*. With translation, introduction, and notes. New York: Columbia University Press.

Yao, Xinzhong. 2013. "Confucian Approaches to Religious Diversity." In *Religious Diversity in Chinese Thought*, edited by P. Schmidt-Leukel and J. Gentz, 65–79. London: Palgrave Macmillan.

Yao, Xinzhong, and Yanxia Zhao. 2010. *Chinese Religion: A Contextual Approach*. London: Continuum.

Yi, Bhikkhuni Liao, and Maria Reis-Habito, eds. 2005. *Listening: Buddhist-Muslim Dialogues 2002–04*. Taipei: Museum of World Religions.

———. 2012. *Heart to Heart: Buddhist-Muslim Encounters in Ladakh*. Taipei: Museum of World Religions.

Yokota, John S. (= Ishihara, John). 1986. "Śākyamuni within the Jōdo Shinshū Tradition." *Pacific World* 2:31–35.

———. 2000. "A Call to Compassion." In *Toward a Contemporary Under-standing of Pure Land Buddhism: Creating a Shin Buddhist Theology in a Religiously Plural World*, edited by D. Hirota, 199–221. Albany: State University of New York Press.

———. 2004. "Nāgārjuna, Shinran, and Whitehead." In *Three Mountains and Seven Rivers: Prof. Musashi Tachikawa's Felicitation Volume*, edited by S. Hino and T. Wada, 249–72. Delhi: Motilal Banarsidass.

———. 2005. "Where beyond Dialogue? Reconsiderations of a Buddhist Pluralist." In *Deep Religious Pluralism*, edited by David R. Griffin, 91–107. Louisville: Westminster John Knox.

Yong, Amos. 2012. *The Cosmic Breath: Spirit and Nature in the Christianity-Buddhism-Science Trialogue*. Leiden: Brill.

Young, Richard Fox. 2005. "The Carpenter-Prēta: An Eighteenth-Century Sinhala-Buddhist Folktale about Jesus." *Asian Folklore Studies* 54:49–68.

Yusuf, Imtiyaz. 2005. "Dialogue between Islam and Buddhism through the Concepts of Tathagata and Nur Muḥammadi." *International Journal of Buddhist Thought & Culture* 5:103–14.

———. 2010a. "Islam and Buddhism Relations from Balkh to Bangkok and Tokyo." *Muslim World* 100:177–86.

———. 2010b. "Islamic Theology of Religious Pluralism: Qur'ān's Attitude towards Other Religions." *Prajñā Vihāra: Journal of Philosophy and Re-ligion* 11 (1): 123–40.

Yusuf, Shaykh Hamza. 2010. "Buddha in the Qur'ān." In *Common Ground between Islam and Buddhism*, edited by R. Shah-Kazemi, 113–36. Louis-ville: Fons Vitae.

Zhiru, Shi. 2013. "Contextualizing Buddhist Approaches to Religious Diversity: When and How Buddhist Intellectuals Address Confucianism and Daoism (3rd–9th c.)." In *Religious Diversity in Chinese Thought*, edited by P. Schmidt-Leukel and J. Gentz, 81–98. Basingstoke: Palgrave Macmillan.

Zürcher, Erik. 2007. *The Buddhist Conquest of China: The Spread and Adaptation of Buddhism in Early Medieval China*. 3rd ed. Leiden: Brill.

Index

Abe, Masao, 87–88, 182, 195, 211, 238
Abhishiktananda, Swami, 19
Abrahamic religions. *See also* Christianity; Islam; Judaism
  exclusivist tendencies in, 53
  pluralism in, 109–10
absolute truth, 83
adhikāra-bheda, 60–61, 64, 70, 86
Advaita Vedānta, 55–56, 69–70, 72, 240
agnosticism, 4n8, 5
Akbar the Great, 64
al-Baghdādī, 'Abd al-Qāhir, 187
al-Dīn, Rashīd, 188–90
Alighieri, Dante, 159
Al-Junayd, 49
al-Khiḍr, 188
al-Maqdisī, Tāhir, 186
al-Sharastānī, 188
Amida Buddhism, 88, 177–79
Amitābha, 177
anekāntavāda, 69, 133–34
anxiety, existential, 10
apophatism, 202
Aquinas, Thomas, 218–20
'Arabī, Ibn, 48
Ariarajah, Wesley, 20
Aristotle, 219
Arjan, Guru, 64
Arkoun, Mohammed, 48
Āryas, 61
Arya Samāj, 65
Askari, Hasan, 44, 50–51, 52, 134, 150, 223
Atay, Rifat, 45
atheism, 2, 3, 164, 167, 171
avatāra, 167
awakening, 166, 170–71, 173
Aydin, Mahmut, 44, 45, 47–48
Ayoub, Mahmoud, 44, 155

Balasuriya, Tissa, 20
Barlaam and Josaphat, story of, 164–66, 187

Barth, Karl, 20, 120, 177–78
Bauschke, Martin, 161
beliefs
  faith and, 22–23, 43
  revision of, 144
Benzhong, Lü, 96
Berger, Peter, 9–10
Besant, Annie, 19n8
Beyond Dialogue: Toward a Mutual Transformation of Christianity and Buddhism (Cobb), 178–79
Bhagavadgītā, 59–60
Bharatiya Janata Party (BJP; Indian People's Party), 67
Bhāvaviveka, 207, 208, 209, 211, 214
Bible
  as inner-Jewish discourse, 17
  theology of religions in, 17
blasphemy, 35–36
blind men and the elephant, parable of, 71–74
Bloom, Alfred, 88
Bodhi, Bhikkhu, 172–73
Bodhisattvas, 166, 176–77, 181, 188, 202
  path of, 83, 84
  virtues of, 215
body of retribution, 168
Book of Changes (Yijing), 95
Brahmo Samāj, 64, 65
Brook, Timothy, 99
Buddha
  awakening of, 171, 173–74
  as Bodhisattva, 176–77
  characterization of, 167–68
  Christian perspectives on, 164–67, 175
  incarnation of 168
  Jesus compared with, 164, 168, 173
  legend of, 166
  as mind from beyond, 173–78, 183
  Muslim portrayal of, 188–89
  presence of, 75–76, 82
  as prophet, 188, 194–96, 198–99

as saintly figure, 164, 167
as savior, 27
Son of God and, 181
as supreme being, 76
supranatural, 177
three bodies of, 168, 170, 175-76, 181-
    82. *See also* Buddha Body
veneration of, 99, 166, 199
as visible *nirvāṇa*, 206
Buddha Body, 205, 206. See also
    dharmakāya
Buddhadāsa, Bhikkhu, 80–82, 89,
    180–81, 199–200, 223
Buddha Germ, 216
buddhahood, 195–96, 203
Buddha Lands, 215–16
Buddha Nature, 82, 144, 168, 168, 202,
    205, 216–17
Buddhism. *See also Chinese Buddhism*;
    Japanese Buddhism; karmic creation;
    Mahāyāna Buddhism; Theravāda
    Buddhism; *Zen Buddhism*
acknowledging the Prophet, 199–203
as atheism, 164, 167, 171
in China, 90–91
Christianity and, 88, 89, 93, 169–71
Confucianism and, 84–85, 91–93,
    95–100
on cosmological arguments and cre-
    ation, 207
Daoism and, 84–85, 90–93, 95–100
on divine creation, 204, 207–11
genesis of, 173–74
on grace, 214
Hinduism and, 61–63, 167, 172
idolatry and, 187, 197–98
inclusivism in, 78, 109
interreligious theology and, 235–36
Judaism and, 34, 37, 40
liberation and, 167
message of, 200
monasticism and, 95–96
moral standards of, 188–89
Muslim perspectives on, 185–90
as mysticism, 172
nontheism of, 197
perspectives on Islam, 190–93
perspectives on Jesus, 179–82
pluralism and, 87–89
salvation and, 81
social responsibility and, 182
on Son of God epithet, 167

spirituality of, 166, 199
superiority claims of, 89, 93, 97
theologically relevant truth for, 132
ultimate reality and, 204–6
Buddhist-Christian dialogue, 182–84, 196
Buddhist-Christian relations, 217–18
Buddhist-Muslim dialogue, 193–203
Buddhist-Muslim relations, 185
Būdhāsaf, 187
Byrne, Peter, 20

Cabezón, José, 170, 215–16
certainty, religious, 10
Cheng, Chung-ying, 104–6
Chengguan (Ch'eng-kuan), 84
Chia, Edmund, 136–37
China
    Christianity in, 101
    interfaith dialogue in, 100–101
    multiple religious participation in,
        99–100
    official religions in, 91, 92
    religious diversity in, 90–91
    religious pluralism in, 100–101
Chinese Buddhism, 84, 91, 96, 110
Chinese religions, ultimate reality in,
    103–4
Ching, Julia, 228, 230
Christ. *See also* Jesus (Jesus Christ)
    as Amida Buddha, 178–79
    uniqueness of, 231
    universal role of, 47–48
Christian-Buddhist dialogue, 182–84, 196
Christian-Buddhist relations, 217–18
Christianity
    Buddhism and, 88, 89, 93, 164–67,
        169–71
    in China, 90, 91–92
    Chinese religious tradition and, 101
    claiming finality, 161–62
    comprising different religions, 231
    Confucianism and, 91–92
    Daoism and, 91–92
    exclusivism of, 17–18, 21
    as heresy, 169
    Hinduism and, 63, 64, 67
    inclusivism of, 17–18, 21, 30
    interreligious theology and, 236
    message of, 200
    as minority community, 18
    on Muḥammad as prophet, 159–61
    oppositions with Islam, 147

pluralism and, 17, 18, 19–21, 24, 27–31, 109
  reason and, 65
  salvation and, 81
  superiority claims of, 24, 26, 31, 232, 241
  world religions and, 114
Christian-Muslim dialogue, 196
Christians and Religious Pluralism: Patterns in the Christian Theology of Religions (Race), 3
Christology, 154
  Chalcedonian, 26–27, 151, 154
  disputes over, 151
  Qur'ānic, 154–56
Clooney, Francis, 30
Cobb, John, 29, 104, 123, 124, 178–79, 237–39, 242
Cohn-Sherbok, Dan, 38
co-inherence, 223
collective identity, 50–51
collective karma, 207–9, 211
Collins, Steven, 205
colonialism, 169
Commedia Divina (Alighieri), 159
common good, joint commitment to, 20
Common Ground Between Islam and Buddhism (Shah-Kazemi), 52, 194, 196–99, 203
Common Word Between Us and You, A, 147, 196
comparative religion, 227–32
  dialogical, 115
  global, 115–16
  personalization of, 116
  phenomenological school, 140
  transformed version of, 115
comparative studies, 232
comparative theology, 29–30, 99, 116–17, 119, 132, 143, 244
compassion, 174–75, 182, 197, 200, 202
complementarity, 106, 134
Comte, Auguste, 2
Confucianism, 84–85, 90–91
  Buddhism and, 91–93, 95–100
  as Chinese state orthodoxy, 97
  Christianity and, 91–92
  Daoism and, 95, 96–100
  dogmatism in, 95
  flexibility of, 95
  political power and, 95
  religious diversity and, 95, 110

superiority claims of, 97
Confucius, 95, 99
Congregation for the Doctrine of the Faith, 28
conventional truth, 83. *See also relative truth, two truths*
Coomaraswamy, Ananda, 197
Copernican revolution, 103
Cornille, Catherine, 140
cosmos, sacred nature of, 237
cosmotheandric unity, 27
cosmotheandrism, 222
Council of Chalcedon, 151. *See also* Christology
covenants, multiple, 39
Cragg, Kenneth, 161
creatio ex nihilo, 218
creation
  alternative theory of, 208
  Buddhist concept of, 211, 212–13
  cosmological arguments and, 209
  divine will and, 220
  doctrine of, 204, 219–20
  justice and, 219
  karmic, 211, 214
  ontological speculation on, 209
  salvation and, 218–19
  synthesizing view on, 217–21
creatio post nihilum, 218
creeds, 142
culture, 226–27

Dabru Emet, 33
Dalai Lama (Fourteenth), 37, 85–86, 181–82, 196
  on a creator God, 204
  on Islam, 200
damnation, for nonbelievers, 21, 25–26
Dao, 94, 111
Daode jing (Laozi), 94
Daoism, 84–85
  Buddhism and, 90–93, 95–100
  Christianity and, 91–92
  Confucianism and, 95, 96–100
  diversity in, 94
  religious diversity and, 110
  superiority claims of, 93–95, 97
Death and Eternal Life (Hick), 118, 119
de Couto, Diogo, 166
deep pluralism, 29
deities, linking of, 59–60
dependence, 46

dependent origination, 239n86
de Silva, Lynn, 19, 176, 182
detachment, 174, 197, 199
dhamma, 73, 74, 82. *See also* Dharma
Dhammapada, 74
Dhammavisuddhi, 78–79
Dharma, 174
    discovery of, 76
    diverse forms of, 82–83
    God and, 81, 200
    revelation of, 61
    understanding of, 72
Dharma body, 168, 175
Dharma gates, 82–83
Dharmakara (Bodhisattva), 178
dharmakāya, 87, 168, 195, 198. *See also*
    Buddha Body
Dharmakīrti, 207
Dharmapala, Anagārika. 169–70, 211
Dharmasiri, Gunapala, 210
Dialectical Theology, 231
dialogical thinking, 40
dialogue theology, 101
Dignity of Difference, The (Sacks), 41
diversity, levels of, 227
divine. *See* God
divine creation. *See* creation
divine creator
    belief in, as spiritually disadvanta-
        geous, 210
    Buddhist critique of, 207–11
divine reality, 23
doctrine, 22, 68
Dominus Iesus (Congregation for the
    Doctrine of the Faith), 28, 110
Dorff, Elliott, 38
Drew, Rose, 234
dual belonging, 234. *See also* multireli-
    gious identity
Dunne, John, 143
Dupuis, Jacques, 28
Durkheim, Emile, 2
Dvaita Vedānta, 56

Eastern meditation, 34
Eastern religions, 19
    pluralism in, 109–10
    superiority claims of, 53
Ecumenical Association of Third World
    Theologians (EATWOT), 20
ecumenical councils, 151
ecumenism, 236

Eliade, Mircea, 229, 236
Elyashiv, Yosef Shalom, 41
emptiness, 205–6n5, 217, 239
Engineer, Asghar Ali, 44, 46
Englert, Winfried Philipp, 164
enlightenment, attainment of, 87
Esack, Farid, 44, 47, 52
eternal truth, 68–69
evil, problem of, 23
exclusivism, 3–7, 12, 17, 28, 111

faith, 200
    beliefs and, 22–23, 43
    expression of, 22–23
    Hick's formula for, 23
    meaning of, 242
    saving nature of, 22
Faith and Belief (Smith), 119
false Christians, 18
fanaticism, 10
fatwas, 52
feminist theology, 20–21
Feuerbach, Ludwig, 2
filial piety, 183
Fletcher, Jeannine Hill, 21
folk religion, 90, 92, 102
forgiveness, 184
Four Noble Truths, 74–75, 80
Fowler, James, 233
Fractal Geometry of Nature, The (Man-
    delbrot), 224
fractals, 9, 223–26
    culture and, 226–27
    nature and, 224–25
    religion and, 230–31
    religious diversity and, 232–45
    self-inverse, 230
Fredericks, James, 30, 119, 124, 125,
    127–28, 140
freedom, 207, 212, 213
fundamentalism, 9, 10

Gandhi, Mahatma, 68, 105–6
Gautama, Siddhārtha. *See Buddha*
Gautama Buddha. See Buddha
genetics, fractal structure and, 226
Gentz, Joachim, 94
Ghazan, Mahmud, 185, 188
Ghazi bin Muḥammad, 147, 196
Gilkey, Langdon, 20, 31
Gillis, Chester, 20
globality, 145

God
  authoritarianism of, 210
  as a Buddha, 167
  cause of, 207–8
  conceptual grasp of, 24–25
  covenants and, 35–37
  creativity of, 238
  Dharma and, 81
  diversity within, 209
  divine play of, 210
  human experience of, 24–25
  immutability of, 209–10
  ineffability of, 25–26, 45
  invisibility of, 153–54
  kingdom of, 24, 152–53
  mercy of, 162
  paradox regarding, 21
  presence of, 39
  responding to non-Christians, 21
  self-revelation of, 48, 131
  submission to, 43
  transcendence of, 25, 33
  understandings of, 56, 72
  as universal love, 21
  unity of, with humans, 27
  universal care of, 35
gods, linkage of, 59
Golden Rule, 102
Golwalkar, Madhav Sadashiv, 66–67
Goossaert, Vincent, 100
Goshen-Gottstein, Alon, 39, 40
Gowans, Christopher, 204–5
grace, 214
Greenberg, Irving, 37, 38
Griffin, David, 104
Griffiths, Paul, 140
Gross, Rita, 87, 201
Guardini, Romano, 173
Guénon, René, 196–97

Hadith Qudsi, 155, 163
Hafez, 49
Haight, Roger, 20, 26–27, 154, 157,
    182–83
Halbfass, Wilhelm, 57
Hamer, Dean, 2
Hanshan Deqing, 84–85
harmony, 95, 98
harmony of the three teachings, 84, 92,
    97–100, 104, 168–69, 175–76, 181,
    182
Hartman, David, 38–39

Hazra, Kanai Lal, 62–63
Hedges, Paul, 132
Hedgewar, Keshav Baliram, 66
Heiler, Friedrich, 228, 229
Heim, Mark, 29, 237, 240–42
Herbert of Cherbury, 19
Heschel, Abraham Joshua, 32–33, 39,
    104–5
Hevajra Tantra, 217
Hick, John, 6, 7, 19–21, 23–27, 30–31,
    33, 37, 45, 49, 54, 72, 101–4,
    118–20, 123–29, 218
hierophany, 236
Hinduism
  Buddhism and, 61–63, 172, 189
  Christianity and, 63, 64, 67
  divine creator in, 172
  exclusivism in, 65
  features of, 57
  inclusivism in, 55–56, 109
  Islam and, 63–64, 67
  Judaism and, 34, 37, 39
  mission of, 67
  as mother of religions, 54–55
  nature of, 66
  pluralism of, 54–58, 64–66, 68–70
  principles of, 57
  salvation and, 110
  spirituality of, 39
  superiority of, 58, 67–68, 70
  theologically relevant truth for, 132
Hindu Theology of Liberation, A (Ram-
    bachan), 70
Hindutva movement, 65, 66–68, 106
Hiremath, R. C., 62–63
Hisamatsu, Shin'ichi, 211
Holenstein, Elmar, 226–27, 233
Holy, experience of, 114
Hosein, Imran Nazar, 190
human body, concepts of, 123–24
Hume, David, 3, 10, 53
Hutchison, John A., 239

ibn al-Fayyumi, Nethanael, 34
Ibn 'Arabī, 203
Ibn-Khālid, 186, 187
iconoclasm, 193
idolatry, 35–36, 150, 187, 190, 197–98
Ikeda, Daisaku, 201
Ikemoto, Hannosuke, 201
impersonae, 25, 29, 123
imported religions, 91–92

incarnation, 26–27, 161, 170, 195–96
  Buddha and, 183
  doctrine of, 26–27
  inlibration and, 156–58
  interreligious approaches to, 138
  Jesus and, 26, 152–54, 157–58, 161
  prophethood and, 198–99
  revelation and, 154, 156–57, 163
inclusivism, 3–7, 12, 17, 110, 111, 135
India
  conversion of, to Christianity, 166
  destiny of, 57
  history of religions in, 55–65
indigenous religions, 90–91
infinite plenitude, 197–98
Ingram, Paul, 19
inlibration, 156–58
Insadi Sūtra, 192
intercultural philosophy, 225–27
intercultural theology, 139
interdependence, 133
Interpretation of Religion, An (Hick), 7
interreligious conflict, 11–12
interreligious dialogue, 6–7
  interreligious theology and, 137, 206
  permanence of, 12
  presuppositions about, 126
  purpose of, 13, 124
  religious pluralism and, 19, 124–29
  stereotypes and, 50–51
  transformation and, 144
interreligious learning, 87
  inclusivism and, 135
  interreligious theology and, 136
interreligious theology, 8–13, 117, 118,
      129, 136–37, 232, 235–36
  comparative work of, 143
  development of, 139
  end of, 145
  incompleteness of, 139
  intercultural philosophy and, 140
  interreligious dialogue and, 137, 206
  interreligious learning and, 136
  methodological issues of, 139–46
  mutuality and, 137
  need for, 11–12
  participants in, 138
  principles of, 130–39
  process of, 138–39
  religious pluralism and, 9–10, 113–14
  significance of, 133
  tasks of, 113–14, 133, 140

theological credit of trust and, 131–33
  transition to, 243
  writings on, 137–38
intersection, intercultural, 226
Iran, Buddhism in, 185
Islam, 18–19
  as Buddhism's fulfillment, 188
  Buddhist perspectives on, 190–93
  in China, 90, 91
  as Christian heresy, 159
  claiming finality, 161–63
  claiming universality, 42
  distinct from *islām*, 43
  exclusive validity of, 43
  foundation of, 42–43
  Hinduism and, 63–64, 67
  Jewish relations with, 34
  interreligious theology and, 235
  message of, 200
  mysticism and, 48–53, 155. *See also*
      Sufism
  oppositions with Christianity, 147
  perspectives of, on Buddhism, 185–90
  pluralism in, 42–53, 109
  prophets' attributes in, 155
  religious boundaries in, 46–47
  salvation and, 81
  spiritual practice of, 199
  spread of, 185
  theologically relevant truth for, 131
  universality of, 47–48
islām, 43–44, 153. *See also* submission
  call to, 47
  practiced in different religions, 50
isolationism, 40
Izutsu, Toshihiko, 202, 217

Jainism, 61, 62, 133–34
James, William, 233
Jāmi' al-Tavārīkh (al-Dīn), 188–90
Japanese Buddhism, 201
Jayatilleke, Kulatissa Nanda, 78
Jesus (Jesus Christ). *See also* Christology
  as a Buddha, 81
  Buddha compared with, 164, 168, 173
  Buddhist perspectives on, 170, 180–82
  crucifixion of, 160, 162
  demonization of, 169–70
  dual natures of, 154
  enlightenment of, 181–82
  as guru, 64
  message of, 184

portrayals of, 169–70
as prophet, 151
representing God's kingdom, 153
as revelation, 33
as savior, 27
as Son of God, 148–51, 180–81
as symbol, 26–27, 154
twofold meaning of, 153–54
Jesus Symbol of God (Haight), 26–27
jihad, 192
Jillette, Penn, 2
John of Damascus, 165
Joshi, Lal Mani, 62–63
Jospe, Raphael, 37
Journal of Comparative Scripture, 104
JuBus, 34, 234
Judaism, 18–19
  Buddhism and, 34 and, 37, 40
  exclusivism and, 35
  Hinduism and, 34, 37 and, 39
  identity of, 32–33
  Islam and, 34
  mystical tradition of, 40
  pluralism and, 32–41 in, 109
  relationship of, with other faiths, 32–34
  special election of, 37
  Sufis and, 34
  superiority claims of, 36
  theologically relevant truth for, 131
  theology of, 33
justice, 183, 201, 213
Juvaini, 188

Kabīr, 64
Kālacakra Tantra, 191–92
Kalkin Cakrin, 191–93
Kalkipurāṇa, 62
Kalsky, Manuela, 21
Kamalaśrī, 188
Kant, Immanuel, 19, 25
Kaplan, Steven, 29
karma
  collective, 207–9, 211
  creation and, 209
  critique of, 212
  deterministic, 212–14
  grace and, 214
karmic creation, 211, 214
Kāśyapa, 92–93
Kaufman, Gordon, 20
Kerr, David, 161
Khan, Uljaytu (Öljeitü), 188

Kiblinger, Kristin, 30, 126
King, Ursula, 21
Klostermaier, Klaus, 61–62
Knitter, Paul, 20, 23–24, 27, 47–48, 52,
  101, 182–83, 184
Kogan, Michael, 34–38
Kristensen, W. Brede, 228
Kumārila, 61
Küng, Hans, 12, 147, 161, 228, 230
Kyung, Chung Hyun, 21

Lamptey, Jerusha Tanner, 46, 223
Langer, Ruth, 35
Laozi, 92, 94, 99
Lee, Yen-Yi, 102–4
Legenhausen, Muhammad, 156–57, 199
Le Saux, Henri, 19
Lessing, Gotthold Ephraim, 19
Leuze, Reinhard, 161
Li, Chenyang, 102
liberation, 3, 176, 183, 205, 207. *See also*
  salvation
  Buddhism and, 167, 172
  ultimate reality and, 217
liberation theology, 20, 52
"Light of Truth, The" (*Satyārtha Prakāśa*;
  Dayananda), 65
logos, 26, 153, 157
Long, Jeffery, 68–69, 70
Lopez, Donald, 166
Lord Lao. *See* Laozi
Lord's Prayer, 152, 153
Lotus-Sūtra, 175
Luther, Martin, 237

Madhyamaka School, 211, 220
Mahāparinibbāna Sutta, 77
Mahāvaṃsa, 62
Mahāyāna Buddhism, 73–74, 168, 177
  on creation, 215
  exclusivism and, 84
  flexibility of, 82–83
  on incarnation, 195
  inclusivism and, 83–84, 86, 87
  Islam and, 186
  pluralism and, 82, 85–87
  on pure mind, 216
  tenets of, 83
  theologically relevant truth for, 131–32
Maimonides, Abraham, 34
Maimonides, Moses, 36
Makransky, John, 86, 182

Mall, Ram Adhar, 225–26
Mandelbrot, Benoît, 223–25
Manichaeism, 90, 91, 93, 187
Marx, Karl, 2, 20
Masnavi (Rūmī), 72
McFaul, Thomas, 112
McGuire, Michael, 2
Meir, Ephraim, 40, 222–23
mercy, 201
merit transfer, 177
Merton, Thomas, 237
Milindapañha, 212, 213
monasticism, 95–96, 166
monocentric pluralism, 29
monotheism, 52–53, 102, 188
Muḥammad
    Buddhist assessment of, 195
    as incarnation, 191–92
    mission of, 47
    as prophet, 148, 158–63, 159–60,
        199–203
    as seal of the prophets, 42
Muḥammad-Reality, 203
multiple religious participation, 99–100
multireligious allegiance, 142
multireligious identity, 11, 100, 234
Muslim-Buddhist dialogue, 193–203
Muslim-Buddhist relations, 52, 185
Muslim-Christian dialogue, 50, 196
mutuality, 137
mysticism, 40
    Buddhism as, 172
    Islamic, 48–53. *See also Sufism*
*Myth of Christian Uniqueness, The:
    Toward a Pluralistic Theology of
    Religions* (Hick), 30–31, 40
Myth of God Incarnate, The (ed. Hick),
    26
*Myth of Religious Superiority, The:
    Multifaith Explorations of Religious
    Pluralism* (Knitter), 31

Nakamura, Hajime, 225
Nānak, Guru, 64
Nasr, Seyyed Hossein, 51, 197
Natural History of Religion, The (Hume),
    53
naturalism, 3–4, 6
natural revelation, 131
Neo-Confucianism, 91, 96
Neo-Hinduism, 57–58, 61, 64–65, 86, 110
Neoplatonism, 51

Nestorians, 18
Nhat Hanh, Thich, 183–84
nibbāna. See *nirvāṇa*
Nicetas of Byzantium, 159
Nichiren Shōnin, 201–2
Nicholas of Cusa. *See* Nicolas Cusanus
Nicholson, Hugh, 119–21, 124
Nicolas Cusanus (Nicholas of Cusa), 19,
    150–51
nirguṇa-bhakti movements, 63–64
nirmāṇakāya, 168
nirvāṇa, nibbāna 72-73, 78, 171–74,
    189n26, 214-16, 239n86, 240
    grace and, 214
    ultimate reality and, 204–6
Noahide laws, 35–37
Noble Eightfold Path, 74, 77–78, 80
nonattachment, 180
nonduality, 197
non-Mahāyāna Buddhism, 186. *See also*
    Theravāda Buddhism
nonreductive pluralism, 42n3
Nostra Aetate (Second Vatican Council),
    160
Nyanaponika, 79, 86

official religion, 91, 92
Ogden, Schubert, 125–26
On Religion (Schleiermacher), 19
otherness
    mysticism and, 40
    potential and, 40
    in the Qur'ān, 46
    religion and, 8
Otto, Rudolf, 233, 245
overlapping, 226

paccekabuddha doctrine, 77
pagans, 18
Pāli canon, 72–74, 79, 80
Pallis, Marco, 197
Palmer, David A., 100
Panikkar, Raimon, 19, 27, 29, 101, 120,
    141–42, 222
Patton, Kimberley, 232
Paul, Gregor, 227
Peng, Guoxiang, 101–2
perennialist school, 51–52, 196–97
perfection, 153
perichōrēsis, 222
personae, 25, 29, 123
phenomenological method, 143n36

phenomenology of religion, 228, 244
philosophy
    intercultural, 227
    process, 69, 104, 123, 128, 238–39
Pieris, Aloysius, 19, 20, 175, 176, 183,
    184, 199
pluralism, 3–5, 17, 111–12
    credibility and, 106
    criticism of, 28–29
    moderate, 45
    possible, 126
    regulated, 101, 106
    religion-specific, 113
Poincaré-chains, 230
polycentric pluralism, 29
polytheism, 53, 149–51
popular religion, 90, 92, 100
postcolonial studies, 116
pratyekabuddha doctrine, 77–80
primal religion, 239
primus-inter-pares pluralism, 67–68, 70,
    86, 110, 113
process philosophy, 69, 104, 123, 128,
    238–39
process theology, 29, 104, 123, 124, 128
Prophet, the, 148, 158–60. *See also*
    Muḥammad
prophethood, 195–96, 203
prophets, 158–59
    associated with books, 189
    Bodhisattvas and, 202
proximate others, 47
Pure Land Buddhism, 88, 214–17
Puruṣa myth, 59

qi, 94, 95
"Questions of King Milinda, The" (*Mil-*
    indapañha), 75–76
Quest for Meaning, The: Developing a
    Philosophy of Pluralism (Ramadan),
    49
Qur'ān
    affirming diversity, 45
    Christology of, 154–56
    criticism of, 65
    God's mercy in, 162
    as mother of all books, 157, 163
    motifs in, 46–47
    revelation in, 48, 163
    salvation and, 81

Race, Alan, 3, 20

Radhakrishnan, 70
Rahman, Fazlur, 157
Rahner, Karl, 120, 214
Ramadan, Tariq, 49, 203
Ramakrishna, 64, 65, 71–72
Ramakrishnaism, 65–66
Ramakrishna Mission, 64, 65–66
Rambachan, Anantanand, 69–70
Rashtriya Swayamsevak Sangh (RSS; Na-
    tional Volunteers Organization), 67
Ratanakul, Pinit, 80n11
Ratzinger, Josef, 53
Real, 23–25, 29, 102–3
reality, unity of, 133–36
reciprocal acceptability, 128
reciprocal illumination, 143–44, 235
regulated pluralism, 101, 106
reincarnation, 110, 207
relatedness, mutual, 46
relative truth, 83, 211, 220
relativism, 4, 9, 10
Religion of the Concrete Spirit, 114–15
religions
    comprising other religions, 233
    concept of, 244
    confessional nature of, 8
    credibility of, 10
    culture and, 227
    devotional, 230
    diversity of, 2, 104. *See also* religious
        diversity
    evolution of, 227
    explanations for, 1–2
    fractals and, 230–31
    future of, 112
    globality of, 145
    gnostic, 230
    interdependence of, 32
    interpenetration of, 115
    interpretations of, 245
    of the law, 230
    magical-sacramental, 230
    modern sense of, 18
    mystical, 228
    nontheistic, 8
    parallels among, 229–30, 233, 235
    parity among, 31
    particularity of, 114
    paths of, hierarchization of, 60
    pluralist integration of, 113
    pluralists' knowledge of, 120–21
    pluralization of, 9

positive assessment of, 34
practice of, 68
prophetic, 228
qualification for, 103
representing whole of religious experi-
    ence, 222
sapiential, 228
science of, 227
self-perception of, 143
spiritual maturity and, 55, 60–61
superiority claims of, 4, 21, 38
studies on, personal nature of, 22
surrender as essence of, 153
titles in, 145
tolerance and, 4–5
traditions of, 22
truth of, 55–56, 141–42
typologies of, 227–30, 237–38
religious diversity
    awareness of, 6
    equality and, 122
    fractal patterns and, 9, 232–45
    hermeneutics and, 49
    hierarchical interpretation of, 60–61
    monocentric pluralism and, 119–24
    naturalists' approach to, 122
    pluralist view of, 111–12
    religious pluralism and, 119–24
    root of, 245
    as supernatural resource, 11
religious ends, 83
religious identity, 40, 50
religious incommensurability, 243–44
religious others, 40, 235
religious pluralism, 28
    critique of, 2–3, 53, 110, 119–24
    emergence of, 19–21
    interreligious dialogue and, 19, 124–29
    interreligious theology and, 9–10
    monocentric, 29, 69, 104, 119, 121,
        128–29, 134–35
    polycentric, 69, 124, 128–29
    as positive assessment, 5–6
    and practice of interreligious theology,
        113–14
    reasons for, 112
    religions' approaches to, 1–2, 6–7
    religious diversity and, 1
    secularization and, 9–10
    testing of, 126
    tradition and, 7–8
    transformation and, 127

validity and, 85
value judgment and, 113
religious psychology, 233
Religious Question in Modern China, The
    (Goossaert and Palmer), 100
responsibility, 207, 212, 213
revealed religions, 52
revelation, 18, 24
    conclusion of, 160
    contextual, 48
    divine communication and, 131
    expression of, 33, 38–39, 45
    Hindu texts and, 61
    historical nature of, 163
    incarnation and, 154, 156–57, 163
    multiple forms of, 39
    natural, 131
    recipients of, 48–49
    Son of God epithet and, 180–81
    validity of, 38
Ricci, Matteo, 169
Richards, Glyn, 20
ritual services, consumption of, 99–100
Roman Catholic Church, rejecting reli-
    gious pluralism, 29
Roy, Rām Mohan, 64
Rubicon Conference, 30–31, 222
Ruether, Rosemary Radford, 19, 21
Rūmī, Jalal al-Din, 48, 49, 72
Russell, Bertrand, 3, 122–23n50

Sachedina, Abdulaziz, 44
Sacks, Jonathan, 38, 41
salvation, 3–4, 29, 80–81, 205
    Buddhism and, 73, 75, 77–78, 172, 180
    compassion and, 177
    concepts of, 132–33
    creation and, 218–19
    faith and, 22
    gradual, 218
    Hinduism and, 59–60, 110
    Islamic perspective on, 44
    karma and, 212
    manifestation of, 22–23
    for non-Jews, 35–36
    paths of, 230
    theology of religions and, 131
    transformation and, 23–24, 27
    ultimate reality and, 124–25
Samartha, Stanley, 19, 127–28
sambhogakāya, 168
saṃsāra, 72, 172

Sanders, Ed, *151, 153*
Saṅghas, 76, 77
sanjiao heyi. See harmony of the three teachings
Śaṅkara, 61
Sanskrit, significance of, 61
Śāntarakṣita, 210
Saraswati, Dayananda, 65
scaling, 233
Schachter-Shalomi, Zalman, 39–40
Schleiermacher, Friedrich, 19
Schomerus, Hilko Wiardo, 230–32
Schoun, Frithjof, 51, 52, 197
Seal of the Prophets, 159
Second Vatican Council, 160
secularization, 9–10
Self, 144–45
selflessness, 81
self-relativization, 111
self-similarities, 224
Sermon on the Mount, 81, 170, 180
Shah-Kazemi, Reza, 51–52, 196, 199, 203
Shaivites, 63
Sharia law, 163
Sharma, Arvind, 54, 143
Shih-erh-men-lun, 208–9, 211
Shikoh, Dara, 64
Shin Buddhism, 177
Siddhārtha, 166. *See also* Buddha
Siddiqui, Ataullah, 44
Siddiqui, Mona, 156, 162
Sierpinski triangle, 223–24
Sikhs, 64
siṃsapā leaves, 80
skillful means, 83, 84, 87
Smith, Huston, 197
Smith, Wilfred Cantwell, 19, 21–23, 26, 30, 43–44, 50, 101, 115–18, 120, 124, 128, 133, 137, 140, 142–43, 145, 156, 161, 206
Solomon, Norman, 38
Son of God, 148, 180–81
    Buddha and, 181
    Buddhist perspectives on, 167
    Christian meaning for, 152
    Islamic understanding of, 148–51, 155–58
sonship, 150, 151–54, 160, 170, 181, 203
Soroush, Abdolkarim, 49, 133
Spirit of God, 152, 155, 156
spiritual growth, stages of, 55–56
spirituality, prophetic, 201

spiritual maturation, 70
submission, 47, 200
Suchocki, Marjorie Hewitt, 21
suffering, 176, 208, 213
Sufism, 34, 48–49, 155, 196–97
superiority claims, 31, 111–12. *See also individual religions*
surrender, 153
Sutta-Nipāta, 73
Suzuki, Daisetz T., 195
Swidler, Leonard, 19, 20, 144
symbolic mediation, 27
symbols, 27, 154, 163
syncretism, 138–39, 145, 234
synod of Diamper, 18
synod of Ephesus, 151n16

Takeda, Ryūsei, 88–89, 124–25, 126
Taliban, 193
Tamils, 62
Tanaka, Kenneth, 88–89
Tathāgatagarbha tradition, 216
Tehranian, Majid, 201
theodicy, 23
theological credit of trust, 131–33
theology, 8, 117, 130. *See also* interreligious theology; theology of religions
    Dialectical, 231
    future of, 11, 115
    revelation and, 131
    tradition-specific, 9
theology of religions, 117
    in the Bible, 17
    Christian, 131
    comparative theology and, 29–30, 132
    including multiple religions, 18–19
    salvation and, 131
    theocentric model of, 103
Theosophists, 19n8
Theravāda Buddhism, 73–74, 186, 204–5, 216
    Christianity and, 169
    enlightened beings in, 77
    exclusivism and, 74–79, 84, 180
    pluralism and, 80–82
    superiority claims of, 74–75, 77
    tenets of, 74–75, 80
Thomas Christians, 18
three bodies teaching. *See* harmony of the three teachings
Three Teaching Halls, 99
Tian, 111

tian-dao, 132
Tiger, Lionel, 2
Tillich, Paul, 19, 114–15, 223, 236
Timothy I (patriarch), 161
Tindal, Matthew, 19
tolerance, 4–5
Torah, as revelation, 33
Towards a World Theology (Smith), 118
Toward a True Kinship of Faiths (Dalai
    Lama), 85
traditional school. *See perennialist school*
transcategoriality, 25–26
transcendence, 3, 24, 167
    affirmation of, 150–51
    experience of, 38
    negation of, 149–51
    religion's relation to, 52
trans-difference, 40–41, 222–23
transformation, mutual, 88
Trinity, 24, 25, 29, 151–54, 161
    dimensions of, 240
    and three bodies of Buddha, 176
    unity of, 241
Troeltsch, Ernst, 19
true nature, 168
True Reality, 205
trust, hermeneutic of, 177–78
truth
    claims of, taking seriously, 13
    expressions of, 6
    in Mahāyāna Buddhism, 83
    religious, 1
    transcendence of, 68
    ranking of, 69
    variety of, 4, 49, 56
twofold commandment, 24
two truths, 83, 85

Udāna, 72
ultimate reality, 3, 103–4
    concepts of, 121–23, 237–38
    creation and, 204
    experience of, 123, 206
    liberation and, 217
    Mahāyāna understanding of, 202
    plurality of, 29
    realization of, 86–87
    religions rooted in, 86
    revelatory presence in, 235
    salvation and, 124–25, 179
    transcendence of, 110–11, 242
ultimate truth, 83

unity of reality, 133–36
Upanishads, 61, 64

Vaishnavism, 59, 63, 191
Valignano, Alexandro, 237
van der Leeuw, Gerardus, 228
Vedānta, 56
Vedas, 61, 63, 65
Vélez de Cea, J. Abraham, 79–80
Vermes, Geza, 153
Vigil, José Maria, 20
Vimalakīrti-Nirdeśa, 215
virgin birth, 150, 152
Visalo, Phra Paisan, 202
Vishva Hindu Parishad (VHP; World
    Hindu Council), 67
Viśiṣṭādvaita Vedānta, 56
Viṣṇupurāṇa, 61–62
Vivekananda, Swami, 54–60, 63–67, 223
Volf, Miroslav, 162
von Brück, Michael, 139
von Stosch, Klaus, 140–41
Vroom, Hendrik, 161

Wach, Joachim, 228, 234
Waldenfels, Bernhard, 226, 227
Wang, Yu, 101–2
Wang, Zhicheng, 101
Wang, Zhihe, 104–6, 223
Ward, Keith, 20, 140
Way of All the Earth, The (Dunne), 143
What Is Scripture? (Smith), 119
Whitehead, Alfred North, 238–39
Wiles, Maurice, 20
Wilfred, Felix, 20
Williams, Paul, 171
willpower, 200
Wimmer, Franz Martin, 227
wisdom, 200
Wong, Wai Yip, 102, 103
Word of God, 48, 156–58
    Jesus as, 26, 153, 155, 156, 161–62, 199
    Qur'ān as, 160, 162, 163
World Council of Churches, 50
World Parliament of Religions, 54–55
world religions, 114
world theology, 30, 117–19
worship, joint, 99

Xi, Zhu, 96
Xiazong, 97, 98
Xiu, Ouyang, 96

Yagi, Seiichi, 19
Yao, Xinzhong, 91, 95
yin-yang, 106, 223
Yokota, John Shunji, 88, 179, 182
Yu, Han, 96
Yuanwu, 167–68
Yuanzhang, Zhu, 97

Yusuf, Imtiyaz, 52

Zen Buddhism, 87–88
Zhao, Yanxia, 91
Zhixu, 168
Zongmi (Tsung-mi), 84
Zoroastrianism, 90, 91, 93